Mobilizing Religion in Middle East Politics

Contrary to the expectations of the secularization theorists, religious political movements rose to prominence in numerous countries across the globe in the past three decades. By examining the conditions that underlie the electoral fortunes of religious actors in democratic regimes, this book contributes to our understanding of this worldwide religious resurgence.

Employing a social movement theory framework, *Mobilizing Religion in Middle East Politics* explores the macro and micro dynamics of successful political mobilization by Sephardic Torah Guardians (Shas) in Israel and the National Outlook Movement in Turkey in the recent decades. In a comparative framework, the book demonstrates how ripe political opportunities, appropriate frames and dense social networks contribute to building popular support in Israel and Turkey. Yusuf Sarfati also assesses the effects of the increasing political power of religious actors on democratic governance and illustrates similarities and differences between the two countries.

Drawing on empirical data from a range of interviews conducted in both Israel and Turkey, this book provides a comparative study of religious politics in two countries that are often thought of as "exceptional cases," and are rarely compared. As such, this book is a welcome contribution for those studying Middle East politics, comparative politics, religious politics, democratization and social movements.

Yusuf Sarfati is an assistant professor of Politics and Government at Illinois State University where he teaches on the comparative politics of the Middle East. He is also the Director of the Middle Eastern and South Asian minor program at ISU. Sarfati's scholarship revolves around religion and politics, identity and citizenship, democratization and social movements.

Routledge Studies in Middle Eastern Politics

1. **Algeria in Transition**
   Ahmed Aghrout with Redha M. Bougherira
2. **Palestinian Refugee Repatriation**
   Edited by Michael Dumper
3. **The International Politics of the Persian Gulf**
   Arshin Adib-Moghaddam
4. **Israeli Politics and the First Palestinian Intifada**
   Eitan Y. Alimi
5. **Democratization in Morocco**
   Lise Storm
6. **Secular and Islamic Politics in Turkey**
   Ümit Cizre
7. **The United States and Iran**
   Sasan Fayazmanesh
8. **Civil Society in Algeria**
   Andrea Liverani
9. **Jordanian–Israeli Relations**
   Mutayyam al O'ran
10. **Kemalism in Turkish Politics**
    Sinan Ciddi
11. **Islamism, Democracy and Liberalism in Turkey**
    William Hale and Ergun Özbudun
12. **Politics and Violence in Israel/Palestine**
    Lev Luis Grinberg
13. **Intra-Jewish Conflict in Israel**
    Sami Shalom Chetrit
14. **Holy Places in the Israeli–Palestinian Conflict**
    Edited by Marshall J. Breger, Yitzhak Reiter and Leonard Hammer
15. **Plurality and Citizenship in Israel**
    Edited by Dan Avnon and Yotam Benziman
16. **Ethnic Politics in Israel**
    As'ad Ghanem
17. **Islamists and Secularists in Egypt**
    Dina Shehata
18. **Political Succession in the Arab World**
    Anthony Billingsley
19. **Turkey's Entente with Israel and Azerbaijan**
    Alexander Murinson

20. **Europe and Tunisia**
Brieg Powel and Larbi Sadiki

21. **Turkish Politics and the Rise of the AKP**
Arda Can Kumbaracibasi

22. **Civil Society and Democratization in the Arab World**
Francesco Cavatorta and Vincent Durac

23. **Politics in Morocco**
Anouar Boukhars

24. **The Second Palestinian Intifada**
Julie M. Norman

25. **Democracy in Turkey**
Ali Resul Usul

26. **Nationalism and Politics in Turkey**
Edited by Marlies Casier and Joost Jongerden

27. **Democracy in the Arab World**
Edited by Samir Makdisi and Ibrahim Elbadawi

28. **Public Management in Israel**
Itzhak Galnoor

29. **Israeli Nationalism**
Uri Ram

30. **NATO and the Middle East**
Mohammed Moustafa Orfy

31. **The Kurds and US Foreign Policy**
Marianna Charountaki

32. **The Iran–Iraq War**
Jerome Donovan

33. **Surveillance and Control in Israel/Palestine**
Edited by Elia Zureik, David Lyon and Yasmeen Abu-Laban

34. **Conflict and Peacemaking in Israel-Palestine**
Sapir Handelman

35. **Arab Minority Nationalism in Israel**
Amal Jamal

36. **The Contradictions of Israeli Citizenship**
Edited by Guy Ben-Porat and Bryan S. Turner

37. **The Arab State and Women's Rights**
Elham Manea

38. **Saudi Maritime Policy**
Hatim Al-Bisher, Selina Stead and Tim Gray

39. **The Arab State**
Adham Saouli

40. **Regime Stability in Saudi Arabia**
Stig Stenslie

41. **Sacred Space in Israel and Palestine**
Edited by Marshall J. Breger, Yitzhak Reiter and Leonard Hammer

42. **The UN and the Arab–Israeli Conflict**
Danilo Di Mauro

43. **Sectarian Conflict in Egypt**
Elizabeth Iskander

44. **Contemporary Morocco**
Edited by Bruce Maddy-Weitzman and Daniel Zisenwine

45. **Political Regimes in the Arab World**
Edited by Ferran Brichs

46. **Arms Control and Iranian Foreign Policy**
Bobi Pirseyedi

47. **Everyday Arab Identity**
Christopher Phillips

48. **Human Rights in Libya**
Giacomina De Bona

49. **Negotiating Political Power in Turkey**
Edited by Elise Massicard and Nicole Watts

50. **Environmental Politics in Egypt**
Jeannie L. Sowers

51. **EU–Turkey Relations in the 21st Century**
Birol Yesilada

52. **Patronage Politics in Egypt**
Mohamed Fahmy Menza

53. **The Making of Lebanese Foreign Policy**
Henrietta Wilkins

54. **The Golan Heights**
Yigal Kipnis

55. **Iranian Foreign Policy since 2001**
Edited by Thomas Juneau and Sam Razavi

56. **Modern Middle East Authoritarianism**
Edited by Noureddine Jebnoun, Mehrdad Kia and Mimi Kirk

57. **Mobilizing Religion in Middle East Politics**
Yusuf Sarfati

Mobilizing Religion in Middle East Politics

A Comparative Study of Israel and Turkey

Yusuf Sarfati

Routledge
Taylor & Francis Group
LONDON AND NEW YORK

First published 2014 by Routledge

2 Park Square, Milton Park, Abingdon, Oxfordshire OX14 4RN
52 Vanderbilt Avenue, New York, NY 10017

Routledge is an imprint of the Taylor & Francis Group, an informa business

First issued in paperback 2019

British Library Cataloguing in Publication Data
A catalogue record for this book is available from the British Library

Library of Congress Cataloging in Publication Data
Sarfati, Yusuf, 1977-
Mobilizing religion in Middle East politics : a comparative study of Israel and Turkey / Yusuf Sarfati.
pages cm
Includes bibliographical references and index.
1. Religion and politics--Middle East. 2. Religion and politics--Israel.
3. Religion and politics--Turkey. 4. Middle East--Politics and government.
5. Turkey--Politics and government. 6. Israel--Politics and government. I. Title.
BL65.P7.S265 2013
322'.109561--dc23
2013004092

ISBN: 978-0-415-54016-2 (hbk)
ISBN: 978-0-8153-6115-2 (pbk)

Typeset in Times New Roman
by Taylor & Francis Books

Contents

Illustrations

Figures

Tables

Acknowledgments

I am indebted to numerous colleagues, friends, and mentors for providing intellectual support as I was completing this manuscript. First, I would like to extend thanks to my mentors at the Ohio State University, Bill Liddle, Carter Findley and Goldie Shabad for providing constructive criticisms and continuous encouragement. Ali Riaz, A. Kadir Yıldırım, Konstantin Vössing, and Marina Carter have read parts of the manuscript at different stages of this project and provided valuable insights. I am particularly indebted to Aviad Rubin who generously read several chapters and offered useful suggestions to improve the quality of this manuscript.

During my field research, I benefited from the insights of Eliezer Don-Yehiya, Menachem Friedman, Shahar Ilan, Yasin Meral, Yoav Peled, Bensiyon Pinto, Asher Susser, Ricki Tessler, Binnaz Toprak and Cemal Uşak, who all were kind enough to take time from their busy schedules to discuss my project and share with me their expertise and resources. Special thanks go to Nissim Leon, who spent considerable time with me explaining the Shas movement and connected me with activists. In my second research trip, Ohad Shaked provided invaluable research assistance by helping me arrange interviews with politicians, taking me to parts of Israel I had never visited, and discussing with me the intricacies of Israeli politics and society. I thank him for his research assistance and camaraderie. Most importantly, I am thankful to the activists from Shas, the National Outlook Movement and other political formations who spent time with me sharing their insights and stories. Without their contributions, this project would never have materialized.

I would also like to thank the Halif family who generously welcomed me to their home during both of my research trips in Israel. My parents and sister in Istanbul showed their continuous support and faith in me at each step of this arduous journey. Last but not least, I thank my partner Lisya Seloni for her continuous encouragement and patience from the start to the finish of this project, even at times when I locked myself in my room writing for hours. Her inspiration and unconditional love kept me going.

Parts of Chapter 8 appeared in 'The politics of religious education in Turkey', in *Religion, Education and Governance in the Middle East* edited by Sai Felicia Krishna-Hensel (Farnham: Ashgate, 2012), pp. 147–72.

Abbreviations

DLP	Democratic Left Party (*Demokratik Sol Parti*)
FP	Felicity Party (*Saadet Partisi*)
JDP	Justice and Development Party (*Adalet ve Kalkınma Partisi*)
JP	Justice Party (*Adalet Partisi*)
MK	Member of Knesset
MP	Motherland Party (*Anavatan Partisi*)
MUSIAD	Independent Industrialists and Businessmen Association (*Müstakil Sanayiciler ve İşadamları Derneği*)
NAP	Nationalist Action Party (*Milliyetçi Hareket Partisi*)
NOM	National Outlook Movement (*Milli Görüş Hareketi*)
NOP	National Order Party (*Milli Düzen Partisi*)
NRP	National Religious Party (*Mifleget Datit Leumit*)
NSC	National Security Council (*Milli Güvenlik Kurulu*)
NSP	National Salvation Party (*Milli Selamet Partisi*)
ÖNDER	Alumni Association of Imam Hatip High Schools (*İmam-Hatip Liseleri Mezunları ve Mensupları Derneği*)
RPP	Republican People's Party (*Cumhuriyet Halk Partisi*)
Shas	Worldwide Sephardic Association of Torah Keepers (*Hitahdut HaSfaradim HaOlamit Shomrei Torah*). Also commonly referred as Sephardic Torah Guardians (*Sfaradim Shomrei Torah*)
SMEs	Small and Medium-scale Enterprises
TPP	True Path Party (*Doğru Yol Partisi*)
VP	Virtue Party (*Fazilet Partisi*)
WP	Welfare Party (*Refah Partisi*)

1 Introduction

In the nineteenth and early twentieth centuries, founders of modern social science, such as August Comte, Karl Marx and Max Weber, all argued, albeit in different ways, that positivism and secular trends would be triumphant in the modern world. For these thinkers religion was antithetical to modernity. According to them secularization was an irreversible process in the modern world, and the role of religion in public and social life would diminish radically with increasing socioeconomic modernization of societies. This was still the hegemonic view among social scientists in the 1950s, 1960s, and even 1970s. Daniel Lerner (1958), Bryan Wilson (1966, 1978), Peter Berger (1967) and David Martin (1979) were part of this theoretical school known as secularization theory. However, at the end of 1970s, religiopolitical movements began to emerge as serious political alternatives in many democratic political systems that had been previously dominated by parties with secular programs. The Christian right became a pivotal actor in contemporary U.S. politics following the rise of the Moral Majority during Ronald Reagan's presidential campaign; ultra-Orthodox and messianic movements have been increasing their popular appeal since the early 1990s in Israel; the Hindu revivalist Bharatiya Janata Party (BJP) has challenged and at certain periods replaced the secular Congress Party in the government of India; and recently Islamist political actors, such as the Freedom and Justice Party (FJP), the political arm of the Muslim Brotherhood in Egypt, and Rashid Ghannushi's Ennahda, have scored sweeping electoral victories in the first competitive elections of the newly emerging democracies of Egypt and Tunisia. These developments show that religion is a significant factor in politics in different corners of the world with different cultural traditions.

Following these political developments, scholarly interest in the study of religious politics has also surged among political scientists. Two main questions have guided the studies of these scholars: Why the sudden rise of religious political activity? How will the strengthening of religious politics affect liberal democracy? Thus, some recent studies have compared the complex interaction between religion and the state in various countries and provide useful typologies.[1] Others have studied the rise of religious parties in both authoritarian and democratic settings,[2] while a group of political scientists focused on the relationship between democratic governance and political religion.[3] Scholars of Middle East politics have also paid particular attention to the assertive role of religion in politics throughout the region. Mohammad Ayoob's *Many Faces of Political Islam*, Robert Lee's *Religion and Politics in the Middle East* and Asef Bayat's *Making Islam Democratic: Social Movements and the Post-Islamic Turn* are three recent studies that focus on religious politics in the region.

Drawing on these debates, this book examines the causes of and conditions for the electoral success of religiopolitical parties in two Middle Eastern democracies, namely Israel and Turkey. The study focuses on the following questions: Why does the electoral strength of religiopolitical actors increase in democratic settings? What are the mechanisms of political mobilization used by religiopolitical actors? What factors facilitate the success of religious parties in democratic politics? What is the effect of the increasing power of religiopolitical actors on democratic governance and stability?

I tackle these questions by discussing the recent political success stories of the Shas movement in Israel and the National Outlook Movement (NOM) in Turkey in the last two decades in comparative perspective. Israel and Turkey provide prolific material for studying these questions. Both countries' governance was founded on modernizing, secularist national ideologies. During state formation, Zionism and Kemalism emerged as hegemonic secular nationalist ideologies with an aim to create a secular citizenry for the newly founded modern nation-states. The Republican People's Party (RPP) in Turkey and Mapai (later the Labor Party) in Israel became founding political parties during the early decades of state formation that promoted the hegemony of secular nationalism in the political, institutional and social arenas. However, in the past two decades in both countries the political power of religious parties has increased significantly.

In Israel, in the 1999 national election, the combined vote share of the religious parties peaked and passed 20 percent of the national vote (see Figure 1.1). In the same election, the Shas party (Sephardic Torah Guardians) became the largest religious political party and the third largest political party by capturing 17 seats in the 120-seat Knesset. The party, which is seen by many as the strongest representative of the Oriental Jews, is still the largest political party in the religious bloc and holds 10 percent of the seats in the Knesset as well as key ministries in the government.

In the 1994 national election in Turkey, the Welfare Party (WP), which was the third political party of Erbakan's NOM, captured the municipalities of Istanbul and Ankara, the two largest cities in Turkey. The party also emerged as the winner of the 1995 national election, and for the first time in the history of the Turkish Republic, a religious party became the bigger partner in a coalition government. Moreover, the Justice and Development Party (JDP), which is an offshoot from the NOM, became the governing party of Turkey winning the 2002 election. The JDP has formed a single-party government in Turkey for the past decade scoring landslide victories in the 2007 and 2011 national elections (see Table 1.1).

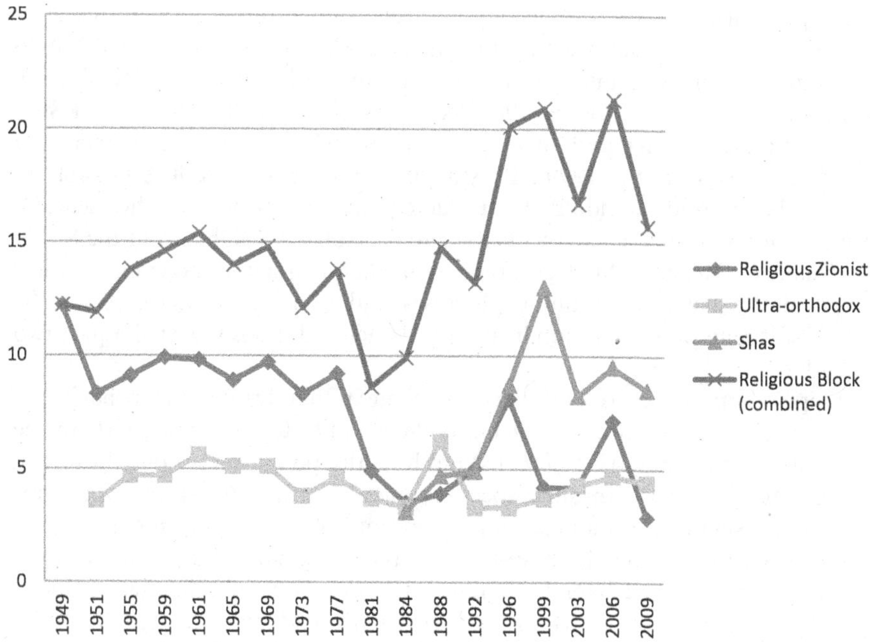

Figure 1.1 Percentage vote share of the religious parties in Israel in the national elections

Table 1.1 Percentage vote share of National Outlook Parties and the JDP in the national elections

Election year	*National Outlook Parties*	*JDP*
1973	11.8	
1977	8.6	
1987	7.2	
1991	16.2	
1995	21.4	
1999	15.4	
2002	2.5	34.4
2007	2.3	46.6
2011	1.8	49.1

Shas and the National Outlook parties not only emerged as political actors, but have also developed into social movements mobilizing masses with elaborate social networks.

These political developments in Turkey and in Israel have not only perplexed political observers, but also created (and still create) high anxiety among the countries' secular publics. In Israel, Shinui emerged as a single-issue party with a secularist agenda and rode the anti-Shas wave in the 2001 elections, while secularist actors in Turkey coalesced around the RPP, judiciary and the army trying to thwart the rise of the Islamists. This book is an attempt to understand the parallel electoral successes of the NOM and Shas in the political arena and their ability to mobilize important segments of their societies since the 1990s. By studying these two cases, it is possible to gain a better understanding of the factors that contribute to the electoral success of religiopolitical actors elsewhere. Borrowing insights from the Social Movement Theory (SMT), I argue that the interaction between political opportunity structures, framing processes and social networks explains the successful religiopolitical mobilization in Israel and Turkey over the past two decades.

Opportunity structures refer to the context that frames the behavior of political actors and enhances or limits their ability to garner support. In the first part of the analysis, I demonstrate how the politicization of a historical sociocultural cleavage through social change, such as rural–urban immigration, increasing literacy, and school integration ripened opportunities for both movements by making the grievances of the marginalized segments in each society more acute (Chapter 3). Later, the inclusion of religious actors in government structures provided an additional set of opportunities for those religious parties by enabling them to gain access to the cultural and material resources of the state (Chapter 4 and Chapter 5). Implementation of neo-liberal economic programs in both countries created further opportunities for both movements as they were able to fill the social vacuum with their extensive welfare provisions. In the case of Turkey, economic liberalization also became an impetus for a new Muslim middle class who actively supported the NOM and later the JDP.

After discussing these contextual factors, the second part of the book focuses on how framing processes mediate between political opportunity structures and collective behavior. In this part, I discuss how religious entrepreneurs construct injustice frames, prognostic frames and empowerment frames to mobilize the masses. These frames were critical for successful mobilization, because they:

1 resonated with the target audiences' sociocultural grievances;
2 were articulated by credible agents (i.e. activists of religious movements); and
3 were disseminated to the larger society through social networks built in poor neighborhoods, development towns, shantytowns, and around schools (Chapter 6, Chapter 7 and Chapter 8).

Social networks acted as mobilizing vehicles not only because they circulated the frames to more people, but also because they have provided welfare to the needy and forged solidarity and trust between constituents, politicians and movement activists.

By focusing on the fortunes of Shas and NOM in democratic elections, I also assess the validity of existing hypotheses on the relationship between democratic governance and religious movements. Many political scientists and lay observers argued that religious discourse and activity is antithetical to a democratic order. The systematic comparison of Israel and Turkey reveals that the relationship between religious politics and democratic governance is multi-layered. Both Shas and the NOM became agents of democratization by empowering the socially and culturally marginalized segments in their respective societies. These religious movements not only carried the economic demands of their constituencies to the national agenda, but also gave effective political voice to the peripheral groups in their societies by constructing a positive identity for Sephardim/pious Muslims. This politics-of-identity paved the way for the recognition of excluded groups' cultural demands in the public arena and restored the sense of pride they lacked in earlier periods. Thus, the experiences of Shas and NOM show that religious movements can become agents of democratic recognition and empowerment by using religion as a meta-narrative to address social exclusion.

On the other hand, the dismissive and divisive political rhetoric Shas and the National Outlook leaders occasionally employed against their political opponents harmed democratic political culture in both political systems. Specifically, the leaders' references to political opponents as non-believers and in some cases their demonization passed the boundaries of civil, democratic debate. Moreover, the increasing political fortunes of the religiopolitical actors instigated a reaction from the secular political actors and led to the intensification of the secular–religious cleavage in both countries. While polarization occurred in both cases, the consequences of this polarization on the democratic order differed in each of the cases.

Lastly, the comparative discussion of Shas and NOM informs us about the sources and degrees of religiopolitical actors' ideological moderation. The political experiences of NOM and Shas show that the widely accepted inclusion–moderation thesis needs to be refined. According to this thesis, political inclusion of religious actors leads to their ideological moderation, while their political exclusion leads to radicalization. In Turkey, the defection of the reformers from NOM in 2001 and the formation of the JDP with a post-Islamist agenda represented the ideological moderation of religiopolitical actors. However, this moderation followed the WP's removal from power during the 28 February Process under pressure from the military and the closure of the WP and the Virtue Party (VP) respectively by the Constitutional Court. Hence, the moderation of the religiopolitical actors followed a period of exclusion. In Israel, Shas moderated to a far lesser extent after the party was kept outside of Ariel Sharon's coalition government of 2003. I argue that in these two cases a rational-actor model better captures the dynamics of moderation than the inclusion–moderation thesis. However, there is also a qualitative difference between the levels of moderation between the two movements. While the JDP parted ways with the Islamism of the

NOM and underwent an ideological transformation, the moderation of Shas was more tactical. I argue that the difference lies in the class bases of both parties.

Methodology and Data Sources

I chose Israel and Turkey as my two cases, because they are dramatically different on a number of political, cultural, economic and institutional levels. As discussed further in Chapter 2, the selection of the Shas movement in Israel and the NOM in Turkey for comparison constitutes a "most different" case design. These two countries differ in their level of economic development, in their level of urbanization, in the relative strength of center parties, in their majority religion, in their institutional arrangements to manage the relationship between religion and state, and in their educational institutional arrangements. Despite these differences, a similar process of religiopolitical mobilization is traced in both countries. The extant literature on Middle Eastern scholarship has treated both Turkey and Israel as "exceptional cases," and most studies on political movements in these countries are based on analysis of single case studies.[4] The comparative focus of this study has advantages over single case studies, since comparison provides leverage to control for alternative explanations and make causal inferences while utilizing rich empirical data derived from primary resources.

Moreover, the discussion of similarities between an Islamic and a Judaic political movement—which is very rare in the literature—reveals that heightened political activism is not unique to Islam as essentialist theories contend. Essentialist scholars define Islam as a monolithic religion tied to unchanging textual sources and attribute religious political activism among Muslims to Islam's political nature.[5] These scholars not only fail to see that there are multiple interpretations of Islam and various manifestations of political Islam, but also discard the plethora of religiopolitical movements in other religious traditions. By studying political Islam in a comparative design with a Judaic movement, this book not only counters essentialist and Orientalist theorization, but also treats religion (or culture in general) as a malleable resource dependent on political context and political agents' interpretations. Thus, an analytically guided comparison of two different cases helps to control for the alternative explanations in the literature and to properly assess the explanatory variables. Yet this guided comparison is not enough to claim causality and make inferences. In order to do this, I will explicate qualitative causal mechanisms and provide a causal narrative. The empirical causal narrative, which forms the heart of this book, is based on my field work in Israel and Turkey. The data for the study primarily come from a series of open-ended interviews I conducted during my year-long research in Turkey (Istanbul and Ankara) and Israel (Jerusalem, Tel Aviv, Petach Tikva, Tiberias and West Bank settlements) in 2006–7 and a month-long research trip in Israel (Sderot, Netivot, Ofakim, Or Yehuda, Elad and Batyam) in the summer of

2012. During my visits, I interviewed political activists from both movements, members of other political parties, government officials, graduates of religious schools, and educators. This qualitative interview material helped me to assess the interests, motives and political agendas of various social and political actors. In addition to the interview data, I conducted a thematic analysis of newspaper archives and secondary literature on both countries. In Israel, I scanned the daily newspapers *Ha'aretz* and *The Jerusalem Post*, as well as the weekly magazine *Jerusalem Report* for the past three decades. In Turkey, I scanned the daily newspapers *Zaman*, *Milli Gazete*, *Tercüman* and *Milliyet* as well as the weekly magazine *Nokta* in the post-1980 period. These archival materials together with the secondary literature from both countries enabled me to situate the interview data in the context of political events and to assess the validity of the claims made by my respondents.

The Overview of the Book

The rest of this book is laid out as follows. Chapter 2 provides the definition of key terms used in the study, lays out the rationale of the comparative research design, and grounds the main argument of the book in the literature on religious politics and democratization. Chapter 3 discusses the formation of a sociocultural cleavage in Turkey and Israel during the formative periods of both countries and the politicization of this cleavage through the processes of social change. In this chapter I delineate the historical evolution of the Sephardi–Ashkenazi cleavage in Israel and the center–periphery cleavage in Turkey during the early state formation. The chapter first describes how the Sephardim faced political, cultural and socioeconomic exclusion when they arrived in Israel in great numbers in the 1950s. When they came into closer contact with the dominant secular Ashkenazi population in the 1970s because of attempts at school integration and faced a backlash from Ashkenazi parents, the sense of exclusion felt by the Sephardim became more acute. In this context, Shas was born as a political party that addressed social and cultural grievances of the Sephardi community living on the periphery. The chapter then draws a parallel narrative for Turkey by describing the Kemalist Westernization project and the political, cultural and socioeconomic exclusion faced by pious Muslims in the villages. When increasing numbers of villagers migrated to cities throughout the 1960s and 1970s, these rural immigrants came into closer contact with secular urbanites. When the established urbanites projected the conservative rural immigrants as the primary source of the cities' problems, such as overcrowding, lack of infrastructure and loss of urban manners, the grievances of the periphery became acute. The NOM emerged in this context and constructed an ideology that addressed the social, cultural and political grievances of the different groups within the periphery.

Chapter 4 discusses how Shas has been incorporated into most coalition governments in Israel since the movement's inception in 1984. Due to this participation in coalition governments Shas gradually established patronage networks in the Interior Ministry, Religious Affairs Ministry, Ministry of Labor and Social Welfare, and Health Ministry. The party's grip on these ministries created a favorable opportunity structure, because Shas used its access to these state resources to add to and consolidate its popular support. Chapter 5 shows how the inclusion of religious actors in the Turkish context boosted the prospects of the Islamist movement in Turkey. The chapter starts with a discussion of the National Salvation Party's inclusion in three coalition governments in the mid to late 1970s and the party's use of government ministries and agencies for patronage. Next, it focuses on the organic relationship cemented between the Hearth of Intellectuals and the military regime (1980–3) and the political activities of the conservative faction under the umbrella of the center-right Motherland Party (1983–91) as evidence of further incorporation of Islamic actors into the state apparatus. The chapter concludes with a discussion of the two-fold consequences of these incorporation policies. On the one hand, religious actors found a receptive environment to increase their public appeal as religion became a hegemonic force while the left was severely repressed. On the other hand, the religious social and political actors criticized the instrumentalization of Islam by the government, and due to this criticism the periphery's support shifted from the conservative center-right Motherland Party to the Islamist Welfare Party in the 1990s.

Chapter 6 discusses how Shas appeals to ultra-Orthodox, traditional and non-observant Sephardim in Israel by blending religious, ethnic and socio-economic messages. These different groups gravitate toward the movement because Shas addresses in various ways the sense of Sephardi marginalization. Moreover, the movement's political motto, *Lehahzir Atara LeYoshna* (Restoring the Crown to its Past Glory), indicates how the movement aims to empower the Sephardim around a religious identity grounded in Sephardi heritage. Shas has become a sociopolitical movement with an expansive popular base, because unlike other religious parties in Israel, it has succeeded in creating a flexible message by adapting to Sephardi local traditions. Shas also used its civil society arms, such as *El Hama'ayan* (To the Source), in order to provide social services to the needy and thereby showed that a religious project can respond to the everyday needs of the marginalized. At the end of the chapter, I evaluate different aspects of the multi-faceted relationship between Shas's politics and democratic stability in Israel.

Chapter 7 discusses how National Outlook activists framed political questions around the concept of injustice and were able to fashion an alliance of the excluded. Peasants, urban poor, Kurds and the Islamic bourgeoisie were all drawn to the Islamist movement because it created an eclectic message that successfully addressed different senses of injustice. The NOM also created a dense web of networks especially in shanty towns that helped to spread its message. The WP and the VP not only addressed the sense of exclusion felt by these diverse groups, but also employed a message of empowerment based on Islamic identity. The chapter ends with a discussion of the transformation of political Islam in Turkey with the establishment of the JDP, and its rise to power.

Chapter 8 is a comparative discussion of the politics of state-funded religious education. In this chapter, I discuss how Shas has built its own education network, namely *Ma'ayan Hahinuch HaTorani* (Wellspring of Torah Education) and secured continuing state funding for it, while in Turkey the NOM has politicized *Imam Hatip* schools, vocational religious schools for the training of imams and preachers. These schools became vehicles for religious mobilization for Shas and NOM, because religious entrepreneurs effectively constructed empowerment and prognostic frames within and around these institutions creating an affirmative religious Sephardi/pious Muslim identity. Moreover, both religious movements used informal social networks formed around these religious schools to disseminate these frames to the larger society, to provide social provisions to the socioeconomically marginalized, and forge links between the religious school graduates and religious party activists.

Notes

1 A. Stepan, 'Religion, Democracy, and the "Twin Tolerations"', *Journal of Democracy*, vol.11, no.4, 2000, 37–57; A. T. Kuru, *Secularism and State Policies toward Religion: The United States, France, and Turkey*, New York: Cambridge University Press, 2009; J. Fox, 'World Separation of Religion and State Into the 21st Century', *Comparative Political Studies*, vol.39, no.5, 2006, 537–69.

2 M. E. Marty and R. S. Appelby (eds.), *Fundamentalisms Observed*, Chicago: University of Chicago Press, 1994; R. Kalyvas, *The Rise of Christian Democracy in Europe*, Ithaca: Cornell University Press, 1996; Z. Munson, 'Islamic Mobilization: Social Movement Theory and the Egyptian Muslim Brotherhood', *The Sociological Quarterly*, vol.42, no.4, 2001, 487–510; C. R. Wickham, *Mobilizing Islam: Religion, Activism and Political Change in Egypt*, New York: Columbia University Press, 2002; C. Hedges, *American Fascists: Christian Right and the War on America*, New York: Free Press, 2007.

3 S. Kalyvas, 'Commitment Problems in Emerging Democracies: The Case of Religious Parties', *Comparative Politics*, vol.32, 2000, 379–98; J. Schwedler, *Faith in Moderation: Islamist Parties in Yemen and Jordan*, New York: Cambridge University Press, 2006; K. Delacoura, *Islamist Terrorism and Democracy in the Middle East*, New York: Cambridge University Press, 2011.

4 D. Lehmann and B. Siebzehner, *Remaking Israeli Judaism: The Challenge of Shas*, London: Oxford University Press, 2006; C. Tuğal, *Passive Revolution: Absorbing the Islamic Challenge to Capitalism*, Stanford: Stanford University Press, 2009; H. Yavuz, *Secularism and Muslim Democracy in Turkey*, New York: Oxford University Press, 2009.

5 B. Lewis, *The Political Language of Islam*, Chicago: Chicago University Press, 1988; S. Huntington, *The Clash of Civilizations and the Remaking of World Order*, New York: Simon & Schuster, 1996.

2 Theoretical Framework

Terminology

A study that examines the causes of and conditions for the electoral success of religious parties needs to answer the question: "What is a religious party?" Most social science studies that discuss religious politics use the term without giving it a clear definition. Defining a religious party as a political entity that uses religious symbols or imagery would be a very broad definition, because most politicians pay lip service to religious symbols on a very superficial level without necessarily embracing any religiopolitical ideology. On the other hand, defining a religious party as a political entity that calls for the radical transformation of the state or one that works for the formation of a theocracy would be a very narrow definition, since many religiopolitical actors use religion as part of their political ideology without explicitly demanding the creation of a religious state. I define a religious party as a political party that takes religion as a reference point for its policy proposals to address the major political problems of its country.[1] I use this definition, because it is flexible enough to include parties that do not explicitly state that they want to create a theocracy but also stringent enough to exclude parties whose leaders only make occasional references to sacred concepts in their speeches. Surely, there are significant differences in the way religious ideology is expressed in the political sphere in Israel and Turkey because of the institutional differences between the two countries' religiopolitical arrangements. In Turkey, which is constitutionally defined as a secular republic, no political party explicitly defines itself as religious because of the Constitutional Court's very stringent interpretation of secularism and the numerous historical examples of political party closures. However, a closer look at the National Outlook Parties' programs and activists' political statements clearly reveal that the NOM is a religious political movement using religion as an important reference point for the solution of major political issues in Turkey. In Israel, on the other hand, Shas and other religious parties, such as the National Religious Party (NRP) or United Torah Judaism, explicitly use religion in their names and party programs due to the Israeli state's accommodationist stance toward religious actors and the lack of a strict secularist ideology as in the case of Turkey.

Attentive readers have probably already recognized that I use the words party and movement interchangeably when I refer to Shas and the NOM. There is surely an important difference between these two concepts. Social movement literature draws a clear distinction between a social movement and political party with regard to their mode of operation, aims and organizational features. Social movements rely mainly on committed adherents, engage in protest actions to create social change and consist of informal networks of groups and organizations. On the other hand, political parties aim to occupy political office, rely on the support of voters and consist of a formal party organization.[2] In the context of this comparative study, it is apt to say that Shas and the National Outlook Parties can be defined as movement-parties. Both Shas and the NOM operate around a committed group of adherents who aim to create concrete social change in their own national contexts and are embedded into their respective societies through dense informal networks. Activists interact with their constituents on a constant basis, not only during election campaigns as most of the other parties do. This is why most of the political activists I interviewed referred to *Tnu'at Shas* (Shas Movement) and *Milli Görüş Hareketi* (National Outlook Movement) when asked about their political party. On the other hand, both of these movements have been participating in national elections through their formal party organization and have been aiming to occupy political office since their establishment. Therefore, throughout the study I refer to these political entities sometimes as social movements and sometimes as political parties depending on which organizational aspect of their identity I want to emphasize at the time.

Research Design

The scholarship on Turkish and Israeli religious politics mostly consists of single case studies, because most scholars consider both Turkish and Israeli cases as "exceptional cases" with idiosyncratic histories and dynamics. There are few studies that integrate Turkish or Israeli domestic political developments into systematic comparative analysis. What is even rarer is the comparison between Israeli and Turkish contexts. One scholarly work that compares religious politics in Israel and Turkey is Sultan Tepe's *Sacred and Secular: Politics of Religion in Israel and Turkey*. Tepe makes an excellent analysis of religious parties' ideologies in Israel and Turkey. In her four-party comparison, she masterfully differentiates between parties that sacralize secular concepts (National Religious Party in Israel and National Action Party in Turkey) and parties that secularize religious traditions (Shas in Israel and the NOM and the JDP in Turkey). Tepe accurately claims that scholars wrongly attribute to the latter parties a radical ideology and define the former as moderate, although explicitly religious parties that secularize their religious traditions tend to be much more flexible ideologically. My study aims to complement Tepe's work because it traces micro-processes of religious mobilization rather than drawing comparisons of party ideologies.

In order to weave the processes of political mobilization into a causal narrative, this book employs a case-oriented comparative method, which is the systematic analysis of a small number of cases.[3] This case-oriented comparative method is both historically interpretative and causally analytic.[4] It differs from a single case study in its emphasis on empirical generalizations rather than on the particularity of each case. Yet, similar to the single-case study approach, this method is still attentive to the empirical details of particular case histories. In my analysis, I use a "most different" case design, one of the various research design strategies employed in case-oriented comparative analysis. In this research design, the cases take the same value on the dependent and independent variables but differ on the values of the alternative explanations.

As summarized in Table 2.1, Israel and Turkey differ in key social, economic, political and institutional variables used to explain the rise of the religiopolitical movements. First of all, there is a significant difference in the level of economic development in each country. While Israel has $31,282 GDP per capita, Turkey has $10,498 GDP per capita as of 2011 and is classified as a medium income country.[5] Both countries also vary in their degree of urbanization. In 2011, 92 percent of Israel's population lived in cities, while in the same year the urbanization rate of Turkey was 71 percent. In terms of human development indicators, Israel is classified as a country with very high human development, while Turkey ranks at the low tier of high human development.

The (diminishing) strength of the mainstream parties is another variable that is used as a potential explanation for the rise of religious politics and intensification of the religious cleavage. According to this explanation, a vote for religious parties represents a protest against the status quo and will change course in the medium term. In Turkey, a sharp downward trend of the mainstream parties' total vote share is clearly observable in the 1990s. The four main center parties (two center left and two center right) captured 82.6 percent of the national vote in the 1991 general elections. Their total vote share dropped to 64.2 percent in the 1995 elections, to 56.1 in the 1999 elections, and finally to 26 and 27 percent in the 2007 and 2011 elections.[6] In Israel, the strength of the center right and center left stagnated in the four elections between 1984 and 1992 and remained in the 70–75 percent range. In the elections between 1996 and 2009, their combined vote share slightly diminished to the 50–60 percent range. In sum, the center parties' power in Turkey has eroded over time, while in Israel, the center parties have lost some of their political power yet still retain a significant share.

Culturally, Turkey is a predominantly Muslim country with Muslims constituting 99 percent of total population, while Israel is a predominantly Jewish country with Jews constituting 76 percent of the Israeli population. Lastly, both countries also differ in their initial institutional arrangements regarding church–state relations as well as education. Israel grants extensive autonomy to all religious groups in conducting their personal affairs. Issues such as

Table 2.1 Most different case design: Differences between Israel and Turkey in alternative explanations

		Israel	*Turkey*
Socioeconomic variables	Economic development (GDP per capita in 2011)	$ 31,282	$ 10,498
	Urbanization (% living in cities in 2011)	Predominantly urban with a very small rural population (92% live in cities)	Urban with a considerable rural population (71% live in cities)
	Human Development Indices ranking by the UNDP	Very High Human Development (ranked 17th worldwide by UNDP)	High Human Development (ranked 92nd worldwide by UNDP)
Political variable	Strength of the mainstream political parties	Stagnant from 1977–1992, slight decline from 1996–2009	Sharp downward decline from 1991 to the 2011 elections
Cultural variable	Dominant religion	Judaism (76% of the total population is Jewish)	Islam (99% of the total population is Muslim)
Institutional variables	State-religion arrangements	Accommodation of religious lifestyles through granting autonomy to religious groups. Certain secular liberties are restricted to accommodate religion in the public sphere	Strict secularism and regulation of religious expression by the state. Certain religious liberties are restricted to maintain secular public sphere
	Education	Multiple educational streams	Unified education system

marriage, divorce, burial or conversions are handled by religious courts of each religious community. The Israeli state also imposes certain restrictions over the secular way of life in order to accommodate religious demands and protect the Jewish character of the state. For instance, public transportation is restricted during Shabbat in certain cities. In contrast, in Turkey the state institutions, such as the Directorate of Religious Affairs, retain significant control over religious affairs. In contrast to Israel, the state restricts certain religious freedoms, such as the wearing of religious symbols in public offices or the right to private religious education, in order to protect the secular character of the state.[7] In terms of electoral systems, Israel has a nation-wide Proportional Representation (PR) system with a 2 percent threshold, which reduces the cost for smaller parties to enter the Knesset and gives the political system a consensual character. While Turkey also implements a PR system (with multi-member districts), the existence of a 10 percent national threshold exerts a majoritarian effect on Turkish politics, particularly after the 2002 elections, when only few parties could have passed the threshold. Institutionally, the educational systems of both countries also differ in fundamental ways. While separate educational systems operate in Israel in order for each cultural group to protect its own communal identity, in Turkey the Law on the Unification of Education demands that there is unified education across the board.

Despite these differences, a similar process in religiopolitical mobilization is traced in both countries. As Barrington Moore (1966) asserts, "comparisons can serve as a rough negative check on accepted historical explanations, and comparative method can lead to new historical generalizations." Yet, control by design is not sufficient to establish causality. Therefore, I delineate a causal narrative that ties the interaction between political opportunity structures, framing processes and social networks to the rise of religiopolitical movements.

New Religious Politics

A close look at the scholarship on the new religious politics reveals that there are three main approaches used to explain the rise of the new religious movements. These three frameworks base their explanations for increasing religiopolitical activism on cultural, socioeconomic and political factors.

Scholars who emphasize the role of culture in the politicization of religion mainly focus on the contemporary rise of political Islam and attribute a unique role to Islam in explaining this phenomenon. Some scholars argue that Islam is more prone to be politicized because there is no separation between religion and politics in Islamic textual sources. According to these scholars, Islamist activism is the result of the interwoven nature of political and religious authority in Islamic praxis since the time of the Prophet Muhammad.[8] The lack of democracy in most Muslim-majority countries is in turn tied to this lack of separation between religious and political leadership. One of the most well-known representatives of this framework is Samuel

Huntington, who argues in *Clash of Civilizations* that Islam and liberal democracy are fundamentally opposed to each other and therefore cannot coexist. An important assumption made by Huntington's and similar studies is that Islam is a hierarchical faith that does not favor individualism or political freedoms.

However, this type of cultural analysis has major flaws. First of all, it assumes a direct link between the state–church separation and democracy. The existence of this type of institutional separation in democratic regimes is a myth, as many well-established European democracies, including England, Sweden, Denmark and Norway, have an official state church, while others, such as Italy and Germany, have been governed by Christian democratic parties at different periods in their political history. In fact, Jonathan Fox (2006) shows in his world-wide comparative study that complete institutional separation between religion and state does not exist in 151 of the 152 countries considered.[9] Fox's and other studies show that secular state apparatus and religious authorities have established various forms and levels of institutional interaction in all democratic settings.

Second, the attribution of an unchanging textual essence to Islam that is independent from historical circumstances is fundamentally problematic. These types of essentialist cultural analyses disregard the fact that religious texts are read and interpreted by social and political agents who base their behavior on their own interpretations of these sources. The interpretations of religious scriptures are shaped by the political, social and historical context in which the individual agents operate. By attributing a monolithic unchanging essence to a religious tradition, these scholars do not only fail to distinguish among multiple interpretations of Islam or various manifestations of political Islam, but also fail to recognize the contemporary rise of religiopolitical movements from other religious traditions. Therefore, it is important to situate the analysis of Islamist movements in a comparative design with political movements from other religious traditions, such as Judaism. One of the main aims of this book is to show that the rise of religious movements is not unique to Islam.

Moreover, cultural essentialist frameworks cannot accommodate political or cultural change in their unidirectional explanations. Historically, several scholars raised similar arguments about the authoritarian nature of Roman Catholicism and its incompatibility with liberal democracy. Yet, changes in the Catholic Church's doctrine during the Second Vatican Council, the rise of Christian democratic parties in Europe, and the Church's pro-democracy position during democratic transitions in the 1980s and 1990s in South Europe, Latin America and Eastern Europe discredited these arguments. Today, few argue that the Catholic doctrines of the medieval period carry the same outlook toward democracy as the Catholic Church of today. There is no reason to assume this for Islam either. Therefore, the questions that need to be asked are not whether Islam is inherently political or whether it is compatible with democracy. The more significant questions to ask are: Under what circumstances is Islam, or for that matter Judaism, politicized? And under what circumstances do Muslims and Jews embrace interpretations that reconcile their faith with democracy?

Scholars who embrace the socioeconomic framework go beyond the essentialism of cultural theories and offer useful insights to answer these questions. This framework is useful in explaining the context in which religious revival occurs. The most well-known socioeconomic explanation provided for the rise of religious political actors is economic deprivation. According to this theory, religious political actors appeal to the economically deprived segments in their society and prosper especially among the urban poor.[10] Those at the margins of the society, the argument goes, are more susceptible to manipulation by religious symbols and therefore serve as a recruitment base for religiopolitical movements. More sophisticated and convincing versions of this theory maintain that the rise of political religion is caused by increased and unrealized expectations.[11] According to these theorists, increasing immigration from rural areas to cities and increasing opportunities for higher education, especially in Middle Eastern countries, creates a highly educated and young population. However, these highly educated youngsters become frustrated, because they cannot find the jobs they expected or cannot find jobs at all. These unemployed or underemployed youngsters become activists in religious movements, because these movements promise a just future grounded in a reimagined Golden Age.

These arguments based on the importance of socioeconomic factors have great merit as they go beyond essentialism and depict the context in which religious movements arise. Most also accurately observe that current religio-political activism is not a return to tradition or a simple religious awakening, but rather an innovative response to current social and economic problems, and therefore represent modern political projects. Yet despite their merit, the socioeconomic explanations fail to emphasize the significance of meaning and meaning-making that is crucial to appeal to the marginalized or dislocated. These theories fail to answer the legitimate question: Why do socialist or radical nationalist parties fail to mobilize the urban poor, the losers of economic globalization or the dislocated masses, while religious parties succeed?

A number of scholars who use socioeconomic explanations provide an answer to this question. They contend that religious movements thrive because they can address the alienation many face in new, unsettling modern settings. In "Desecularization of the World: A Global Overview," Peter Berger (1999) emphasizes the link between socioeconomic modernization and the rise of new religious politics: "Modernity tends to undermine the taken-for-granted certainties by which people lived through most of history. This is an uncomfortable state of affairs, for many an intolerable one, and religious movements that claim to give certainty have great appeal."[12] A similar observation is made by Ali Riaz who ties the current rise of the religious movements in South Asia to the mental and physical dislocation created by the forces of globalization. As Riaz put it: "The appeal of religious identity is a result of ontological insecurity and existential uncertainty faced by individuals because of the pace and nature of globalization in recent decades."[13] Similarly, Amin Maalouf asserts that globalization prompts people living in the non-Western world to associate their core existence with attachment to their religion because the pace of change instigated by the process of cultural globalization is enormous, and this is almost always associated with Western cultural imperialism. As Maalouf contends:

> The ever-increasing speed of globalization undoubtedly reinforces, by way of reaction, people's need for identity. And because of the existential anguish that accompanies such sudden changes it also strengthens their need for spirituality. But only religious allegiance meets, or at least seeks to meet, both of these needs.[14]

These scholars make a plausible argument when maintaining that religious ideologies—different from their secular counterparts—can provide certainty and meaningful answers to existential questions raised by dislocated individuals in an insecure, globalizing world. Yet, this argument is still not sufficient to explain the prominence of religious politics in a fast globalizing world. Why would dislocated people not simply embrace a more ascetic religious lifestyle or return to religiosity, rather than supporting religiopolitical projects? In other words, why would we expect the losers of globalization to embrace an activist interpretation of their faith, rather than an ascetic one? In order to understand how dislocation, alienation or existential insecurities lead to support for religiopolitical projects, one needs to take into consideration how religious entrepreneurs frame ideas, create meaning and politicize grievances. These framing processes are crucial to establish a link between socioeconomic context and religiopolitical mobilization. As I will discuss later, this is one of the main aims of this book.

The third main approach emphasizes purely political factors in the strengthening of religious movements. Ergun Özbudun, for instance, argues that the weakness of center parties was the main reason for the de facto rise of the Welfare Party in Turkey in the 1990s.[15] Since the mainstream parties of the center were not successful in solving long-lasting economic problems, the religious right emerged as the only untried alternative. According to this thesis, a vote for religious parties is not ideologically based but merely a protest vote due to the poor performance of the center parties. Similarly, many scholars tie the concomitant rise of religious movements in post-colonial countries in the recent decades across different regions and economic stages to the crisis of hegemony of secularist nation-building projects.[16] In the Middle East, for instance, the ideologies that challenged the West in the post-independence period, namely liberal nationalism, Nasser's socialist Arab nationalism, and Ba'athism, could not fulfill their promises of economic growth, stable and representative political institutions, and international strength. Thus, "[t]he failure of these models was a major driver for the rise of the

Islamist model – the concept that 'Islam is the answer.'"[17] This type of political approach suffers from similar weaknesses with the socioeconomic approach. While it offers important insights about the political context which provides a foundation for the rise of religiopolitical projects, it does not to take into account the use of religious idioms in the construction of ideologies which tie the political context to collective action. As with the socioeconomic approach, it fails to explain the role of religious entrepreneurs in creating meaning and circulating these new ideas to the society in order to garner support for their religiopolitical projects. I argue that the Social Movement Theory (SMT) provides a fuller picture of religiopolitical activism, and to this approach I now turn my attention in the next section.

SMT and Religious Mobilization in the Middle East

SMT emphasizes the importance of political opportunity structures, framing processes—including identity formation—and social networks in explaining protest movements and different types of contentious politics. While most SMT theorists focus on one or the other of these three theoretical aspects in explaining political mobilization, there is a need to advance more comprehensive theories that look at the interaction between the three aspects.[18] An approach that is grounded in the interaction of these three concepts goes beyond the limitations of the cultural, socioeconomic and political approaches discussed above. In this book, I claim that the Shas movement and the NOM were successful in political mobilization because the political opportunity structure in both countries was ripe, religious entrepreneurs constructed frames transforming grievances into political capital, and finally religiopolitical movements connected these frames to the everyday life of citizens through dense social networks formed in poor neighborhoods, development towns, shantytowns, and around religious schools.

Currently, there is an emerging trend in Middle Eastern Studies whereby social scientists use the theoretical tools of SMT to explain religious activism, particularly Islamism, in various contexts in the region.[19] For Middle Eastern Studies, this dialogue with the SMT is productive because it enriches the study of religious activism in the region by incorporating the tools of mainstream political science and moving beyond claims of Middle Eastern and/or Islamic exceptionalism. This is a positive scholarly development, because "until recently Islamism had been excluded from the mode of inquiry developed by social movement theorists in the West."[20] This novelty should not, however, be perceived as a one-way street, where conceptual tools of Western academia are uncritically appropriated to undercover political dynamics in the non-Western world. As I try to show in the following empirical chapters of the book, studying religiopolitical movements in two different Middle Eastern cases through an SMT framework contributes to this theoretical tradition not only by advancing the scope of the cases beyond the Western context, but also by testing different arguments developed in this theoretical tradition and contributing to theory building.

One of the main limitations of the scholarship on social movements in the Western context has been the priority given to the political process and institutional sites associated with the state. The political process model with its emphasis on the importance of political opportunity structures is a good example of this approach. These approaches usually conceptualize the state and society as two sides of a binary and therefore fall short in understanding the religiopolitical movements in the Middle East. In contrast, the collective public enactment of one's piety through particular religious practices, such as veiling, can transform the society through identity formation in citizens' everyday life practices without necessarily asserting any claim on formal politics.[21] As Tuğal (2009) aptly claims, the study of Islamism in Turkey requires attentiveness to both state structures and identity formation in everyday practices and informal networks.[22] Following Tuğal's advice, in my study of the NOM in Turkey and the Shas movement in Israel, I will analyze the actions of social movements as they pertain to both formal political mechanisms and aspects of identity formation in civil society. This approach also has resonance with Joel Migdal's "State-in-society" approach which views state–society interaction as an iterative process transforming both social groups and the state through accommodation, bargaining and new-boundary creation.[23]

The political opportunity structure (POS), which is also known as the political process model, suggests that prospects for political mobilization are context-dependent. Political entrepreneurs do not operate in a vacuum, rather the sociopolitical context facilitates or restrains social movement mobilization by setting the grievances around which activists mobilize—advantaging some claims and disadvantaging others.[24] Among other things, the political opportunity structures might include the nature of political cleavages, access to influential allies within the government, and increasing political access to the state's resources. Political opportunities are exogenous factors to the activities of social movements. It is important to note that the state, as a political actor, can influence the prospects of social movements by facilitating or preventing access to valuable resources.[25]

In accordance with the POS model, a closer look at the Israeli and Turkish cases reveal that religious mobilization in both countries has been facilitated by the politicization of a historical sociocultural cleavage, which sharpened sociocultural grievances of Sephardim and pious Muslims. Moreover, the secular state elites' incorporation of religious actors into the state created a new political opportunity by providing access for religious entrepreneurs to the cultural and material resources of the state. The beginning of neo-liberal restructuring in Israel in 1977 and in Turkey in 1980 also constituted a POS by weakening the welfare systems for the poor and allowing the religiopolitical movements to appeal to the losers of neo-liberalism by forming informal welfare institutions. In the case of Turkey, the state's provision of export incentives during neo-liberal structuring also paved the way for the strengthening of Anatolian Tigers, small and medium sized enterprises from Anatolia, who formed an Islamic middle class and became the engine of Islamism in Turkey in the 1990s and 2000s.

It is important to note at this point that my definition of a "political opportunity structure" is more expansive than the way the concept is employed by most theorists of the political process model. Most such theorists prioritize the role of political institutions and political elites, such as the existence of elite allies within the state apparatus, while neglecting to analyze the role of societal factors as potential sources of opportunity for the mobilizational capacity of social movements.[26] In this study—in addition to political institutions—I discuss the role of societal modernization—such as rural–urban migration, increasing literacy rates and school integration—that politicize a dormant political cleavage and therefore create a favorable context for oppositional social movements as well as the transition to neo-liberalism that undermines welfare provisions and changes the class dynamics of society.

However, a sole focus on political opportunities leaves out the significant role played by religious entrepreneurs who are key in translating opportunities into mobilization.[27] Framing literature is useful to establish this link.[28] Framing processes address the importance of ideas and meaning-making in politics. A frame can be defined as "a schemata of interpretation that enable individuals to locate, perceive, identify, and label occurrences within their life space and the world at large."[29] As agents of signification, movement activists have to articulate and disseminate frames of understanding that resonate with (potential) constituents.[30] These frames help to diagnose problems, attribute responsibility, as well as "suggest action pathways to remedy problems."[31]

In Israel and Turkey, I pinpoint three different types of frames that the religiopolitical movements use to appeal to potential constituents. First, *injustice frames*[32] identify the victims in a societal setting, emphasize their victimization and attribute blame to certain sociopolitical actors. Second, what I call *empowerment frames* provide followers as well as potential followers with cognitive tools to overcome their victimhood and construct a positive collective identity. Thus empowerment frames are important in understanding processes of identity formation. Lastly, *prognostic frames*[33] propose a solution to the diagnosed problem. Shas, the NOM and to a certain extent the JDP succeeded in portraying Sephardim/pious Muslims as victims at the hands of secular states, empowered potential constituents by creating pride around Sephardi/pious Muslim identity, and proposed a religious way of life as a remedy for societal decay caused by hyper-modernization. In both countries, these frames gained credibility among the potential constituents because they had *resonance*[34] with everyday life-experiences of the marginalized.

Explication of the social networks formed around religious schools constitutes the last piece of the puzzle for religiopolitical mobilization. Vertical networks solve collective action dilemmas, increase communication flow among members, embody past successes at collaboration, and foster norms of reciprocity as well as interpersonal trust.[35] These social networks "need to be considered in any assessment of *religious* movements since they provide a vehicle for recruitment, facilitate the consolidation of their material and social bases, and offer general support and solidarity."[36] In Israel and Turkey, social networks formed by religiopolitical movements play two important roles. First, they provide social provisions for the economically disadvantaged, mainly the poor Sephardim in Israel and the economically strained peripheral populations in Turkey. By providing basic goods and services through these informal networks, the religious activists in both countries can demonstrate that a religiously inspired organization can solve the everyday problems of the marginalized. This function of the religiopolitical movements in Israel and Turkey is not different from the provision of social services by other religious movements such as Hamas in Palestine, Hizballah in Lebanon or the Muslim Brotherhood in Egypt. Second, networks built in poor neighborhoods, development towns, shantytowns, and around religious schools provide a space that connects activists, potential activists and potential constituents across space. This function of the social networks, such as the *El Ham'ayan* or *Milli Gençlik Vakfı* (National Youth Foundation), is similar to other social networks studied by scholars, formed around medical clinics,[37] prayer circles[38] and churches.[39] These informal networks are significant for political mobilization because they facilitate recruitment by circulating the mobilizing frames among potential recruits or supporters in the larger society.

Religious Politics and Democracy: A Debate

A comparative analysis of the concomitant rise of religiopolitical movements in Israel and Turkey provides an opportunity to address some of the debates in the social science literature surrounding the relationship between democracy and religion because both countries have democratic regimes with sizeable religiopolitical actors. One of the heated debates in the social sciences revolves around the question of whether it is possible for religious teachings and democracy to coexist. Some scholars have investigated whether, theoretically, certain religious traditions (and today the debate is mainly focused on Islam) are compatible with democracy. Those who answer this question negatively argue that religions are governed by absolute dogma, while democracy requires an adherence to the pluralist rules of the game and bargaining with political actors representing multiple worldviews. Therefore, the argument goes, democracy and religion cannot coexist in the political arena, and the latter needs to be relegated to the private sphere. This argument is challenged by other scholars, who argue that democracy can be legitimized by concepts authentic to religious teachings. For instance, many scholars have analyzed Islamic concepts, such as *shura* (consultation), *ijma* (consensus) and *ijtihad* (independent analysis) to show that Islam authentically contains the basic doctrines for the justification of liberal democracy, pluralism and human rights.[40] Others argue that religious traditions are multi-vocal, and the question of whether any religion is compatible with democracy hinges not on an analysis of religious texts, but on political struggles between actors who interpret their religion democratically and actors who interpret their religious teachings in an undemocratic fashion.[41] In other words, as Bayat asserts, "discourse is not power unless given material force."[42] Therefore, it is more apt to focus on the political ideologies, discursive practices as well as political and social constituents of religiopolitical actors within democratic political systems in order to evaluate the religion–democracy compatibility debate, rather than engaging in theological discussions.

Some scholars argue that religiopolitical actors do not have any place in a democratic system, because they advocate political ideologies that are inherently antidemocratic and are therefore unable to adhere to democratic values and practices.[43] Daniel Pipes (1995) maintains that religious parties participating in democratic elections are using the democratic system to come to power and to establish an authoritarian theocracy from above. The evidence from the empirical cases discussed in this book does not support these claims. While the leaders from both Shas and the National Outlook parties have occasionally made illiberal, exclusionary and even inciting statements against their political opponents undermining democratic political culture, both participated in the democratic game, engaged in democratic bargaining, and accepted the institutional constraints of their respective democratic systems even when they were in government. Both movements have also utilized religious concepts and idioms in order to appeal to their constituents. Yet, this use of religious idioms is not inherently undemocratic. Rather, these religious concepts, as further discussed in Chapters 6, 7 and 8, provide a form of communication between these political actors and societal groups for whom religious idioms constitute an important part of their daily lives. Some of the novel interpretations of religious teachings, such as Shas's use of *pikuah nefesh* to legitimate the Oslo Peace Process, can even challenge the status quo and lead to more inclusionary demands.

Moreover, many of the religious discourses employed by both movements serve a democratic function by empowering peripheral groups and offering them a voice in the center of politics in their societies. In this regard, these religiopolitical actors have something in common with the social protest movements of the 1960s and 1970s which fought for recognition of differences in the public sphere. Until the 1960s, social groups fought to gain equal legal and political rights in the political arena. Many thought that gaining equal rights would lead to the concept of equal citizenship and the inclusion of disadvantaged groups (i.e. blacks, women, cultural minorities) into the political system. This demand for legal equality was blind to particularities—it was color-blind, gender-blind and culture-blind. In other words, all the disadvantaged groups were to be included into the mold of citizenship "in spite of their differences." Participation in the public sphere presupposed casting aside one's differences and assumed a neutral national political sphere based on universal values. Yet, when these groups acquired equal legal and political rights, it became apparent that the rules and practices of the public sphere were very much dominated by the norms and codes of the privileged groups.

Thus, political inclusion in such a political sphere required assimilation to those norms and codes. Hence, the oppressed groups, which acquired equal legal and political rights, were still at a disadvantage and lacked meaningful access to political power.

As a response to the inadequacies of this homogenizing politics, a new understanding of social justice was developed. This demand for social justice was based on the recognition of differences (i.e. racial, religious, gender-based, cultural) in the public and political spheres.[44] Hence, minorities did not accept being included "in spite of their differences" to a public sphere that was dominated by the rules and norms of the privileged groups; rather, they demanded to participate "with their differences" or as "different members" in their national political community. Trends of cultural globalization that had started to undermine the power of the nation-state in the 1970s also contributed to the emergence of this politics of difference.

The Shas movement in Israel and the NOM in Turkey show some limited similarities to new social movements that represent culturally oppressed groups. Both movements and their civil society arms try to carve ideological spaces where they assert a group specificity and pride against ideals of assimilation.[45] For instance, the new language that Shas employs for the articulation of a religious Sephardi identity in the political sphere challenges the Ashkenazi-dominant secular Zionist identity, which was the bearer of cultural homogenization in Israel. In the civil society Shas constructs pride around Sephardi traditions in education and popular culture through civil society organizations, such as its school network, *Ma'ayan Hahinuch Hatorani* or its newspaper *Yom LeYom*. Similarly in Turkey, the NOM and later the JDP articulated a new Islamic identity, which challenged the cultural homogenization of secular Kemalist nationalism. This Islamic identity was not only manifested in the political sphere through the statements of the party activists or affiliated government officials, but also in the civil society through the proliferation of Islamic media outlets, NGOs, business associations (i.e. MUSIAD), labor unions and Islamized social spaces, especially after the 1980s. These sociopolitical expressions of difference are significant for the deepening of democracy in both contexts in that they led to the social and political recognition of the culturally marginalized peripheral groups in previously homogenous and exclusionary public spaces.

Another debate in the democratization literature focuses on the relationship between a political regime's approach toward religiopolitical actors and the ideology of those actors. According to the moderation–inclusion thesis, religiopolitical actors that are allowed to participate in competitive contestation moderate their demands because by being part of the electoral process they learn values essential to democracy, such as bargaining and compromise.[46] Over time, many religious activists internalize more fundamental values to democracy, such as pluralism and respect for human rights. On the other hand, exclusion from the political system creates feelings of alienation, frustration and prompts religiopolitical actors to embrace more radical ideological positions.

While the moderation–inclusion thesis makes a convincing argument, the evidence from the Turkish and Israeli cases does not support it. In Turkey, the main moderation of religiopolitical actors occurred when the JDP broke with the Islamist ideology of National Outlook and emerged as a post-Islamist party. Yet, this moderation followed the removal of the WP from power by a "soft coup" and the closure of the WP and VP respectively by the Constitutional Court in the aftermath. Hence, the moderation of the religiopolitical actors followed a period of exclusion. However, it is important to understand the nature of exclusion in Turkey and how its interpretation by religiopolitical actors might differ from other cases. Unlike in other countries (i.e. Algeria in 1991, Egypt and Tunisia in the 2000s), in Turkey, exclusion does not mean violent state repression and/or total exclusion from elections. Despite the fact that the parties of National Outlook were closed down by the Constitutional Court, the religiopolitical actors knew from past experiences and a history of protracted democratic regimes that they could reorganize themselves in the political field. Moreover, they were already adapted to the rules of competitive elections from their 30 years of participation in Turkish democracy, despite their momentary exclusion from the political system at the end of the 1990s. Hence, the JDP leadership rationally decided that it would be in their best long-term interest to continue to participate in the Turkish political system with a more moderate agenda in order to avoid similar exclusionary reactions from the state institutions.

In Israel, the Shas party underwent a moderation of rhetoric to a far lesser extent in the past decade. This moderation did not follow any change in the political regime's approach toward Shas. Rather, the Shas leadership's decision to tone down some of its uncompromising rhetoric was based on an assessment of the political events. The vocal secular opposition against the party spearheaded by the secularist Shinui and Shas's exclusion from Ariel Sharon's government in 2003 played an important role in this assessment. Thus, both in Turkey and Israel, interest-calculation rather than inclusion explains the moderation of religiopolitical actors. In both cases, moderation occurred when religious actors acted as rational agents and decided—after an assessment of the political climate—that a change of strategy would be in their long-term interest. However, there is a qualitative difference between the ideological moderation of the JDP and strategic moderation of Shas. The difference can be explained when the social bases of the two are assessed.

Lastly, the Israeli and Turkish cases illustrate that the electoral strengthening of religious parties in countries with strong secular traditions can have an adverse effect on stability of democracy. The rise of the Welfare Party to power in 1996, and the Shas party's winning of an unprecedented 17 mandates in the Knesset in the 1999 election, increased the anxiety of secular segments in both countries. This anxiety instigated the formation of secular blocs against the WP (and later against the JDP) and Shas, and this has led to the polarization of politics around the secular–religious divide. While both countries observed polarization, the effects of this polarization differed in each case, which requires further explanation.

Notes

1 A similar definition is suggested by S. Tepe, *Beyond Sacred and Secular: Politics of Religion in Israel and Turkey*, Stanford: Stanford University Press, 2008, p. 18.
2 D. Rucht, 'The Impact of National Contexts on Movement Structures: A Cross-Movement and Cross-National Comparison', in D. McAdam, J. McCarthy and M. Zald (eds.), *Comparative Perspectives on Social Movements: Political Opportunities, Mobilizing Structures, and Cultural Framings*, New York: Cambridge University Press, 1996, p. 187.
3 D. Collier, 'The Comparative Method', in A. Finter (ed.), *Political Science: The State of the Discipline II*, Washington, D.C.: American Political Science Association, 1993, pp. 105–19.
4 C. J. Ragin, *The Comparative Method: Moving beyond Qualitative and Quantitative Strategies*, Berkeley: University of California Press, 1987, p. 35.
5 The GDP per capita and urbanization figures are taken from the World Bank's 2011 Databank. The data is available at http://data.worldbank.org/indicator/NY.GDP.PCAP.CD.
The figures for HDI, which is a combination of measures of life expectancy, literacy, educational attainment and GDP per capita, is taken from the UNDP. It is available at http://hdrstats.undp.org/countries/.
6 One can plausibly claim that the JDP has reshaped the center and become the new center-right party. While this might be an accurate observation, it still does not validate the protest hypothesis, which claims that the popular support for the religious parties would be ethereal and return to the center-right parties.
7 For a recent study that investigates the root causes of the different approaches toward religion in the public sphere in Israel and Turkey see A. Rubin, 'The Status of Religion in Emergent Political Regimes: Lessons from Turkey and Israel', *Nations and Nationalism*, 2012, 1–20.
8 B. Lewis, *The Political Language of Islam*, Chicago: Chicago University Press, 1988; W. Zartman, 'Democracy and Islam, the Cultural Dialectic', *Annals of the Academy of Political and Social Science*, vol.524, 1992, 181–91; B. Lewis, *What Went Wrong: The Clash between Islam and Modernity in the Middle East*, New York: Oxford University Press, 2002.
9 J. Fox, 'World Separation of Religion and State Into the 21st Century', *Comparative Political Studies*, vol.39, no.5, 2006, 537–69.
10 F. Ahmad, 'Islamic Reassertion in Turkey', *Third World Quarterly*, vol.10. no.2, 1988, 750–69; F. Ahmad, 'Politics and Islam in Modern Turkey', *Middle Eastern Studies*, vol.27, no.1, 1991, 3–21.
11 A. Richards and J. Waterbury, *A Political Economy of the Middle East*, Boulder: Westview Press, 1996; N. Keddie, 'New Religious Politics: Where, When, and Why do Fundamentalisms Appear?', *Comparative Studies in Society and History*, vol.40, no.4, 1998, 696–723; C. L. Brown, *Religion and State: The Muslim Approach to Politics*, New York: Columbia University Press, 2000.
12 P. Berger, 'Desecularization of the World: A Global Overview', in P. Berger (ed.), *The Desecularization of the World: Resurgent Religion and World Politics*, Grand Rapids: Eerdmans Publishing, 1999, p. 10.
13 A. Riaz, 'Three Arguments about the Religion-Politics Nexus', in A. Riaz (ed.), *Religion and Politics in South Asia*, London: Routledge, 2010, p. 9.
14 A. Maalouf, *In the Name of Identity: Violence and the Need to Belong*, New York: Penguin Books, 2003, p. 93.

15 E. Özbudun, 'The Institutional Decline of Parties in Turkey', in L. Diamond and R. Gunther (eds.), *Political Parties and Democracy*, Baltimore: Johns Hopkins University Press, 2001, pp. 238–65.
16 A. Riaz, '"God Willing": The Politics and Ideology of Islamism in Bangladesh', *Comparative Studies of South Asia, Africa, and the Middle East*, vol.23, no.1&2, 2003, 301–20; F. Keyman, 'On the Relation between Global Modernity and Nationalism: The Crisis of Hegemony and (Islamic) Identity in Turkey', *New Perspectives on Turkey*, vol.13, 1995, 93–120.
17 A. M. Rabasa, 'Overview', in A. M. Rabasa (ed.), *The Muslim World after 9/11*, Arlington, VA: Rand Corporation, 2004, p. 36.
18 D. McAdam, J. McCarthy and M. N. Zald, 'Introduction: Opportunities, Mobilizing Structures, and Framing Processes-toward a Synthetic Comparative Perspective on Social Movements', in D. McAdam, J. McCarthy and M. Zald (eds.), *Comparative Perspectives on Social Movements: Political Opportunities, Mobilizing Structures, and Cultural Framings*, New York: Cambridge University Press, 1996, p. 6.
19 See, for example, Z. Munson, 'Islamic Mobilization: Social Movement Theory and the Egyptian Muslim Brotherhood', *The Sociological Quarterly*, vol.42, no.4, 2001, 487–510; C. R. Wickham, *Mobilizing Islam: Religion, Activism and Political Change in Egypt*, New York: Columbia University Press, 2002; Q. Wiktorowicz (ed.), *Islamic Activism: A Social Movement Theory*, Bloomington: Indiana University Press, 2004; Banu Eligür, *The Mobilization of Political Islam in Turkey*, New York: Cambridge University Press, 2010.
20 A. Bayat, 'Islamism and Social Movement Theory', *Third World Quarterly*, vol.26, no.6, 2005, 892.
21 For a fascinating example see Saba Mahmood, *Politics of Piety: The Islamic Revival and the Feminist Subject*, Princeton: Princeton University Press, 2005.
22 C. Tuğal, 'Transforming Everyday Life: Islamism and Social Movement Theory', *Theory and Society*, vol.38, 2009, 423–58.
23 J. Migdal, *State in Society: Studying How States and Societies Transform and Constitute One Another*, New York: Cambridge University Press, 2001.
24 D. S. Meyer, 'Protest and Political Opportunities', *Annual Review of Sociology*, vol.30, 2004, 127–8.
25 Ibid., p. 131.
26 D. Rucht, 'The Impact of National Contexts', p. 185.
27 D. S. Meyer, 'Protest and Political Opportunities', p. 138.
28 D. Snow, E. B. Rochford, S. K. Worden and R. D. Benford, 'Frame Alignment Processes, Micromobilization, and Movement Participation', *American Sociological Review*, vol.51, no.4, 1986, 464–81; D. A. Snow and R. D. Benford, 'Ideology, Frame Resonance, and Participant Mobilization', *International Social Movement Research*, vol.1, 1988, 197–217; R. D. Benford and D. Snow, 'Framing Processes and Social Movements: An Overview and Assessment', *Annual Review of Sociology*, vol.26, 2000, 611–39.
29 D. Snow, E. B. Rochford, S. K. Worden and R. D. Benford, 'Frame Alignment Processes', p. 464.
30 Q. Wiktorowicz, 'Introduction: Islamic Activism and Social Movement Theory', p. 15.
31 Mayer N. Zald, 'Culture, Ideology, and Strategic Framing', in D. McAdam, J. McCarthy and M. Zald (eds.), *Comparative Perspectives on Social Movements: Political Opportunities, Mobilizing Structures, and Cultural Framings*, New York: Cambridge University Press, 1996, p. 265.
32 W. Gamson, B. Fireman and S. Rytina, *Encounters with Unjust Authority*, Homewood: Dorsey Press, 1982.
33 R. D. Benford and D. Snow, 'Framing Processes', pp. 616–17.

34 D. A. Snow and R. D. Benford, 'Ideology, Frame Resonance'.
35 R. Putnam, *Making Democracy Work Civic Traditions in Modern Italy*, Princeton: Princeton University Press, 1994, pp. 173–5.
36 D. Singerman, 'The Networked World of Islamist Social Movements', in Q. Wicktorowicz (ed.), *Islamic Activism: A Social Movement Theory*, Bloomington: Indiana University Press, 2004, p. 155. Italics are mine.
37 J. Clark, 'Social Movement Theory and Patron-Clientelism: Islamic Social Institutions and the Middle Class in Egypt, Jordan, and Yemen', *Comparative Political Studies*, vol.37, no.8, 2004, 941–68.
38 C. R. Wickham, 'Interests, Ideas, and Islamist Outreach in Egypt', in Q. Wicktorowicz (ed.), *Islamic Activism: A Social Movement Theory*, Bloomington: Indiana University Press, 2004, pp. 231–49.
39 D. McAdam, *Political Process and the Development of Black Insurgency, 1930–1970*, Chicago: University of Chicago Press, 1982.
40 J. Esposito and J. Voll, *Islam and Democracy*, New York: Oxford University Press, 1996; A. Mousalli, *The Islamic Quest for Democracy, Pluralism, and Human Right*, Gainesville: The University of Florida Press, 2003; K. Abou El Fadl, *Islam and the Challenge of Democracy*, J. Cohen and D. Chasman (eds.), Princeton: Princeton University Press, 2004.
41 A. Bayat, *Making Islam Democratic: Social Movements and the Post-Islamist Turn*, Stanford: Stanford University Press, 2007.
42 Ibid., p. 6.
43 B. Tibi, 'Why they Can't be Democratic', *Journal of Democracy*, vol.19, no. 3, 2008, 43–48.
44 I. M. Young, *Justice and the Politics of Difference*, Princeton: Princeton University Press, 1990; I. M. Young, *Inclusion and Democracy*, Oxford: Oxford University Press, 2000; C. Taylor, 'The Politics of Recognition', in A. Gutmann (ed.), *Multiculturalism: Examining the Politics of Recognition*, Princeton: Princeton University Press, 1994, pp. 25–74; E. Kiss, 'Democracy and the Politics of Recognition', in I. Shapiro and C. Hacker-Cordón (eds.), *Democracy's Edges*, Cambridge: Cambridge University Press, 1999, pp. 193–209.
45 I. M. Young, 'Polity and Group Difference: A Critique of the Ideal of Universal Citizenship', *Ethics*, vol.99, no.2, 1989, 251.
46 C. R. Wickham, 'The Path to Moderation: Strategy and Learning in the Formation of Egypt's Wasat Party', *Comparative Politics*, vol.36, no.2, 2004, 205–28; J. Schwedler, *Faith in Moderation: Islamist Parties in Jordan and Yemen*, Cambridge: Cambridge University Press, 2006.

3 Setting the Stage

The Creation and Politicization of Sociocultural Cleavages in Israel and Turkey

Understanding the historical evolution of state-religion arrangements and sociocultural cleavages in a country is key to any discussion of contemporary religiopolitical mobilization. The interaction between state elites, religious authorities and political actors shape the public sphere and construct many of the cultural and social references that constitute the political actors' referential repertoire. The Israeli and Turkish states have dealt differently with the issue of religion's public role and created dissimilar mechanisms to deal with the question of religious authority during their formative periods. The Turkish state tried to minimize the role of religion in public institutions and embraced a strict secularist approach similar to the French *laïcité* in an attempt to legitimize its political authority by drawing a sharp contrast with the *ancien regime* that is the Ottoman Empire. While most of the public manifestations of religion were eradicated with new reforms, the Turkish state also aimed to control and singularize the interpretation of religious authority through its newly formed Directorate of Religious Affairs (*Diyanet İşleri Başkanlığı*). The Israeli state was much more concerned with winning the support of different religious groups at a time when its own existence was in jeopardy. In order to ensure the support of all sections of Jewish society, the Zionist elites sought to accommodate different Judaic subcultures within the public sphere through granting autonomy to modern Orthodox and ultra-Orthodox actors in a number of institutions.

Despite these contrasts, in both countries secular modernizers dominated state institutions for decades after state formation, and this reality led to the creation of a similar sociocultural cleavage both in Israel and Turkey. In Israel, an ethnic divide between Ashkenazim and Sephardim (see definitions and further details below), which cuts across the already existing secular–religious categories between secular, modern Orthodox, and ultra-Orthodox Jews was formed with the immigration of large numbers of Jews from Muslim countries in the 1950s. Similarly, during the formative period of the new republic in Turkey (1923–46), a sociocultural hierarchy was created with a modernist center and a more conservative periphery. The discussion below aims to illustrate how processes of social change politicized these cleavages and thereby created ripe political opportunities for new political players, such as Shas and the NOM.

Religion-State Arrangements in Israel during State Formation

Cultural, political and religious diversity has characterized the Jewish population in Palestine since the new *Yishuv*[1] era. The diversity was institutionalized in what is known as an enclave system. Political parties operated as the major facilitators of social services in the Yishuv, and therefore separation was established in different spheres of life, including schools, youth movements, and neighborhoods. This institutionalized fragmentation during the *Yishuv* continued in the post-independence era. For the purposes of state-religion arrangements, there were three significant institutionalized political trends in the *Yishuv*: Labor Zionism, Ultra-Orthodoxy and Religious Zionism.

Increasing trends of nationalist sentiment in Europe and the persecution of Jews in various European countries in the eighteenth and nineteenth centuries became catalysts for the formation of the modern secular Jewish nationalism, known as Zionism. The Zionist movement was spearheaded by the intellectual elites of European Jewry, such as Theodor Herzl and Max Nordau, who were heavily influenced by the norms and values of *Haskalah* (Jewish Enlightenment). During the *Yishuv* era, especially after the start of the British mandate in Palestine, Labor Zionism emerged as the dominant stream within the Zionist movement. Labor Zionists, whose most important leaders came to Palestine during the second *aliyah*,[2] not only aimed to create a secular Jewish state in Palestine, a territory Jews claim to have an ancestral attachment to, but also to radically transform the life of the Jews in Palestine according to principles of socialism, equality, nationalism and secularism. Important ideologues of the movement, such as Aaron David Gordon, promoted Jewish agriculture and manual work as a way to transform Jews from a "parasitic group of people" to an "independent self-sufficient nation."[3] Moreover, productive Jewish agriculture would confirm Jews' right to inhabit the land, which was described by the Labor ideologues as "poor, desolate, abandoned … and almost uninhabited."[4] Grounded in this ideology, Labor Zionists built most of Israel's foundational political and social institutions, including the Mapai (*Mifleget Poelei Eretz Yisrael*, the party of the laborers of the land of Israel, which became the Labor Party in 1968), Haganah (later the Israeli Defense Forces), Histadrut (General Federation of Laborers in the land of Israel), and the kibbutzim (collectivist agricultural settlements). While Zionism was first and foremost a secular nationalist movement based on political considerations, religion was used as a motif in strengthening nationalism and fostering the creation of the "new Jew." The selection of Magen David (the star of David) as the symbol of the Israeli flag, the use of the seven-branch menorah, another ancient religious symbol, as the national emblem, and the use of the word Zion (a biblical synonym for Jerusalem) in describing the nationalist movement reflect some of the ways in which religion was selectively utilized to forge a common national identity.[5]

For the ultra-Orthodox community, also known as *Haredim* (literally, those who fear God), this lip service to Jewish religion in national identity was never sufficient for designating a political entity as Jewish. The ultra-Orthodox, who lived in the ghettoized communities in Europe and in the holy cities of Jerusalem, Hebron, Safed and Tiberias in Palestine during the pre-*Yishuv* period, perceived Judaism as a divine mandate. According to the ultra-Orthodox, legitimate Jewish identity could only be expressed by living a life based on private and public observance of *halacha* (Jewish law).[6] The ultra-Orthodox sector started to develop its separate institutions as a reaction to the effective institutions created by Zionist settlers from Europe during the new *Yishuv*. The formation of the first ultra-Orthodox political party, *Agudat Yisrael*, in 1912 was the first step in the formation of separate ultra-Orthodox institutions. Moshe Blau, who became the head of the *Agudat Yisrael*'s Palestine branch in 1919, spearheaded the creation of separate *Agudah* schools, *Agudah* courts, *Agudah* rabbinic institutions and *Agudah* civil authorities.[7] These institutions were the first symbols of the resistance on the part of the ultra-Orthodox against integration to the mainstream secular public.

The ultra-Orthodox also challenged the legitimacy of any Jewish political entity built by the Zionist movement because the idea of a Jewish reawakening by secular figures ran against their belief of messianic redemption. The unification of the Jewish people could, they contended, only be achieved by the coming of the Messiah, "who would restore sovereignty to the Jewish people in its land, the Land of Israel."[8] According to one interpretation of ultra-Orthodoxy, God imposed three oaths on the Jewish people: two of which were not to rebel against the non-Jews and not to collectively immigrate to the land of Israel before the coming of the Messiah.[9] Therefore the ultra-Orthodox interpreted the attempts of the Zionist movement to foster a national reawakening in Palestine as "forcing the end" by human agency rather than divine mandate.[10] Rabbi Schneerson explains this position succinctly:

> In order to infuse our brethren with the idea of being "a nation" and an independent polity … the Zionists must give nationalism precedence over the Torah, because it is known that those who cling to the Torah and the commandments are not likely to change and accept another identity, especially such as implied by their own power … Hence, in order to implement their idea, the Zionists must distort the essence of [Jewishness] in order to get [the Jews] to assume a different identity.[11]

In addition to the anti-Zionist ultra-Orthodox and the Labor Zionists, religious Zionists constituted the third significant group during the *Yishuv* era. Religious Zionists were mainly Jews pursuing an Orthodox life, while at the same time embracing the ideals of the Zionist movement in a national Jewish reawakening. Religious Zionism, which represented a middle ground between the secular Mapai and the anti-Zionist Agudat Yisrael because of its synthesis of Orthodoxy and Zionism, was organized in the political party *Mizrachi*[12] from 1902 on. One of the influential ideologues of *Mizrachi*, Rabbi Avraham Kook, created a novel synthesis of Orthodoxy and Zionism that reconciles messianic Judaism with the secular Zionist project. According to Kook, the Zionist project fulfilled God's plan of redemption despite being led by secular actors and a secular ideology. According to Kook's interpretation, secular Zionists were propelled and guided by Divine Providence without being cognizant of it. Formation of the Zionist settlements in Palestine was part of the messianic process and "Zionism was a stage in God's plan," while the Zionist pioneers were "good sinners" and "principled evildoers."[13]

Partly grounded in this theology of Avraam Kook, Religious Zionists accepted the legitimacy of the proposed Jewish state. *Mizrachi* actively participated in the World Zionist Organization and the National Board (*Va'ad Leumi*), the main Jewish governing apparatus in Palestine during the British mandate, while Agudat Yisrael stayed out of these bodies and refused any funding for its autonomous institutions until 1947. Before the founding of the state, the main challenge for the Labor Zionists was to convince the ultra-Orthodox to accept the proposed Jewish state or at least not to forestall its creation. To that end, David Ben-Gurion, together with two functionaries in the Jewish Agency, sent a letter offering concessions to the ultra-Orthodox to Agudat Yisrael's leadership. This document, which is also known as the status quo agreement, assured Agudat Yisrael that the cultural survival of the ultra-Orthodox would not be in jeopardy in the new Jewish state. According to the letter:

1 the matters of personal status, such as marriage and divorce, will be handled solely by the orthodox Rabbinate in the Jewish sector (in order to prevent any schism within the Jewish people);
2 the Shabbat will be a legal day of rest in Israel and its sanctity shall be preserved;
3 the ultra-Orthodox will have autonomy in running their educational institutions; and
4 *Kashrut* (Jewish dietary laws) will be kept in all kitchens opened by the state.[14]

Based on these concessions, the ultra-Orthodox did not oppose the establishment of the state and accepted, although hesitantly, inclusion in the political process. The provisions of the status quo document were honored by successive governments after the creation of the state of Israel and still form the basis of a careful political balance between secular and ultra-Orthodox political actors in Israel. This symbolized Israel's opposition to separation of church and state as a principal of the political regime and opened the door to accommodation of religious groups in the public sphere.[15]

Western vs. Eastern Jews: New Immigration Waves (1950s and 1960s) and the Creation of an Ethnic Hierarchy in Israel

Despite the religious and political divisions between them, the secular, modern Orthodox (Religious Zionist), and ultra-Orthodox communities were all predominantly Ashkenazim (Jews of European origin), because Jews from Europe constituted close to 90 percent of the Jewish population in Palestine when the State of Israel was established in 1948.[16] All of the formative institutions in the secular and religious sectors and the leadership positions were established by Ashkenazim. However, Israel's demographics changed dramatically with the arrival of large numbers of *Sephardim* (Jews from the Middle East and North Africa).[17] From 1948 to 1956, a total of 450,000 Jews arrived in Israel from Asia and Africa, compared to 360,000 Jews from Europe and America.[18]

Although these immigrants came from many different countries, such as Morocco, Iran, Iraq, Egypt, Turkey, Libya, Tunisia, Yemen, etc., and from various ethnic backgrounds, once they arrived in Israel, they were subsumed under the category "*Mizrahi*" (Easterner). In the eyes of the Ashkenazi founders, who saw themselves as the bearers of Western Enlightenment values, Easterner had a derogatory meaning, and even the labeling itself was indicative of a new cultural hierarchy that was in the process of formation between the two groups. This distinction between the Ashkenazim and Sephardim created a long-lasting ethno-cultural cleavage in Israeli society. The Sephardim were attached to the cultural norms of the societies from which they had emigrated. For instance, many of them spoke Judeo-Arabic and listened to Oriental music. Their sense of Jewishness was interwoven with the culture in which they had been raised, and many of them conceived their identity as "part of a larger Judeo-Islamic cultural fabric."[19] This "Easternness" was perceived to undermine the image of the "new Jew" that the Labor Zionists were trying so hard to construct. Furthermore, the ideology of Zionism as secular Jewish nationalism was alien to most of the Sephardi newcomers. Many of them did not come to Israel for ideological reasons, but in hope of a better life or to escape oppression. The sense of religiosity of the Sephardim did not fit in the established categories of the secular–religious divide in the predominantly Ashkenazi society of Israel. Most of the Sephardic Jews considered themselves religious and observed basic religious commandments, such as eating kosher or attending the synagogue on Shabbat. However, their religious observance was intermeshed with popular religious practices and was not sufficiently strict according to the standards of the ultra-Orthodox and the modern Orthodox in Israel. Therefore, most Sephardim in Israel are today defined as "*masorti*" (traditional), as distinct both from "secular" and "religious" categories.[20]

As a result of official resistance to these differences, the Sephardim had to undergo some humiliating practices. For instance, some Yemenite children had their side locks cut off, so that they would look like their Ashkenazi counterparts, or entire families were sanitized with pesticides in the airports.[21] Moreover, the Oriental culture of the Sephardim was devalued by the Ashkenazi establishment, and they were forced to assimilate to mainstream Israeli society, which was heavily influenced by Ashkenazi practices. The statements of early Israeli political leaders reveal this discriminatory mindset developed by the Ashkenazi Zionist establishment. Remarks made by David Ben-Gurion in 1949 clearly demonstrate this orientation:

> those [Jews] from Morocco had no education. Their customs are those of Arabs. They love their wives, but they beat them ... Maybe in the third generation something will appear from the Oriental Jews that is [a] little different. But I don't see it yet. The Moroccan Jew has taken a lot from the Moroccan Arabs. The culture of Morocco I would not like to have here. And I don't see what contribution present [Jewish] Persians have to make ... We do not want Israelis to become Arabs. We are in duty bound to fight against the spirit of the Levant, which corrupts individuals and societies, and preserve the authentic Jewish values as they crystallized in the [European] Diaspora.[22]

These remarks by the most influential politician in Israel in the immediate aftermath of the establishment of the state are rather telling. They, and many similar remarks by the political elite, indicate that Orientalism as a colonial ideology had penetrated the minds of the Israeli leadership in regards with the Eastern Jewry. The Orientalist hierarchy between the "rational" West as the colonizer and the East as the "backward" colonized was reproduced within the Jewish population in Israel between the Ashkenazim and *Mizrahim*. This type of paternalistic attitude toward Oriental Jewry has a long history among the European Jewry. For instance, the French Jewry established *Alliance Israélite Universelle*, a school network, in 1860 with an aim to "liberate" the Oriental Jews living among Muslim communities from their "state of ignorance" through providing education in French language, culture and thought.[23] *Alliance* schools, which became quite prevalent among Jewish communities in Morocco, Tunisia, Iran and Turkey in the first decades of the twentieth century, treated the heritage languages of these communities, such as Arabic, Judeo-Arabic or Judeo-Spanish, as relics of a tradition-bound past in need of erasure. Building on this intellectual and colonialist heritage, the Ashkenazi elite in Israel prioritized the values of the European Diaspora in the formation of the Jewish state's national values, and therefore cultural assimilation of the "inferior" *Mizrahim* became a deliberate goal of the government. Zalman Shazar, the two-time president of Israel, described the dangers of Mizrahi immigration during his service in the Jewish Agency Executive in 1951 in these terms:

> An *Aliyah* has come to us who never knew the taste of high school, and they are unused to so much education, to so much learning ... Suppose

> that, ok, we can bring them to graduate primary schools, but what will the level be then, what will the *yishuv* be like, would we be able to be a light for the gentiles? … Will the *yishuv* in Israel survive without more Europeans and Anglo-Saxons, Jews like us?[24]

Other public officials, such as the head of the Jewish Agency's Youth and Pioneer Department Moshe Kol, argued for age and quantity restrictions to Sephardi immigration in order to be able to assimilate the Oriental newcomers to Ashkenazi values:

> In Morocco, Tunisia, and Persia some half a million Jews live, and from these countries we must pick youths and pioneers aged 13–14. This will be cheaper, and we can educate them, and they would be able to absorb their families more easily within two or three years. Otherwise, we may find ourselves drowning in a Levantine ocean, and the country will become a Levantine country.[25]

Sammy Samoha, a world-known Sephardi sociologist who immigrated to Israel from Iraq in the early years of the state, describes how the Zionists used the concept of ingathering of the exiles (*mizug galuyot*) to stress an imagined unity among the Jews. This supposed unity among Jews was used as a national construct to assimilate Mizrahim into mainstream Israeli national norms defined by Ashkenazi practices:

> We were told not to speak Arabic, but we didn't know Hebrew. Everything was strange. My father went from being a railroad official in Baghdad to an unskilled nobody. We suffered a terrible loss of identity. Looking back, I'd call it cultural repression. Behind their lofty ideals of "one people", they were acting superior, paternalistic.[26]

The paternalistic and derogatory attitude toward Mizrahi culture persisted among the Israeli elite long after state formation. Twenty years after the establishment of the state Prime Minister Golda Meir's statement upon the arrival of a number of new Russian immigrants was revealing:

> You are the real Jews. We have been waiting for you for twenty-five years. You speak Yiddish! … Every loyal Jew must speak Yiddish, for he who does not know Yiddish is not a Jew. You are a superior breed-you will provide us with heroes.[27]

The Russian immigrants did not just receive a warmer welcome in words, but also in public policies. The cultural marginalization of the Sephardim was exacerbated by spatial isolation. Most of the Sephardi newcomers were placed in temporary immigrant camps, called *ma'abarot*, and in peripheral towns, called "development towns." These towns, created as part of Israel's absorption policy, "were far removed from the Israeli urban centers. The towns were populated through the provision of public housing to (mainly Mizrahi) homeless and dependent immigrants who had little other residential choices."[28] In addition to their geographic marginality, the socioeconomic indicators in these development towns were significantly poorer compared to other parts of the country. Soon, they resembled dilapidated ethnic ghettos with lower wages, a younger population, lower literacy rates, poor schools, higher delinquency rates, higher levels of unemployment, and poor social services.[29] Even in 2000, the average income in development towns was 80 percent of Israel's average and the percentage of welfare recipients was twice the Israeli average.[30] The development towns with a very high concentration of Sephardi Jews, such as Dimona, Kiryat Shmona and Kiryat Gat, also face a net out-migration, which makes ethnic residential segregation more acute.[31] Until the early 1990s, when significant numbers of Russian immigrants started to arrive in Israel, Sephardi residents made up more than 80 percent of the population in these development towns. Moreover, ethnic segregation at the neighborhood level continues to be a reality in the mid-sized and big cities. Despite some integration in certain urban centers, many pockets of poverty, which were created at the peripheries of mid-sized cities or unpopular inner-city neighborhoods of big cities, are still populated predominantly by Sephardim.[32]

Due to this history of structural disadvantage, an ethnic gap still exists today in many social and economic indicators, even among second generation Ashkenazim and Sephardim. Although the gap between the two groups has decreased in years of schooling, significant inequalities continue to persist in income, in holding prestigious jobs, and participation in higher education. According to 2009 figures provided by Central Bureau of Statistics in Israel, 39 percent first generation Ashkenazi immigrants and 55 percent second generation Ashkenazi immigrants held white-collar jobs, while for first generation and second generation Sephardi immigrants the corresponding figures were 22 and 34 percent.[33] Sephardim are also overwhelmingly underrepresented among the intellectual, artistic and cultural leaders in the country.[34]

Moreover, the percentage of Sephardim who continue to higher education is significantly lower than the percentage of Ashkenazim in universities. Figure 3.1 shows that both first and second generation immigrants from Asian and African countries are far less likely to attend a university than first and second generation immigrants from European and American countries. Similarly, second generation Ashkenazi immigrants are more likely to receive a university degree compared to youth born of Israeli parents, while second generation Sephardi youth lag significantly behind them. Since higher education is the most important determinant of income, the lack of a higher education for most Sephardi youth has an adverse impact on their future life prospects. Longitudinal data suggest that the earning gap between second generation Ashkenazi men and Mizrahi men has actually increased in 1975–2001.[35] Because of the persistence of these socioeconomic inequalities

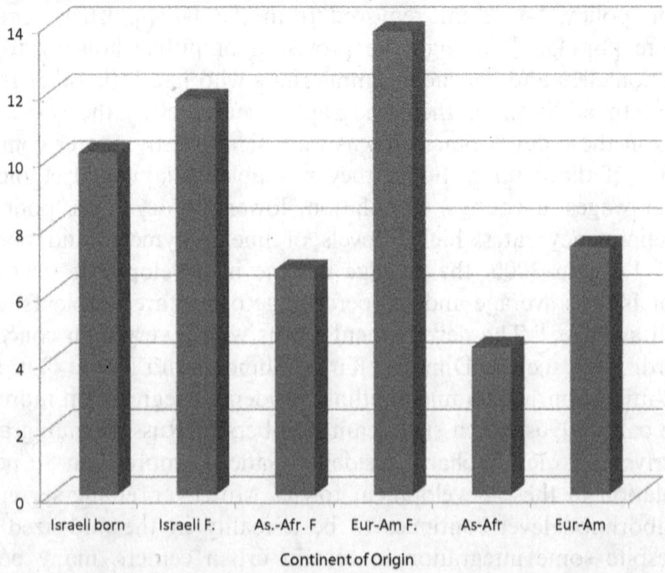

Figure 3.1 Percentage of university-age youth in higher education according to father's country of origin.

Source: *Statistical Abstract of Israel*, 2002. In the census, there is no question about respondents' ethnic identity, but there is a question regarding respondent's father's origins, which can be a proxy for ethnic identity. Following are the definitions of the terms in the figures: As-Afr: Students who are first generation immigrants and born in Asia or Africa; Eur-Am: Students who are first generation immigrants and born in Europe or America; As.-Afr. F: Students who are born in Israel as second generation immigrants to parents from Asia or Africa; Eur-Am F: Students who are born in Israel as second generation immigrants to parents from Europe or America; Israeli F: Students whose fathers are born in Israel; Israeli born: All students born in Israel

ethnicity is still salient in Israel and impacts the opportunities of most second generation Sephardim.

School Integration and Politicization of Sephardi Grievances

The sociocultural cleavage between Ashkenazim and Sephardim had important repercussions for the education system. In Israel, three main school streams operated since the passage of the State Education Law in 1953. According to this law, the Zionist educational streams[36] of the *Yishuv* period were merged into a *secular state education* system, while the Religious Zionist educational stream was transformed into a *state religious education* system. Unlike these two streams that operated under the Education Ministry, the ultra-Orthodox educational institutions of Agudat Yisrael did not become official institutions, although the education provided by most of them is recognized by the Israeli state. In the early years of Mizrahi immigration, the children of Sephardi immigrants had to attend one of these three streams. With increasing school attendance of the Sephardim, it became apparent that Sephardi children faced some type of discrimination in all three educational streams.

The ethnic hierarchy between Ashkenazim and Sephardim was—and still is—most apparent in ultra-Orthodox educational institutions. Many of the Agudah schools have been implementing quotas that limit the admission of Sephardi children. For instance, the most prestigious ultra-Orthodox girls' school Beit Yaacov still imposes a 30–35 percent quota for students from Sephardi families. These quotas, which are mainly constructed by listing the ethnic origin of the registering students, survive up to today despite drawing strong criticism from the Sephardi community and civil rights groups.[37] A recent controversy that has surfaced in Emmanuel, a predominantly Haredi settlement town in West Bank, is indicative of the discrimination Sephardim face in Haredi schools. One Sephardi parent petitioned the Supreme Court, because the elementary Beit Yaacov school her daughter attended implemented segregation between strictly observant girls who were mainly from Ashkenazi families and the rest who were predominantly Sephardim.[38] The segregation in the school was enforced by erecting a wall between different tracks and assigning "separate entrances, separate teachers, separate rooms, separate playgrounds and even different uniforms for the two groups of girls."[39] When the Supreme Court ruled to integrate the schools, the Ashkenazi parents resisted the ruling and integration in the school. When they were incarcerated en masse for disobeying the decision of the court, tens of thousands of Ashkenazi Haredim supported the parents and protested in the streets of Jerusalem and Bnei Brak.[40] As this and similar incidents show, many Ashkenazi Haredim see Sephardi Haredim as inferior and avoid any attempts to mingle with them. Many of the central figures, who played an important role in the establishment of the Shas party, such as the first party chairman Ariyeh Deri and the party's spiritual leader Rabbi Ovadia Yosef's son David Yosef, were educated in the Ashkenazi yeshivas of the Agudah network and felt this ethnic discrimination first hand. Moreover, in the Agudah network the number of religious high schools and *yeshivas*[41] specifically catering to the Sephardim was inadequate, and existing Sephardi institutions were very poorly funded. The closing of the Sephardi yeshivas due to a lack of funding under the Agudah network is one of the main reasons that prompted the birth of Shas.[42]

The difficulties Sephardim faced in the state-secular system were mainly caused by the curriculum of the schools that was predicated on Orientalist meta-narratives of secular Zionism. The culture of Sephardi children was alien to the Zionists, and this posed an important challenge to the curriculum. Mizrahim were represented as backward and inferior in school textbooks until 1967, when the textbooks were rewritten.[43] The following passage from a history textbook taught in secular-state schools in the late 1960s is a good example of the Orientalist imagery used toward Mizrahim:

> While European Judaism goes through a stormy revolutionary process, and while a new important powerful Jewish center emerges across the ocean, some eight hundred thousand members of Jewish communities in the backward Muslim countries of Asia and Africa—formerly strongholds of Jewish culture—are submitted to the double burden of Oriental tyranny and Muslim zealousness, enclosed for the most part in their special quarters, limited to a few professions, especially as artisans and peddlers, frozen in their ways, deep in a spiritual sleep. The masses of populace lived in degenerate poverty, spoke like the commoners, and those who inhabited faraway districts, removed from the highway of modern history (including the inhabitants of Kurdistan, and of the Iranian plateaus, cave dwellers in the Atlas mountains, or oases on the edge of the Sahara) were on an even lower level, their way of life, their cultural level much like those of their half-savage Muslim neighbors. The absolute majority of the Jews were ignorant, and much like their neighbors, steeped in bizarre superstitions. Public life was entirely petrified, not a trace could be found of any social movement whatsoever (even the memory of Shabbetaianism has been already wiped out!), no trace of an ideological struggle or any living aspiration, except for a heavenly longing for the coming of the Messiah.[44]

The exposure of the Sephardi pupils to this type of Orientalist representations in formative years did not only pressure them to shed their cultural heritage, but also created profound feelings of social inferiority vis-à-vis their Ashkenazi peers. Even today, Zionist historiography scarcely pays any attention to the histories of the Sephardim. For instance, little mention is made of the fact that major Sephardi texts in philosophy, linguistics, poetry and medicine were produced when Jews were living in Arab lands.[45]

In addition to their cultural misrecognition, Sephardi children also struggled in terms of academic achievement because of their lower socioeconomic standing. A tracking system was introduced to deal with this achievement gap. According to this system, students took a scholastic aptitude test in the ninth grade and were placed either in a non-academic vocational track[46] or in an academic track. Due to the academic achievement gap between the two groups vocational tracks were predominantly filled with Sephardim, while Ashkenazim constituted the overwhelming majority in the academic tracks. This early placement in a vocational track significantly hindered the Sephardi pupils' ability to continue to higher education. Therefore, despite the increase in the rate of post-primary education, the proportion of Sephardim entering higher education has remained stable at about 15 percent as compared with about 40 percent for the Ashkenazim in the 1980s.[47] Even in the mid-1990s, most of the Jewish students who could not pass the national matriculation examination were Sephardim.[48]

The greatest ethnic tension surfaced in the state-religious education system, because the percentage of the Sephardi pupils in the state-religious schools was greater than in the two other school streams. After their arrival, Sephardi parents who defined themselves as *masorti* (traditional) preferred to send their children to the state-religious schools because they wanted their children to receive some level of religious formation in the school. However, due to ethnic segregation of the neighborhoods there was significant segregation between Ashkenazi and Sephardi students in state-religious schools throughout the 1950s and 1960s.

After some discussions at the Education Ministry and Knesset regarding possibilities for school integration, in 1963 Joshua Prawer prepared an Education Reform Program for the Education Ministry that aimed to integrate Sephardi and Ashkenazi pupils in public schools and close the ethnic achievement gap. In 1968 a large majority in the Knesset approved a bill endorsing the integration of public schools as an educational goal.[49]

However, the passage of this bill by the Israeli parliament did not mean that the Education Minister would follow strict policies to enforce integration, such as bussing students from low opportunity neighborhoods to schools in high opportunity neighborhoods. In January 1976 it was decided that school integration would not be enforced, but authority would be given to district directors and local authorities to guide the process of rearranging school districts if they deemed it necessary in their region.[50] Subsequently many battles have been fought between Ashkenazi and Sephardi parents in the state-religious system over school integration at the local level.

Many modern Orthodox Ashkenazi parents believe that integration of Sephardim would negatively impact upon the quality of education in their schools. Moreover, many of the Ashkenazim perceive the integration of their children with *masorti* Sephardim as a threat toward their own religious way of life. This concern is expressed cogently by an official in the state-religious education:

> The religious modern Orthodox and the *masortim* go to the same state-religious schools. But the religious modern Orthodox also have their limits, if there are too many *masortim* [in the school], especially more *masortim* than religious (*datiim*). The question is very complicated, but most of the time its hinges on Shabbath … Most of the *masortim* are going to the synagogue and saying the Kiddush. The question is whether you are going to the synagogue and then coming back and driving the car or watching the game. … If they [the *masortim*] are more secular than religious, then this has an important impact on the climate of the school, and the regular religious are not ready to live in such a climate. Hence, many problems are caused based on that. Especially in Petach Tikva, this created a big crisis.[51]

Hence, the modern Orthodox community perceives the growing numbers of *masorti* pupils in state-religious schools as endangering their own religious way of life. The changing climate within these schools leads them to believe that they are losing a historically won collective right, namely that of having an autonomous educational stream. Because of this threat perception—similar to the secular schools—a tracking system was introduced as a defensive strategy against integration. In this tracking system, vocational tracks were predominantly filled with Sephardi pupils, while the academic tracks were often filled by Ashkenazi pupils.[52] More importantly, a separate private religious school network, *Noam*, was established by Ashkenazi modern Orthodox parents who broke away from the state-religious education in 1972. *Noam* schools did not accept any Sephardim in their schools because they were seen as the root cause of diminishing quality of education and loosening of religious observance in the state-religious schools. The parents preferred to pay for the private education of their children rather than see them integrate with the *masorti* Sephardim.[53] Due to the flight of a significant number of Ashkenazi pupils to the *Noam* schools, the percentage of Sephardi students within the remaining state-religious schools increased significantly, and this caused more problems. As one modern Orthodox parent explained:

> When they opened *Noam* in Petach Tikva, all the [modern Orthodox] families, let's call them good families—including mine—said that *Noam* is a better Orthodox school. [They said] let's send our children there ... So when it [the student composition in the state religious school] was seventy percent from Kfar Ganim [a modern Orthodox neighborhood] and thirty percent from Shaariya [a Sephardi neighborhood], it was O.K. Then thirty to forty good families sent their children to *Noam*. Now they [Sephardi students] were seventy percent and we were thirty percent ... Now this is not integration. Because thirty years ago they told us that they need integration, so that they can learn with students from higher socioeconomic backgrounds ... The idea of integration is that you take seventy to eighty percent from a good community and you take twenty percent from a low socio-economic community, so that the strong [socioeconomically advanced] group can elevate the [socioeconomically] low group. Once it becomes the other way around ... They bring us down.[54]

This and similar reactions against school integration by Ashkenazi parents made the cultural grievances felt by the Sephardim more acute and politicized the sociocultural divide between Ashkenazim and Sephardim. This politicization created a ripe political opportunity for a political actor that could capitalize on this sociocultural resentment. As I discuss later, the Shas movement did exactly that.

Religion-State Arrangements in Turkey during State Formation

In order to understand the relationship between religious and political authority during state formation in Turkey, it is necessary to briefly mention religion's role in Ottoman politics and political changes during the late Ottoman Empire. The Ottoman Empire was not a religious state, although religion served several important political functions. Religious communities, including Muslims, Greek Orthodox, Armenian Orthodox and Jews, were officially recognized as *millets*, and given legal autonomy in managing their communal affairs, including charitable activities and education. Religious courts of each community had jurisdiction over issues related to personal status law, while issues related to state administration, taxation and international relations were dealt with by imperial laws, known as *kannunnames*,[55] and administered through state courts.

For the Muslim subjects of the Empire, who constituted the majority, the Ottoman state acted as the protector of orthodox Islam in the world.[56] In the eyes of his Muslim subjects, Islam served as a significant source of legitimacy for the Ottoman sultan. The *ulama* (religious scholars) played an important role in constructing this religiopolitical legitimacy, because they were functionaries of the state. From the Şehy-ül-Islam, who acted as the Minister of Religion at the top of the hierarchy, to the kadıs, who were the judges in local religious courts, these religious functionaries exerted important control over education and the judiciary, and thus "indirectly ensured the state's control of social life."[57] Moreover, Islam served as a source of social cohesion and forged horizontal ties among the Muslim subjects.[58]

Starting with the eighteenth century, Ottoman governments began to centralize and modernize the state institutions as a response to Europe's military and economic superiority as well as to fight against centrifugal tendencies in the Empire. While the early reformers Selim III (1789–1807) and Mahmud II (1808–39) focused on reforming the military and administrative apparatus, later reformers from the *Tanzimat* period (1839–76) onwards implemented more aggressive reforms adopting Western political, legal and educational institutions. Shariah law was limited and codified along European lines in 1865–88, a new penal code granting legal equality to Muslims and non-Muslims was introduced, and secular *nizamiye* courts were established in 1869 to deal with cases involving non-Muslims.[59] On the educational front, a three-tier secular school system was introduced which expanded the secular *Rüşdiye* (elementary schools) opened during the rule of Mahmud II and added civilian high schools called *idadiye* and colleges called *sultaniye*.[60] The political reforms that started with the promulgation of the *Gülhane* Edict in 1836, culminated in the introduction of the first Ottoman constitution in December 1876 and elections to the first popular Ottoman assembly in 1877. While the First Constitutional Period (1876–8) did not last long because of the dissolution of parliament by Sultan Abdulhamid II in 1878, it became "an important precedent to the Second Constitutional Period (1908–18)."[61]

During the reform periods, three major ideological outlooks emerged among the reformist state elites to prevent the disintegration of the Empire, namely Ottomanism, Islamism and Turkism. For the *Tanizmat* reformers the best way to preserve the territorial and demographic unity of the Empire was to create a civic bond among different groups based on shared citizenship. This ideology that came to be known as Ottomanism was visible in the *Gülhane* Edict (1839), which extended the reforms to all subjects irrespective of religion and the Reform Edict (1856), which created equal obligations for Muslims and non-Muslims for military service, equal opportunities for state employment as well as admission to state schools. The aim of Ottomanism was to stem the rising nationalist tendencies among the ethno-religious minorities in the Empire by bringing together all ethnic elements around a common Ottoman citizenship. However, the loss of Christian-majority territories in the Balkans after the Turko-Russian war of 1877–8 was a sign that the ideology of Ottomanism was not succeeding.[62]

Abdulhamid II (1876–1908) adopted Islamism as a new political plan to hold together Ottoman Muslims.[63] He made prominent religious figures, including Jamaleddin Al-Afghani, permanent residents in his court and employed his title caliph more often than his predecessors in order to appeal to Muslims world-wide.[64] As Abdulhamid himself put it: "The title of Amir-ul Muslimin [caliph] should be given priority everywhere and every time. The title 'Ottoman ruler' should take the second place because the state's social structure and politics is built on religious principles."[65] He also built the Hijaz railway to connect the capital of the Empire with Mecca and Medina, the most holy cities of Islam.[66]

Despite these efforts, the Empire continued to lose territory, and minority nationalisms continued to flourish, including among non-Turkish Muslims, such as Albanians and Arabs. Nationalist sentiment developed lastly among the Turks and only as a reaction toward the centrifugal minority nationalisms. Yusuf Akçura, one of the first Turkist thinkers, argues in his famous article, "Three Kind[s] of Policy," published in the periodical *Türk*, that Ottomanism and Islamism both failed as political ideologies to hold together the Empire.[67] Instead of these failed ideologies Akçura suggests a "national policy based on the Turkish race."[68] Later Ziya Gökalp developed a cultural Turkism, where he defined a nation as a group with shared language, shared culture, shared education and shared sentiments.[69] For Gökalp, the nation was the most developed societal group and the national ideal could not be replaced by the broader ideal of *ummah* (community of religious believers) or by the narrower ideal of the family.[70] According to Gökalp, the lack of a national ideal among Turks resulted in the "disintegration of economic, religious and political institutions of the Empire."[71] Therefore, for Gökalp the discovery and cultivation of a national consciousness and ideal among Turks was imperative. Turkism first flourished in cultural and literary venues, such as the periodicals Turk (*Türk*), Turkish Homeland (*Türk Yurdu*) and Turkish Association (*Türk Derneği*). Committee of Union and Progress (CUP) leaders embraced Turkism only toward the end of the Empire, especially after the traumatic losses in the Balkan Wars.

Early Republic and Secularization (1923–46)

Following the disintegration of the Empire and the war of national independence, the Republic of Turkey was founded in 1923. The founders, known as Republicans, came from the Ottoman bureaucratic and military class. The new state apparatus remarkably "retained an estimated 93 percent of the Ottoman military officers and 85 percent of the civilian administrators."[72] The secularist, Westernist and elitist worldview of the Republicans was the culmination of the political culture created among the higher echelons of the bureaucracy during the implementation of reform efforts in the late Ottoman era. Kemalism, the official ideology of the new regime, interweaved the cultural Turkism of Gökalp with secularization and cultural Westernization. Like Zionist pioneers in Israel, Turkey's Republican elites aimed to secularize and modernize Turkish society by implementing top-down reforms.

Some of those reforms aimed to weaken the power of religion in the public sphere. On 3 March 1924 the institution of the caliphate together with religious courts and religious schools (*medreses*) were all abolished. In 1925, Republicans also outlawed all the religious orders and dervish lodges to curb the social power of any non-official religious institution. The day of rest was changed from Friday to Saturday afternoon and Sunday in 1935. The constitutional article declaring Islam the official religion of the state was removed in 1928, and finally the principle of secularism (*laiklik*) was enshrined in the constitution in 1937.[73]

However, the Republican elites were careful not to directly attack Islam. According to Atatürk's public statements, Islam was fully compatible with progress and science. Yet a misguided interpretation of Islam that had been disseminated through existing religious institutions constituted a threat to Turkey's advancement toward civilization and needed to be erased. Therefore, the new Republic complemented its full scale assault on organized religion with the creation of a reformed and strictly state-controlled version of Islam. To this end, a Directorate of Religious Affairs was instituted in 1924 under the prime minister to replace the Ottoman religious hierarchy. However, unlike the Ottoman religious hierarchy, the Directorate had nothing to do with the application or interpretation of the law, but was solely responsible for providing religious services to Muslim citizens, including the appointment of personnel to places of worship all over the country. The next year, the Turkish Grand National Assembly commissioned a Turkish translation of the Qur'an.[74] In 1932, the calls to prayer were required to be made in Turkish in place of Arabic.[75] The aim of these policies was to create a Turkified and reformed Islam that would be firmly under the authority of the state and aid the Republicans in the construction of the new Turkish nationhood. The need for the Turkification of religious worship had already been articulated during the late Ottoman period by intellectuals, such as Abdullah Cevdet and Ziya Gökalp. According to Abdullah Cevdet, Turkish worship was an essential step in the reformation of Islam along the lines of the Protestant Reformation.[76]

Another important pillar of the new Republic's political project was cultural Westernization. For the Republican elites, "being modern" was closely aligned with adopting Western cultural practices. The adoption of the Gregorian calendar in place of the lunar calendar (1925), the introduction of the Latin alphabet in place of the Arabic alphabet (1928), and the banning of the traditional fez in favor of Western style hats (1928) were all steps toward the creation of a new Turkish nation, whose culture was in line with the Western world. The official stance of the Republican People's Party (RPP) was to label the local and more Islamic culture of the masses as relics from the dark ages and deny any ethnic or religious differences in Anatolia.[77] Accordingly, many religious and oriental cultural practices were debased, while Western cultural practices were depicted as superior. For instance, while the performance of Oriental music in public was banned, Village Institutes (*Köy Enstitüleri*) were formed in order to socialize villagers to a Westernized Turkish culture.[78] Similarly, Mustafa Kemal presented the adoption of the Latin alphabet during the Turkish language reform as a break from the grip of Oriental culture and a move toward European civilization:

> So long as Turkish was written from right to left, it could never properly express the ideals of European civilization. The picturesque involutions and intricacies of Arabic script afforded a psychological background to the Oriental mentality which stood as the real enemy of the Republic.[79]

The adoption of the Latin alphabet represented the Republican aim to sever any association with the Ottoman-Islamic past and to create a secular Turkish identity closely aligned with Europe. Kemal's comments on the adoption of the Latin alphabet also reveal how much outward appearance and forms were interconnected with the content of modernity in the minds of the Republicans. The following statements of Mustafa Kemal on the abandonment of traditional Ottoman headgear constitute yet another example of the construction of the East–West and primitive–civilized binaries through outward appearance:

> Gentlemen, it was necessary to abolish the fez, which sat on the heads of our nation as an emblem of ignorance, negligence, fanaticism, and hatred of progress and civilization, to accept in its place the hat, the headgear used by the whole civilized world, and in this way to demonstrate that the Turkish nation, in its mentality as in other respects, in no way diverges from civilized social life.[80]

As the above statements reveal, Republican elites saw traditional cultural practices as the main reason for the decline of the Ottoman Empire and the underdevelopment of Turkey. Women and their attire also played a significant symbolic role to represent the new regime's progressive image and the negation of the Ottoman-Islamic past. In 1926 with the implementation of the Turkish Civil Code, modeled after the Swiss Civil Code, the Islamic practice of polygamy was outlawed, women were granted equal rights in divorce and child custody cases,[81] and in 1934 women were granted suffrage. During these reforms, the abandonment of veiling was actively encouraged by the regime. For the Republicans, both the veil and traditional gender norms were hurdles to be passed in achieving the Republic's goal of "advancing to the level of contemporary civilization." In one of his speeches in Kastamonu, Mustafa Kemal directly addressed this issue:

> In some places I have seen women who put a piece of cloth or a towel or something like it over their heads to hide their faces, and who turn their backs or huddle themselves on the ground when a man passes by. What is the meaning and sense of this behaviour? Gentlemen, can the mothers and daughters of a civilized nation adopt this strange manner, this barbarous posture? It is a spectacle that makes the nation an object of ridicule. It must be remedied at once.[82]

For the Republican elites unveiled women "reinforced the movement toward Westernist civilization in a Muslim society previously dependent upon the isolation of women."[83] Hence, the Republican regime constructed its "civilized," Western image by publicizing photographs of women unveiled, women athletes in sports uniforms, and men and women intermingling in tea salons and at Republican balls. As Jenny White explains:

> Since the new Republican woman presented the modern, secular, Westernized state, she was expected to behave and dress in what the state defined as a modern, Western manner. Women who felt that their religious beliefs required them to dress modestly and cover their heads ... were not accepted into this Republican sisterhood and were alternately reviled as the uncivilized primitive.[84]

This derogatory view of the elites toward traditional dress and behavior was also replicated toward village life. Many examples can be found in the artistic productions of the period, such as Yakup Kadri Karaosmanoğlu's famous novel *Yaban*, where the villagers are portrayed as uncivilized primitives by the protagonist Ahmet Celal who moves to a village after becoming a war veteran. These Orientalist discourses and representations constructed a binary between a "primitive," "backwards" periphery and "civilized," "enlightened" center in the public sphere and became the source of a cultural hierarchy.

However, Republicans' aim to transform the Islamic way of life to a Westernized way of life did not completely succeed, and the inculcation of the Kemalist ideals of secularization, progress and positivism did not penetrate the entire Turkish society, especially in the villages, which were far from the big cities. The cultural idioms associated with Islam survived in the daily lives of the masses,[85] and Islamic consciousness remained the foundation of communal identity among large segments of society.[86] Accordingly, a duality between the more traditional, Islamic masses residing in the villages and the secular, Westernized elites residing in the big cities was created. This duality in Turkey paralleled the drift between the Oriental Sephardim and secular Ashkenazim in Israel. This division, which is known as the center–periphery cleavage,[87] became one of the most important divisions in Turkish social and political life in the multiparty period.

The economic policies of the Republican elites also produced stark socio-economic disparities between the center and the periphery. The twin economic aims of the Turkish state in its formative period were to build a domestic industrial base and to create a national middle class anchored in ethnically Turkish elements. Starting with the great depression, the Turkish state implemented a state-led industrialization program, which came to be known as *etatism*. In 1929–39, the RPP implemented protective measures to reduce the import of consumer goods and promoted the creation of infant industries by easing the import of intermediary goods.[88] These policies led to major industrialization in the big cities. Annual growth rate of industrial production in 1933–9 passed 10 percent.[89] The state bureaucrats, who controlled the main thrust of economic activity, reaped most of the economic benefits.[90] In 1931–40, 72.4 percent of all the new firms were established by state bureaucrats.[91] State-led economic initiatives, such as the founding of Sümerbank in 1933 and Etibank in 1935, were designed to benefit the new industrial middle class.[92] On the other hand, industrialization efforts heavily taxed and exploited the agricultural sector, and the farmers emerged as the main losers of the state's economic policies.[93] The government bought crops, such as wheat, sugar beet or cotton, from the small farmers under market price and sold them at great profit after processing.[94] The exploitation of the agricultural sector continued during the years of World War II. In 1944, the passage of the Soil Products' Tax (*Toprak Mahsülleri Vergisi*), a flat tax of 10 percent on all agricultural products, created a very heavy burden for the poor and small farmers. At the end of the war, the agricultural sector, which constituted 85 percent of the Turkish population at the time, harbored much resentment against the state.[95] By undertaking extensive state-led economic initiatives, the young Turkish state had managed to transform socioeconomic life in the big cities. Yet, at the end of the same period the periphery was not only culturally and politically marginalized, but also socioeconomically disadvantaged and dependent on the center.

The Encounter between the Periphery and the Center during the Multiparty Period: Failed Attempts at Integration

Turkey's transition to a multiparty democracy in 1946 marked the end of the one-party regime and ushered in a new political era under the government of the Democratic Party (DP) (1950–60). The DP, which was led by RPP defectors Adnan Menderes and Celal Bayar, pursued a liberal economic policy during its political tenure. With assistance received from the Marshall

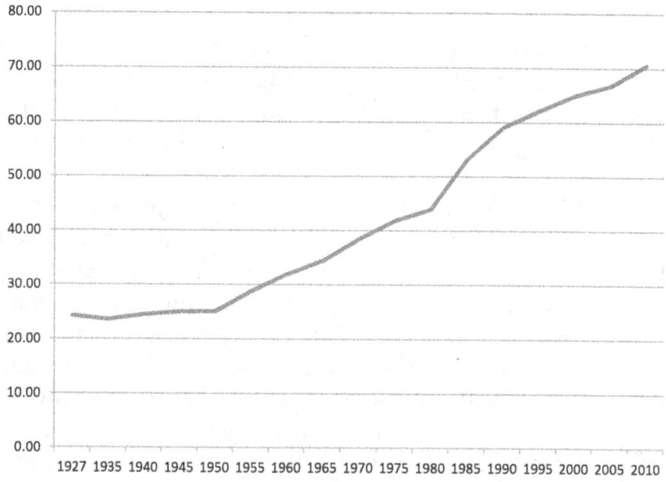

Figure 3.2 Share of the population living in urban areas as percentage of total population in Turkey in 1927–2010.
Sources: Turkish Statistical Institute; "World Urbanization Prospects, 2011 Revision" United Nations

Plan, mechanization of agriculture became pervasive. The number of tractors in Turkey skyrocketed from 1,750 in 1947 to 44,144 in 1957.[96] Increasing mechanization led to a decreasing need for agricultural labor and also threw small farmers out of business.[97] The newly unemployed villagers started to migrate to the major cities in great numbers.[98] The DP's expansion of the road network also contributed to the rural–urban migration.[99] In his classic anthropological account, Daniel Lerner (1958) portrayed the changes that took place in Balgat, a village near Ankara, during the first four years of DP rule. Lerner's account vividly describes how the newly built roads and increased bus transportation services changed societal dynamics in the rural areas and enabled the villagers to gain easier access to the urban areas.[100]

This increasing rural–urban migration meant that the periphery was moving closer to the center. As seen in Figure 3.2, rural–urban migration accelerated significantly in the 1980s and 1990s, especially with the reduction of agricultural subsidies during Turgut Özal's governments. The proportion of Turkish citizens residing in urban areas increased from 25 percent of the entire population in 1950 to 44 percent in 1980 and to 70.5 in 2010.

However, the state did not have sufficient resources to provide an urban development plan for the integration of the newcomers. Most of the rural migrants lived in shanties called *gecekondu* (literally meaning put up by night indicating how fast they were erected). These shanties were often built on state land without any legal permit and without any infrastructural plans. They were erected overnight because of a legal loophole that made it impossible for the state authorities to tear down a building if it was completed (basically, if it had a roof) between dusk and dawn without having been noticed by the authorities. Rather than tearing down the building, the state authorities had to start proceedings in the legal system. Often, the erection of the shanties was carried out close to election time, so that squatters could request amnesty from politicians and receive legal permits and/or other services for their *gecekondus.*

The first squatter settlements were built on the outskirts of the cities, although today many of them are incorporated into city centers due to urban outgrowth. When they were built, these settlements were characterized by poverty, by a large number of young residents, and by too many infrastructural problems, such as lack of sewerage, transportation, paved roads, clean water or electricity.[101] Most of the *gecekondu* dwellers were employed in the informal economy with no social security. The men usually worked as street vendors, construction workers or *dolmuş* (collective taxi) drivers, while the women either produced for the market in their homes or became servants in upper-middle class homes. Hence, despite their physical closeness to the center, these settlements still constituted a periphery, this time the "urban periphery."[102]

Despite their socioeconomic marginality in the major metropolitan areas of Turkey, the first generation *gecekondu* dwellers were optimistic about city life. Kemal Karpat's (1976) extensive study of three squatter settlements in Istanbul shows that the *gecekondu* residents, who mostly migrated to the cities for better economic and educational opportunities, earned on average more than the villagers, yet significantly less than the established urbanites. The migrants had a positive attitude toward the city, because of this increase in their income.[103] Moreover, 92 percent of those interviewed were optimistic about the future of their children due to expansive economic and educational opportunities.[104]

However, the optimism of the first generation *gecekondu* dwellers did not extend to the second and third generations, because the opportunities for the *gecekondu* dwellers did not improve parallel to their expectations. The city-born youngsters "were stuck at the level of their parents' low-income, low-prestige jobs in industries that had advanced beyond them."[105] Second and third generation *gecekondu* residents were more cognizant of their lack of economic opportunities and the discriminatory outlook of the established urbanites toward them.

In addition to this, some of the middle class urbanites started to move to suburbs of the major cities in the 1990s. Because of this movement toward the new suburbs, the *gecekondu* dwellers witnessed the growth of middle or upper class settlements in their backyards. Suburbanization led to closer contact between *gecekondu* dwellers and the established urbanites in the cities. This closer contact increased the awareness of the *gecekondu* residents of the social and cultural gulf that existed between themselves and the urban elites.

One of the spaces where daily encounters between rural migrants and the established urbanites took place was middle class apartments, where rural migrant men took jobs as doorkeepers (*kapıcı*) and their wives worked as maids.[106] Doorkeepers and their families lived in cramped, dark basements and undertook mundane chores, such as buying groceries, cleaning the apartment building, taking out the garbage, or moving furniture.[107] The following accounts of doorkeepers' wives are emblematic of the position accorded them by their employers:

> You are home-bound; you can't leave home for a visit for your enjoyment. You are like a prisoner. They see you as a dog on their doorstep, we are beneath them/they hold us in low esteem. They say we don't know how to eat food (meal-time behavior); they say our homes smell.
>
> They despise doorkeepers. They warn their children, "Don't play with doorkeepers' kids, they would contaminate you with microbes" ... We're humans too, only our appearance do not fit theirs.[108]

These intimate encounters made the rural migrants more cognizant of the cultural hierarchy that was formed between them and the urbanites. This awareness continued with the younger generations, as many children replaced their parents as the doorkeepers of the apartment buildings.

Another important factor that exacerbated the sociocultural frustration of rural migrants in the 1990s was the narratives that were created around *gecekondu* dwellers in the public space. In the 1990s with the help of the proliferation of media outlets in Turkey, the degrading term "*varoşlu*" replaced the more neutral term "*gecekondu* dweller."[109] Erman explains how the representation of the *gecekondu* dwellers changed significantly in the 1990s:

> The *gecekondu*/migrant population is not constructed any more as a rural population that failed to become urban, but as a population that is attacking the city, its values, its political institutions and, more importantly, the very core of its ideology (a secular and democratic society built on consensus and unity) and its social order ... [Urban dwellers stigmatized] people of rural origin as the "threatening Other", as the "dangerous and violent Other" and as the illegal occupiers and holders by force not only of some city space (that is, the *gecekondu* land), but today also of the social, cultural and political space.[110]

The urban elites blamed the *gecekondu* dwellers not only for ruralizing the city, for the mounting infrastructural problems, for overcrowding, for diminishing high urban manners, and for increasing criminal activity, but also for posing a cultural and political threat to their very existence. The increasing presence of the rural migrants and their corruption of the high urban manners in the urban landscape were labeled in mainstream middle class narratives as "invasion" (*istila*) and "siege" (*kuşatma*).[111] A new musical genre known as *arabesk*—songs casually mixing popular Western and Egyptian rhythms—became very popular among the low-income rural migrants, and despised by the urban elites so much that it was banned from state television and radio for defying established tastes and categories.[112] Starting in the mid-1980s, the usage of the term *arabesk* was expanded to groups who were deemed incapable of adopting the cultural habits of the bourgeoisie and took pleasure in "vulgar" and "tasteless" art forms.[113]

These derogatory depictions became much more prevalent in the 1990s, because the number of the rural migrants and *gecekondu* dwellers sky-rocketed, and the urban problems of the earlier periods snowballed. In the 1980s, 55 percent of Ankara, 70 percent of Istanbul and 50 percent of Izmir lived in *gecekondus.*[114] Another study conducted in 1993 showed the number of *gecekondus* as 1.6 million with almost three-quarters of a million in Ankara, Istanbul and Izmir alone. According to estimates the *gecekondu* dwellers constituted 17 percent of the national electorate at the time.[115] By the year 2000, the *gecekondu* residents in Istanbul constituted 75 percent of the city's total population.[116]

Conclusion

Both in Israel and Turkey a sociocultural divide was forged in the early years of state formation. The sociocultural hierarchy between the Ashkenazim and Sephardim was politicized when the two groups came into closer contact following attempts at school integration in the 1970s. When these attempts created a backlash on the part of the Ashkenazi parents and increased the frustrations of the Sephardim, the sociocultural divide was politicized.

In Turkey, the sociocultural divide between the periphery and the center that can be traced back to the early republican period, was transformed with increasing rural–urban migration. The relations between rural migrants and established urbanites became much tenser in the 1990s when both groups came into closer contact with the erection of suburban neighborhoods near *gecekondu* areas. When the negative representations of the rural migrants became part of the mainstream middle class urban discourse and depicted the *gecekondu* dwellers as a cultural threat to their own existence, the grievances of the second and third generation rural migrants, who already found it hard to climb the economic ladder due to stagnant opportunities, became more acute.

The politicization of the Ashkenazi–Sephardi cleavage in Israel and the center–periphery cleavage in Turkey created ripe political opportunities for religiopolitical actors, who successfully transformed those grievances to political capital through constructing appropriate frames. Chapters 6, 7 and 8 will discuss how religious movements in both countries used religion as a meta-narrative in framing those grievances and building political support.

Notes

1 The word *Yishuv* refers to the Jewish residents of Palestine prior to the establishment of the State of Israel. Old *Yishuv* refers to the Jewish settlements that existed

in Palestine prior to the arrival of the Zionist pioneers. The New *Yishuv* refers to the Jewish settlements that were formed by Zionist settlers from 1881 onwards.

2 *Aliyah* refers to Jewish immigration to the Land of Israel. Literally the word means "ascent."

3 Z. Sternhel, *The Founding Myths of Israel: Nationalism, Socialism, and the Making of the Jewish State*, Princeton: Princeton University Press, 1998, p. 48.

4 Ibid., p. 69.

5 R. D. Lee, *Religion and Politics in the Middle East: Identity, Ideology, Institutions, and Attitudes*, Boulder: Westview Press, 2010, p. 126.

6 M. Friedman, 'The Ultra-Orthodox and Israeli Society', in J. Peters and K. Kyle (eds.), *Whither Israel: The Domestic Challenges*, London: I. B. Tauris & Company, 1993, p. 179.

7 For more information on the creation of separate ultra-orthodox institutions in the *Yishuv*, see N. J. Efron, *Real Jews: Secular Versus Ultra-Orthodox and the Struggle for Jewish Identity in Israel*, New York: Basic Books, 2003, pp. 16–56.

8 M. Friedman, 'The Ultra-Orthodox', p. 179.

9 I. Shahak and N. Mezvinsky, *Jewish Fundamentalism in Israel*, London: Pluto Press, 2004, p. 18.

10 A. Ravitzky, *Messianism, Zionism, and Jewish Religious Radicalism*, Chicago: University of Chicago Press, 1999, p. 15.

11 S. Z. Landau and J. Rabinowitz (eds.), *Or la-yesharim*, Warsaw, 1900, p. 658. Quoted in A. Ravitzky, *Messianism, Zionism*, p. 16.

12 *Mizrachi* is an abbreviation for *Mercaz Ruhani* (spiritual center). The word should not be confused with the term *Mizrahi*, which means Easterner and is used to describe Jews who immigrated to Israel from Middle East and North Africa.

13 G. Gorenberg, *The Accidental Empire: Israel and the Birth of Settlements, 1967–1977*, New York: Times Books, 2006, pp. 21–2. Quoted in M. Munson, 'Gush Emunim and the Israeli Settlers of the Occupied Territories: A Social Movement Approach', *Strategic Insights*, 2008.

14 E. Don-Yehiya, *Religion and Political Accommodation in Israel*, Jerusalem: The Floersheimer Institute for Policy Studies, 1999, p. 41; N. J. Efron, *Real Jews*, p. 44.

15 A. Rubin, 'The Status of Religion in Emergent Political Regimes: Lessons from Turkey and Israel', *Nations and Nationalism*, 2012, 1–20.

16 E. B. Rafael and S. Sharot, *Ethnicity, Religion, and Class in Israeli Society*, Cambridge: Cambridge University Press, 1991, p. 27.

17 The distinction between the terms Sephardi and Ashkenazi does not strictly correspond to the distinction between European Jews and Jews from the Middle East and Africa. For instance, Jews from the Balkans were Sephardim, and the Jews of Southern Africa are Ashkenazim. Moreover Sephardic Jews originated from Spain, a European country. There are further complications with the category "Sephardi." The literal meaning of the word is Spanish in Hebrew. While most of the Jews who were expelled from Christian Spain came to the Ottoman Empire and then settled in countries ruled by Muslims, there were other Jewish communities already living under Muslim empires. These communities are known as *Mizrahi* (Easterner) Jews, different than Sephardim. Yet, in Israel these two groups are often conflated and a plethora of names are used to describe them, such as *Edot HaMizrach* (Eastern Communities), Arab Jews, Jews of Dar-ul Islam, Middle Eastern Jews, Oriental Jews, etc. I will primarily use the term Sephardi to describe Jews from Asia and Africa, because this term is used in Israel by the communities themselves and by Shas. At times, I switch to *Mizrahi* when I think it is a better descriptive.

18 *Statistical Abstract of Israel* 1978, Jerusalem: Israel Central Bureau of Statistics, in J. Allouche, *The Oriental Communities in Israel, 1948–2003: The Social and*

Cultural Creation of an Ethnic Group, Geneva: Institut universitaire de hautes études internationals, 2003, p. 24.

19 E. Shohat, 'Perspectives on Mizrachiut. The Shaping of Mizrahi Studies: A Relational Approach', *Israel Studies Forum*, vol.17, no.2, 2002, 87.

20 For a sociological discussion see Y. Yadgar, 'Jewish Secularism and Ethno-National Identity in Israel: The Traditionist Critique', *Journal of Contemporary Religion*, vol.26, no.3, 2011, 467–81.

21 G. N. Giladi, *Discord in Zion: Conflict Between Ashkenazi & Sephardi Jews in Israel*, London: Scorpion Publishing, 1990, p. 103. Quoted in J. Massad, 'Zionism's Internal Others: Israel and the Oriental Jews', *Journal of Palestine Studies*, vol.25, no.4, 1996, 56.

22 Z. Zohar, 'Sephardim and Oriental Jews in Israel: Rethinking the Sociopolitical Paradigm', in Z. Zohar (ed.), *Sephardic and Mizrahi Jewry: From Golden Age of Spain to Modern Times*, New York: New York University Press, 2005, p. 305; S. Smooha, *Israel, Pluralism and Conflict*, Berkeley: University of California Press, 1978, pp. 86–8. Quoted in J. Massad, 'Zionism's Internal Others', p. 57.

23 A. Rodrigue, *Images of Sephardi and Eastern Jewries in Transition: The Teachers of the Alliance Israélite Universelle, 1860–1939*, Seattle: University of Washington Press, 1993, p. 7; E. Benbassa and A. Rodrigue, *Sephardi Jewry: A History of the Judeo-Spanish Community, 14th-20th Century*, Berkeley: University of California Press, 2000, p. 83.

24 Quoted in S. S. Chetrit, *Intra-Jewish Conflict in Israel: White Jews, Black Jews*, London: Routledge, 2010, p. 35.

25 Quoted in ibid., p. 36.

26 Sammy Smooha quoted in D. Rosenthal, *Ordinary People in an Extraordinary Land: The Israelis*, New York: Free Press, 2003, p. 116.

27 G. N. Giladi, *Discord in Zion*, p. 255.

28 E. Tzfadia and O. Yiftachel, 'Between Urban and National: Political Mobilization among Mizrahim in Israel's "Development Towns"', *Cities*, vol.21, no.1, 2004, 45.

29 J. Allouche, *The Oriental Communities in Israel*, p. 34.

30 E. Tzafadia, 'Public Policy and Identity Formation: The Experience of Mizrahim in Israel's Development Towns', *The Journal for the Study of Sephardic and Mizrahi Jewry*, 2007, 61.

31 C. Goldscheider, *Israel's Changing Society Population, Ethnicity, and Development*, Boulder: Westview Press, 2002, pp. 123–4.

32 A. Gonen, 'The Changing Ethnic Geography of Israeli Cities', in A. Weingrod (ed.), *Studies in Israeli Ethnicity: After the Ingathering*, New York: Gordon & Breach, 1985, pp. 25–37.

33 *Statistical Abstract of Israel 2010*. White-collar jobs are defined as academic professionals, associate professional and technicians, and managers.

34 E. Illouz, 'Begin's Legacy: Enough of Ethnicity', *Ha'aretz*, 22 February 2012.

35 Y. Haberfeld and Y. Cohen, 'Gender, Ethnic, and National Earnings Gaps in Israel: The Role of Rising Inequality', *Social Science Research*, vol.36, 2007, 654–72.

36 Educational streams refer to different school systems that operate with different curricula and educational philosophies. A more detailed discussion is given in Chapter 8.

37 S. Ackerman, 'Do Agudat Yisrael Schools Bar Sephardim?', *The Jerusalem Post*, 26 October 1990; T. Rotem, 'Sorry, Rejected; your Grandmother's Sephardi', *Ha'aretz*, 5 August 2003.

38 L. Derfner, 'This is a Religious War', *The Jerusalem Post*, 11 June 2010.

39 R. Eglash, 'Is the Fight in Emmanuel over Racism or Religious Freedom?', *The Jerusalem Post*, 18 June 2010.

40 J. Mandel and A. Selig, 'Haredi Masses Hail Emmanuel Fathers En Route to Jail', *The Jerusalem Post*, 18 June 2010.

41 Religious post-secondary institutions.

42 Interview with Roni Huri, 13 December 2006. Huri studied in a Sephardi yeshiva under the Agudah network and then became a Shas activist.

43 D. Rosenthal, *Ordinary People*, pp. 116–17.

44 S. Horowitz, *A Brief History of the People of Israel: The Modern Period*, Haifa: Harealy Halvri School, 1966, pp. 169–70. Quoted in S. S. Chetrit, *Intra-Jewish Conflict,* pp. 34–5.

45 E. Shohat, 'The Invention of Mizrachim', *Journal of Palestine Studies*, vol.29, no.1, 1999, 6–8.

46 Tracks refer to different specialization fields (academic or vocational) within the same high school.

47 Y. Shavit, 'Segregation, Tracking, and the Educational Attainment of Minorities: Arabs and Mizrahi Jews in Israel', *American Sociological Review*, vol.55, no.1, 1990, 115–26.

48 Z. Zameret, 'Fifty Years of Education in the State of Israel', Israel Ministry of Foreign Affairs, 1998. Online. Available at www.mfa.gov.il/MFA/History/Modern%20History/Israel%20at%2050/Fifty%20Years%20of%20Education%20in%20the%20State%20of%20Israel (accessed 3 December 2008)

49 N. Blass and B. Amir, 'Integration in Education: the Development of a Policy', in Y. Amir and S. Sharan (eds.), *School Desegregation: Cross-cultural Perspectives*, Hillsdale, NJ: Lawrence Erlbaum Associates Publishers, 1984, pp. 63–98.

50 Ibid., p. 72.

51 Interview with Rami Hoffenberg, the head of state-religious education in Petach Tikva, 4 December 2006.

52 In 1995, the head of the Religious Education Council, Matityahu Dagan, abolished most of the vocational tracks within the state-religious schools because of the tracking system's effects on ethnic disparities.

53 The *Noam* school system refused to come under the authority of the state-religious system after is formation. After long negotiations for more than two decades, most of the *Noam* schools accepted to be part of the state-religious education system. As part of the deal, they also agreed to accept a certain number of Sephardim to their schools.

54 Interview with Yehuda Lanskron, 13 December 2006. The formation of the *Noam* schools not only exacerbated existing problems in the state-religious schools, but also signified the creation of a new lifestyle within the religious Zionist community. The families around the *Noam* schools adopted some of the cultural norms of the ultra-orthodox, such as growing earlocks and segregating themselves in neighborhoods while still trying to keep their religious Zionist identity. Therefore they are named as *haredi-leumiim*, meaning ultra-orthodox nationalist. This trend created an important cultural split and internal debate within the religious Zionist community.

55 Ş. Hanioğlu, *A Brief History of the Late Ottoman Empire*, Princeton: Princeton University Press, 2008, p. 18.

56 E. Zürcher, *Turkey: A Modern History*, London: I. B. Tauris, 2004, p. 11.

57 Ş. Mardin, 'Religion and Secularism in Turkey', in E. Özbudun and A. Kazancıgil (eds.), *Atatürk: Founder of Modern Turkey*, Hamden: Archon Book, 1981, p. 194.

58 H. Yavuz, *Islamic Political Identity in Turkey*, New York: Oxford University Press, 2003, p. 40.

59 E. Zürcher, *Turkey*, p. 61.

60 Ibid., p. 62.

61 Ş. Hanioğlu, *A Brief History*, p. 121.

62 L. C. Brown, *Religion and State: The Muslim Approach to Politics*, New York: Columbia University Press, 2000, p. 108.

63 K. H. Karpat, *Politicization of Islam: Reconstructing Identity, State, Faith, and Community in the Late Ottoman Empire*, New York: Oxford University Press, 2001, p. 174.

64 C. V. Findley, *Turkey, Islam, Nationalism, and Modernity: A History, 1789–2007*, New Haven: Yale University Press, 2010, p. 149.
65 Sultan Abdulhamid, *Siyasi Hatıratım*, Ismet Bozdağ (ed.), Istanbul, 1974. Quoted in K. H. Karpat, *Politicization of Islam*, p. 177.
66 C. V. Findley, *Turkey, Islam, Nationalism*, p. 150. While the railway connected Istanbul to Medina, it did not reach Mecca due to difficulties in construction during World War I.
67 B. Lewis, *The Emergence of Modern Turkey*, New York: Oxford University Press, 2002, p. 326.
68 Ibid., pp. 326–7.
69 T. Parla, *Ziya Gökalp, Kemalizm ve Türkiye'de Korporatizm*, Istanbul: Iletişim, 1989, pp. 75–6.
70 Z. Gökalp, *Türkleşmek, İslamlaşmak, Muasırlaşmak*, F. Kaynak (ed.), Istanbul: Eflatun, 2004, p. 19.
71 Ibid., p. 19.
72 D. Rustow, 'Atatürk as an Institution Builder', in E. Özbudun and A. Kazancıgil (eds.), *Atatürk: Founder of Modern Turkey*, Hamden: Archon Book, 1981, p. 73. Quoted in L. Anderson, 'The State in the Middle East and North Africa', *Comparative Politics*, vol.20, no.1, 1987, 5.
73 Ş. Hanioğlu, *Atatürk: An Intellectual Biography*, Princeton: Princeton University Press, 2011, pp. 157–8.
74 Ibid., p. 154.
75 Ibid., p. 155.
76 A. İ. Demir, *Cumhuriyet Dönemi Aydınlarının İslam'a Bakışı*, Istanbul: Ensar Neşriyat, 2004, pp. 224–5.
77 Ş. Mardin, 'Türkiye Siyasasını Açıklayabilecek Bir Anahtar: Merkez-Çevre İlişkileri', in M. Türköne and T. Önder (eds.), *Şerif Mardin Bütün Eserleri 6: Türkiye'de Toplum ve Siyaset*, Istanbul: İletişim Yayınları, 2004, p. 65.
78 Ş. Mardin, 'Religion and Secularism in Turkey', in A. Hourani, P. S. Khoury and M.C. Wilson (eds.), *The Modern Middle East*, Berkeley: University of California Press, 1993, p. 371.
79 Y. Çolak, 'Language Policy and Official Ideology in Early Republican Turkey', *Middle Eastern Studies*, vol.40, no.6, 2004, 73.
80 K. Atatürk, *Nutuk*. Cited in B. Lewis, *The Emergence of Modern Turkey*, p. 268.
81 D. A. Kandiyoti, 'Emancipated but Unliberated? Reflections on the Turkish Case', *Feminist Studies*, vol.13, no.2, 1987, 320.
82 *Atatürk'ün Söylev ve Demeçleri*. Cited in B. Lewis, *The Emergence of Modern Turkey*, p. 271.
83 N. Göle, *The Forbidden Modern: Civilization and Veiling*, Ann Arbor: Michigan University Press, 1997, p. 73.
84 J. B. White, 'State Feminism, Modernization, and the Turkish Republican Woman', *NWSA Journal*, vol.15, no.3, 2003, 157–8.
85 Ibid., pp. 372–3.
86 H. Yavuz, *Islamic Political Identity*, p. 55.
87 The general distinction between the center and the periphery was first introduced by Edward Shils in E. A. Shils, 'Centre and Periphery', in *The Logic of Personal Knowledge: Essays Presented to Michael Polanyi on his Seventieth Birthday*, London: Routledge, 1961 and further elaborated in E. A. Shils, *Center and Periphery: Essays in Macrosociology*, Chicago: University of Chicago Press, 1975. The division between the center and the periphery is applied to Turkish politics by Şerif Mardin. See Ş. Mardin, 'Center-Periphery Relations: A Key to Turkish Politics', *Daedalus*, 1973, 169–90.
88 D. Barlas, *Etatism and Diplomacy in Turkey: Economic and Foreign Policy Strategies in an Uncertain World, 1929–1939*, New York: Brill, 1998, p. 87.

89 K. Boratav, 'Kemalist Economic Policies and Etatism', in E. Özbudun and A. Kazancıgil (eds.), *Atatürk: Founder of Modern Turkey*, Hamden: Archon Book, 1981, p. 179.
90 Ç. Keyder, *Türkiye'de Devlet ve Sınıflar*, Istanbul: İletişim, 2000, p. 147.
91 Ibid., p. 149.
92 F. Ahmad, 'The Political Economy of Kemalism', in E. Özbudun and A. Kazancıgil (eds.), *Atatürk: Founder of Modern Turkey*, Hamden: Archon Book, 1981, p. 160.
93 Ç. Keyder, *Türkiye'de Devlet ve Sınıflar*, p. 150.
94 K. Boratav, 'İktisat Tarihi', in S. Akşin, B. Tanör and K. Boratav (eds.), *Yakınçağ Türkiye Tarihi 1908–1980*, Istanbul: Milliyet Yayınları, 2003, p. 335.
95 S. Gürsel, 'Cumhuriyet Döneminde Türkiye Ekonomisi', in M. Tunçay (ed.), *75 yılda düşünceler tartışmalar*, Istanbul: Türk Tarih Vakfı Yayınları, 1999, p. 142.
96 F. Ahmad, *Demokrasi Sürecinde Türkiye (1945–1980)*, Istanbul: Hil Yayın, 1992, p. 140.
97 Ibid., pp. 140–1.
98 M. C. Yalçıntan and A. E. Erbaş, 'Impacts of "Gecekondu" on the Electoral Geography of Istanbul', *International Labor & Working-Class History*, vol.64, 2003, 92–3.
99 Y. Atasoy, *Turkey, Islamists and Democracy: Transition and Globalization in a Muslim State*, London: I. B. Tauris, 2005, p. 93.
100 D. Lerner, *The Passing of the Traditional Society Modernizing the Middle East*, Glencoe: The Free Press, 1958, pp. 19–42.
101 Ibid., pp. 99–100.
102 T. Erman and A. Eken, 'The "Other of the Other" and "Unregulated Territories" in the Urban Periphery: Gecekondu Violence in the 2000s with a Focus on the Esenler Case, Istanbul', *Cities*, vol.21, no.1, 2004, 58.
103 K. Karpat, *The Gecekondu: Rural Migration and Urbanization*, New York: Cambridge University Press, 1976, pp. 105–6.
104 Ibid., pp. 107–9.
105 T. Şenyapılı, *A New Stage of Gecekondu Housing in İstanbul: Development of İstanbul Metropolitan Area and Low Cost Housing*, İstanbul: Turkish Social Science Association, Municipality of Greater İstanbul and IULA-EMME Publication, 1992, quoted in J. White, *Mobilization in Turkey: A Study in Vernacular Politics*, Seattle: University of Washington Press, 2002, p. 82.
106 G. Özyeğin, 'The Doorkeeper, the Maid and the Tenant: Troubling Encounters in the Turkish Urban Landscape', in D. Kandiyoti and A. Saktanber (eds.), *Fragments of Culture: The Everyday of Modern Turkey*, New Brunswick: Rutger University Press, 2002, pp. 43–72.
107 Ibid., pp. 46–8.
108 Ibid., p. 49.
109 T. Erman, 'The Politics of Squatter (*Gecekondu*) Studies in Turkey: The Changing Representations of Rural Migrants in the Academic Discourse', *Urban Studies*, vol.38, no.7, 2001, 983–1002.
110 Ibid., pp. 996–7.
111 A. Öncü, 'Global Consumerism, Sexuality as Public Spectacle, and the Cultural Remapping of Istanbul in the 1990s', in D. Kandiyoti and A. Saktanber (eds.), *Fragments of Culture: The Everyday of Modern Turkey*, New Brunswick: Rutger University Press, 2002, p. 184.
112 Ibid., p. 185.
113 Ibid., pp. 185–6.
114 A. Buğra, 'The Immoral Economy of Housing in Turkey', *International Journal of Urban and Regional Research*, vol.22, no.2, 1998, 283–302.
115 Ş. I. Özler, 'The Political Choices of Urban Squatters in National Elections', *Turkish Studies*, vol.1, no.2, 2000, 40.
116 M. C. Yalçıntan and A. E. Erbaş, 'Impacts of Gecekondu', p. 94.

4 State Incorporation of Shas as Expanding Political Opportunity

Political Representation of Sephardim Prior to the Formation of Shas

The formation of Shas in 1983 was a watershed for the representation of Sephardim in Israeli politics, since Sephardim did not have a significant voice in the mainstream political parties before the establishment of the Shas movement. In the 1950s and 1960s, new Sephardi immigrants gave their electoral support to the governing parties. Until 1977, the Mapai dominated Israeli politics by acquiring the plurality of the votes in each election and heading every single government as the senior coalition partner. Mapai strategically included the religious Zionist National Religious Party (NRP) as its junior coalition partner in all of these governments. This partnership, known as the "historical alliance," was convenient for both parties because the NRP could have control on issues pertaining to its religious agenda (e.g. Religious Zionist education, religious laws), and Labor could implement its agenda on national issues (e.g. foreign policy, economic policy, etc.) Because of these parties' tight grip on the allocation of state resources, especially Mapai's control of the absorption services, Sephardim supported Mapai and the NRP in the early years of Israel. However, Sephardi support for the governing Labor Party was not ideologically driven but based on a patron–client relationship between the government and the new Sephardi immigrants.[1] When the social and cultural resentment of the Sephardim grew in the 1970s as explained in Chapter 3, they became more and more critical of Mapai, which they associated with the Ashkenazi establishment. According to the Sephardim, the Ashkenazi establishment prevented their social mobility and thwarted their meaningful political representation. Therefore, while first generation Sephardim accepted the premises of Labor Zionism as the only means of expression for the ideals of Jewish nationalism and modernization[2] and overwhelmingly voted for the Labor Party, second and third generation Sephardim changed their allegiance from Labor to right-wing Herut (later Likud).

This change of allegiance was the expression of a protest against the established order. The center right Likud appealed to the Sephardim by meshing traditionalist values into an uncompromising Jewish nationalism. Although Likud did not define itself as a religious party, it projected a positive view of Jewish tradition and supported the strengthening of the role of religion in public life.[3] Menachem Begin, the leader of Likud at the time, made it clear in his public speeches that he saw Jewish tradition as one of the main elements of Israel's civil religion.[4] Begin directly appealed to the Mizrahim and thereby challenged one of the basic tenets of Labor Zionism, namely ingathering of the exiles (*mizug galuyot*), a myth that helped to sustain the cultural hierarchy between Sephardim and Ashkenazim. While the Sephardim perceived the Labor Party as representing an elite class detached from the sensitivities of Oriental Jewry, they saw Menachem Begin as a more approachable leader with traditional values and as more amenable to Sephardi interests. The words of a Sephardic Jew in a development town, Beith Shemesh, reveal why the Sephardim tended to favour the Likud during Begin's leadership period:

> The Mapainiks just wiped out everything that is imprinted on a person. As if it was all nonsense. And then they put what they wanted into him. From that ideology of theirs. Like we were some kind of dirt. Ben-Gurion himself called us the dust of the earth. That's written in Bar Zohar's book about Ben-Gurion. But now that Begin's here, believe me, my parents can stand up straight, with pride, and dignity. I'm not religious either, but my parents are; they're traditional, and Begin has respect for their beliefs. Your whole problem is that you don't realize that Begin is prime minister. For you he's garbage, not prime minister.[5]

As these remarks show, support for Likud was not only prompted by Sephardic sociocultural frustrations or Likud's image as a traditional party, but also by the perception that Begin was an outsider figure for the establishment. Therefore, it was easier for the Sephardim, who felt that they were outsiders themselves, to associate with such a figure. Sephardim's change of support became most visible in the 1977 elections when Likud formed the government for the first time in Israel's political history. The percentage of Sephardim voting for Likud rose from 22 percent in the 1969 elections to 65 percent in the 1977 elections and 71 percent in the 1981 elections.[6] Considering that Sephardim constituted 55 percent of the entire Jewish population in Israel, this was definitely a deciding factor in Likud's accession to power.[7]

Despite the fact that Sephardi votes carried Likud to political success, the number of Sephardim in the higher echelons of the bureaucracy and governmental positions did not increase significantly after the formation of the first Likud-led coalition government.[8] While some Sephardi figures, such as David Levy and Moshe Katsav in Likud or Aharon Abuhatzera in the NRP, climbed to the upper echelons of their parties, proportionally the number of influential Sephardi politicians considerably lagged behind the Ashkenazi. Moreover, the number of Sephardi Members of Knesset (MKs), although increasing steadily as percentage of all MKs, always significantly lagged behind the percentage of

Table 4.1 Percentage of Sephardi MKs among all the Jewish MKs before Shas

Year	*1949*	*1951*	*1955*	*1959*	*1961*	*1965*	*1969*	*1973*	*1977*	*1981*
Number of Jewish MKs	118	112	113	113	114	113	113	114	113	116
Number of Sephardi MKs	8	7	10	14	14	21	17	19	22	28
Percentage of Sephardi MKs among Jewish MKs	7	6	9	12	12	19	15	17	19	24

Source: Adapted from J. Allouche, *The Oriental Communities in Israel, 1948–2003: The Social and Cultural Creation of an Ethnic Group*, Geneva: Institut universitaire de hautes études internationals, 2003, p. 108. The percentages are calculated by the author.

Ashkenazi MKs, although the Sephardim constituted over half of the Jewish electorate in the beginning of 1980s (see Table 4.1).

Oriental communities started to show signs of disenchantment with the Likud governments in the mid-1980s, because their expectations of significant social and economic improvement did not materialize.[9] This paved the way for the emergence of Sephardi parties, like Tami and Shas. Sephardim made greater political advances during Shas's participation in successive coalition governments. The deputy director of *El Hama'ayan* explains the difference between Shas and Likud from the perspective of the Sephardim:

> I was driving in a cab, and the cab-driver was a non-religious Sephardi, and he told me that he votes for Shas. And I asked him "Why do you vote for Shas?" He said because it is the only movement that delivers to its public … What they [Shas politicians] do is for their own constituents. The more political power we have, the more we can do both about general things, but also about things that are important particularly for us [Sephardim]. Today we have our own representatives in the municipal councils, we have deputy mayors, or mayors. And with them we can influence more policies. We can have the strings … In the past we chose Likud for example, it is not that I could not request anything from him [a Likud mayor], but it is not the same as to go to your own representative in the municipality. It is another way of getting power.[10]

As the remarks of this Shas activist reveal, although Sephardim felt a closer affinity to Likud compared to Labor, Likud was only perceived by them as a temporary home. It was not until the formation of Shas that more Sephardim were placed in political power positions, who explicitly claimed to represent Sephardi interests.

Sephardi Representation in Ethnic Lists and Religious Parties in 1948–84

In the wake of state formation, mainstream political parties supported ethnic Sephardi organizations in the national elections. For instance, in the first Knesset, Mapai supported the Sephardic Federation, and the General Zionists supported the Yemenite List.[11] Yet after the first two elections, this practice of supporting semi-independent lists of candidates was gradually replaced by offering Sephardi leaders "safe places" from the lists of major parties.[12] In 1955–81 the Sephardi parties failed to pass the one percent threshold and receive Knesset representation (see Table 4.2).[13] In the 1950s and 1960s, the practice of running independent ethnic parties was portrayed as separatism and a betrayal of the Zionist ideal of ingathering of the exiles. In the public and political discourse, a stigma was attached to mentioning ethnicity as a source of political mobilization as this contradicted the official melting pot ideology perpetuated by the Ashkenazi Zionist founders.

Some Sephardim also found refuge in the religious parties and participated both in Agudat Yisrael and in the NRP. While Agudah mainly attracted the Haredi Sephardim, who have a long history in Ottoman Palestine which predates the Zionist settlements, the Sephardim who supported the NRP were mainly traditional (*masorti*) Jews. These traditional Jews preferred to support the NRP, which presented itself as a moderate party bridging the differences between the secular and religious publics.[14] However, despite the fact that the Sephardim constituted a significant part of the NRP's constituency, the number of Sephardi MKs in the party was always negligible.

The alliance of the Sephardim with the ultra-Orthodox and Religious Zionist parties started to crumble in the 1980s with the defection of major figures from these parties. Three major events ultimately paved the way for the formation of Shas. The first transformative event occurred within the religious Zionist camp when Aharon Abuhatzeira, who served as the Minister for Religious Affairs and Social Welfare Minister under the NRP, broke off from

Table 4.2 Ethnic parties and political representation until the advent of Shas

Election	*Vote share and Knesset representation*
1949	Sephardic Union (3.5%, 4 MKs) Yemenite Association (1%, 1 MK)
1951	Sephardic Union (1.8%, 1 MK) Yemenite Association (1.2%, 1 MK)
1981	Tami (2.3%, 3 MKs)
1984	Tami (1.5%, 1 MK) Shas (3.1%, 4 MKs)

Source: H. Herzog, 'Political Factionalism: The Case of Ethnic Lists in Israel', *The Western Political Quarterly*, vol.39, no.2, 1986, 289. Note: Ethnic Sephardi parties did not receive enough votes to get elected in the Knesset elections between 1951 and 1981.

the party on 25 May 1981, shortly before the elections for the tenth Knesset. Abuhatzeira's defection was a protest at the lack of Sephardi candidates nominated from higher places in the election list. Abuhatzeira, who is of Moroccan origin and related to the famous rabbinic Abuhatzeria clan, immediately formed Tami (Movement for Israeli Tradition) and received financial support from the Sephardi Swiss millionaire Nissim Gaon. In the 1981 election, Tami scored a major success by garnering 2.3 percent of the national vote and putting three representatives into the Knesset. This was a major blow to the NRP, which lost half of its parliamentary representation and shrank to six seats in the Knesset. Tami's main support came from development towns with big Mizrahi populations and other towns with high concentrations of Moroccan Jews, such as Ashkelon and Ramla. In these settings, entire party branches defected from the NRP and moved to Tami.[15] Furthermore, the ethnic segregation of synagogues helped Tami, because in the very short period between its formation and the elections—in the absence of an institutionalized party structure—it was able to use Sephardic synagogues as an efficient means of political mobilization.[16]

In the tenth Knesset, the party followed a populist agenda and tried to represent the poor segments of the Sephardi public. Tami opposed budget cuts in welfare, health and education and filled the posts in its ministries with Sephardim.[17] Aharon Uzan, one of the party's leaders, stated that the main aim of Tami was to undo the wrongs made to the North Africans in particular, and to the Sephardim in general and to place as many Sephardim as possible in power positions.[18] However, in the 1984 elections, the party lost two of its Knesset seats and merged with Likud before the 1988 elections. One of the major reasons for Tami's demise was corruption charges brought against Aharon Abuhatzeira and Nissim Gaon. Moreover, Tami failed to empower its constituency by producing a positive Sephardi identity, because it primarily focused on the socioeconomic problems of the Mizrahim and only paid lip service to the cultural marginalization *Edot HaMizrah* faced. Nevertheless, Tami contributed to the rise of a Sephardi political consciousness and paved the way for the formation of Shas by starting the divorce of the Sephardi networks, including Sephardi synagogues, influential Oriental rabbis, and Mizrahi rank and file, from the Religious Zionist camp.

Another catalytic event that played a key role in the formation of Shas was the dispute over the term-limits of the chief rabbis. In 1983, Rabbi Shlomo Goren, the Ashkenazi Chief Rabbi of Israel, made a deal with the governing NRP to amend the election rules for the chief rabbi position. According to the deal, chief rabbis would be elected for one ten-year period instead of the customary five-year periods. The new rules restricted the service to one term, unlike the prior arrangement which allowed for a chief rabbi to get elected multiple times with no limit. Sephardi Chief Rabbi Ovadia Yosef strongly opposed this change, which harmed his long-term interests. Yosef, who commanded the reverence of most Sephardim due to his extensive religious knowledge and charisma, would probably have been successful in every election in his lifetime. Despite protests by Ovadia Yosef, the new election rules were instituted, and he lost his position as the Sephardic Chief Rabbi on 16 March 1983. After this incident, Yosef channeled his resentment into gathering political support and forming a new political party.

Parallel to this development there had also been an internal Sephardi revolt within the ultra-Orthodox Agudat Yisrael. A newly emerging Haredi Sephardi elite within the *yeshivas* and *kollels* (*yeshivas* for married men) of the Agudat Yisrael started to show signs of discontent because the party leadership allocated minimal funding to the Sephardi religious and educational institutions within the party's network, although Agudat Yisrael had increased its budget for its religious institutions during its participation in Begin's coalition governments.[19] The Ashkenazi leadership denied Sephardi demands to increase the level of funding for Sephardi educational institutions within Agudah. There were additional factors that fueled the disenchantment of the Haredi Sephardim. For instance, Yiddish was used in all internal dealings signifying the Ashkenazi character of the party. Sephardim were denied top positions in the party and never became Knesset members. Sephardi Haredim also faced discrimination in Agudah schools and even in the marriage choices of the Ashkenazi Haredi families. When these simmering concerns peaked before the Jerusalem municipal elections in 1983, prominent Sephardi yeshiva students within the ranks of Agudat Yisrael, such as Nissim Zeev and Raphael Pinhasi, rebelled against the party leadership and created a political formation, which they called Shas. The disgruntled Ovadia Yosef used this opportunity and threw his support behind this new political party during the municipal elections. This newly formed list did surprisingly well in the Jerusalem municipal elections and won three seats in the City Council. In the same year, more candidates for Shas lists ran in smaller cities, such as Tiberias and Bnei Barak, and some successes were recorded.[20] In February 1984, Ovadia Yosef announced the creation of the national Shas. He explained the rationale behind the formation of the party in plain terms: "The religious parties never gave fair representation to Sephardim, although much of their support came from observant Sephardim."[21]

Sephardic Torah Guardians: A New Political Voice for Sephardim

The Hebrew letters that form the name of Shas (*shin and samech*) are an acronym for the Talmud, namely *Shisha Sedarim* (the six sections of the Talmud). While the party's full name is the Worldwide Sephardic Association of Torah Keepers (*Hitahdut HaSfaradim HaOlamit Shomrei Torah*), many refer to it with the shorter name Sephardic Torah Guardians (*Sfaradim Shomrei Torah*).

Shas is similar to other Haredi parties with regard to party hierarchy. As with the Council of Torah Sages [Greats] (*Moetzet Gdolei HaTorah*) of Agudat Israel, the ultimate decision-making power in Shas lies in the hands of the Council of Torah Sages [Wise] (*Moetzet Chachmei HaTorah*), which meets at least once a month. The current members of the council are Rabbi Ovadia Yosef, Rabbi Moshe Maya, Rabbi Shimon Badani, Rabbi Shalom Cohen and general secretary of the council, Rabbi Raphael Pinhasi.[22] The party's Knesset members, who are always ultra-Orthodox Sephardim, bring impending political questions to the agenda of the council, and the rabbis in the council give the ultimate decisions on these questions. Although there is no formal hierarchy among the four members of the council, it is Rabbi Ovadia Yosef who holds the ultimate authority within the council and in the party.

Born in Baghdad in 1920, Rabbi Ovadia Yosef came to Jerusalem at the age of four and studied the Torah in a number of religious institutions including the famous old Sephardi yeshiva Porat Yosef in Jerusalem, known for the rigor of its education.[23] In his twenties Yosef became a judge (*dayan*) in the Sephardi rabbinical court in Cairo and later rose fast in the Torah world, becoming Chief Rabbi of Tel Aviv in 1968 and serving as the Chief Sephardi Rabbi of Israel in 1973–83.[24] Today, Rabbi Ovadia Yosef is the unequivocal religious authority within the Sephardi world.[25] He also holds a much respected position within the Ashkenazi ultra-Orthodox community.

However, Yosef was not the sole leader of the party in the initial years, and for a period of time he worked as the protégé of Rabbi Eliezer Shach. During its establishment, Shas profited from the internal strife between the *Hassidim* and *Mitnagdim* within the Agudat Yisrael.[26] Rabbi Eliezer Shach, the leader of the *Mitnagdim* and the head of the Lithuanian Pozneh Yeshiva in Bnei Brak, supported the formation of Shas, because he was concerned that the Haredi Sephardim were increasingly influenced by the Hassidic trends within the Agudah. By supporting Shas as a Sephardi party against Agudah, Shach wanted to show the Hassidic elements within Agudah that they needed to pay more attention to *Mitnagdim* or otherwise lose support.[27] Since many of the rabbis who formed Shas were students in the Pozneh Yeshiva, they did not have trouble accepting the spiritual guidance of Shach, who was also Yosef's senior.

However, the relations between Rabbi Shach and Rabbi Yosef were severed when Shach openly criticized the autonomous political activities of the Sephardi ultra-Orthodox sector in a public speech in 1992: "the Sephardim are not ready yet to manage affairs of religion and state … they are growing and developing and returning to their roots, but they still need more time to learn."[28] After these patronizing statements, Ovadia Yosef cut Shas's ties to Shach and proclaimed the party's total autonomy from the Lithuanian *Mitnagdim*. Shas activists used Rabbi Shach's paternalistic statements to galvanize the development towns against him by playing these remarks through loudspeakers again and again.[29] On the other hand, Shach followers harassed Shas activists in their synagogues and neighborhoods in response to Yosef's decision to break from the tutelage of Rabbi Shach.[30] In the following elections, Shas achieved significant electoral victories and emerged as the biggest political party within the religious camp, easily surpassing Shach's party The Flag of Torah (*Degel Hatorah*) and Agudat Yisrael, which later united under the banner United Torah Judaism (*Yahadut HaTorah*).

Reinterpreting Zionism and Ultra-Orthodoxy: Shas's Engagement with the Zionist State

If one of the primary objectives of Shas is to establish the dignity of Sephardi Jewry in Israel through religious and cultural revival, the other is to address the social marginalization of the poor Sephardim through welfare assistance (see Chapter 6). One of the reasons why Shas succeeded in these objectives was its inclusion in the coalition governments of Israel and its creation of robust patronage networks around its ministries. The party participated in all except three coalition governments in the past 30 years,[31] always occupying important ministerial positions. The fragmentation of the Israeli political system and specifically the relative equality of the center left and center right's political fortunes after the 1977 national elections turned the religious parties in Israel into kingmakers, because both the left and right center parties depended on the smaller religious parties to form viable coalition governments. It is undeniable that Shas's participation in the coalition governments created both cultural and material resources which the party very successfully channeled to its supporters.

It was possible for Shas to participate in coalition governments and occupy ministries, because the party leadership introduced a novel interpretation of the ultra-Orthodox Israelis' engagement with the Zionist state institutions. As discussed in the previous chapter, Agudah parties declined to occupy any ministries in the government, because this act alone would be seen as granting legitimacy to the State of Israel, which, according to the ultra-Orthodox, was not a legitimate Jewish state run according to *halacha*. In order to balance the need to be part of the political process and maintain religio-ideological consistency, Agudah Knesset members either received the post of deputy minister or acted as heads of Knesset committees, but never became ministers. This way they could claim that they were not fully participating in the workings of a secular government while being able to deliver some services to their own constituencies. They were keen to differentiate their political stance from Zionist political actors who saw Israel as a secular Jewish political entity.

Shas, on the other hand, has been ideologically much more pragmatic than Agudah in its stance toward the Israeli state and never explicitly rejected Zionism (see Chapter 6 for an extended discussion). This differing ideological stance toward the Israeli state is summed up by a Shas activist:

> Now according to Rav Ovadia Yosef we are part of the State [*Medina*]. We are here because God wanted us to be here. But if anything does not go by the Torah, we try to change it. We only go by the line of the Torah. The moment Torah tells us to do something, we have to do it. This is why we get the Interior Ministry, the Ministry of Communication, etc. and we make changes according to the Torah. This is Zionism for us.[32]

This novel interpretation of Zionism, which differs significantly from previous Haredi attitudes toward the Zionist entity, gave Shas the leverage to become a major player in the coalition governments by occupying critical ministerial positions, including the Ministry of Religious Affairs, Interior Ministry, Ministry of Labor and Social Welfare, Ministry of Housing and Construction, Ministry of Health, and Ministry of Communication. For instance, when negotiations between Kadima's Tzipi Livni and Shas representatives to form a new coalition failed in 2008, and Israel headed for early elections, Rabbi Ovadia Yosef summarized in simple terms Shas's strategy with regards to participation in the next coalition government during one of his weekly sermons:

> Now we have the Knesset elections ahead of us. If we gain 15 [seats], or if we are 18, how good it will be. Whoever is prime minister, would love to have them. He would receive them honorably. He would do anything he is told. "Give us the Housing Ministry." "You are welcome to it." "Give us the Social Affairs Ministry." "Sure thing." "Give us the Education Ministry." "You can have it." If they [Shas MKs] are strong, they could demand anything.[33]

These statements of Rabbi Ovadia Yosef reveal that the Shas leadership is well aware of the virtuous relationship between its command over governmental resources and the party's electoral success. Ovadia Yosef and the party leadership know that their incorporation into the government is a favorable political opportunity. The more governmental resources Shas commands, the more it allocates resources to Sephardi needs, and this increases the party's popularity among the Sephardim. This popularity, in turn, increases the party's electoral strength and concomitantly the number of its MKs gives Shas a better bargaining position in coalition negotiations to demand the ministries Shas needs.

State Incorporation as Expanding Political Opportunity

The political ascendance of Shas in the 1980s went hand in hand with the declining fortunes of the religious Zionist NRP. As discussed in the previous chapter, the NRP acted as the junior coalition partner to the Labor Party until the earthquake elections of 1977. After Shas's first participation in national elections in 1984 and the subsequent realignment of the religious camp, Shas began to gradually replace the NRP as the main religious player in the coalition governments and acquired control of the ministries which had been historically NRP strongholds (see Table 4.3). After the Six Day War, the NRP was pulled into the orbit of *Gush Emunim* (Bloc of the Faithful), the far right settler movement for whom the settlement of the occupied territories constituted a religious duty. Due to this ideological shift toward messianic territorial expansionism, the NRP neglected other issues which historically the party had defended, such as education, social provisions and welfare of the religious Zionist community. This ideological shift not only led to the

Table 4.3 The ministries and deputy ministerships Shas occupied in the coalition governments in 1984–2013[1]

Time period	*Prime Minister/large coalition partner*	*Ministries of Shas*	*Deputy ministerships of Shas*
1984–6	Shimon Peres (Labor-Likud)	Interior Ministry (Yitzhak Haim Peres)	Ministry of Labor and Social Welfare (Raphael Pinhasi) (1985–6)
1986–8	Yitzhak Shamir (Likud-Labor)	Interior Ministry (Yitzhak Haim Peres) (1986–7) Ministry without Portfolio (Yitzhak Haim Peres) (1987–8)	Ministry of Labor and Social Welfare (Raphael Pinhasi)
1988–90	Yitzhak Shamir (Likud–Labor)	Interior Ministry (Ariyeh Deri) Immigrant Absorption Ministry (Yitzhak Haim Peres)	Interior Ministry (Raphael Pinhasi) (1990)
1990–2	Yitzhak Shamir (Likud)	Interior Ministry (Ariyeh Deri) Immigrant Absorption Ministry (Yitzhak Haim Peres)	Ministry of Finance (Joseph Azran)
1992–5	Yitzhak Rabin (Labor)	Interior Ministry (Ariyeh Deri) (1992–3) Ministry without Portfolio (Ariyeh Deri) (1993)	Ministry of Education and Culture (Moshe Maya) (1992–3) Ministry of Finance (Raphael Pinhasi) (1992) Ministry of Housing and Construction (Arieh Gamliel) (1992–3) Ministry of Religious Affairs (Raphael Pinhasi) (1992–3)
1995–6	Shimon Peres (Labor)		
1996–9	Benjamin Netanyahu (Likud)	Ministry of Labor and Social Welfare (Eli Yishai) Interior Ministry (Eliyahu Suissa) Ministry of Religious Affairs (Eliyahu Suissa) (1996–7; 1998–9)	Ministry of Health (Shlomo Benizri) Ministry of Religious Affairs (Arieh Gamliel)

Table 4.3 (Continued)

Time period	*Prime Minister/large coalition partner*	*Ministries of Shas*	*Deputy ministerships of Shas*
1999–2001	Ehud Barak (Labor)	Ministry of Labor and Social Welfare (Eli Yishai) (1999–2000) Ministry of Health (Shlomo Benizri) (1999–2000) Ministry of National Infrastructure (Eliyahu Suissa) (1999–2000) Ministry of Religious Affairs (Yitzhak Cohen) (1999–2000)	Ministry of Communications (Yitzhak Vaknin) (1999–2000) Ministry of Education (Meshulam Nahari) (1999–2000) Ministry of Finance (Nissim Dahan) (1999–2000)
2001–3	Ariel Sharon (Likud-Labor)	Interior Ministry (Eli Yishai) Ministry of Religious Affairs (Asher Ohana) Ministry of Labor and Social Welfare (Shlomo Benizri) Ministry of Jerusalem Affairs (Eliyahu Suissa) Ministry of Health (Nissim Dahan)	Deputy Prime Minister (Eli Yishai) Ministry of Education (Meshulam Nahari) Ministry of Finance (Yitzhak Cohen) Ministry of Labor and Social Welfare (David Azoulay) Interior Ministry (Yitzhak Vaknin)
2003–6	Ariel Sharon (Likud)		
2006–9	Ehud Olmert (Kadima)	Ministry of Communications (Ariel Atas) Ministry of Industry, Trade, and Labor (Eli Yishai) Ministry of Religious Services (Yitzhak Cohen) (2008–9) Ministry without Portfolio (Meshulam Nahari) Ministry without Portfolio (Yitzhak Cohen) (2006–8)*	Deputy Prime Minister (Eli Yishai)

2009–13	Benjamin Netanyahu (Likud)	Interior Ministry (Eli Yishai) Ministry of Housing and Construction (Ariel Atas) Ministry of Religious Services (Yaakov Margi)	Deputy Prime Minister (Eli Yishai) Deputy Minister of Finance (Yitzhak Cohen)

[1]The data in the table is compiled by the author. Source: Knesset Website, available at http://www.knesset.gov.il/govt/eng/GovtByNumber_eng.asp
*Yitzhak Cohen was responsible for religious affairs, a department under the office of the prime minister, at the time. In 2008 this department was reinstituted as the Ministry of Religious Services and Cohen became the minister of religious services.

NRP's political decline, but also created a social vacuum that was later successfully filled by Shas through its civil society organizations.

The primary former NRP stronghold that Shas captured was the Interior Ministry, which veteran NRP chairman Yosef Burg headed until 1984. Afterwards, Shas consistently sought the ministry in coalition negotiations and occupied it for most of the next ten years. Shas's control of the Interior Ministry provided the movement with both cultural and material resources. Culturally, the authority of the ministry over the civil status registration of Israeli citizens gives the party controlling the ministry some say over the "Jewish identity" of the Israeli state. As discussed in Chapter 3, all matters of personal status, such as marriage, divorce, or burial, are handled by religious courts of the respective religious communities in Israel. Within the Jewish community, the Orthodox Chief Rabbinate and the rabbinical courts have a monopoly over the handling of these questions. However, the Interior Ministry also has some discretion, because the officials in the ministry are responsible for registering matters of status change. This duality sometimes creates tensions, particularly for secular Jews who evade Orthodox religious practices—e.g. by having a secular marriage in Cyprus and registering their status change in the interior ministry—and for religious converts to Judaism who request Israeli citizenship based on the Law of Return.[34] Therefore, occupying the ministry gives Shas some leverage on deciding issues that would have an effect on the "Jewish" character of the Israeli state.

A case in point is the controversy over the registration of Soshana Miller, who was converted to Judaism in a Reform congregation in the United States and then applied for Israeli citizenship. While she was granted Israeli citizenship, the officials in the Interior Ministry refused to register her as a "Jew." When this administrative fait accompli of the Shas-controlled ministry was overruled by the Supreme Court, the Interior Minister Yitzhak Peretz insisted that the word "convert" be added next to the category of religion in Miller's identity card.[35] This started an uproar among the Reform and Conservative congregations in Israel and abroad. Finally, the Supreme Court denied the Interior Ministry the right to add the word "convert" next to someone's religion in identity cards.[36] To protest this decision, Peretz, who was also the chairman of Shas, resigned from his post as Interior Minister. In his resignation letter he revealed clearly his party's position on the strict interpretation of Judaism:

> The High Court of Justice [Supreme Court] demanded that I list a non-Jew as a Jew … As a Jew and a rabbi loyal to the tradition and Bible of Israel, I have declared and declare again that my hand will never ever sign for a fraudulent conversion that was not conducted according to the *Halacha*.[37]

Similar controversies surfaced during Shas's command of the ministry regarding the citizenship status of Jewish immigrants from the former Soviet Union in the beginning of the 1990s, because many of these immigrants lacked necessary documentation to prove either that their mothers were Jewish or that they had undergone a proper conversion to Judaism.[38] As will be discussed further in Chapter 6, this intolerant behavior of Shas toward Russian immigrants harmed ethnic relations between Russian newcomers and Sephardi residents, especially in the development towns.

Shas's hardline stance in recent debates on the policy toward African immigrants also showcases how the movement has been using its command over the Interior Ministry as a cultural anchor. Many non-Jewish immigrants have come to Israel in the past ten years from Eritrea, Somalia, and South Sudan as civil war refugees or economic immigrants by crossing the Sinai border. In 2011, Interior Minister Eli Yishai spearheaded a furious political campaign against the undocumented East African immigrants. Yishai repeatedly called the undocumented immigrants "infiltrators," claimed that they pose a threat to the national unity of the Jewish people and tied them to increasing crime despite the fact that the crime rate among this group is not above the national average.[39] As a result of Yishai's efforts, several bills were passed through the Knesset that led to major crackdowns on different African communities, their deportation from Israel, and the restriction of their right to appeal residency status claims.[40] The Shas party platform also advocates a "closed door policy" for foreign workers in order to protect the rights of vulnerable [Jewish] populations in Israel.[41] A Shas activist from Or Yehuda passionately explained to me in an interview the significance of Yishai's decision to deport undocumented immigrant workers:

> We saw in the past month the mess with the foreign workers … [The Interior Minister Eli Yishai] took care that the natural increase in foreign workers would be stopped; he took care that the color of the land of Israel would remain a Jewish color … It was the greatest threat, that in every corner, in every place in Israel they [the undocumented workers

> from Sudan and Eretria] found a comfortable niche to live. In this manner, when they marry, have kids, raise them, there's a threat to the Jewish people in the land of Israel. It's bad enough that we have the Muslims and the Arabs. Should we bring in foreign workers from Eritrea and from all sorts of other places? It is an existential threat, very simple.[42]

These statements reveal how Shas activists try to present non-Jewish immigration from Africa as a question of ultimate cultural survival for the Jewish state. The activist's claim to preserve the color of Israel through deportation of Africans is an allusion to the skin color of the African immigrants and reflects the racist attitude embraced by the party leadership. One might be surprised how a Sephardi party claiming to represent a discriminated minority would embrace such a position. I would argue that this uncompromising stance toward the African undocumented immigrants is not solely a cultural stance but has a firm basis in socioeconomic structures. Many of the undocumented immigrants find themselves at the bottom of the economic ladder and work for much cheaper wages than the average unskilled worker in Israel. The employment of undocumented African immigrants as unskilled workers disproportionally hurts working-class Mizrahim from the development towns who also compete for the same semi-skilled and unskilled jobs. It is not a surprise that many residents living in the development towns of Negev, such as Netivot, Sderot or Ofakim, also mention increasing undocumented immigration from Africa as one of the biggest social problems.[43] Shas's aggressive opposition toward immigration is rooted in this politico-material reality, as working-class Mizrahim from the development towns constitute an important profile of the party's constituency. As Yoav Peled cogently illustrated there is a close relation between the socioeconomic hierarchy and political culture in Israel.[44] According to Peled, Mizrahim in Israel constitute a semi-peripheral position between the dominant Ashkenazim and peripheral Palestinians, and Shas emphasizes a politicized Judaism in order to elevate the position of Mizrahim in Israel.[45] The undocumented Africans constitute yet another marginalized peripheral group below the Mizrahim in the socioeconomic ladder and Shas's hostile attitude toward this group—similar to its hostile stance toward the Palestinians—through an emphasis on the Judaic character of Israel represents a willingness to protect the socioeconomic turf of the Mizrahim vis-à-vis the undocumented immigrant workers and to establish a closer status association with the dominant group.

In addition to using the Interior Ministry as a cultural resource, Shas also channeled material resources to its own constituency through forming clientelistic networks around the ministry. The political patronage provided through the Interior Ministry peaked during Ariyeh Deri's ministry (1988–93). In Israel, the Interior Ministry has the authority to fund municipal councils, which have to use these funds for local needs, while the funding to religious institutions is allocated by the Ministry of Religious Affairs via the religious councils. During his ministry, Deri bypassed these laws systematically by making allocations to municipal councils conditional on handing some of these funds to religious institutions affiliated with Shas.[46] In this process of illegal allocations, Deri used his political power over municipal funds. As a Jerusalem municipal council member explained: "Deri will approve, let's say, 5 million NIS [New Israeli Shekel] for municipal needs and then tack on another 1 million NIS for religious institutions."[47] According to some accounts, Deri had diverted every year 100 million NIS, close to a quarter of the Interior Ministry's budget, to religious institutions close to Shas.[48] As a result of these and similar illegal practices, Deri and four of his friends were convicted in 1999 for bribe-taking, aggravated fraud, breach of trust, and falsifying corporate documents.[49] Most of these unlawful practices involved Shas affiliated voluntary non-profit organizations that inappropriately diverted funds.

Throughout the 1990s, the Ministry of Religious Affairs, another NRP stronghold in the pre-1984 era, operated as a fiefdom of Shas. Raphael Pinhasi became the Deputy Minister of Religious Affairs for the first time in 1992, but considering that the ministry was headed by the then prime minister Yitzhak Rabin, it was clear that the strings of the institution belonged to Shas through Pinhasi. Thereafter, Shas MKs served as Minister of Religious Affairs in five coalition governments. The ministry, whose major responsibility is to regulate the provision of religious services to citizens, commands some influence in the political economy of the Jewish religious sector. The minister appoints 45 percent of the members of each local religious council, which manages local synagogues, ritual baths (*mikva'ot*) and kashrut enforcement services for businesses. Moreover, the ministry distributes funds to voluntary non-profit organizations (*amutot*), which provide religious activities such as evening Torah classes for adults, and partially subsidizes full-time yeshiva students, whose sole occupation is studying the Toraḥ. Yet, the central significance of the ministry for Shas lies in its control over the funding for and appointment of a vast number of jobs in the religious sector, such as local chief rabbis, kosher food inspectors, ritual bath managers, religious court judges, and yeshiva school administrators. These jobs are especially vital for the survival of the Sephardi ultra-Orthodox community, who rarely receive any skills necessary for the mainstream job market. As one secular Israeli journalist critical of the ultra-Orthodox says: "The religious councils have a lot of jobs, [they are] a big price. We are talking about a community that doesn't learn to work. They have to work in these jobs."[50] While there have lately been some attempts to integrate the ultra-Orthodox into mainstream economics, such as the opening of a new girls' college by Shas (more in Chapter 8), the comments cited above reflect a persistent reality for the Haredim in Israel, especially regarding their dependence on state-created jobs or subsidies from abroad.

In the 1980s, before Shas took control of the ministry, its budget was miniscule and amounted only to a couple of hundred thousand NIS.[51] In the 1990s, the ministry's budget skyrocketed, rising to 240 million NIS in 1990,[52]

1.2 billion NIS in the fiscal year 1996,[53] 1.6 billion NIS in 1997,[54] and over four billion NIS in 2001.[55]

Through its grip on the ministry that commanded an ever-growing budget and employment opportunities in the religious sector, Shas was also able to create an elaborate patronage network. To begin with, the ability of the minister to appoint almost half of the members of the religious councils gave the party the opportunity to fill these positions with its own supporters and also use these councils' political authority to favor Shas-based institutions, such as Sephardi synagogues and ritual baths. Moreover, Shas became (in)famous for overfunding its own voluntary non-profit organizations with public monies from the ministry. Until 1999, the ministry had discretion over allocating special funds to voluntary non-profit organizations to support Torah study. When Shimon Shetreet from the Labor Party took the ministry from Shas in the middle of the Rabin government in July 1993, he declared that almost the entire annual budget set aside for Torah and Haredi culture was already spent, and that the money had been distributed to Shas institutions.[56] Most of these overfunded voluntary non-profit institutions are run by figures very close to the party's leadership structure. For example during the 1999 budget year, *Yahaveh Da'at* headed by Rabbi Ovadia Yosef's son David Yosef, *Ma'or Yisrael* headed by another of Yosef's sons Moshe Yosef, *Or Hamizrach* headed by yet another son of Yosef Avraham Yosef, and *Rosh Pina* an institution run by Ariyeh Deri's brother Nissim Deri, all received preferential funding from the Ministry of Religious Affairs for their "outstanding" work totaling two million NIS.[57] The assessment of "outstanding work" was evidently based on political criteria. Moreover, under Shas leadership the ministry was able to transfer funds to many fictitious entities. An audit by the State Comptroller[58]Miriam Ben-Porat revealed that in 1998, 30 percent of the yeshivas that received funding from the ministry were either fictitious or already closed by the time of funding. In addition, more than a fourth of the yeshiva students registered for funding did not exist at the time of the audit.[59] The funding of the teachers in the *Ma'ayan Hahinuch HaTorani* network (more in Chapter 8) was another tool through which the Ministry of Religious Affairs was used to disproportionally fund Shas-related organizations. While the teachers in the *Ma'ayan* schools were funded through the Education Ministry due to their status as educational workers, they were also funded by the Ministry of Religious Affairs, because they were also registered as full-time yeshiva students, whose sole occupation is studying the Torah.[60] A Jerusalem District Labor Court defined this practice as "the fraudulent obtaining of moneys from the State authorities on the basis of misrepresentations."[61] In order to prevent the exposure of its fraudulent practices to the larger public, Shas inserted special provisions into the contracts of the teachers working in the *Ma'ayan* network stipulating that any dispute between the school and the teachers should be taken to the ultra-Orthodox run religious courts rather than to any government-run secular courts.[62] Hence it was not surprising that the budget Shas-affiliated civil society institutions received from the ministry rose exponentially from 21.3 million NIS in 1991 to 888 million NIS in 1998.[63]

To prevent Shas from using the ministry as a pipeline for its own institutional growth and to alleviate increasing criticism from the secular public, the government under Ehud Barak introduced in September 1999 a new regulation package for the funding transferred by the ministry to voluntary non-profit organizations requiring accountability and transparency.[64] Despite these new regulations, Shas continued its law-evading practices of transferring government funds to its own organizations thanks to the party's political clout in the coalition governments.

The transformation of the Religious Affairs Ministry to a pipeline for Shas-affiliated organizations and the party's simultaneous electoral success instigated bitter reactions from other political actors, primarily the Religious Zionist NRP as well as secular parties, who view the ultra-Orthodox as their eternal foes. The NRP, who emerged as the major loser from Shas's control of the Religious Affairs Ministry, tried to resist this new reality and attempted to regain the control of the ministry. During the cohabitation of Shas and the NRP in two coalition governments in the late 1990s, this demand led to important political crises. The first dispute broke during the formation of the 1996 coalition government, when both parties demanded the same ministry from Benjamin Netanyahu. At the end of long negotiations the dispute was resolved by an agreement, which effectively split the ministry. According to this agreement each party appointed one deputy minister and the ministership rotated every year between the two parties. During the formation of the Barak government in 1999, the same dispute surfaced between both parties. This time however Shas emerged victorious thanks to its stronger representation in the Knesset. While Shas received the ministry, it also agreed to appoint the deputy minister and the director general from a list submitted to it by the NRP.

The vast amount of state patronage channeled to Shas constituencies by the Religious Affairs Ministry also created resentment on the part of the secular public. As a consequence, the strictly-secularist Shinui party ran on a platform promising the abolition of the Religious Affairs Ministry in the 1999 and 2003 national elections. When Shinui increased its electoral power by scoring a considerable electoral success and joined the coalition government after the 2003 national elections—which was conditional on Shas's exclusion from the coalition—it delivered its promise and abrogated the ministry in 2004. The various tasks of the Religious Affairs Ministry were distributed among other ministries. Control of the rabbinical courts was attached to the Ministry of Justice, handling of the holy places was passed to the Minister of Tourism, and the management of the religious councils and burial societies were placed under the authority of the prime minister. Shinui was able to deliver this promise, because Shas was not part of the coalition government in 2003–6. However, the Religious Affairs Ministry was reinstated under the name Ministry of Religious Services in 2008, and Yitzhak Cohen, a Shas

MK, became its new head. The abolition and reinstatement of the ministry is a testament to the politicization of this political institution and its continuing salience for the project of Shas.

Economic Liberalization and Dismantling of the Welfare State as Political Opportunity

In addition to the Interior Ministry and the Ministry of Religious Affairs, Shas also tried to acquire government positions that would assist the party to implement its socioeconomic agenda. The control of the Labor and Social Welfare Ministry and the Ministry of Health provided Shas with an opportunity to distribute vital resources to two groups that form the backbone of Shas's electoral support, namely poor Mizrahim and ultra-Orthodox Sephardim. It is important to note that Shas did not approach the material problems of the lower social classes with a social-democratic lens. Rather than distributing funds to the needy to alleviate their poverty, to create economic opportunities that would lessen their economic vulnerability, and help them to move up in the socioeconomic ladder, Shas distributed welfare services in a partisan manner, primarily by channeling resources to Shas-affiliated non-profit organizations, which increased poor groups' dependency.

It is important to point out that the economic restructuring of the Israeli economy in the 1980s provided a social vacuum that Shas filled in the late 1980s and 1990s by providing welfare through its ministries to its own constituents. The Israeli economy underwent a neo-liberal restructuring starting with the Likud government of 1977 and crystallizing during the national unity government's (Labor-Likud) implementation of the Economic Stabilization Plan in 1985. This transition occurred in tandem with the global shift toward neo-liberal economics and needs to be considered as part of Israel's full integration into the international capitalist system. Among other measures, the Economic Stabilization Plan of 1985 included severe cuts in government subsidies and spending, dramatic wage restraint, devaluation of the Israeli shekel, and liberalization of the trade system.[65] Essentially these measures meant the dismantling of the welfare state built during the first three decades of Israel. Economic policies of successive governments eroded substantial social protections by cutting back consumer subsidies on food and public transportation, reducing child allowances and restricting eligibility rules for unemployment insurance.[66] Privatization of state economic enterprises and the elimination of regional development incentives led to the retrenchment of the state and threatened to "substantially erode direct and indirect subsidies to housing, employment and public services in peripheral 'development towns'."[67] This new neo-liberal economic reality created a political opportunity for Shas, because it contributed to the economic vulnerability of Mizrahim residing in development towns as well as the ultra-Orthodox Jews, two groups that form the core of Shas's electoral support. By tending to the needs of these groups, who were further impoverished by a transition to economic liberalism, through its grip over ministries and through its civil society organizations (more in Chapters 6 and 8), Shas filled an important vacuum that emerged as a result of the cutback of the Israeli welfare state. Transition to neo-liberalism and the dismantling of the social contracts between governments and citizens all around the world has been a contributing factor in the emergence of new religious politics. As Nikkie Keddie (1998) claims, "expansive developments in capitalism (the main element of globalization) which have increased total production but are highly uneven by region, class, race, and gender [have favored the recent rise of religiopolitics]."[68]

In this context of economic liberalization, Eli Yishai ran the Ministry of Labor and Social Welfare (1996–2000) in a partisan manner by catering to the needs of Shas's clientele. Immediately after the ministry came under the control of Shas, there was a change in the courses offered to the unemployed to increase their skills. The number of "retraining courses in 'Jewish' professions – circumcisers, scribes, ritual slaughterers and such – jumped from eight to 52."[69] It is clear that most of these jobs in the religious sector are of foremost benefit for the ultra-Orthodox. Moreover, in 1999 Yishai allocated ten million NIS to an ultra-Orthodox charity organization, called *Matan*, in order to locate distressed ultra-Orthodox children and to place them into state-run boarding schools.[70] According to the accounts of the ministry, social workers outside of the ultra-Orthodox community did not know how to handle these children. Hence, it was not surprising that, in 1999, more than half of the children designated as "in poverty" came from the ultra-Orthodox community.[71] In the same year, the State Comptroller's critical report revealed that the Ministry of Labor and Social Welfare under Yishai turned a blind eye to the registration requirement of Haredi boarding schools and provided monthly funding to over 60 Haredi boarding schools without a proper license.[72] The same report indicated that some of these unregistered institutions were also funded by the Religious Affairs Ministry, leading to a law-evading practice known as "double dipping."[73] That this funding to religious schools constituted almost 70 percent of the ministry's annual budget drew sharp criticism from opposition secular parties. As a Shinui MK claimed: "there are unemployed, poor, handicapped, and what have you, and the Labor and Social Affairs Ministry takes the money and sends it to yeshivot."[74]

The Health Ministry under Shlomo Benizri operated in a similar fashion. One of the first promises of Benizri, when he became Health Minister in 1999, was that he would appoint hospital rabbis and kashrut supervisors.[75] Rather than strengthening the health services for everyone, Benizri also allocated money to partisan non-profit organizations. The complaints of an MK from the secular Shinui critical of Benizri's methods shed light on such patronage practices:

> If someone wanted to offer dental treatment and apply universal socio-economic standards, I'd be all for it. The Health Ministry could build clinics, then go into the schools and offer the care to children who need

> it, many of them Arabs. But they are creating a private organization, funded by the Health Ministry. There's little doubt that it will have a big picture of the Shas spiritual leader, Rabbi Ovadia Yosef, in the clinic. Is that the way to spend state money?[76]

In 2001 alone, the Ministry of Health supported 161 non-profit organizations, and distributed them funds totaling 32 million NIS.[77]

The institutionalization of clientelism within state institutions had important material consequences for the constituencies Shas claims to represent. Shas played an important role in the *Haredization* of the Sephardi community in Israel by creating a culture of segregation and state-dependency. More than any other religious movement in Israel, Rabbi Ovadia Yosef and Shas promote the return to religion among traditional and secular Sephardim adding to the size of the ultra-Orthodox Sephardi community (more in Chapter 6). The fertility rate of the ultra-Orthodox sector among the Sephardim increased from 4.57 children per family in 1980–4 to 7.24 children per family in 1994–6, surpassing any other sector—including the Ashkenazi ultra-Orthodox—in Israeli society.[78] Similarly, for men aged 25–52 the percent of the Sephardi ultra-Orthodox population studying full-time in yeshivas increased from 38 percent to 56 percent, surpassing the percentage of full-time yeshiva students among the Ashkenazi ultra-Orthodox population.[79] These material changes in the lives of the ultra-Orthodox Sephardi population in the first ten years of Shas's existence indicate how the party's aggressive transfer of state resources to its constituencies had a significant social impact. The ultra-Orthodox Sephardim affiliated with Shas institutions became more and more dependent on state resources, because their livelihood was dependent either on state stipends or jobs offered by the Religious Affairs Ministry and the Chief Rabbinate.

The poor strata of non-ultra-Orthodox Sephardim also became more dependent on state resources in two ways. First, there is an important trend within the traditional Sephardi population to send their children to schools affiliated with *Ma'ayan Hahinuch Hatorani* because of the socioeconomic incentives (more in Chapter 8). It is very unlikely that graduates from the *Ma'ayan* schools enter the mainstream workforce, although there are exceptions.

Second, Shas's control of the Labor and Social Welfare Ministry created a new culture of state dependency in terms of the provision of welfare measures. Unlike programmatic social democratic parties that define welfare benefits in the context of social rights, Shas saw the welfare benefits, such as child allowances, employment benefits or health services, in the context of clientelism. Therefore, the disadvantaged Sephardim received welfare only in return for supporting the Shas party, not as a matter of citizen rights.

Those policies of Shas worked almost as a self-fulfilling prophecy. The party thwarted the effective integration of the ultra-Orthodox Sephardim into the workforce and the upward mobility of the non-ultra-Orthodox poor-Sephardim on the socioeconomic ladder. On the other hand, it offered state-subsidized jobs and welfare benefits to these groups and satisfied their short-term demands through its control of the key government ministries. This is exactly what David Lehmann and Batia Siebzehner (2008) call "self-exclusion as a strategy of inclusion." While Shas offers a path of political inclusion for Sephardim through political representation in the center of politics, it does so by thickening the social barriers between Sephardim and the rest of the Israeli society.[80] This is similar to what Gunther Roth defines as "negative integration" referring to "partial political and economic inclusion combined with alternative cultural and social existence."[81]

Hence, Shas created a Sephardi community that would permanently need the party in power in order to receive these short-term benefits. Unlike the successful integration of the modern Orthodox community into Israeli society in the 1950s and 1960s through the policies of the NRP, Shas does not work for the full socioeconomic integration of the Sephardi community. By providing short-term benefits to its constituents through governmental patronage, the party makes sure that this rather marginalized constituency becomes permanently dependent on the political fortunes of Shas.

Conclusion

Shas's inclusion in successive coalition governments provided the party a political opportunity by granting access to important governmental resources. Through its grip on the Interior Ministry, Shas could claim that it acted to "protect the Jewish character" of the Israeli state, while its occupation of the Interior and Religious Affairs Ministries proved to be critical for creating extensive patronage networks. Shas channeled legal and extra-legal funds to its affiliated civil society organizations and established control over the religious economic sector. Neo-liberal restructuring of Israeli economy created another POS by retrenching Israel's welfare state in the 1980s. Shas filled the subsequent social vacuum by providing social welfare to poor and ultra-Orthodox Sephardim through its control of the Labor and Social Welfare and the Health Ministries. While clientelistic politics attend to the short-term economic needs of vulnerable Sephardim, the trends toward cultural segregation and state dependency prevent prospects for upward mobility.

Notes

1 G. N. Giladi, *Discord in Zion: Conflict Between Ashkenazi & Sephardi Jews in Israel*, London: Scorpion Publishing, 1990, pp. 106–7.
2 D. J. Elazar, *The Other Jews: The Sephardim Today*, New York: Basic Books, 1989, p. 49.
3 E. Don-Yehiya, 'Religion, Social Cleavages, and Electoral Behavior: The Religious Parties in the Elections', in D. J. Elazar and S. Sandler (eds.), *Who's the Boss in Israel?: Israel at the Polls, 1988–9*, Detroit: Wayne State University Press, 1992, p. 110.
4 D. J. Elazar, *The Other Jews*, p. 68.
5 A. Oz, *In the Land of Israel*, New York: Harcourt Brace Jovanovich Publishers, Inc., 1983, p. 34.

6 M. Tessler, 'The Political Right in Israel: Its Origins, Growth, and Prospects', *Journal of Palestine Studies*, vol.15, no.2, 1986, 45.
7 S. Smooha, *Israel, Pluralism and Conflict*, Berkeley: University of California Press, 1978, p. 281.
8 J. Allouche, *The Oriental Communities in Israel, 1948–2003: The Social and Cultural Creation of an Ethnic Group,* Geneva: Institut universitaire de hautes études internationals, 2003, p. 44.
9 E. Don-Yehiya, 'Religion, Social Cleavages, and Electoral Behavior', p. 126.
10 Interview with Nisim Cohen, deputy Director of *El Hama'ayan*, Jerusalem, 12 December 2006.
11 H. Herzog, 'Political Factionalism: The Case of Ethnic Lists in Israel', *The Western Political Quarterly*, vol.39, no.2, 296.
12 Ibid., pp. 297–8.
13 Ibid., p. 288.
14 In its election campaigns, the party argued that it is a bridge (*gesher*) between the Zionist secular constituents and ultra-orthodox religious constituents and can restore peace and stability in the state of Israel.
15 M. Friedman, 'The NRP in Transition—Behind the Party's Electoral Decline', in D. Caspi, A. Diskin and E. Guttman (eds.), The Roots of Begin's Success, London: Croom Helm, 1983, p. 291.
16 Ibid., p. 293.
17 I. Greilsammer, 'Campaign Strategies of the Israeli Religious Parties, 1981–84', in A. Arian and M. Shamir (eds.), *The Elections in Israel 1984*, Jerusalem: Ramat Publishing, 1986, p. 89.
18 Interview with Aharon Uzan, *Jerusalem Post Magazine*, 18 June 1981.
19 A. Rabinovich, 'Rising Star: The Post's Abraham Rabinovich Examines the Origins of the Movement', *The Jerusalem Post*, 13 April 1984. Quoted in J. Abadi, 'Ethnicity and Religion in Israeli Politics: Emergence of the Shas Party', in S. C. Saha (ed.), *Religious Fundamentalism in the Contemporary World Critical Social and Political Issues*, New York: Lexington Books, 2004, p. 239.
20 J. Abadi, 'Ethnicity and Religion in Israeli Politics', p. 239.
21 I. Greilsammer, 'Campaign Strategies of the Israeli Religious Parties', p. 84.
22 'Moezet Hachamim'. Online. Available at http://shas.org.il/Web/He/Council/Default.aspx [Hebrew] (accessed 10 June 2012).
23 Y. Mirsky, 'Rav Ovadia', *Jewish Ideas Daily*, 12 October 2010. Online. Available at www.jewishideasdaily.com/734/features/rav-ovadia/; 'Maran Rav Ovadia Yosef'. Online. Available at http://shas.org.il/Web/He/Council/Maran/118.aspx [Hebrew] (accessed 10 June 2012).
24 B. Lau, 'From Shop to Top "Maran Ovadia Yosef: Habiografia" by Nitzan Chen and Anshel Pfeffer', *Ha'aretz*, 1 October 2004; Y. Mirsky, 'Rav Ovadia', *Jewish Ideas Daily*, 12 October 2010; 'Maran Rav Ovadia Yosef'. Online. Available at http://shas.org.il/Web/He/Council/Maran/118.aspx [Hebrew] (accessed 10 June 2012).
25 During the course of Shas's political career, some Sephardic rabbis tried to challenge Rabbi Ovadia Yosef but have always failed. For instance Agudah tried to draw Sephardi constituencies to its list by placing Shas defector Rabbi Yitzhak Peretz in second place on its national list in the 1992 elections. In the 2003 elections, Rabbi Yossi Kedourie formed a new Sephardi party with the name *Ahavat Yisrael*. These attempts failed to attract any significant support from the constituency of Shas. Very recently Shas MK Rabbi Haim Amsalem was expelled from Shas when he publicly questioned some of Yosef's positions. Amsalem formed his party named "*Am Shalem*" (Whole Nation). The polls conducted before the 2013 legislative elections indicate that political support for *Am Shalem* is weak and the party is unlikely to pose any significant threat to Shas.

26 *Mitnagdim* literally means those who oppose. *Mitnagdim* are known for their emphasis on bookish learning and analytical thinking as opposed to the emphasis on mysticism by the *Hassidim*.
27 S. C. Heilman, 'The Orthodox, the Ultra-Orthodox, and the Elections for the Twelfth Knesset', in A. Arian and M. Shamir (eds.), *The Elections in Israel-1988*, Boulder: Westview Press, 1990, pp. 146–7. Shach also formed and supported another splinter party from the Agudah, namely The Flag of Torah (*Degel Hatorah*).
28 A. Willis, 'Shas-The Sephardic Torah Guardians: Religious "Movement" and Political Power', in A. Arian and M. Shamir (eds.), *The Elections in Israel-1992*, New York: SUNY Press, 1995, p. 129.
29 M. B. Shapiro, 'Mi Yosef ad Yosef Lo Kam ke-Yosef', *Meorot*, vol.6. no.1, 2006, 6.
30 I. Shahak and N. Mezvinsky, *Jewish Fundamentalism in Israel*, London: Pluto Press, 1999, pp. 53–4.
31 Shas left the twenty-fifth government led by the Labor Party on 14 September 1993 and did not join the twenty-sixth government that was formed after Rabin's assassination and lasted only seven months (22 November 1995–18 June 1996). The other government that did not include Shas was the thirtieth government of Israel led by Likud (28 February 2003–4 May 2006).
32 Interview with Shas chairman of Barkan branch Roni Huri, Barkan, 11 December 2006.
33 'Israel's Shas Accuses Kadima, Livni of "Racism"; Coalition Options Viewed', *Maariv*, 28 November 2009.
34 The "Law of Return" in Israel stipulates that anyone who is a Jew can get Israeli citizenship. According to the law, a Jew is defined as someone who is born of a Jewish mother or who is converted to Judaism. There is heated political discussion about the religious legitimacy of the conversions performed by the Reform and Conservative movements. Most ultra-Orthodox politicians in Israel argue that these conversions are not done according to *halacha* (Jewish law). Therefore, they claim that the converts should not be accepted as authentic Jews.
35 D. Izenberg, 'Ministry of Interior Wants to Single Out Converts to Judaism', *The Associated Press*, 25 June 1986.
36 'Israeli Court Upholds a Convert', *The New York Times*, 3 December 1986; I. Murray, 'Israel Court Upsets Minister', *The Times*, 4 December 1986.
37 'Israeli Interior Minister Quits to Protest Ruling', *The New York Times*, 1 January 1987.
38 For Shas leaders' statements questioning immigrants' Judaism see: H. Keinon, 'Deri: Law of Return Must be Made Tougher', *The Jerusalem Post*, 20 July 1990; A. Wallfish, 'Ministry Plans to Weed Out "Non-Jewish" Soviet Aliya', *The Jerusalem Post*, 6 March 1991; H. Shapiro and A. Wallfish, 'Interior Minister Deri Calls Report of Ruling Inaccurate Olim Must Prove Jewishness "Back Four Generations", Rules Ovadia Yosef', *The Jerusalem Post*, 28 June 1991.
39 'NGO Slams Yishai over Refugee Remarks', *The Jerusalem Post*, 9 December 2011; B. Hartman, 'Jerusalem, Juba Work on Building "City" in S. Sudan for Returning African Migrants', *The Jerusalem Post*, 28 December 2011; 'Israel's Interior Minister: All African Migrants should be Jailed', *Ha'aretz*, 16 May 2012; 'Yishai on Migrant Arrests: This is just the First Step', *The Jerusalem Post*, 11 June 2012.
40 For more on the bills that severely penalize immigrants who enter Israel without documentation and Israeli citizens who in any way aid the undocumented immigrants in Israel, see: D. Weiler-Polak, 'Israel Enacts Law Allowing Authorities to Detain Illegal Migrants for up to 3 Years', *Ha'aretz*, 3 June 2012; B. Hartman, 'Israel to Draft Law to Stop "Infiltrators Funds"', *The Jerusalem Post*, 9 July 2012; T. Zarchin, 'Knesset Bill would Deny Migrants Right to Appeal Deportation', *Ha'aretz*, 23 July 2012.

41 'Document of Principles'. Online. Available at http://shas.org.il/Web/He/About/Platform/Default.aspx [Hebrew] (accessed 12 August 2012).
42 Interview with Shas chairman of Or Yehuda branch Uzi Aharon, Or Yehuda, 25 June 2012.
43 Interviews with residents of Netivot by the author.
44 Y. Peled, 'Towards a Redefinition of Jewish Nationalism in Israel? The Enigma of *Shas*', *Ethnic and Racial Studies*, vol.21, no.1, 1998, 703–27.
45 Ibid.
46 'For the State Comptroller', *The Jerusalem Post*, 27 November 1989.
47 D. Izenberg, 'Deri: Interior Desecrator?', *The Jerusalem Post*, 25 May 1990.
48 D. Krivine, 'Awash with Funds', *The Jerusalem Post*, 30 March 1990.
49 I. Levin and H. Magen, 'Deri Convicted of Bribery, Fraud', *Globes-Israel's Business Arena*, 17 March 1999.
50 Interview with Shahar Ilan, 8 October 2006. Ilan is the former *Ha'aretz* correspondent on religious affairs. Currently he serves as the president of the non-profit organization, *Hiddush – For Religious Freedom and Equality.*
51 D. Krivine, 'Awash with Funds', *The Jerusalem Post*, 30 March 1990.
52 Ibid.
53 A. Asa-El, 'Tip of a Fiscal Iceberg', *The Jerusalem Post*, 12 July 1996.
54 Z. Lavi, 'Finance Committee Resubmits Religious Affairs Ministry Budget Proposal', *Globes-Israel's Business Arena*, 17 December 1996.
55 'See Where Some of Your Money Goes', *Ha'aretz*, 14 February 2001.
56 'Sorry State of Religious Affairs', *The Jerusalem Post*, 23 July 1996. Note that before Sheetrit the ministry was headed by the then prime minister Yitzhak Rabin, but essentially it was run by the deputy minister Raphael Pinhasi from Shas.
57 S. Ilan, 'It's Easier to get Funding if you're in Rabbi Ovadia Yosef's Family', *Ha'aretz*, 3 November 1999; S. Ilan, 'Some Torah Institutions are more Equal than Others', *Ha'aretz*, 3 November 1999.
58 State Comptroller in Israel is an institution which is responsible for reviewing and supervising government policies.
59 S. L. 'Sappir Making It Kosher', *The Jerusalem Report*, 13 August 2001.
60 S. Dekalo, 'Jerusalem Court: Shas Education Network Fraudulently Obtained Duplicate State Payments', *Globes-Israel's Business Arena*, 30 June 1999.
61 Ibid.
62 Ibid.
63 R. Tesler, *Beshem hashem: Shas ve hamahapecha hadatit*, Jerusalem: Keter Publishing, 2003, p. 411.
64 N. Strasler, 'Who's Holding the Short End of the Stick?', *Ha'aretz*, 2 March 2000.
65 A. Dowty, *The Jewish State a Century Later*, Berkeley: University of California Press, 2001, p. 126.
66 M. Shalev, 'Have Globalization and Liberalization "Normalized" Israel's Political Economy?', *Israel Affairs*, vol.5, no.2–3, 1998, 134.
67 Ibid., p. 135.
68 N. R. Keddie, 'New Religious Politics: Where, When, and Why do Fundamentalisms Appear?', *Comparative Studies in Society and History*, vol.40, no.4, 1998, 699.
69 L. Derfner, 'What's Par for the Course', *The Jerusalem Post*, 18 September 1998.
70 A. Golan, 'Not by Soup Alone', *Ha'aretz*, 25 November 1999.
71 Ibid.
72 D. Izenberg and D. Zev Harris, 'Waste, Mismanagement Plagued Jubilee Fest', *The Jerusalem Post*, 27 April 1999.
73 Ibid.
74 Interview with Shinui MK Yosef Partizky in N. Gilbert, 'Crusader in the Knesset', *The Jerusalem Post*, 14 January 2000.

75 G. Samet, 'Bye-bye Social Reform', *Ha'aretz*, 30 July 1999.
76 Interview with Shinui MK Yosef Partizky in S. L. 'Sappir Making it Kosher', *The Jerusalem Report*, 13 August 2001.
77 Ibid.
78 E. Berman, 'Sect, Subsidy and Sacrifice: An Economist's View of Ultra-Orthodox Jews', *NBER Working Papers*, 6712, National Bureau of Economic Research Inc., 1998, 37.
79 Ibid., p. 35.
80 D. Lehmann and B. Siebzehner, 'Self-Exclusion as a Strategy of Inclusion: The Case of Shas', *Citizenship Studies*, vol.12, no.3, 2008, 233–47.
81 G. Roth, *The Social Democrats in Imperial Germany: A Study in Working-Class Isolation and National Integration*, Somerville: Bedminster Press, 1963. Cited in A. Bayat, *Making Islam Democratic: Social Movements and the Post-Islamist Turn*, Stanford: Stanford University Press, 2007, p. 20.

5 State Incorporation of Religious Actors in Turkey in the 1970s and 1980s

Political Representation of the Periphery and the Advent of the NOM

Until the 1970s, center-right parties appealed to the periphery in Turkey without embracing an explicit religious political ideology. While the RPP was perceived as an elitist party representative of the center's ideology, the DP in 1950–60, and the Justice Party (JP) in 1961–70 received political support from the periphery. Like the Likud Party, which appealed to the Sephardim in Israel by embracing traditional values, the center-right parties in Turkey were more amenable to the cultural sensitivities of the periphery without taking an explicitly religious character. Although Süleyman Demirel's center-right JP contained a religious group led by Saadettin Bilgiç, this group never achieved a powerful enough position within the party to be able to influence major policy decisions.[1]

The birth of the NOM is linked to the frustrations of a group of politicians with the center-right parties at the end of the 1960s. In 1969, Necmettin Erbakan and 17 of his friends declared their candidacy as independents or were nominated from other center-right parties with the aim of forming a parliamentary group after the elections. Despite the fact that only Erbakan was elected to the Great National Assembly (GNA) from Konya as an independent member, this group of candidates formed the core of the Independents Movement (*Bağımsızlar Hareketi*) that developed into the NOM. From his years as the president of the Union of Chambers and Stock Exchanges of Turkey (*Türkiye Odalar ve Borsalar Birliği, TOBB*), Erbakan was known as the champion of the interests of the Anatolian small merchants against the big industrialists in the major cities. By using this economic divide within the center right, he formed his new political movement, the NOM.

On 26 January 1970 Erbakan founded the National Order Party (NOP) with the organizational help of the Nakshibendi Sheikh Mehmet Zahid Kotku from the İskenderpaşa Order. Many of the prominent figures from the İskenderpaşa Order played an active role in the formation of the NOP and its successor National Salvation Party (NSP).[2] Kotku provided not only an electoral base for Erbakan, but also the social networks of his Nakshibendi

Order for the political mobilization efforts of the NOP. In return, Erbakan emphasized his *biat* (obeisance) to Kotku and claimed that his political activities were in line with the will of the Sheikh and the teachings of his order.

Despite these close relations between the İskenderpaşa Order and the NOM, the parties of the NOM do not intertwine religious and political authority as Shas does in Israel. The leaders of the NOM asserted independence from religious authority structures as their party gradually commanded more influence over significant segments of the Turkish population. The İskenderpaşa Order ultimately parted ways with the NOM in 1990, when Esad Coşan, the leader of the İskenderpaşa Order at the time, became increasingly disillusioned with Erbakan and his politicization of Islam.[3] Coşan declared his suspension of support for the NOM in a speech he delivered to his followers.[4]

The political life of the NOP did not last long, and the party was shut down by the Constitutional Court on 20 May 1971. According to the decision of the Constitutional Court, the NOP "acted against the principles of the secular nature of the state and the protection of Atatürk's reforms."[5] The closure marked the first of the multiple politico-legal clashes between religious actors and the secularist coalition consisting of the higher judiciary and military. However, Erbakan and his friends were unfazed and reorganized the NOM under five different political parties, namely the NOP, the NSP, the Welfare Party (WP), the Virtue Party (VP) and the Felicity Party (FP).

In addition to these five parties, two major splits occurred within the NOM. The new generation within the VP, led by Recep Tayyip Erdoğan, Abdullah Gül and Bülent Arınç broke away from the NOM in 2001, and formed the Justice and Development Party (JDP) in 2001. Although the JDP incorporated significant segments of the party grassroots and networks from the VP, the leaders explicitly broke with the ideological program of the National Outlook and embraced a post-Islamist ideological stance (for more

Table 5.1 The National Outlook Parties and their leaders

Name of party	*Leader-period*
National Order Party	Necmettin Erbakan (1970–1)
National Salvation Party	Süleyman Arif Emre (1972–3) Necmettin Erbakan (1973–80)
Welfare Party	Ahmet Tekdal (1983–7) Necmettin Erbakan (1987–98)
Virtue Party	Recai Kutan (1997–2001)
Felicity Party	Recai Kutan (2001–8) Numan Kurtulmuş (2008–10) Necmettin Erbakan (2010–11) Mustafa Kamalak (2011–today)

Table 5.2 Offshoots of the NOM and their leaders

Name of party	*Leader-period*
Justice and Development Party	Recep Tayyip Erdoğan (2001–today)
The People's Voice Party	Numan Kurtulmuş (2010–12)

Note: The People's Voice Party was closed down by its own leaders on 19 September 2012 and united with the JDP.

information on the JDP, see Chapter 7). Moreover, a group of left-leaning activists splintered from the NOM and formed the People's Voice Party (*Halkın Sesi Partisi*) in November 2010, which joined the JDP after two years.

The NSP in the Coalition Governments (1974–8)

When the NOP was dissolved, Erbakan formed the NSP on 11 October 1972. In 1973, the NSP for the first time participated in national elections and sent 48 Members of Parliament (MPs) to the GNA by capturing 11.8 percent of the vote. Yet, what was more important than its electoral success was NSP's participation in the three coalition governments in the hyper-volatile years of Turkish politics between the two military interventions. In addition to being the champion of the economic interests of the small merchants in Anatolia against the big industrialists in Ankara and Istanbul, the NSP also embraced a moral-religious agenda. Accordingly, the party's twin goals were material development (*maddi kalkınma*) and spiritual development (*manevi kalkınma*) as reflected in its party program. On 24 January 1974 to many observers' surprise Erbakan joined a coalition government with the RPP.

The provisions of the coalition agreement reveal that NSP's socioeconomic goals became part of the government's agenda. Some of the articles of the coalition agreement reflected those goals:

> the implementation of a regional industrialization program according to criteria of social justice and regional balances; the formation of an industrial bank within the Ministry of Industry; the development of national war and arms industry; putting caps on the profits of foreign investment; legalization of the already built illegal squatter-settlements in the major cities.[6]

These provisions were indicative of the government's desire to create a national economy based on heavy industry without hurting the small industrialists in the small cities; the NSP's desire to create an independent nationalist economic system that is less dependent on international capitalism; and the goal of integrating the *gecekondu* residents into the city life. In order to fulfill these aims, the NSP received seven ministries, including the Ministry of Justice, Interior Ministry and Ministry of Industry.[7]

Holding the Ministry of Industry was particularly instrumental for the fulfillment of NSP's goal of material development through pervasive industrialization in Anatolia. Therefore, the NSP requested the same ministry in all three coalition governments, in which it participated. The NSP leaders continuously declared that pervasive heavy industrialization was a sine qua non for creating a strong, independent "Great Turkey" that would refashion the glorious past of the Ottoman Empire.[8]

In addition to its goal of material development, the NSP also implemented policies that were concordant with its goal of spiritual development.[9] To this end, the party held onto government agencies, such as the Directorate of the Religious Affairs and General Directorate of Vaqf (*Vakıflar Genel Müdürlüğü*). During its participation in the coalition government, the NSP set aside funding in the national budget for more than 5,000 additional Quranic course teachers and imams.[10] It also inserted morality lessons to all elementary, middle and high schools; opened the middle-school sections of the *Imam Hatip* schools;[11] and opened 29 more of these schools bringing their total number to 101 (further discussion in Chapter 8).

The government resigned 11 months after its formation due to difficulties between the two parties, and Ecevit's belief that an early election would give the RPP a mandate to rule alone. However, the parliament did not decide to hold early elections, and after an independent senator's unsuccessful attempt to form the government, the first "Nationalist Front" government, a coalition between right-wing parties in the parliament, was formed. The Hearth of Intellectuals, a think-tank comprised of conservative-nationalist university professors, played a significant role in the configuration of this nationalist alliance. The Hearth members tried to synthesize Turkish nationalism with Islamic values and projected the RPP, which embraced a more social-democratic position with its "left of center" program, as the biggest threat to the future of Turkey. Therefore the Hearth members opposed divisions within the right, and worked hard to construct an alliance between all right-wing parties, namely the center-right JP, the ultra-nationalist Nationalist Action Party (NAP), the elitist Republican Trust Party (RTP) and the Islamist NSP.[12]

Consequently, the NSP became again a "key"[13] member of the coalition government in 1975, and the party's twin goals were clearly visible both in the coalition agreement and the policy initiatives of the government. According to the coalition agreement:

> the morality lessons in the elementary and high schools will be foremost taught according to their philosophy by the graduates of the divinity faculty, Institute of Islamic Higher Education or *Imam Hatip* schools; educational curriculum will be purged from elements not suiting Turkish national culture;[14] the place of religious functionaries in our society will be recognized by utilizing them in our social and economic development.[15]

The NSP also tried to give the graduates from the *Imam Hatip* schools the opportunity to become officers in the Turkish army, but failed in its attempt.[16]

In order to fulfill its promise of material development, the NSP undertook a heavy industrialization program and started to build factories in many of the peripheral cities. Şevket Kazan, the Minister of Labour from the NSP at the time, explains the industrialization effort of his party:

> At that time [during the first Nationalist Front government], Turkey was developing. If you look at the map of Turkey, you can see that there were factories all over. Especially, in eastern Turkey. Meat factories, milk factories, fodder factories, sugar factories. Why here? Because there was animal husbandry, so animal husbandry develops as well as employment is provided. In addition to those, there were other factories, for example airplane engine factories. In Diyarbakır TUSAŞ was built. The foundations of concrete factories were laid … For example in Mazi the emphasis was put on facilities for coal reserves. Hence in all of Turkey heavy industry moves were made, foundations were laid, but we could not stay in the government for long.[17]

Parallel to these claims the NSP pressured the JP to put into the 1977 budget an extra $1.8 billion investment for heavy industrialization and to significantly increase the number of the NSP staff in bureaucratic positions.[18] Erbakan threatened the JP to quit the coalition and to form a new coalition with the RPP if its demands were not met.[19] Yet due to early elections that were held in June of 1977, the NSP could not harvest the results of that year's budget and its industrialization proposals. Moreover, Erbakan's too frequent factory openings without sufficient infrastructural plans became points of criticism and ridicule in parts of the media.

In the 1977 election NSP's national vote share fell from 11.8 percent to 8.7 percent, and the number of NSP members in the parliament decreased from 48 to 24. While NSP activists claimed that the abrupt halt of their heavy industrialization program was the sole reason for the erosion of public support in the elections, internal conflicts within the party were an important factor. In the aftermath of the elections the NSP participated in the second Nationalist Front government, but the life of this government was less than four months.

The NSP's involvement in the coalition governments was important for two main reasons. First, participating in the governments—particularly in the coalition government with the RPP—helped the party to improve its public image. The NSP erased its previous image of being a threat to the secular regime, when its predecessor NOP was shut down by the Constitutional Court in 1971. Erbakan's movement showed that it could fulfill important political functions, including governing the state. Second, occupying important ministries and government agencies provided the NSP the opportunity to create patronage networks within state institutions, such as the

State Planning Organization (*Devlet Planlama Teşkilatı*). Important segments of the NSP's political and bureaucratic staff joined the center-right Motherland Party (*Anavatan Partisi*) (MP) and were promoted to decision-making positions within the state during the democratic era following the military government.

The Co-optation of Islam by the Military Regime: Institutionalization of the Turkish-Islamic Synthesis (1980–3)

On 12 September 1980 the military overthrew the civilian government and suspended democratic politics. During the following three years the military establishment ruled Turkey through the National Security Council (NSC) and transformed political institutions by rewriting the constitution and changing the legal status of political parties. The NSC banned all parties that operated in the pre-coup period from politics under the pretext that political polarization between left and right and the uncompromising attitudes of party leaders were responsible for growing instability and political violence in the country. While the military targeted both the right and the left political formations, the socialists and the leftist Kurdish nationalists became the foremost political victims of the regime.

During its time in power, the military developed a closer relationship to religion and redefined nationalism by co-opting certain elements of Islam. To many, this came as a surprise, as the military establishment had been the bulwark of Turkish secularism since the proclamation of the republic. The military leaders envisioned that promoting a benign form of Islam could create some type of brotherhood within the Turkish society that had been torn by ideological polarization and violence in the latter half of the 1970s.[20] Thus, the junta used Islam as an instrument of social control.

The military's co-optation of Islam can be analyzed on three levels. First, the military establishment nurtured a symbiotic relationship with the conservative Hearth of Intellectuals especially in designing the cultural policies of the state. Second, it altered national policy regarding religious education. Finally, the head of the state, Kenan Evren, frequently used Islam in his speeches to legitimize the authoritarian policies of the military regime.

As discussed above, the Hearth of Intellectuals was a think-tank formed in 1970 by conservative academicians in order to counter the intellectual hegemony of the left in the universities and among the youth. Their aim was to promote the idea of "native intellectuals" against the cosmopolitan left intellectuals and to become the trusted, organic intelligentsia of the regime.[21] One of the most important projects of the Hearth was the "Turkish-Islamic Synthesis," namely the creation of a new historical narrative by intermeshing Turkish nationalism with Islamic culture. The authoritarianism of the military years produced an important window of opportunity for the Hearth, which was an elitist association with a statist aim of transforming the society from the top down according to its own ideology. Since the ideology of the

Hearth suited the junta's aims, the members and ideas of the Hearth were incorporated into the institutional reform efforts of the new regime.

On 23 October 1981, a new legislative body was formed with the name Consultation Assembly (*Danışma Meclisi*) under the auspices of the NSC.[22] The primary responsibility of the Consultation Assembly, members of which were closely screened and appointed by the NSC, was the preparation of proposals for a new constitution.[23] The NSC still held the ultimate authority for the finalization of the constitutional provisions.[24] During the preparation of the constitution, it was prohibited to submit recommendations to the Preparatory Committee of the Consultation Assembly in the name of any institution or association. Despite the ban, the Hearth submitted its own draft directly to the NSC. Moreover, two of the members of the Preparatory Committee, namely Şener Akyol and Yılmaz Altuğ, were members of the Hearth.[25]

The new constitution, which further restricted democratic liberties and placed the future of the political regime under the tutelage of the military, was ratified by a plebiscite on 7 November 1982. After the ratification of the constitution, the president of the Hearth stated in an interview that "the constitution and their draft overlapped 75–80 percent."[26] In another interview in 1987 he added:

> Yes, certainly we have supported [the coup of] 12 September. We supported its constitution. It is true that some of the proposals were suggested by members of the Hearth of Intellectuals. Therefore, it is true that we have problems with the scientific community, which demands significant changes in the [1982] constitution.[27]

In addition to the Hearth's influence on the preparation of the constitution, the junta appointed members of the Hearth to important positions in the bureaucracy. For example the State Planning Organization, responsible for the formulation of the five-year plans including the public education and culture policy, was filled with the members of the Hearth.[28] In 1983, the State Planning Organization published a "Report on National Culture" (*Milli Kültür Raporu*) that became the basis of the culture and education policies of the "Fifth Five-Year Development Plan." This document, prepared mostly by the professors who belonged to the Hearth, suggested a number of methods to incorporate religion into the promotion of national consciousness.[29]

The program included the following articles on cultural planning:

> i)The state needs to make religious and moral planning, and to create a "religious map" of Turkey; ii) The importance of religion and morality needs to be emphasized through public communication mediums, and in formal education; iii) The workers need to work with a religious devotion; iv) The cultural policies of the republican era need to be changed. Due to these policies, which did not support religious life, we could not

> respond to the complex problems that emerged during industrialization; v) We need to encourage our people with spiritual education, religious and moral discipline, and national and historical consciousness; vi) Materialistic worldviews like pragmatism or positivism need to be removed from the curriculum of education.[30]

As these statements make clear, the state elites depicted the lack of religion in the previous periods as a fundamental problem and aimed to create a religious consciousness in harmony with Turkish nationalism in order to create law-abiding future citizens. The reference to the need for the workers to work with religious devotion aimed to curtail the Marxist and revolutionary tendencies prominent among the workers in the 1970s. Moreover, the report adopted an antagonistic tone not only toward extreme left ideologies—which it saw as the source of political polarization of the previous era—but also criticized rationalist and materialistic worldviews.

Another venue for the dissemination of the Hearth's ideology within the state was the Atatürk Culture, Language and History Higher Institution (*Atatürk Kültür, Dil ve Tarih Yüksek Kurumu*) formed under article 134 of the 1982 constitution. This institution was responsible for coordinating the activities of the Turkish Historical Society (*Türk Tarih Kurumu*) and the Turkish Language Society (*Türk Dil Kurumu*). Thanks to the Hearth members appointed to the higher echelons of this newly formed institution, the Turkish-Islamic Synthesis became a source for the state's official historical narratives. In a report that the institution prepared in June 1986, Kemalism was defined "as a movement that directs the Turkish-Islamic culture to a new synthesis with the Western culture."[31] Due to this novel interpretation of Kemalism, the Turkish-Islamic Synthesis, alongside the secular version of Kemalist ideology, informed the narratives of the history and "religious culture and knowledge of morals" books prepared for elementary and high schools between 1980 and 1993.[32] When reading this new interpretation of Turkish history, students were reminded, among other things, about the parallels between Atatürk and the Prophet Muhammad with regard to their skillful statesmanship and military heroism.[33]

In addition to the increasing presence of Hearth members within the state institutions, the new religious nationalism was also promoted by the military establishment itself. The General Staff published a three-volume work, *Atatürkçülük*, which explained among other things the compatibility of Atatürk's views with Islamic teachings. The self-declared aim of these three volumes was "to guarantee that the future generations are systematically educated according to a national morality based on Atatürkist principles and become good citizens, who embrace this ideology."[34] Thus, these three volumes were published "in order to provide source materials to the 'History of Atatürkism and Reform' classes taught in the educational institutions."[35] Some sections in these source materials prepared for the education of primary and secondary students demonstrate how Atatürkist principles were reinterpreted by the military establishment in the aftermath of the 1980 coup. For instance, under a section entitled "Atatürk and the religion of Islam" it is stated:

> Atatürkism understands and practices the basic tenets of Islam according to the Qur'an and Prophet Muhammad's path. These words belong to Atatürk: "I believe in my religion as I believe in reality. [It] does not contain anything contrary to consciousness or progress. Yet among this Asian nation [referring to the Turks' pre-Islamic, Central Asian origins] that gave Turkey its independence, there is also a more complex, more artificial religion that is full of empty beliefs. These illiterates, these helpless people will be emancipated, when time comes."[36]

On the one hand, the paragraph conveys to the reader that Atatürk's principles are fully compatible with the Qur'an and the Prophet Muhammad's teachings—albeit without explaining how this compatibility works. On the other hand, it also asserts that the state should fight against a superstitious version of Islam. While the military incorporated the ideology of the Hearth and very selective elements of Islam in its cultural policies, it also acted severely against members of the closed NSP by prosecuting them in Military Martial Law Courts. For the military leaders, any religiopolitical ideology outside the state was harmful and manipulative, while they, as the guardians of the state, had the obligation to protect, disseminate and control the true form of Islam. The following quotation from the same volume reflects a similar idea:

> In Qur'an, shura 22, Verse 17 it is stated that "God will give his final judgment on the judgment day between the believers, the Jews, the Sabians, the Christians, the Magians, and those, who worship others besides God. The truth is God is witness over all things." According to this clear statement, God did not give to anyone, to any religious or worldly institution the authority to control his commandments and to punish individuals due to their religious activities. There is no coercion in Islam. Atatürkism, which accepts the necessity of religion for the individual and the society, foresees the struggle against religious bigotry, the abolition of false religious institutions, the education of healthy religious functionaries, and the control of religious education in order to prevent religion's control over institutions that are out of its jurisdiction.[37]

In addition to the publication of these three volumes, a new Department of Propagation (*İrşad Dairesi*) was formed in the Directorate of Religious Affairs with an aim to promote this new national consciousness based on the alliance between nationalism and religion.[38] The military establishment also made effective use of the media for the dissemination of religious consciousness by increasing the number of religious programs on national television, the only television broadcast in Turkey until 1990.

As part of its strategy to co-opt Islam, the military regime also tinkered with the education system. In 1981, several ministers and the Director of Religious Affairs submitted a report with the title "Religious Education and the Abuse of Religion" (*Din Eğitimi ve Din İstismarı*) to the NSC.[39] Among other things the report stated that the elective nature of religious classes in primary and secondary education had created divisions among students, and prevented the forging of national solidarity.[40] The report also added that the lack of religious instruction had led many people to unofficial religious education, and this benefited some groups that worked against the state. Consequently, it suggested that the civic and voluntary religion classes should be combined and made compulsory.[41] The generals heeded the advice of the report's authors and inserted a provision into the 1982 constitution making religious education compulsory in primary and secondary schools.[42] Necati Öztürk, the director of general religious education at the time, explains the aim of these newly instituted "Culture of Religion and Knowledge of Moral" (*Din Kültürü ve Ahlak Bilgisi*) classes:

> Compulsory religious education will conform to Atatürk's principle of secularism by not mixing religion with the affairs of state. Such courses will meet the needs of family and community, as they are designed to fill the void in our children by imparting knowledge of morality and faith with a scientific bent. From a sociological point of view, the school is an extension of society; it reflects society's characteristics. A school devoid of the mores and values of its society cannot be considered an educational institution. It is thus impossible to ignore the fact of religion present in the mores and values of Turkish society.
>
> Religious instruction in our schools is grounded on three general aims. (1) The individual aim: Religious sentiment has its place in the developmental stages of the child. (2) The historical and cultural aim: Compulsory education for the new generation must promote a self-identification with our history, literature, art – in short, with our national culture – through scientific and emotional modes of appreciation. (3) The social aim: Education must take into account the role religion plays in interpersonal and intergroup relations.[43]

These statements reflect the conception of society the generals and the Hearth were trying to promote. According to Öztürk, religion could play a role in smoothing the tense intergroup relations that Turkey inherited from the pre-coup period by creating some type of Islamic brotherhood. Moreover, the compulsory religion classes could help students to internalize the moral values of a unified Turkish society in the present, as well as to identify with their national heritage.

President Kenan Evren, a pious believer and the son of a prayer leader, also used quotations from the Qur'an to give advice to the citizens on matters varying from how to dress to how to pray. During one of his speeches in

Malatya in 1981, Evren said "People ask me about why we made religious education compulsory. As I have said many times before, secularism does not mean atheism … We made religious education compulsory so that our children would not be brainwashed with superstitions."[44]

Furthermore, he emphasized the importance of religion as a source of unity rather than conflict, as he states:

> There is no distinction in our religion, such as Alevism or Sunnism. We cannot make distinctions between Alevi or Sunni. We are a nation that believes in the same religion, in the same book, in the same prophet and in the same God. Whoever makes this distinction should be punished. Here the most important job belongs to our teachers and religious preachers. If we teach our children in the schools that we belong to the same religion, they will not make these distinctions, once they grow up.[45]

Evren often emphasized that state-taught Islam is an important source of unity and a bulwark against the misguided attempts of those who try to politicize religion. This attitude noticeably overlooks the fact that his junta was politicizing Islam for different purposes. During their three-year reign, the generals employed Islam as a tool in their de-politicization agenda into the once politically and ideologically torn society. They selectively referred to Islam in their policies and injected it into an Atatürkist national narrative. The main aim was to create an organically united society with no important distinctions along religious, ethnic, class or ideological lines.

A New Democratic Era and the Motherland Party Governments (1983–91)

The military regime handed over the political power to the civilians when it held general elections on 6 November 1983. The political parties of the turbulent pre-1980 era and their new incarnations were barred from running in the first highly restrictive multiparty elections. The MP headed by Turgut Özal received 45.2 percent of the vote and earned a comfortable majority in the parliament despite president Evren's open criticism of the MP on national television a few days before the elections.

During the MP governments (1983–91), Turkey went through a gradual transition to democracy and implemented a neo-liberal economic agenda. In this period, two sets of political opportunity structures opened up for the Islamists in Turkey. First, Özal embraced an export-led growth strategy that paved the way for the embourgeoisement of Islam. Many of the small and medium-scale enterprises (SMEs) located in Anatolian provinces increased their capital accumulation in this period. These businesses that came from the periphery synthesized their religious conservatism with this new middle class status and became one of the main drivers of the NOM in the 1990s.

Second, the incorporation of religious actors into the state apparatus continued during the MP governments. Under its umbrella, the MP included former NSP members who influenced important legislation and policy. This inclusion triggered a double movement in the political arena. On the one hand, state institutions, such as the Education Ministry, the national television network, and the Ataturk Culture, Language and History Higher Institution, continued to constitute institutional sites where a conservative outlook was promoted. As a consequence, religious social actors found a receptive environment to increase their public appeal in the post-1980 era, whereas the left has been heavily suppressed. On the other hand, the attempts of the MP and the previous military regime to co-opt Islam drew criticism from societal actors. WP activists, religious newspapers and Islamist intellectuals criticized the MP for instrumentalizing a watered-down Islam. As a result of these criticisms, the periphery's support gradually shifted from the conservative MP to the Islamist WP in the 1990s.

Neo-Liberal Restructuring and the Emergence of a Pious Muslim Middle Class

The transition to neo-liberalism began under military rule, when Turgut Özal served as the Deputy Minister responsible for economic matters. The pace of liberalization accelerated during the MP governments, when Özal became prime minister. While the new economic structuring included several standard neo-liberal policy instruments, such as the passage to the floating exchange rate system and import liberalization, the government also utilized significant measures, such as export tax rebates, export subsidies, and low interest credits that aimed to encourage export growth.[46] Thus, during this period of neo-liberal economics, state intervention in the economy did not solely disappear, rather it changed direction.[47] One observer labeled this strategy "unorthodox liberalism," pointing out the system's contradictions. These new economic instruments dramatically changed the incentive structure for businesses. As a result, the ratio of exports to GNP increased from 5 percent in 1980 to 14.4 percent in 1989, while the ratio of industrial exports to total exports skyrocketed from a mere 6 percent in 1980 to 77.80 percent in 1991.[48]

This new economic restructuring has mainly benefited the SMEs in provincial cities. A major boom in production and capital accumulation was observed for companies in Anatolian cities, such as Konya, Yozgat, Denizli, Çorum, Aksaray and Gaziantep after the 1980s.[49] Most were run by conservative businessmen who had taken political refuge in the NOM in the 1970s. When these businessmen became wealthier, they started to synthesize their Islamic, conservative values with their new class position and formed a new Islamic middle class, who became the carrier of the WP and later JDP (for further discussion see Chapter 7).

The economic power of this new religious middle class was crystallized in 1990 with the establishment of a new economic business association, the

Independent Industrialists and Businessmen Association (*Müstakil Sanayici ve İşadamları Derneği*) (MUSIAD). As the representative of the SMEs from the periphery, MUSIAD challenged the dominance of the Turkish Industrialists and Businessmen Association (*Türkiye Sanayici ve İşadamları Derneği*) (TUSIAD), which represents the big industrialists primarily from Istanbul who became rich during the implementation of Import Substitution Industrialization (ISI) in the 1970s. Today, MUSIAD has over 5,600 members, who employ 1.2 million workers and contribute 17 billion dollars to Turkey's exports.[50] MUSIAD is "founded on Islamic principles, which include feelings of trust and solidarity, the primacy of community over the individual, the discourse of the just self over the self-interested actor, and the privileged status of ethical codes over individual morality."[51] By integrating these Islamic values into a free-market ideology, the business association presents itself as an alternative to the amoral, liberal capitalist development model.[52]

Another major economic opportunity that has benefited Islamic capital was the proliferation of interest-free banking under the MP governments. Two days after it came to power, the first MP government passed a decree permitting the formation of "private financial institutions," which refers to interest-free banking in the Turkish context.[53] While these private financial institutions, such as Al Baraka Türk, Faysal Finans and Kuveyt Türk, were first formed by foreign investment from Saudi Arabia and Kuwait, the Islamic bourgeoisie from Anatolia started to participate in its ownership after some time.[54] Prominent MP members, such as the prime minister's brother Korkut Özal and the head of MP's Istanbul organization Eymen Topbaş, also became partners in these special financial institutions.[55]

Turgut Özal also played a role in synthesizing religion and liberal economics. Özal was a practicing believer and a member of the Nakshibendi order (*ehl-i tarik*). On the other hand, his degrees in electrical engineering and economics, his tenure in the State Planning Organization and his familiarity with world economics made him a competent technocrat who used cost–benefit analysis in approaching political subjects. During his premiership, he successfully defined ideological and political issues in a technical manner and created a "new professional politician," who thought as a rational, neutral technocrat.[56] In several instances, he did not hesitate to combine his personal piety with this technocratic vision and explained economic subjects with Islamic concepts:

> Order in Islam is based on the concept of unity (*tevhid*). In this order everything has a specific place and function, and moves in an organic relation according to certain rules. In the contemporary context what we mean by an organic relation is a functioning free market with its basic principles … There have always been similarities in the Western and Islamic market principles. First of all, both of them are free. In the Islamic market the prices are set freely and by the market mechanism as well. The

> Islamic market is superior in dealing with the formation of monopolies. On the one hand there is almsgiving (*zekat*) and on the other hand the principle of profit sharing instead of interest prevents monopolies.[57]

Factions within the Motherland Party

Although the MP governments established civilian control over the political regime, there were several ideological continuities with the military period. For instance the idea of creating an "organic unity" in Turkish society, which was one of the main pillars of the military regime's ideology, was endorsed by the program and policies of the MP. Özal stated in many of his speeches that the ideological, divisive understanding of politics of the pre-coup era should be abandoned. To that end, he embraced a Weberian, technocratic rationalism and defined politics as "competition for service to the society" in his party's program. The recourse to technocratic, non-ideological politics coupled with neo-liberal economic policies has created a yuppie class, dubbed the "Özalist youth," who place personal well-being over commitments to political ideologies. This yuppie consumerism and the new neo-liberal economic ideals were in line with the growing global trends of the 1980s.

Another way in which Özal promoted brotherly unity in Turkish politics was by claiming that the MP was merging four different tendencies in the society. Accordingly, in its party program the MP defined itself as a party that is nationalist, conservative, committed to free market enterprise,[58] and to social justice. In order to achieve this eclectic ideological goal, Özal recruited politicians from the four main pre-coup political parties which represented different ideological agendas, namely the center-left RPP, the center-right JP, the ultra-nationalist NAP and the Islamist NSP. The new motto of the party became "the unification of the four tendencies under the roof of Motherland." One of the founders of the party explained this with an anecdote:

> Mr. Turgut [Özal] has read a poem in the first party congress: "The rightist calls us leftist, the leftist calls us rightist. We neither belong to this nor to that, we belong both to this and that" ... The Western media has presented us as progressive conservative. We thought, and decided that we would not use even this label; we would not divide the nation. The aim of politics is not to divide the nation, [the aim is] to unify, to heal the wounds, to bring the rightist and the leftist under the roof of the same party.[59]

Despite this "politics without ideology" rhetoric and an effort to assimilate all the four ideological tendencies into Motherland's pragmatist worldview, party congresses triggered political competition among the four factions for the party leadership. The three powerful factions within the party were the conservative faction, the nationalist faction and the liberal faction. These factions were not firm groups with fixed policy agendas, and boundaries between them were fluid. Membership was based more on past political commitments and lifestyle than well-developed programmatic differences. As one former MP minister explains:

> In MP, the distinction between conservative, nationalist, and liberal was not based on ideology ... the distinction between liberals and conservatives was a nonsensical distinction based on people's lifestyles. For instance the liberals used to define their liberalism by sipping whisky in the five-star hotels, while we defined our conservatism by going to the Friday prayer ... This was an artificial distinction. If we look according to the roots, the conservative group came from the old Justice Party and the NSP. ... The individuals who are known as liberals in our party were rather social democrats, hence people with RPP roots. This group was labeling itself as "liberal". Additionally they did not have any nationalistic or conservative worries. Mr. Turgut [Özal] was interestingly a very pragmatic person, he was practical.[60]

This account partly reflects the political culture in Turkey, where symbols and rituals can sometimes determine political commitments more than well-established programs. The competition between those factions helped the media and the society to situate the ideology of the government, and recognize in which direction the governing party was moving. From the appointment of a bureaucrat to the interpretation of a law, anything could start a friction between the different factions. The liberals, for instance, were very insistent on the annulment of articles 141 and 142 of the Turkish penal code, since these articles interfered with freedom of speech. On the other hand, the conservative wing was more vocal on the need to get rid of article 163, which was restrictive of religious freedoms. Similarly, conservatives were at the forefront of the passage of a bill that would get rid of the ban on the headscarf in educational institutions.[61]

The Conservative Wing of the MP and its Relation to State Institutions

The incorporation of religious actors into state institutions constituted a marked continuity between the military regime and the MP governments. Turgut Özal, who himself ran as a candidate from the NSP during the 1977 national elections in İzmir but failed to get elected, appointed many bureaucrats or mayors from the closed NSP to bureaucratic positions during his premiership. Özal took the entire team of his brother Korkut Özal, who served as the Interior Minister from the NSP in 1977–8, and brought its members into important positions in the bureaucracy and party organization.[62] Patronage networks were formed and became especially active in the police department under the interior ministry of Abdülkadir Aksu and in the Ministry of Agriculture, Forest and Rural Affairs under Hüsnü Doğan.

The operation of these patronage networks troubled others in the MP so much that Mustafa Taşar, an influential MP, argued in a memo written to Özal that Erbakan's WP was benefiting from MP's government through the appointment of its supporters to key positions in the bureaucracy.[63]

During the MP governments, conservative politicians obtained positions that could potentially influence cultural politics. The first three of the four education ministers under the MP were members of the conservative faction.[64] According to Hasan Celal Güzel, Minister of Education in 1987–9, Özal intentionally appointed conservatives to this position in order give the periphery the message that the education of their children was in the hands of people with proper moral values.[65]

When asked how he implemented conservatism at the policy level, Hasan Celal Güzel talked about a synthesis between modernity and Turkish-Islamic values:

> I said that we need to make peace between Asım and Haluk. As you know Asım's generation is [that of] the discourse of Mehmet Akif … This is a nationalist, patriotic generation that holds to its own cultural values … Haluk is Tevfik Fikret's son, who later changed his religion. … The poems that Tevfik Fikret wrote for his son are also beautiful. There, Tevfik Fikret expresses a humanist understanding, and Haluk is in a way a world citizen. This conflict between Mehmet Akif and Tevfik Fikret passed to future generations. On the one hand, there was a nationalist-conservative understanding, on the other hand a liberal, humanist understanding that is open to the left. First, I said I would unite, reconcile these two understandings … Second I mentioned a youth holding the Qur'an in his hand and wearing a space suit. And then I explained these two symbols: a youth who would not forget his identity, his essence, but would be open to science and development.[66]

Hasan Celal Güzel's description of reconciling two different worldviews is in line with Özal's aim of bringing together different worldviews under the roof of the party. His portrayal of the youth with space clothes and the Qur'an represents MP governments' attempts to modernize Turkey technologically on the one hand, and to protect the moral values of Turkish society on the other. Vehbi Dinçerler, the first Minister of Education in the MP government, also referred to a synthesis:

> When you go to Japan, they do their weddings with clothes from thousands of years ago, they give salutes like they did thousands of years ago. The upbringing of the children, the perfection of their family life … The protection of the family life is one of the main pillars of our conservatism … This is why we tried to prevent everything that would create a chasm between the parents and the children. For instance we put in place a restriction on selling alcohol to the youth under 18 … As the

> minister of education, I played an important role on passing this restriction ... When we brought this restriction, we also prohibited selling beer in the villages. If anyone wants [to buy alcohol], he can go to the city and buy it from there ... This was the sharpest thing [we did] according to our program.[67]

By alluding to Japan, Dinçerler emphasized the dual aims of the Motherland Party that Güzel described above. Yet according to Dinçerler, there was a need to enact laws that would ensure the preservation of the moral values of the Turkish society. During his education ministry, he banned the opening of new bars within 200 meters of schools, sport clubs and mosques.[68] In the realm of education, Dinçerler was also active in promoting a religious worldview. For instance, he put creationism into the school books as an alternative to the evolutionary theory of Darwin. According to him, evolution was taught to the students as a law in the biology classes, and this practice hinted to the students that there could be a contradiction between science and religion.[69] In order to prevent this, Dinçerler sent a report to the schools on 25 March 1985, and demanded that "the evolutionary theory of Charles Darwin should not be thought as a law in the course books."[70] Moreover, Dinçerler forged close relations with the Christian right in the United States and invited creationist scholars to Istanbul for a conference.[71] His ministry promoted creationism and "intelligent design" in school curriculums by translating books written by these Christian right groups in the United States, publishing, and distributing them to secondary school teachers.[72] His Ministry of Education also published books written by Turkish scholars on the same subject.[73]

The conservative policies of the MP were not restricted to the realm of education, but extended to other spheres. For instance, in 1986 the government passed the "law for protecting minors from harmful publications" (*Küçükleri Muzır Neşriyattan Koruma Kanunu*) and formed an 11-member censorship committee that would supervise the suitability of written publications for the spiritual development of children. Accordingly, the committee restricted the sale of certain publications, which would be labeled "harmful for children," to designated shops, and breach of the law carried significant monetary fines.[74]

The MP also took a proactive stance in protecting the institution of family that it defined as a basic pillar of a healthy society in its party program. With the initiative of the conservative Minister of State, Cemil Çiçek, the government passed a decree law for the formation of a "Family Research Institution" in 1989. One of the first activities of this institution was to prepare a serial named "Home" for the national television, which was the only available TV station at the time.

The theme of the serial reveals how state television was used as a site for the construction of a conservative ideology. The heroine of the serial, the wife of a woodcarver, led a happy life as a housewife and mother until she was attracted to the dynamic lifestyle of her friend, a single businesswoman. As she started to spend more time with her and to engage in social activities, she realized that she was neglecting her family. At the end of the serial she understood that her friend was lonely and the life she chose was wrong. Therefore she decided to continue her life as a happy housewife.[75] By presenting the proper role of women as breeders and homemakers, the plot frames women's work outside of the home as a threat to the natural order of things, an all-too-familiar justification historically used to exclude women from the public sphere.

The formation of 12 public "Family Consultation Centers" headed by Melih Gökçek[76] followed the opening of the Family Research Institution. One of the main aims of these centers was the preservation of the extended Muslim family.[77] The main activity of these centers was to offer consultation to partners who were considering divorce and to convince them to continue their marriage. Since divorce was still a taboo in Turkey at the time, and many women saw it as a last resort, progressive circles criticized these policies of the government. Feminists claimed that the aim of these centers was to pressure vulnerable women to stay in insupportable marriages. On 2 November 1989 40 feminists symbolically filed for divorce in order to protest these centers. The Minister of State, Cemil Çiçek's response was harsh: "Feminism corrupts the order of the family … Like drug addiction, feminism is a deviation."[78]

Mehmet Keçeciler, the leader of the conservative faction within the MP summed up the aim of the conservatives in designing this type of legislation:

> The type of person, who believes that he will need to account for his actions after his death, is actually a good type of citizen. It is much easier to govern such a person and to direct him to goodness. It is harder to govern people, who do not believe in anything or in any value. This is why the [political] order that the conservative people would form in Turkey could develop much better.[79]

By linking the fear of God to the state's ability to govern, these remarks show the striking similarity between the military regime's use of Islam as a tool of de-politicization and the aspiration of conservatives within the MP.

During the MP governments the Hearth's influence within state institutions continued. Important ministers—such as Hasan Celal Güzel and Kazım Oksay—were members of the Hearth. In the Fourth Nationalists' Congress prepared by the Hearth in January 1987, two ministers (Dinçerler and Güzel) and the vice head of the Grand National Assembly from the MP delivered speeches. Turgut Özal, as the prime minister, sent a congratulatory message to the congress.[80] The permanent staff of public universities, the Higher Education Council, and the Turkish Radio and Television Corporation (TRT) were filled with members of Hearth.[81] The Education Ministry had all textbooks completely revised to conform to the tenets of the Turkish-Islamic Synthesis, and the new textbooks emphasized "the alliance between the military and religion as native to the Turks' cultural essence."[82] While the MP has constructed a religious conservatism through these bureaucratic appointments, passage of conservative legislation, and the statements of the conservative members, the power balance in the MP started to shift with Özal's ascendance to the presidency.

Özal's Presidency and the Struggle for Hegemony within the MP

Competition between different factions intensified in the MP in the late 1980s. For instance, during the second party congress in 1988, the conservative and nationalist factions made what was dubbed as a "holy alliance" against the liberals in the election for the Central Decision Making and Executive Board. Turgut Özal reacted pragmatically to intraparty competition and tried to craft a balance between different factions during his tenure as prime minister. However, this balance started to crumble as soon as he declared his decision to become a candidate for president in 1989.

Yıldırım Akbulut, a low-profile, non-ideological MP, and the former speaker of the GNA, replaced Özal as prime minister in November 1989. Akbulut was a mere puppet and Özal effectively controlled his decisions during the former's premiership. However, since Akbulut was not a competent leader and Özal lost his official ties to the MP, the liberals and the conservatives soon started to compete for control of the party. The leadership race in the Istanbul party congress in February 1991 was a vivid example of this competition. The liberals nominated Semra Özal, Turgut Özal's wife known as the secular aunt (*laik yenge*) who has never hidden her antipathy toward the conservatives within the MP. Turgut Özal saw his wife's nomination as an opportunity for regaining his waning control over the party organization and harshly criticized the conservatives with these words:

> I prefer that the MP should stay as a modern, secular, reconciliatory party. The indispensable elements of a constitutional democracy are political parties. If one of them, particularly the one with a majority, is in danger of conquest by obsessed people, who desire to go back to the pre-Islamic *jahiliyyah*[83] times, I would definitely support anyone, who is standing by modernism, women's rights, and secularism.[84]

In addition to Özal's harsh criticism, Akbulut removed Hüsnü Doğan, a prominent conservative, from his post as Minister of Defense because Doğan took an openly critical stance against Semra Özal's nomination.[85] Akbulut also reduced the powers of other conservative ministries. Conservative members within the MP reacted to the words of Özal and to other attempts to weaken the powers of conservative ministers within the government. For instance, one conservative member within the party stated:

> Under normal circumstances Özal would not exclude the conservatives. Thanks to them, [the MP] got all the votes and formed the government.

> Until today they have fought together. A person does not throw away the foundation of the building … The one who denounces his origin engages in wrongful behavior … It is wrong that [Özal] changes sides.[86]

On 28 February 1991, at the Istanbul party congress, which was full of tension, arm-twisting and irregularities, Semra Özal was elected chair of the Istanbul organization. At the national congress which convened the following month, the former foreign minister Mesut Yılmaz, the liberal candidate, became chairman of the party. Yılmaz was not willing to share his power with anyone and effectively pulled the MP out of the orbit of Özal. More importantly, Yılmaz's election signaled that the MP was losing its conservative character. Immediately after his election, Yılmaz emphasized the waning power of the conservatives: "It is a happy development for Turkey that the use of religion, which is very important for our people, for political purposes is not credited even in a rightist party."[87]

In the upcoming national elections in October 1991, when the conservatives were nominated from weak places in the party lists, some openly criticized the developments within the party. Cemil Çiçek, who served as the minister of state in 1987–91, openly criticized the purge of the conservatives from the party, and declared publicly that he would vote for the WP in the next national elections.[88] Erbakan accused the MP of becoming a "masonic party" due to the ridding of all of religious members from the party organization.[89] Similarly, columnists in religious newspapers were furious, and many held Özal responsible from intentionally undermining the conservative identity of the MP during the Istanbul party congress.[90] Ahmet Taşgetiren wrote a long diatribe against Özal in the daily *Zaman*, where he argued that the primary reason for Özal's ascendancy to the prime ministership and afterwards to the presidency was his piety. According to Taşgetiren, many conservative MP activists convinced people to vote for the MP by depicting a prime minister who was doing his daily prayers, so that ordinary people would identify with him. People also approved his presidency, since—contrary to prior presidents, who were all ex-military men—a pious president was appealing to the man on the street. Yet Taşgetiren claimed that Özal's direct attack against his conservative colleagues was simply inexcusable and constituted an example of backstabbing.[91]

Even the Hearth of Intellectuals withdrew its political support from the MP. Its president, Nevzat Yalçıntaş, worked hard for an electoral alliance between the Islamist WP, the ultra-nationalist NAP, and the small Reformist Democracy Party (RDP) for the 1991 national elections. Once the three parties agreed to form an alliance under the roof of the WP for the national election, the Hearth declared its full support for the WP thinking that only this "holy alliance"[92] could secure the representation of their ideals.

In the 1991 national elections, MP's vote share shrank to 24.1 percent, while the WP doubled its national vote share from previous elections receiving 16.2 percent of the vote. After a failed attempt by Keçeciler to run for the chairmanship of the MP in 1992, many conservatives as well as party organizations resigned from the MP en masse.[93] Following these resignations, an open letter on the first page of *Milli Gazete* invited these conservatives "to their real home, next to their brothers."[94] Many joined the WP in the following years, which strengthened the WP organizationally as well as electorally.[95] Thereafter, the Islamist WP became the new center of attention for conservative constituencies and constantly increased its vote share until its remarkable successes in the 1994 municipal election and 1995 national elections.

Religious Intellectuals and a Critique of the State Co-optation of Islam

After firmly establishing his authority in the MP, Mesut Yılmaz enlisted Ali Coşkun and Korkut Özal, both heavy-weight conservatives, to boost his party's conservative outlook prior to the 1995 elections. Yet, these were futile moves because the MP's conservatism had been long discredited in the eyes of the electorate. One of the main reasons for this was the principled criticism posed toward co-optation of religion by Islamist intellectuals.

These intellectuals helped to construct a narrative that projected the instrumental incorporation of selective elements from Islam into the official state ideology and inclusion of token religious figures as measures aiming to tame the rising authentic Islamist tide. According to this line of criticism, state co-optation of religion was harmful to religion as it corrupted people's understanding of the authentic Islam. When asked how the WP differed from the conservative MP, Bahri Zengin, the most influential ideologue within the NOM and the author of numerous books, responded:

> Throughout history, particularly during the time of the prophet, it is clearly observed [that] the movements that are first weak, but have very strong ideas, are countered by their opposites. However later, when these opposites appear to be insufficient, and these movements get stronger, they are countered by their likes. And to differentiate these similar movements is a more difficult job; it is the job of professionals.[96]

Zengin, who served as the head of the publicity campaign of the WP in 1985–7 and 1990–3, argued that the aim of the MP was just to appear religious and to hinder the increasing Islamic awareness that the NOM represented in Turkish society. Zengin also mentioned that the WP activists had very clearly communicated to the voters that the MP was just a bad imitation of the NOM.

There were also independent Islamist intellectuals, who criticized the practices of co-optation. Ali Bulaç, arguably the most influential Islamist intellectual in Turkey, implicitly objects to the idea of a Turkish-Islamic Synthesis adopted as the official ideological narrative in the aftermath of the 1980 coup d'état.

In his book *Religion and Modernism*, he categorically denounces nationalization of religion in any context:

> Those who want to see and present Islam as the religion of the Middle Eastern nations are making the mistake of blocking this universal salvation message by restricting it to limits of a geographical and historical region. Hence the most vivid evidence of this is the idea of spiritual community in Islam that transcends the concept of nation and accepts the *umma* as the correct and ultimate aim.[97]

Bulaç also takes issue with the instrumental use of religion by the military and MP governments: "[The great powers of the world system] are trying to neutralize religion in the Islamic world by 'Islamization' … Here the aim is to promote the functional role of an 'anti-Islamic Islam'."[98] According to Bulaç, the incorporation of religion into state institutions by secular elites was an attempt to tame the Islamic tide that was on the rise in the Muslim world. At the time, such political efforts were clearly visible in other Muslim-majority countries as well. Anwar Sadat's co-optation of Islamist student associations in university campuses in Egypt and his self-designation as the "believer president," Zia-ul Haq's Islamization of Pakistan's legal and political system under his military rule, and Suharto's alliance with the Association of Indonesian Muslim Intellectuals in the last decade of his military dictatorship are some examples. While the left argued that the United States and other world powers encouraged the co-optation of Islam in order to contain Soviet Union and the ideological threat of communism, many Islamists, including Bulaç, read it as an attempt by the United States to diffuse the challenge posed by the ascendance of political Islam to American global hegemony.

Abdurrahman Dilipak, another Islamist intellectual, directly targets the compulsory religion classes initiated by the military government:

> The aim [of the military government] is to raise a type of Muslim who would be in harmony with the state. [The aim is] to determine the standards of the new Turkish Muslim, to prohibit the religion outside of this standard … The rightists do not want to propagate and strengthen religion. … [their aim is] to interpret the religion anew and to standardize it.[99]

In his book Dilipak deciphers the intentions of the military government in installing compulsory religion classes in the curriculum. According to Dilipak's interpretations, the aim of these classes was to use religion instrumentally to create a complacent citizenry. Dilipak is also critical of Hearth's Turkish-Islamic Synthesis that justified Turkish nationalism by using Islam:

> Our religion is not Atatürk's religion, but Allah's religion. There cannot be an Atatürk-Islam synthesis, as there cannot be a Turkish-Islamic

> synthesis. We don't have the will to dilute our religion, with others' beliefs and thoughts. They should not try to Kemalize our religion.[100]

Dilipak sees any attempt to incorporate selective elements of Islam into secular ideologies as the contamination of religious practices. In this vein, he differentiates between what he sees as "authentic" and "fake" interpretations of Islam in the political arena and argues that the military regime's policies as well as the MP's conservatism were not authentic. This type of criticism also shows that state co-optation of religion might create a sense of grievance among religious segments if it is perceived as "perverting the real meaning of religion." The critique of the religious intellectuals played an important role in framing the policies of the military period and the MP as contamination of the true meaning of Islam.

However, Dilipak also recognizes the unintended consequences of these compulsory classes instituted by the Turkish state:

> Despite everything, people's attempts to alter religion is in vain ... Sometimes Allah makes the infidels [to] serve Islam. They [the generals who attempted to use Islam] were hoping for something else ... Sometimes we might not exactly know what is beneficial and what is harmful for us ... We know what they have desired, but what they have hoped for did not materialize ... They have presented such a shallow religion, so that people started to search for the real religion ... Teachers did not limit themselves to the information within these books, and in many schools these classes led to the correct manifestation of Islam.[101]

Dilipak's argument is a vivid example of the dynamic interaction that occurs between state and social actors. According to the author, the generals' attempt to create an Atatürkist youth by using Islam engendered students' interest in what he sees as the "correct" manifestation of religion. Whatever the military regime aimed to achieve by instituting the compulsory religious classes seems to have backfired, as it opened a space for the articulation of a critique of secularism. Dilipak's critique reveals that ideas that are embedded into state institutions to create hegemony do not always produce intended political outcomes, because opposition groups outside the state rearticulate and reappropriate these ideas in order to challenge the state's official ideology.

Conclusion

In Turkey, incorporation of religious actors into the government and high-level bureaucratic institutions started in 1974 and continued throughout the 1980s. During its coalition membership in the Ecevit government and in the two Nationalist Front governments in the 1970s, the NSP was recognized as a legitimate political actor in Turkish politics, and Erbakan's party used its ministries and governmental agencies to create patronage networks, which survived into the post-1980 period. The military government (1980–3), which ended the tumultuous era of the coalitions and street violence, incorporated selective elements from Islam in its nationalism in order to forge an organically unified society. It was during this time that the Hearth of Intellectuals' ideology of Turkish-Islamic Synthesis started to shape the cultural and educational policies of the regime.

The MP governments (1983–91) also included a conservative faction—part of which was Korkut Özal's team from the NSP—within the government and continued the close relationship between the Hearth and the state. Although the MP was composed of different factions, the party succeeded in presenting itself as a conservative party to religious constituents in various spaces. Like Shas in Israel, during this period, the conservative faction within the MP used the cultural resources of the state. State institutions such as the education ministry, national television, family consultation centers, or Ataturk Culture, Language and History Higher Institution emerged as institutional sites where a conservative ideology was constructed and communicated to the larger public. This created a ripe political opportunity for the religious social and political actors outside of the state to increase their public appeal.

On the other hand, the instrumental use of religion by the state triggered a totally different dynamic. Autonomous religious actors, such as religious newspapers, the WP and Islamist intellectuals criticized MP policies and the military's instrumental use of Islam. While some protested the weakening of conservative influence within the MP, Islamist intellectuals claimed that both the military government's use of Islam and MP's lip service to conservative constituents contaminated the authenticity of Islamic expression. These criticisms depressed MP's support among religious actors, and the WP gradually emerged as the new center of attention for the strengthened religious actors. At the same time, the gradual resignation of conservatives from the MP and their movement to the WP added to the latter's organizational and political strength.

Notes

1 Saadettin Bilgiç assumed the post of acting party chairman briefly in 1964 after the party's first leader Ragıp Gümüşpala died. Yet Süleyman Demirel won the elections for the chairmanship in the first party congress held in the same year.

2 M. E. Yaşar, 'Dergah'tan Parti'ye, Vakıf'tan Şirkete Bir Kimliğin Oluşumu ve Dönüşumü: İskenderpaşa Cemaati', in Yasin Aktay (ed.), *İslamcılık*, Istanbul: İletişim, 2004, p. 331.

3 Ibid., p. 338.

4 The speech of Esad Coşan delivered on 26 May 1990. Quoted in R. Çakır, *Ayet ve Slogan Türkiye'de İslami Oluşumlar*, Istanbul: Metis Yayınları, 1990, pp. 48–54.

5 The decision of the Constitutional Court is available at www.belgenet.com/dava/mnp_dava.html.

6 'I. Ecevit Hükümeti Koalisyon Protokolü (CHP-MSP)'. Online. Available at www.tbmm.gov.tr/hukumetler/KP37.htm.

7 'I. Ecevit Hükümeti Koalisyon Protokolü (CHP-MSP)'. Online. Available at www.tbmm.gov.tr/hukumetler/KP37.htm. For the entire list of the ministries and government agencies see the 7th and 10th articles of the coalition agreement.
8 'Erbakan: 10 Yılda Harp Silahlarımızı Kendimiz Yapacağız', *Milliyet*, 11 May 1977.
9 'Erbakan, 'Manevi kalkınma için adımlar atılacaktır' dedi', *Milliyet*, 14 March 1974.
10 A. Y. Sarıbay, *Türkiye'de Modernleşme Din ve Parti Politikasi: Millî Selâmet Partisi Örnek Olayı*, Istanbul: Alan Yayınları, 1985, p. 190.
11 Ibid., p. 190; S. Yalçın, *Hangi Erbakan?* Istanbul: Başak Yayınları, 1994, p. 97.
12 E. Alper and O. S. Göral, 'Aydınlar Ocağı', in A. Çiğdem (ed.), *Muhafazakârlık*, Istanbul: İletişim Yayınları, 2003, pp. 583–9.
13 The NSP's party emblem was a key. Many political observers made the analogy between the NSP's critical role in the coalitions and the symbol of the party.
14 The Turkish word "*milli*" is translated as national in English. It stems from the root nation (*millet*). However, in Ottoman Turkish, the word was used to describe different religious communities in the Ottoman Empire. Accordingly, the NSP also uses the word "*millet*" for describing a religious community rather than an ethnic or civic nation. Hence the word "*milli*" in the "*milli kültür*" (national culture) has religious connotations for NSP activists and their constituency.
15 'IV. Demirel Hükümeti Koalisyon Protokolü (AP-MSP-MHP – CGP)'. Online. Available at www.tbmm.gov.tr/hukumetler/KP39.htm.
16 F. Ahmad, *Demokrasi Sürecinde Türkiye (1945–1980)*, Istanbul: Hil Yayın, 1992, pp. 383–4.
17 Interview with Şevket Kazan, 2 March 2007.
18 'Bütçe için AP ile', *Milliyet*, 27 November 1976.
19 'Sanayi ödemeleri konmazsa MSP bütçeyi imzalamayacak', *Milliyet*, 25 November 1976.
20 B. Toprak and F. Birtek, 'The Conflictual Agendas of Neo-Liberal Reconstruction and the Rise of Islamic Politics in Turkey: The Hazards of Rewriting Modernity', *Praxis International*, vol.13, 1993, 192–212.
21 Y. Taşkın, 'Muhafazakâr Bir Proje Olarak Türk-İslam Sentezi', in A. Çiğdem (ed.), *Muhafazakârlık*, Istanbul: İletişim Yayınları, 2003, p. 389.
22 'Danışma Meclisi Açıldı', *Milliyet*, 24 October 1981.
23 'Danışma Meclisinin İlk Hedefi: Anayasa', *Milliyet*, 17 October 1981.
24 B. Tanör, *Siyasal Tarih (1980–1995)*, in S. Akşin (ed.), *Türkiye Tarihi 5: Bugünkü Türkiye 1980–2003*, Istanbul: Cem Yayınevi, 2005, p. 42.
25 T. Bora and K. Can, '12 Eylül'ün resmi ideolojisi, faşist entelejensiya ve "Türk-İslam Sentezi', *Birikim*, vol.18, 1990, 27.
26 M. Umur and T. Bora, 'Türk-İslam Masonları', *Yeni Gündem*, 22 February 1987. Cited in E. Alper and O. S. Göral, 'Aydınlar Ocağı', p. 587.
27 Interview with Süleyman Yalçın, *Nokta*, 12 October 1987, p. 21.
28 S. Kaplan, '"Religious Nationalism": A Textbook Case from Turkey', *Comparative Studies of South Asia, Africa and the Middle East*, vol.25, no.3, 2005, 666.
29 V. Timuroğlu, *12 Eylül'ün Eğitim ve Kültür Politikasi Türk-İslam Sentezi*, Istanbul: Başak Yayınları, 1991, p. 91.
30 *Milli Kültür Raporu*, in ibid., pp. 88–9. Translation is mine.
31 T. Bora and K. Can, '12 Eylül'ün resmi ideolojisi', p. 33.
32 For a systematic analysis of how the historical narrative of Turkish nationalism was transformed and incorporated Islamic idioms in the aftermath of the 1980 coup, see E. Copeaux, *Tarih Ders Kitaplarında (1931–1993) Türk Tarih Tezinden Türk-İslam Sentezine*, A. Berktay (trans.), Istanbul: Tarih Vakfı Yurt Yayınları, 2000.
33 Ibid., p. 310; S. Kaplan, 'Religious Nationalism', pp. 672–3.

34 K. Evren, 'Preface', in Genelkurmay Başkanlığı (General Staff), *Atatürkçülük*, vol.1, Istanbul: Milli Eğitim Basımevi, 1988, p. I.
35 Ibid., p. I.
36 Genelkurmay Başkanlığı (General Staff), *Atatürkçülük*, vol.3, Istanbul, Milli Eğitim Basımevi, 1988, p. 234.
37 Ibid., p. 230.
38 H. Yavuz, *Islamic Political Identity in Turkey*, New York: Oxford University Press, 2003, pp. 69–70.
39 '12 Eylül'ün Din Raporu', *Milliyet*, 19 March 1989. The signatories of the report included, the Minister of State Mehmet Özgüneş, the Minister of Justice Cevdet Menteş, the Minister of the Interior Selahaddin Çetiner, the Minister of Education Hasan Sağlam, the Minister of Rural Administration and Cooperatives Münir Güney, the Minister of Sport and Youth Vecdi Özgül, and the Director of Religious Affairs Tayyar Altıkulaç.
40 'Din Eğitimi, Laiklik ve Ötesi', *Nokta*, 26 March 1989, p. 19.
41 A. Dilipak, *Bu Din Benim Dinim Değil*, Istanbul: İşaret Yayınları, 1991, p. 132.
42 Article 24 of the 1982 constitution stated that "education and instruction in religion and ethics shall be conducted under state supervision and control. Instruction in religious culture and moral education shall be compulsory in the curricula of primary and secondary schools."
43 *Milliyet*, 30 August 1981. Quoted in P. J. Magnarella, *Human Materialism: A Model of Sociocultural Systems and a Strategy for Analysis*, Gainesville: University Press of Florida, 1993, pp. 106–7.
44 B. Oran, *Kenan Evren'in Yazılmamış Anıları*, Ankara: Bilgi Yayınevi, 1989, p. 87. Translation is mine.
45 From Evren's speech in Antakya on 13 March 1983. In K. Evren, *Türkiye Cumhuriyeti Cumhurbaşkanı Kenan Evren'in Söylev ve Demeçleri/12 Eylül 1982–9 Kasım 1983*, Ankara: TBMM Basımevi, 1985, pp. 197–8. Translation is mine.
46 Z. Öniş, 'The Political Economy of Export-Oriented Industrialization in Turkey', in Ç. Balım (ed.), *Turkey: Political, Economic, and Social Challenges in the 1990s*, Leiden: Brill, 1995, p. 115.
47 A. Buğra, 'Political Sources of Uncertainty in Business Life', in M. Heper (ed.), *Strong State and Economic Interest Groups: The Post-1980 Turkish Experience*, New York: Walter de Gruyter, 1991, pp. 156–9.
48 Z. Öniş, 'The Political Economy of Export-Oriented Industrialization', p. 114.
49 Ö. Demir, M. Acar and M. Toprak, 'Anatolian Tigers or Islamic Capital: Prospects and Challenges', *Middle Eastern Studies*, vol.40, no.6, 2004, 168.
50 'Musiad Kimdir?'. Online. Available at www.musiadfair.com/tr/musiadnedir.php.
51 E. Özbudun and F. Keyman, 'Cultural Globalization in Turkey: Actors, Discourses, Strategies', in P. Berger and S. Huntington (eds.), *Cultural Globalization in the Contemporary World*, New York: Oxford University Press, 2002, pp. 307–8.
52 Ibid., p. 308.
53 Y. Arat, 'Social Change and the 1983 Governing Elite in Turkey', in M. Kıray (ed.), *Structural Change in Turkish Society*, Bloomington: Indiana University Press, 1991, p. 172.
54 Ö. Demir, M. Acar and M. Toprak, 'Anatolian Tigers', p. 171.
55 Y. Arat, 'Social Change and the 1983 Governing Elite', p. 172.
56 *Yeni Gündem*, 1 April 1985, in T. Parla, *Türkiye'nin Siyasal Rejimi 1980–1989*, Istanbul: İletişim Yayınları, 1995.
57 From Özal's speech delivered in Paris in the *Islam and West* conference, Paris, 14 November 1985. Quoted in H. Cemal, *Özal Hikayesi*, Ankara: Bilgi Yayınevi, 1989, p. 153. Translation is mine.
58 During my interviews, one MP member stated that Özal preferred the concept "committed to free market enterprise" rather than liberal, because liberal was a

foreign term for most Turkish citizens. He also added that Özal was afraid that using the concept "liberal" would give an impression to the citizenry as if the party was contradicting its other tenet, "conservatism."

59 Interview with Mehmet Keçeciler, 21 February 2007.

60 Interview with Hasan Celal Güzel, 13 February 2007.

61 The MP passed a bill that established liberty of dress in higher education in 1990. The intent of the bill was to enable girls with headscarves to enter universities. After its passage, the bill was sent to the Constitutional Court by president Kenan Evren. Although the bill was not found unconstitutional by the court, the judges added a footnote claiming that this bill cannot be interpreted against the dress code of the Turkish revolution. In the aftermath of this Constitutional Court decision, this footnote is interpreted as a ban on headscarves in higher education. As will be discussed further in Chapter 7, the issue of wearing headscarves in universities and public institutions is still a contested political and legal issue in Turkey.

62 Interview with Korkut Özal. In M. A. Birand and S. Yalçın, *The Özal: Bir Davanın Öyküsü*, Istanbul: Doğan Kitapçılık, 2001, pp. 173–4.

63 M. Seçkin, 'Taşar Raporu: 'Çağdaş beklentiler partimizi aşıyor', *Nokta*, 18 November 1990, pp. 20–1.

64 The first Minister of Education, Youth and Sport was Vehbi Dinçerler, who served in 1983–5. In 1985 Özal replaced him with Metin Emiroğlu, who served in 1985–7. Hasan Celal Güzel succeeded Metin Emiroğlu in 1987 and served until 1989 in this post. Avni Akyol was the Minister of Education in the last two years of the MP government. Only Akyol did not belong to the conservative faction within the MP. In the following sections more will be said as to how the conservatives in MP started to lose their influence and were eventually purged from the party, especially after Özal left the MP in November 1989.

65 Interview with Hasan Celal Güzel on 13 February 2007.

66 Ibid.

67 Interview with Vehbi Dinçerler on 7 February 2007.

68 B. Toprak, 'The State, Politics and Religion in Turkey', in M. Heper and A. Evin (eds.), *State, Democracy and Military: Turkey in the 1980s*, New York: W. de Gruyter, 1988, p. 132.

69 'Darwin Tartışması: Aslını inkâr eden … ', *Nokta*, 14 April 1985.

70 Quoted from the Education Ministry's website: www.byegm.gov.tr/YAYINLARIMIZ/AyinTarihi/1985/mart1985.htm. In his later interviews Dinçerler claimed that his aim was to include both evolutionist and creationist theories in the curriculum so that the students would learn different theories about the origin of humans.

71 'Historic Creation Conference in Turkey', *Acts and Facts*, vol.21, no.12, 1992.

72 Ibid.; T. Ediş, 'Islamic Creationism in Turkey', *Creation/Evolution*, vol.34, no.1, 1994, 1–12. Two of these books translated by Turkish academics were: D. T. Gish, *Yaratılış Evrim ve Halk Eğitimi*, Ankara: Milli Eğitim Basımevi, 1985; Henry M. Morris, *Yaratılış Modeli*, Ankara: Milli Eğitim Basımevi, 1985.

73 I. Yılmaz and S. Uzunoğlu, *Alternatif Biyolojiye Doğru*, Ankara: Milli Eğitim Basımevi, 1985; A. Tatlı, *Evrim ve Yaratılış*, Ankara: Milli Eğitim Basımevi, 1985.

74 'ANAP'ın Tasarısı: Basın Tehdit Altında', *Nokta*, 23 February 1986.

75 A. Kapan, 'Cemil Çiçek'in Aileyi Kurtarma Harekatı', *Birikim*, vol.20, 1990, 74.

76 Melih Gökçek was a government bureaucrat in 1989–91 from the MP. He was transferred to the WP before the 1991 elections. He was elected to parliament in 1991 from the WP, and became the mayor of Ankara in 1994. Today he is a JDP member and serving his fourth term as the mayor of Turkey's capital.

77 *Nokta*, November 11 1990.

78 A. Kapan, 'Cemil Çiçek'in', p. 74.
79 Interview with Mehmet Keçeciler, 21 February 2007.
80 E. Copeaux, *Tarih Ders Kitaplarında*, p. 63. Although Özal never became an official member of the Hearth, he was very close to the social circles around this group. For instance he outlined his famous January 24 economic program at one of Hearth's meetings in April 1979.
81 E. Alper and O. S. Göral, 'Aydınlar Ocağı', p. 587.
82 S. Kaplan, 'Din-u Devlet All Over Again? The Politics of Military Secularism and Religious Militarism in Turkey', *International Journal of Middle East Studies*, vol.34, 2002, 121.
83 *Jahiliyyah* refers to the condition of the Arabs in pre-Islamic Arabia. The word literally means the state of ignorance.
84 Sabah, 2 March 1991 quoted in A. Taşgetiren, 'Yeni Özal karşınızda … ', *Zaman*, 6 March 1991.
85 Hüsnü Doğan was Turgut Özal's cousin and one of the prominent founders of the MP. Since the formation of the party, he has been very close to Özal. Despite this background, the relationship between the two soured over Semra Özal's candidacy and Özal's adversarial behavior toward the conservatives during the MP's Istanbul congress.
86 M. Ünal, 'Böyle vefa olur mu?', *Zaman*, 8 March 1991.
87 'Mesut Yılmaz ile Söyleşi: Genç bir politikacının başbakan olarak portresi', *Nokta*, 30 June 1991.
88 'ANAP kurucusu Cemil Çiçek: Özal dostlarıyla düşmanlarını karıştırdı', *Tercüman*, 11 October 1991.
89 'Erbakan: Diğer Partiler Diskotek Zihniyetli', *Tercüman*, 3 October 1991.
90 F. Koru, 'Ne oluyoruz, nereye götürülüyoruz?', *Zaman*, 3 March 1991.
91 A. Taşgetiren, 'Yeni Özal karşınızda … ', *Zaman*, 6 March 1991.
92 The electoral alliance between these parties was named the holy alliance by the three parties and by the media throughout the campaign.
93 In these elections, Turgut Özal, who realized that he had lost his control over the MP to Mesut Yılmaz, supported Mehmet Keçeciler's candidacy. This move by Özal was interpreted by the religious sector as a last gasp attempt to use the conservatives to control the MP. For criticisms see Z. Ceyhan, 'Daha önceleri nerelerdeydiniz?', *Milli Gazete*, 19 November 1992 and 'Özal takunyalarını mı arıyor', *Milli Gazete*, 21 November 1992.
94 İ. İspirli, 'ANAP'lı Muhafazakârlara Açık Mektup', *Milli Gazete*, 2 December 1992.
95 Mehmet Altınsoy, one of MP's founders and the former mayor of Ankara, Abdülkadir Aksu, the former Minister of Interior, Vehbi Gül, the mayor of Samsun and Melih Gökçek were the most well-known political figures who joined WP after resigning from the MP. In addition to these figures, entire party organizations left MP and joined WP in 1991–95. Mehmet Keçeciler never joined the WP and returned to MP.
96 Interview with Bahri Zengin, 7 March 2007.
97 A. Bulaç, *Din ve Modernizm: Tarihin Kırılma Anında Tufan*, Istanbul: Endülüs Yayınları, 1990, p. 243.
98 Ibid., p. 236.
99 A. Dilipak, *Bu Din Benim Dinim Değil: 'Resmi Din' Öğretisine Eleştirel Bir Yaklaşım*, Istanbul: İşaret Yayınları, 1991, pp. 52–3.
100 Ibid., p. 82.
101 Ibid., p. 67.

6 The Politics of Shas

What makes Shas a social movement, and more than just a political party, is its message that creates a sense of belonging and empowerment among its supporters, its elaborate grassroots network all around the country, and its dedicated grassroots activists. Today, Shas operates party branches in 106 cities in Israel and runs an elaborate network that consists of its numerous civil society arms, including *Ma'ayan Hahinuch Hatorani*, *Meonot Margalit*, *Bnei Hayyil*, *Margalit Em B'Yisrael* and *El Hama'ayan*.[1] These organizations play a critical role in linking Shas to the populace by providing various social services. *Ma'ayan Hahinuch Hatorani* and *Meonot Margalit* provide formal education to school age children and preschoolers respectively. *Bnei Hayyil* is the youth arm of Shas, while *Margalit Em B'Yisrael* constitutes the women's branch within the movement. *El Hama'ayan* operates clubs in 2000 locations in Israel, where it provides informal education during after-school hours to children aged between seven and seventeen. In these clubs, children from poor socioeconomic backgrounds find shelter, play simple games, get help with their homework, and learn about Jewish values.[2] In addition to these civil society organizations, the movement has a weekly newspaper, *Yom LeYom*, which covers current Israeli politics, movement news, speeches of Rabbi Ovadia Yosef, and the weekly Torah portion.[3] Shas-affiliated individuals also sponsor a number of pirate radio stations, such as *Kol HaEmet* and *Arutz 2000*, which broadcast religious programs and party propaganda.

Although Shas is popularly known as an ultra-Orthodox political entity, it draws support from various segments of the Sephardi population. According to estimations, 25 percent[4] to 30 percent[5] of Shas's voter base consists of ultra-Orthodox Sephardim. The core activists of the party also come from this group—mainly rabbis and yeshiva students—as well as the new religious returnees. The students studying in the Sephardi yeshivas work very dedicatedly for the electoral campaign of Shas with the encouragement of their rabbis, and most of the religious returnees follow Yosef's advice in political activism during election times. A second group that plays a significant role in the movement's popular and electoral success is traditional Sephardim, who are not strictly observant and deemed to have "soft" religiosity, but nevertheless feel great reverence toward Sephardi rabbis.[6] A survey conducted in

Table 6.1 Vote share of Shas in selected development towns in the last five national elections

	1992	*1996*	*1999*	*2003*	*2006*	*2009*
National	4.9	8.7	13	8.2	9.5	8.5
Ashdod	10.4	17	24.1	14	17.1	14.8
Ofakim	19.3	24.3	31.3	21.8	22.2	20.9
Kiryat Shmona	6.3	14.8	22.2	12	14.3	11
Dimona	11.3	27.9	33.7	17	17	16.7
Or Yehuda	16.7	29.3	31.9	20	25	19.3
Sderot	12.9	19.5	22.6	14	15	13.2
Ramle	10	19.8	28.4	16.1	20.4	15.8
BeitShean	9.6	21.1	40.6	25.4	30	22.9

2000 finds that 57 percent of Shas supporters define themselves as religious and traditional.[7] Lastly, 13 percent of Shas voters define themselves as secular.[8] These non-religious supporters mainly come from low-income Sephardim. While some are drawn to Shas because of the pride they feel from being part of a movement associated with an ethnic identity, others support Shas because of the social provisions they receive through Shas's civil society organizations. A closer look at the vote share of the party across several elections shows that Shas has a much stronger electoral showing in development towns, where the low-income Sephardim constitute an important section of the residents (see Table 6.1).

In order to mobilize Sephardim from different walks of life, Shas formulates an eclectic ideology which addresses its constituencies' ethnic and religious sensitivities as well as social and economic concerns. Below, I explore different frames Shas activists construct in order to tap into the grievances of Sephardim as well as the grassroots networks through which Shas accesses actual and potential supporters.

Shas as a Religious Movement

In addition to its political significance, Shas represents a movement of "religious revival." At the center of Shas's religious identity lies the spiritual and *halachic* authority of Rabbi Ovadia Yosef and his religious activism. Departing from the ultra-Orthodox Lithuanian Ashkenazim emphasis on theoretical textual analysis known as *pilpul*, Yosef focuses on *halacha* (the Jewish legal code) that is geared toward practice. One of Yosef's main aims is to create a Sephardi elite that would succeed him in rabbinical authority. In order to convert this aim to reality, Yosef trains a cadre of ultra-Orthodox rabbis and specifically rabbinic judges (*dayanim*), who can take over his role as a rabbi, judge and arbiter.[9] As one scholar notes, Shas movement's popular success went hand in hand with Ovadia Yosef's efforts in the religio-legal field:

> It remains difficult to evaluate the whole of Rav Ovadia Yosef's halakhic work or its success, although in certain instances the matter has undoubtedly been resolved. For example, with respect to the [ethnic] origin of rabbinical judges (*dayanim*) in the state of Israel: if, in the past, Rav Ovadia Yosef had to demand that in each court (*beit din*) there be at least one Sephardic judge, today the situation is entirely reversed … Clearly, this revolution in the rabbinical courts is connected to the dramatic rise of the Shas movement.[10]

According to Yosef, the formation of this Sephardic religious elite is a step toward the creation of a society in which the Sephardi authorities become prominent within the *halachic* world. In this ideal society, religious authority should be based on Rabbi Yosef Karo's famous work *Shulhan Aruch*.[11] As Yosef stipulates, Karo's book became the most authoritative codification of Jewish law in the world when it was written in the sixteenth century. However, again according to Yosef, the Sephardi rabbis gradually lost ground in the world of *halacha* to Ashkenazi rabbinic authorities:

> It is known that the Sephardi chief rabbis before me were subordinated to their colleagues, the Ashkenazic rabbis. And for the sake of peace, they said nothing, but I, who am not subordinate, praise God, will uphold my mission to restore the crown to its former glory and ordered that the ruling of *Maran* [Rabbi Yosef Karo] be adopted.[12]

Restoring the crown to its past glory (*Lehahzir atara leyoshna*) has been the main motto of Shas since the movement's inception. The motto appears in various spaces, including on posters hanging in Sephardi homes, weekly Torah pamphlets, bumper stickers and electoral posters, and became a catch-all phrase indicating the movement's identity. For Shas activists and supporters this sentence has multiple meanings and its interpretation differs from one to another. Some see in this sentence a religious revival and the recreation of a glorious religious past that the Sephardic Jews possessed in the Iberian Peninsula before their expulsion. As an ultra-Orthodox Shas activist from Elad explains:

> [M]any years ago, the world of Sephardi Torah was the source, but because of the inquisition and because of the expulsion from Spain, the world of Sephardi Torah got contaminated, it split up, and it was forgotten … 800 years ago, there was Rambam … he lived in Morocco, he lived in Spain. He was one of the biggest rabbinic authorities for the World of Sephardi Torah. Rabbi Yisthak Alfasi, he was the rabbinic authority in Morocco. We acted according to his *psakim*[13] (religious legal rulings). Even today we act according to his religious edicts. From that time on because of the Inquisition and because of the expulsion from Spain, the Sephardi World of Torah got divided. Some went to Iraq,

> some went to Morocco, some went here and there. And there remained no *Gdolei Torah* (Torah Sages) left. Now for the past thirty five years, Rabbi Ovadia Yosef is fighting to return the crown to its past glory. What was once, he is trying to make it anew. He is trying to renew this … And today, blessed by God, there are many Sephardi yeshivas, many Torah scholars, many Sephardi Torah Wise.[14]

According to scholars, the recreation of an imagined, idealized past is one of the distinguishing characteristics of new religiopolitical movements.[15] Religiopolitical movements—or as some scholars call it fundamentalism—inculcate among their followers the idea that a return to a past when the sources of religious authority reigned supreme—whether this past is in the seventh-century Arabian Peninsula, nineteenth-century America, or eleventh-century Spain—would be a panacea for the ills of their societies.[16] Ultimately, this is not a "return" to the past, but rather an attempt to reimagine the past by selectively appropriating certain concepts, traditions and practices associated with that historical period. Shas's success lies in the fact that this image of a glorious past in Andalucia being a cure all resonates with the life situation of many Sephardim in Israel. In the parlance of Social Movement Theory (SMT), this attempt to imagine an idealized past amounts to a prognostic frame which attempts to offer a solution to the Sephardim's discontent in regard to social injustice, economic inequality and cultural erasure.

Yet others equate Shas's aim of returning the crown to its past glory with a sense of dignity. As the local chairman of Shas in Bat Yam explains:

> [Once] … the Sephardi world was more powerful than the Ashkenazi world. Our great rabbis ruled here in Israel, the Sephardi rabbis. There was honor. The *hahambaşı*—they'd call the chief Sephardi rabbi the *hahambaşı*—was the leader in the land of Israel. We say we want to return the crown to its past glory, we want the honor of the Sephardim to be like it was once upon a time, when we had real honor. We have a large, broad tradition, which they didn't teach us, because we'd go to Ashkenazi institutions and they teach us about Ashkenazi rabbis: the Chofetz Haim, or Haim of Brisk, about all of the Ashkenazim. About Sephardim, Rabbi Yosef Karo, the Ben Ish Hai, they didn't teach us about all of those people because everyone in charge was Ashkenazi. In order for the Sephardim to wake up and realize that their rabbis were in fact great and serious, [we need] to return the crown to its past glory—returning the honor of the Sephardim.[17]

The above statements reveal how the Shas activist frames the movement's goal of bringing back the glorious days around a sense of ideational empowerment by associating it with the dignity of Sephardim. This type of empowerment frame provides the tools for many Sephardim to overcome their perceived victimhood at the hands of the Ashkenazim and create pride around a newly created positive collective identity. Still others give a more practical meaning to "*lehahzir atara leyoshna*" and see it simply as following the legal advice of Yosef in daily religious praxis. For them, the significance of Shas lies in the revival of the Sephardi tradition, whether it is on rules of animal slaughter, dress code, or how to behave toward family members. This sentiment is voiced by the deputy director of *El Hama'ayan*:

> This is the real thing: Introducing the right *psakim* (religious legal rulings) by the Sephardim and the right methods. According to me this is the meaning of *lehahzir atara leyoshna*. And we make those available through our brochures. This was part of the revolution. What is returning the crown to its past glory? It is to go according to what *Maran* Ovadia Yosef teaches.[18]

In line with the above quotation, Shas, Shas-affiliated yeshivas and kollels, and the movement's other civil society entities transmit many of the *halachic* rulings and Torah commentaries of Rabbi Ovadia Yosef to ordinary Sephardim. Shas publishes and subsidizes special prayer books or seasonal guides to the laws of holidays with Yosef's picture on the cover.[19] Many of Yosef's televised Torah lectures are broadcast on screens around the country.[20] Therefore, Ovadia Yosef's religio-legal goal goes beyond the education of a small rabbinical elite and becomes the education of the masses through neighborhood *halachic* class, wall posters in synagogues, or leaflets distributed to members of Sephardi congregations.[21] According to Nissim Leon, Ovadia Yosef grounds this "door-to-door approach" of *halacha* in the concept "*zikui harabim*," which asks yeshiva students and community rabbis not to act solely as experts, but to use their religious knowledge for public guidance and enabling the masses to attain religious merit.[22] One Shas activist expressed this sense of religious duty rather powerfully:

> I am of course the long arm of Rav Ovadia. He installed me here and everything I do is through him … Most of our activities are for the sake of God, they are Torah-based … We see it as a *mitzvah* (commandment). Beside it being a *mitzvah*, we see it as a mission.[23]

Framing their work for Shas as a *mitzvah* creates ideational incentives for the activists, because this installs in them a sense of religious duty in their political undertakings unseen in the secular parties. Shas also benefits from Yosef's charisma and religious authority among Sephardi voters. Rabbi Ovadia Yosef uses religious texts and symbolism from biblical history to frame Shas's political messages. For instance an election poster before the 2003 national elections displayed Rabbi Ovadia Yosef's picture with the sentence: "Those who are for God follow me," a use of the call of the Hasmonean leader Matityahu against the Greeks in the second century B.C.[24] Similarly, Yosef and Rabbis around his circle use Saturday evening sermons on the eve of elections to get their congregations out to vote:

> Many people have the common misconception that this commandment (*mitzvah*) can be fulfilled only by dying for G-d's sake. True, martyrdom carries with it untold reward: "No soul can stand in the same quarters as those killed by the government" (Pesahim 50a). But, in essence, anyone who increases the honor of G-d, whoever plays a role in strengthening the honor of G-d, has earned the merit of the greatest *mitzvah* in the Torah … In two weeks, every Israeli citizen is invited behind the curtain, to stand before a pile of ballots. Quite frankly, a single vote has a minuscule chance of swaying the election in any given direction. No government official has ever won by a single vote. However, in the Heavens everything is calculated differently. If there is a list of G-d fearing individuals, who observe the Torah, remain loyal to the faith and to the authority of Torah scholars, who are committed to maintaining the Jewish image of the State, to the proliferation of Torah institutions, the increase of Torah education, implanting Torah values, people who believe in the Creator and insist that the *yeshivot* receive money along with the universities, that public Torah classes be subsidized along with the sport functions, theaters and concerts – how sad it is that in a Jewish state such fights are necessary – then in the heavens it will be recorded that such-and-such person joined the ranks and took part in the sanctification of G-d's name. He merits the greatest *mitzvah* of all, in a single moment. If one does not take advantage of this simple *mitzvah*, how can he justify not having participated in this sanctification of (G-d's) name (*kiddush Hashem*).[25]

One of the peculiar strengths of Shas lies in the appeal of its religious message—fashioned by an ultra-Orthodox core—to traditional Sephardim who don't embrace an ultra-Orthodox way of life. Many traditional Sephardim support the party, since, irrespective of their level of religious practice, they show a great reverence toward their religious leaders.[26] A Shas activist explains the significance of the concept of *Emunat Hachamim* (Faith in the Sages) in the popularity of Shas among traditional Sephardim:

> How can traditional Sephardim vote for Rav Ovadia who is *Haredi* (ultra-orthodox)? The Sephardim have *Emunat Hachamim* (Faith in the Sages) … They see him as a spiritual exemplar. They love him and elect him. God Forbid, if Rav Ovadia Yosef would not be with Shas, it would have shrunk to 4 mandates.[27]

Faith in the Sages, which means following the advice of one's rabbi in social, political or personal spheres, has been around for millennia among the Sephardi Disapora communities. It is this reverence felt toward Rabbi Ovadia Yosef, as well as to other local Sephardi Rabbis loosely associated with the party, that draws many traditional Sephardim toward Shas. In this instance, Shas capitalizes on a Sephardic religious tradition in accessing a wider audience.

Another way in which Shas reaches out to the masses outside of its ultra-Orthodox core is by incorporating elements of folk religion in its mobilization efforts. For instance the movement distributes stickers with "blessing over the home" or "prayer for the road" before elections.[28] Furthermore, Shas recruited Rabbi Yitzhak Kedouri, a revered elderly Kabbalist, for its election campaigns in 1992 and 1996. Kedouri not only appeared side by side with Rabbi Ovadia Yosef in Shas rallies, but also became famous for distributing *kameot* (lucky charms) before the elections to potential Shas voters.[29] These practices appealed to the sensitivities of the traditional Sephardim whose religiosity is very much tied to folk practices, such as visiting the tombs of religious sages. Secularist political actors criticized this practice, claiming that Shas was buying people's votes in exchange for religious favors, and therefore the General Election Committee ordered Shas to refrain from using lucky charms during its election campaigns.[30] Despite this prohibition, Shas continues to use these folk customs during election periods.[31] These mobilization strategies reveal that despite its ultra-Orthodox identity Shas accommodates unorthodox practices such as belief in luck charms and saint worship in order to reach out to traditional Sephardim. The accommodation of these heterodox practices in mobilization efforts gives Shas an edge over the Ashkenazi religious formations, such as the modern Orthodox NRP and ultra-Orthodox Agudah parties, who have more rigid criteria in differentiating between insiders and outsiders. As a NRP activist frankly admitted:

> Rabbi Ovadia Yosef is a wise man, who knows the Torah, who knows the society, and who also knows what the public wants … We [at the National Religious Party] are more closed, like the ultra-orthodox. … If there is someone, who throws away the *kippa* (skullcap), among us [the National Religious Party], he is done. But he [Rabbi Ovadia Yosef] said to him [the person who threw away his *kippa*]: you can be one of us … So he brought everyone together and recognized their traditions … I think this is very healthy.[32]

The acceptance of individuals from heterogeneous religious backgrounds is indeed a deliberate strategy of the Shas leadership. This strategy partly stems from the moderation that has characterized the religious authorities of the Sephardi congregations in the Muslim world in the past two centuries.[33] Even Rabbi Ovadia Yosef, building on this moderate legacy of Sephardi rabbis, formulates more lenient *halachic* rulings in order to answer the needs of the Sephardim and to enable a larger number of Sephardim to stay connected with religion.[34] This moderation of religious authorities is also interrelated with the fluid nature of religiosity within Sephardi social formations. As a Shas activist mentions, there is a marked heterogeneity among Sephardi families:

> Now the families that support us, they do celebrate the religious festivals, they are Zionist, they are engaged in everything. For example in a

> Sephardi family like mine it is possible that there is one secular, one *dos* [slang for religious], one traditional. By the Agudah [Yisrael], there is no such thing. In a family either you are a *Haredi* or not. You cannot be a Zionist, it creates conflict. In our constituents there is no such thing. They all go together well.[35]

This fluidity of the Sephạrdi families is also instrumental in the linkage Shas forges with the *hazarah betshuva* (religious returnee) movement. A religious returnee is a Jewish person who comes from a non-religious background, but returns to religious observance by adopting the ultra-Orthodox way of life. During the early 1980s, the returnee phenomenon reawakened in Israel, and there has been a steep increase in the number of non-observant Jews who have embraced the ultra-Orthodox way of life since then.[36] The *Teshuvah* phenomenon occurs both among the Ashkenazi and Sephardi communities. However, the ultra-Orthodox Ashkenazim consider the returnees as less deserving of respect than people who have been observant all their life, perceive them suspiciously, and discriminate against them in different aspects of life, particularly in marriage decisions.[37] In contrast, Shas made these returnees a central part of its political network by recruiting them into important positions within the movement. Many of the grassroots activists I interviewed proudly mentioned that they have returned to religion before they started to work for Shas. There are also returnees who have risen to the highest levels in the party, such as the Knesset member and three-time minister Shlomo Benizri. To that end, Shas supports many yeshivas dedicated to returnees, most famously "Light of Life" (*Or Hachayim*) yeshiva led by Rabbi Reuven Elbaz. It also uses popular means, such as broadcasting Saturday sermons by Rabbi Ovadia Yosef through radio stations catering to religious returnees, organizing mass public gatherings in stadiums to bring back mainly low income traditional Sephardi youth to religious observance, or holding annual "repentance awakening gatherings."[38]

Hence, Shas has succeeded in creating what Nissim Leon calls a "culture of repentance" in the Sephardi community that overcomes the rigid distinction between the insiders and outsiders.[39] The graduated nature of Shas membership lies in the continuity between the religious returnees, those who are strengthening their religious observance (*mithazkim*), and those who are not observant, but have the potential to return to religion.[40] The statements of Rabbi Yitzhak Peretz, the first chairman of Shas, affirm this view: "[the traditional Sephardim] deep-down feel that Torah should be the law of the land despite the fact that they are not very observant."[41] Peretz's statements reveal that Shas includes less observant traditional Sephardim in an ultra-Orthodox movement with the stipulation that these Jews have the potential to become observant due to their historical cultural background. This configuration where the movement membership consists of three fluid gradations creates an advantage for Shas over other religious parties (both ultra-Orthodox and modern Orthodox), because the graduated nature of the commitment to the ideology and public activities of Shas overcomes the rigid separation between members and non-members in the Ashkenazi world. This heterogeneity in the movement's structure and flexibility in recruitment overcomes many of the obstacles that political movements with rigid ideologies face in building mass-membership.[42] A Shas activist from the south explains in simple terms this fluidity and the critical role religious returnees play for mobilization:

> Now, for those religious returnees it is much easier to connect with the secular public, because he [the returnee] says "I was your friend, I was a secular a month ago. Come and live like me, see how this works." They have a lot of power and form a *bridge* between the secular public and the ultra-orthodox public … Shas does all the seminars for religious returnees, before Shas there was no such thing. Who did all this? It is the Shas movement. Religious returnees connect the seculars to the ultra-orthodox. This is in itself a very big thing.[43]

The "bridge" metaphor the activist employed to describe the significance of the returnees in connecting the ultra-Orthodox and secular worlds aptly depicts the role of Shas as a gateway for many non-observant Sephardim to the ultra-Orthodox way of life. In addition to its own seminars and returnee conferences, there is also close affiliation between Shas and popular media figures who lead returnee events similar to those of the tele-evangelists in the United States. Rabbi Amnon Yitzhak, a Yemenite Jew, who leads a Bnei Brak-based organization named *Shofar*, is a case in point.[44] Yitzhak draws many young and poor Sephardim back into religious observance through his humorous, charismatic personality and stories, which he shares through public meetings and numerous video clips and tapes.[45] These tapes not only invite the listeners to return to religion, but also produce injustice frames that blame Labor Zionism for the separation of the Sephardi Jews from their traditional roots, their secularization and their socioeconomic marginalization. Like Amnon Yitzhak, other returnee preachers, such as Nissim Yagen, Daniel Zar, Haim Rabi and Yosef Mugrabi, became popular in Sephardi homes in the 1990s through the distribution of videotapes.[46] In addition to the dissemination of these injustice frames, the creation of an extensive videocassette culture works as a cognitive network that helps to form a sense of community and solidarity among Sephardi listeners and overcomes the "geographical distance and the political difficulty of conveying the message."[47]

Unlike many modern mass political parties, Shas's organizational structure is extremely diffuse. This decentralized organizational structure draws on several components. The ultra-Orthodox Sephardi rabbis and yeshiva students in the immediate orbit of Rabbi Ovadia Yosef work with a sense of religious duty and loyally disseminate his message during and between elections. Folk figures, such as Baba Baruch or the late mystic Rabbi Kedouri, maintain a loose connection to Shas circles. The popular *hazara betshuva* events and the returnee preachers' popularized videotapes also form fluid networks that build social power for the project of Shas. In addition to circulating the religious message of the Shas movement, these networks are also instrumental in creating a new ethnic consciousness among Sephardim.

The Ethnic Face of Shas

Shas draws many non-observant Sephardim to its ranks due to its ethnic message which addresses the historic ethnic grievances of Sephardim. Shas employs various discursive and material strategies to highlight ethnic inequalities in Israel. For instance, the movement's leaders point out that the Sephardim constitute the huge majority of prison inmates in the state of Israel,[48] while among Sephardim in Diaspora communities incarceration is not a problem. Similarly they focus on increased drug use among the poor Sephardi youth in the development towns as a social problem. In these narratives of ethnic inequality, the blame is squarely placed on the secular Zionist establishment in Israel. A free weekend paper published by Shas's civil society arm *El Hama'ayan* and distributed in synagogues every Shabbat provides an example of such a narrative:

> The founders of the state didn't want us from the beginning. They dreamed of bringing Russian and Polish Jewry here. The Holocaust disturbed their plans, and they had to fill up the area. So what did they do? They brought our fathers here. Did they think about them? Come on! They only thought about themselves and their visions … They dreamed about Israelis cut off from their heritage, so they tore it away from us … Why, and by what right? Don't ask; they didn't ask themselves.[49]

According to this injustice frame, the Sephardim became second-class citizens once they arrived in Israel. The main reason for this, the narrative goes, was the self-serving goals of the Ashkenazi political leaders and their total neglect of the Sephardi lifestyle. Grassroots Shas activists tell similar personal stories when explaining the treatment of Sephardim in the first three decades of Israel. As one activist says:

> The Labor Party was here in the government for the first twenty years. So it was impossible for people coming from other backgrounds to enter and rise in this system. Sephardim were always water carriers of the state. My father paved the roads and my mother was a cleaner in a hospital … For reasons of security, when the Sephardim came, the state has settled them in the periphery close to borders. It is Netivot, it is Sderot, it is Beit Shan, Yeruham, to settle the Negev, Kiryat Shmona. In these places there was no university, there were no good teachers. There was no good education. So from the start, the Sephardim could not come to higher positions.[50]

Yet the appeal of Shas's ethnic message lies not only in its emphasis on the structural disadvantages the Sephardim have been facing in the state of Israel, but also in its efforts to create a positive Sephardi identity. This is the main difference of Shas from other failed ethnic political formations, such as the radical Black Panthers or traditional Tami.[51] For many non-observant Sephardim Shas represents the reestablishment of Sephardi pride. For instance, a leaflet, which was distributed before the 1992 election and juxtaposed a picture of the Ramle prison with a class of Torah-studying children, gives the message that voting for Shas leads to the transformation of a marginalized group of incarcerated youth to a proud, pious Sephardi generation.[52] What is depicted in this and similar materials is not mere political propaganda. The movement works closely with prison inmates in order to reintegrate them into society by drawing them close to religion.

For instance, *El Hama'ayan* works with disadvantaged youth from poor neighborhoods and offers free extra-curricular activities to keep them out of trouble. As the director of *El Hama'ayan* explains:

> Rather than sitting in the jail, we create for them [youth from poor families] a space to be in … For example, there was this kid who came from a broken family, a family that has real issues. When I tried to bring him here [to *El Hama'ayan*], his father reacted and said that "you are stealing my kid." Later, he [the kid] decided by himself to join our activities and became a *hazara betshuva*, not because we asked him to do, but because he chose it. And later his father, who was first telling me that I was stealing his son, came to me and said "[T]hank you, until now I did not know I had a son. I treated him like a dog. Now I understand I have a real son thanks to you."[53]

Although there is an important element of political propaganda in this story, it is nevertheless revealing of how the Shas movement undertakes activities with transformative potential for the underprivileged. By depicting the return to religion as a solution to the problems faced by the disadvantaged—in this example to repair a broken family with an unhealthy parent–child relationship—*El Hama'ayan* demonstrates how a religious volunteer organization can find solutions to the everyday difficulties of the marginalized. Therefore, the movement upholds its discourse of creating Sephardi pride with concrete social deeds.

In addition to these local stories, Shas also employs ethnic frames at the national level during election campaigns. The political campaign around the process of investigation and ultimately the imprisonment of Ariyeh Deri is the most dramatic example. As discussed in Chapter 4, Ariyeh Deri had been tried for receiving bribes and money from government-funded yeshivas during his tenure as Minister of the Interior. The trial came to an end just before the 1999 elections, when the District Court of Jerusalem announced the indictment of Ariyeh Deri. Long before the trial was over, Rabbi Ovadia Yosef declared that Deri was innocent. In his weekly sermons, he repeatedly asserted that Deri was convicted based on one witness testimony, while the *halacha* requires at least the testament of two witnesses. This led to the "Deri is innocent" campaign that was circulated through Shas's media network. In this campaign Shas activists asserted that Deri's indictment clearly signified the persecution of a successful Sephardi politician from a modest background by the affluent Ashkenazi establishment represented by the Court.

This message of ethnic injustice was bolstered by Shas's successful use of symbolism. Shas rallies were full of slogans that equated Aryeh Deri's trial with the infamous trial of Alfred Dreyfus, who was a Jewish military officer persecuted unjustly by the French authorities at the end of the nineteenth century. Shas distributed tens of thousands of copies of a videotape, named "J'accuse,"[54] which referred to Emile Zola's famous letter criticizing French authorities for anti-Semitism during the Dreyfus trial. In this videotape, Deri accused the Supreme Court justices of not trying him properly and persecuting him unjustly, simply because he was a Moroccan Jew. Deri equates his struggle with the struggles of the impoverished Sephardi youngsters and narrates:

> There's a small group of people in Israel who feel they own the country. They took our youngsters in the hundreds of thousands, cut them off from their rabbis and their families. A whole generation sprouted without ties to Judaism. They degenerated to a life of drugs.[55]

While Deri associates himself with the low-class Sephardi youth, the videotape depicts the luxurious homes of the District Court Judges who convicted him. Thus, the ethnic message of the videotape was strengthened by an overlapping message based on class difference between the Ashkenazi judges and the Sephardi underclass.

This message of the tape was reinforced by the statements of Shas party officials and the emotional reactions of Shas supporters. The Minister of Interior Eliayhu Suissa criticized the court with these words: "It's always the 'black man' that's the scapegoat. As a minister, I am obliged to honor the justice system, but if it were up to me, I wouldn't agree to be tried by it."[56] Another Shas MK directly connected the court's decision with Shas's future electoral prospects: "The more they persecute us, the better we do in the polls."[57] As one of my interviewees who worked during the 1999 election campaign mentioned Ariyeh Deri deliberately invested most of Shas's electoral funds in the creation and dissemination of this videotape. This strategy seems to have worked well as the videotape became extremely popular among Sephardi constituents. In Tel Aviv's Carmel Market, many stalls that were run by traditional Sephardim distributed the videotape for free prior to the elections.[58] Shas supporters and other Sephardim also showed solidarity with Deri and accused the state institutions of being ethnically biased against them. As one youngster attending a Shas rally asserted: "I'm not an Israeli,

I'm a Sephardi Jew. Israeli is Ashkenazi."[59] As this Shas voter's reaction shows, the political campaign around Deri's trial deepened the ethnic division between the secular Ashkenazim and Sephardim within Israeli society. Shas capitalized on this sense of division and used the trial as a political asset during the 1999 national election campaign which brought the party a record number of 17 seats in the Knesset.

Starting from the mid-1990s Shas also leveled its political criticism at another group in Israeli society, namely Russian immigrants.[60] With the dissolution of the Soviet Union, Jews from the Soviet successor states migrated to Israel in great numbers. In the year 1990 alone, the volume of Russian immigrants increased the Jewish population of Israel by 5 percent.[61] In 1990–2000, close to 900,000 Russian immigrants arrived.[62] This immigration wave altered the ethnic demographics in the development towns fundamentally, when most Russian immigrants settled in the periphery. In 1990–2000 the overall population of the development towns increased by 20 percent due to the influx of Russian immigrants, and the percentage of the Sephardim in these development towns fell from 75 percent to 61 percent.[63]

Subsequently, both groups started to compete with each other for the allocation of already scarce resources in these peripheral towns. This competition was translated into political rivalry between Shas and the Russian parties *Yisrael Ba'aliyah* (Israel in Ascendance) and *Yisrael Beiteinu* (Israel is our Home) both at local and national levels. One of the most memorable campaign ads used by *Yisrael Ba'aliyah* before the 1999 elections read: "Interior Ministry under Shas's Control? No! Interior Ministry under Nash (Our) Control."[64] With this ad the Russian immigrant party demanded the Interior Ministry, which Shas habitually used to allocate crucial resources to its own followers (see Chapter 4 for more).[65]

This competition induced by structural forces soon turned into a cultural conflict. There is an important cultural divide between the Sephardim and the Russian immigrants, most of whom lead very secular lifestyles. For instance the Interior Minister Eliyahu Suissa from Shas—similar to his predecessor Ariyeh Deri—placed many difficulties in the way of obtaining citizenship rights for Russian immigrants who the Shas party leadership argued were not Jewish according to *halacha*. In its TV broadcasts, Shas claimed that *Yisrael Ba'aliyah* demanded the control of the ministry so as to allow prostitutes and criminals from the former Soviet Union into the State of Israel.[66] Furthermore, the local party leadership in Beith Shemesh staged a big anti-Russian political rally against the operations of a Russian-owned butcher's shop that sold pork.[67] In this rally, Shasniks enraged Russian immigrants by calling them: "hundreds of thousands of Gentiles flooding the land with pork, prostitution, impurity and filth."[68] Referring to the Russian immigrants, the head rabbi of one of the Shas yeshivas said that Israel is "awash with Gentiles who have no connection with Judaism and awash with abomination."[69] Similar rallies were staged in other cities, such as Ashdod, Ber Sheva and Ashkelon. This heated rhetoric around ethnicity benefited both Shas and the Russian

Table 6.2 Vote share of Russian immigrant parties and Shas in selected cities in the 1996–9 national elections

City	*Russian parties 1996*	*Russian parties 1999*	*Shas 1996*	*Shas 1999*
Ashdod	18	22.6	16.8	24.1
Ashkelon	16.5	21	10.6	21.3
Dimona	6.6	13.8	27.3	33.7
Kiryat Gat	15.1	20.5	14	26.1
Migdal Haemek	12.2	19.4	11.5	22.2
Netivot	9.1	18.2	26.2	43.5
Or Akiva	18.3	24.9	21	31
Sderot	9.8	21.5	19.3	22.6
Shlomi	12.2	20.4	17.5	31.6

Adapted from E. Bick, 'Shas Phenomenon and Religious Parties in the 1999 Elections', *Israel Affairs*, vol.7, no.4, 2001,72.

immigrant parties. As Table 6.2 shows, both sides increased their vote share in the 1999 election in towns with a high concentration of Sephardi and Russian immigrant residents.

While in the past decade, the relationship between these two ethnic communities has improved, during national election times the uncivil rhetoric around ethnic conflict flares up. For instance, a few days before the 2009 national elections, Ovadia Yosef unleashed a virulent attack against *Yisrael Beiteinu* during one of his weekly sermons:

> These are people who do not have Torah, people who want civil marriages, shops that sell pork, and the army enlistment of yeshiva students … My heart is heavy. Heaven forbid people support them. This is completely forbidden. Whoever does so commits an intolerable sin. Whoever does so supports Satan and the evil inclination.[70]

In spite of these harsh comments during election time, both parties became partners in the Netanyahu coalition government formed in the aftermath of the elections and have been working together in one of the longest lasting governments in Israel's history.

Shas as a Social Welfare Provider

Machapecha (revolution) is one of the major slogans employed by Shas to communicate its message. While some interpret this revolution as religious or ethnic revitalization as explained earlier, others perceive it as socioeconomic upheaval. Shas has been very deliberate in using a populist rhetoric in the socioeconomic realm and pushing for policy changes that would benefit the poor. Its "Document of Principles" states that promoting social justice is one of the twin goals of the movement.[71] Furthermore, the document engages in a critique of neo-liberal economic philosophy by arguing that the adoption of free-market economic policies, the glorification of globalization as a value system and the privatization of welfare services harm Jewish values of equality, justice and compassion by increasing economic inequality, poverty, unemployment and social gaps.[72]

To remedy these economic injustices, the document proposes several measures including turning Israel into a welfare state, providing economic incentives for working mothers and daycare centers, increasing the minimum wage, maintaining the purchasing power of pensions provided by the National Insurance Agency, creating more subsidized public housing for vulnerable populations, and improving child allowances.[73] The provision of child allowances for big families is one of the measures that Shas consistently emphasizes in fulfilling its social agenda, because it is particularly critical for the subsistence of ultra-Orthodox Sephardim who have large families and few sources of income. Therefore, Shas spearheaded legislation that increased the child allowances or at times threatened to leave the government when its demands to raise child allowances were not met, such as its refusal to reenter the Livni-led Kadima coalition in 2008 that forced Tzipi Livni to call for early elections for February 2009. As a Shas minister explained in an interview:

> Today, with Israel's economy, which is a fairly strong economy—among the strongest economies in the world—it is possible to give a glance at the lower classes [who] were badly hurt over the last years … The direct care for families is the child allowances, or call it what you want. The important thing is that a poor family or a poor child will directly receive support from Israel. This is his budget. His allowance is the only thing that can save him from his terrible distress.[74]

This and other egalitarian socioeconomic messages became the focus of the party's 2006 and 2013 election campaigns and foreshadowed the ethnic and religious messages of Shas during this election period.[75] In the 2006 national election campaign Shas delineated a "social road plan" that emphasized the importance of adopting poverty reduction measures.[76] A videotaped advertisement prepared by Shas shows the image of a hungry boy in tears and discusses the pervasive effects of poverty in the life of youngsters.[77] The words of the party's jingle during this election period also revolve around themes of poverty and social justice:

> Brothers, vote Shas
> Brothers, vote Shas
> You chose life, let's vote Shas
> No more poor people / no more hungry people
> We're sick of the games / only Shas will help the needy
> This is a party with security / Shas keeps its promises
> You will be blessed for this choice / the blessing of the righteous.[78]

While this populist rhetoric is helpful to attract some support from low-income Mizrahim, Shas's main strength stems from its local grassroots initiatives that translate anti-poverty rhetoric into everyday practice. In the 1990s, Shas opened "discount markets" where poor families could buy clothes and shoes under market prices. Moreover, Shas activists provide free meals for needy families during holidays and religious rites of passage, such as brit milah (circumcision) or bar mitzvah ceremonies. In many poor neighborhoods, Shas and *El Hama'ayan* gained the respect of the community for helping drug addicts to overcome their addiction and become functioning members of the society. Operating mostly in urban slums and development towns, Shas's daycare centers provide very cheap services and keep the toddlers until 4 p.m. which makes it appealing to working parents.[79] Small-scale initiatives spearheaded by idealistic local activists abound. For instance in Bat Yam, local Shas activists started a "warm home" program, where they deliver 300 hot meals for needy children, and a "backpack project" which provides school supplies to children starting first grade.[80] Students in Shas-affiliated yeshivas provide daily tutoring to elementary school pupils who otherwise could not afford any private tutors.[81] Another local activist in Ofakim, a development town in Negev, was proud of the recent opening of a new youth club delivering extra-curricular activities to ultra-Orthodox children and the building of a brand new library.[82] He was especially happy because the Interior Minister Eli Yishai was present during the opening ceremony.

The Interior Minister's opening of a youth club in this peripheral town is an example of the close relations the party leaders try to forge with their constituents, especially those residing in disadvantaged areas. Many Shas activists claim that the public can see eye to eye with the Shas leaders (*mul ha'eynayim*). This perception partly stems from the modest background of Shas activists. Most of the influential figures in the movement rose to political prominence from disadvantaged backgrounds. Rabbi Ovadia Yosef was raised in a poor family in the Beit Yisrael neighborhood in Jerusalem and lived in deprived conditions until his mid-thirties when he found permanent employment in the rabbinical courts.[83] The current party chairman Eli Yishai was the son of a construction worker and used to work on construction sites in his youth.[84] Morocco-born Aryeh Deri migrated to Israel when he was nine years old and grew up in a poor family. He studied in several religious schools, including the famous Yosef Porat and Hebron yeshivas in Jerusalem, where he excelled in Torah studies and was discovered by Ovadia Yosef. In 1988, 29-year-old Deri became the youngest minister in the history of Israel. One of the ex-Shas activists from the South explains Deri's significance for the grassroots-building efforts of Shas:

> [Aryeh Deri] is not just a regular person. He has built a movement … He was a man of deeds … Ariyeh Deri knew how to go to the field, how to go down to the level of the people. He knew how to warm up to people,

> to convince people, to knock on the doors, to convince them to vote. He [knows how to] market the Torah, the values of the movement.[85]

In sum, the movement's populist socioeconomic message convinces many people because the movement's promises are translated into practice through numerous national and local welfare initiatives and circulated by political entrepreneurs, who have credibility in the public's eyes because of their modest backgrounds and close affinity with the masses.

Novel Political Positions and Shas: Reshaping the Israeli Political Spectrum

Shas's entry onto the political scene has challenged the classical distinction made for political parties in Israel's political spectrum between the Zionist and non-Zionist as well as left and right.[86] In the immediate aftermath of its formation, many observers labeled Shas a non-Zionist political party because of its ultra-Orthodox leadership. However, the pragmatic ideology of Shas and the statements of the party leadership soon revealed that the party's stance on Zionism was not so straightforward. The first chairman of the party, Rabbi Yitzhak Peretz, asserts his party's stance on Zionism in its early days:

> If Zionism means love for *Eretz Yisrael* (Land of Israel), making sacrifices for it, and willingness to live here at all times and under all conditions, then we are super-Zionists. But if it means abolishing any part of the *halacha* for the alleged needs of the state, or as part of the concept of the state, then we're as far from Zionism as East from West.[87]

Peretz's statements show that Shas does not define Zionism as an ideological precept, but rather as an emotional attachment to the Land of Israel and a willingness to make sacrifices for it. Hence, for Peretz an elusive ideal, namely *Ahavat Yisrael* (Love of Israel), becomes the main basis of Shas's support for Zionism. Another Shas activist from the periphery voiced a similar sentiment when he made a connection between Shas's social activism in the peripheral towns and the movement's position on Zionism:

> There is no party that is more Zionist than Shas. I will give you an example. Who comes to live in Ofakim? Who? [Who comes to live in] Ofakim, Netivot, Yeruham, Sderot, Dimona? First and foremost it is [the] Shas movement. We settle in the Negev, we improve the economy. The same [is true] with the periphery in the North. Who goes to live there? People like us. We settle the place, build houses, bring populations here. Whose vision was this? [The vision] of David Ben Gurion … The Negev is blooming [an attribution to Ben Gurion's vision for Negev]. We don't go and live in America, we don't go and live in India. We stay here, we live here and we travel around here. Is there more Zionism than this?[88]

This passionate statement linking the movement's efforts to improve the social conditions of the communities in the periphery to the concept of Zionism appropriates some of the early Zionist imagery in settling and tilling the land. However, this loose emotional appeal to the love of the land is not systematically developed in Shas's worldview and therefore differs considerably from other Zionist movements which developed coherent ideological narratives to explain their Zionist credentials. For instance, as explained in Chapter 3 the religious Zionist NRP articulated a synthesis between Jewish orthodoxy and Zionism by defining the creation of the Israeli state as a step toward redemption.

The lack of ideological coherency on Zionism allows Shas activists and supporters to give multiple meanings to the concept. For instance, some Shas activists blend their understanding of Zionism with popular religious beliefs. The following statement of a Shas activist shows how religious beliefs are used to promote the party's definition of Zionism:

> We are the true Zionists. We say in our prayers every day, in the *Amidah:* "bring back the presence (*shehina*) to Zion." We pray every day for going back to Zion. Those, who are calling themselves the real Zionists, are not true Zionists. Jews, who have suggested that Jews go to Uganda are not Zionists. Zion is the name for Israel. The Zionists first would come to Israel.[89]

Defining Zionism not on the ideological level, but on the popular-emotional level is particularly appealing to traditional Sephardim who form a significant part of Shas's constituency. The synagogues of the traditional Sephardim customarily include the prayer for IDF soldiers in their prayer books and cite them during their religious services.[90] Rabbi Ovadia Yosef has even permitted the citation of the *Hallel* prayer—which is usually recited for Jewish religious holidays—on Independence Day, albeit without any blessing.[91] Both of these practices differ from ultra-Orthodox Ashkenazi practices. Rabbi Ovadia Yosef also differs from his ultra-Orthodox counterparts in his stance toward the army. Prior to Memorial Day in 2012, Yosef offered a special remembrance prayer to the fallen IDF soldiers and mentioned the significance of the army for Torah study: "G-d should bless the IDF soldiers who stand on guard for our benefit. Without them, we could not learn Torah … G-d should preserve them and keep them alive and well."[92] This is not surprising considering that most Shas supporters complete army service. As one prominent Shas MK asserts: "Of course Shas is a Zionist party. For example 14 percent of the army votes for Shas. People who believe in *Bnei Torah* (people of the Torah), go to the army."[93] Thus, it should come to no surprise that in 2010, Shas became the first ultra-Orthodox movement to join the World Zionist Organization.[94]

Shas's placement in the left–right spectrum with regards to territorial nationalism and peace process also evades easy categorization. Since the Six Day War, parties of the right have been broadly defined as those who take a position of maximalist territorial nationalism and non-conciliation toward Palestinians, while parties of the left are seen as those more amenable to the principle of reconciliation with Palestinians on the basis of territorial concessions. While the religious parties were seen as the natural allies of the "rightist" camp opposing any land for peace arrangements, Shas has joined the left-leaning government composed of Labor and Meretz under the premiership of Yitzhak Rabin in 1992 and supported the initiation of the Oslo Peace Process.

The party's support for the peace process was justified by Rabbi Ovadia Yosef's *psika*, "Ceding Territory of the Land of Israel in Order to Save Lives."[95] In this novel *halachic* ruling, Yosef first discusses the opinions of security experts in the context of giving West Bank and Gaza to the Palestinians, and says that there are different opinions as to how a potential peace agreement would affect the security of Jews living in Israel.[96] Later, the Rabbi discusses the significance of various biblical injunctions, including those of settling the Land of Israel and *pikuah nefesh* (saving Jewish lives). Yosef concludes that if ceding the West Bank and Gaza would bring true peace and security to Jewish citizens of Israel, then these territories should be handed over to Palestinians, because the biblical commandment *pikuah nefesh* (saving Jewish lives) overrides any other biblical commandment, including that of settling the Land of Israel.[97] Yosef received severe criticism from other religiopolitical parties and prominent rabbinical figures for embracing this position and taking this dovish stance.[98]

Yosef's innovative *halachic* ruling shows that religious texts can be read in multiple ways when making inferences for political decisions. Yosef's *psika*, "Ceding Territory of the Land of Israel in Order to Save Lives," reveals that interpretation of religious texts can enhance progressive, democratic policies by supporting less dogmatic positions. Moreover, it challenges normative positions which assert that mixing religious and political argumentation necessarily leads to rigid and undemocratic political positions. Pragmatically, Yosef's *psika* provided the Shas leadership with the flexibility to ally itself with the left whenever it deems it politically expedient. Shas's pragmatic stance on peace for land coupled with the party leadership's original synthesis between ultra-Orthodoxy and Zionism show that Shas carved itself a new ideological space and also reshaped the classical categories of the Israeli political spectrum.

Shas and Democratic Governance

The political trajectory of Shas in the past three decades shows that the relationship between religious parties and democratic governance is many-sided. Four main lessons can be drawn from the relationship between Shas and the quality of democratic governance in Israel.

First of all, by becoming the champion of Sephardi concerns Shas has emerged as a major force in reshaping the lives of Sephardim, particularly those at the periphery. Thanks to Shas's political prominence, the number and percentage of Sephardi representatives at the national and local level has increased significantly in the past three decades. This increased political representation has also led other political actors to pay more attention to Sephardi concerns in order to compete with Shas for this particular constituency. Thus, Shas has played an important role in deepening the quality of democracy, particularly with regards to pluralism, by channeling the concerns of a peripheral group to the center of politics. However, Shas's significance does not only lie in a quantitative increase in Sephardi representation in the Knesset, but in enhanced recognition of an assertive ethnic Sephardi identity in the public sphere. In the first three decades of Israel, Sephardi parties were largely perceived as sectarian formations undermining the Zionist ideal of Ingathering of the Exiles. The cultural project of Shas that claims to revive the Sephardi Golden Age and the construction of empowerment frames by the movement activists posed a serious challenge to this ideal of cultural homogenization. Hence, by expressing pride in their Sephardi heritage in public, Shas followers asserted their difference and challenged the assumptions of culture-blindness in Israel's political sphere. This celebration of the Sephardi identity shows Shas's critical role in the political recognition of a Sephardi identity, which amounts to a demand to be treated as equal while preserving one's difference from the dominant secular-Ashkenazi norms.

In contrast to this positive role played by Shas in highlighting Sephardi concerns and creating a positive public identity, the language the party leaders occasionally employ against their opponents undermines liberal-democratic political culture and civil discourse. Some of the Shas leaders—and especially Rabbi Ovadia Yosef—have not refrained from denigrating their political opponents by using religious texts or attacking the basic human rights of groups with whom they disagree.

In the political arena, the vilifying rhetoric targeted the secularist parties and the judges of the Supreme Court. The secularist parties, such as Meretz, Shinui, and currently Yesh Atid, had been the arch political rivals of Shas on the issue of the religion–state relationship. To indicate his disagreements with political figures from these parties, Ovadia Yosef uses hyperbole with uncivil language that would be counted as hate speech in many liberal democracies. For instance, while Shulamit Aloni from Meretz served as the Education Minister in the Rabin government, he promised "to declare a celebration and throw a banquet the day that wicked woman Shulamit Aloni dies."[99] Similarly, when Yossi Sarid served as the Education Minister in Ehud Barak's coalition government, Yosef gave one of his most hate-filled speeches against Sarid to indicate his protest over Sarid's educational philosophy:

> God has sorely tried us. He brought upon us this Yossi Sarid, this Satan, may his name be erased! And how can we continue to restrain ourselves, how much more can we take? How can we continue to suffer from this wicked person? God will uproot him just as he uproots Amalek, that is how he will uproot him. Haman is cursed? Yossi Sarid is cursed! ...

> Where is his sense, what does he want to do? He wants Mahmoud Darwish? That's his sense? Where is his sense? Doesn't it pain him that the secular Jews don't know Torah? That they don't know how to say the Shema Yisrael. No. It pains him that they don't know Mahmoud Darwish. God will confound his plans and strike his thoughts. He will repay him as he deserves. Just as He showed us with Haman's death. The revenge wrought upon Haman will be wrought upon him. And when you say "Cursed is Haman" after the reading of the Book of Esther, say too "Cursed is Yossi Sarid, Yossi … Darwish."[100]

Those statements, which were made after Yossi Sarid proposed including two poems from the famous Palestinian poet Mahmoud Darwish in the high school curriculum, show how religious texts can be selectively used to vilify political opponents. Yosef likens Yossi Sarid to the biblical figure Haman, the main villain in the book of Esther who tries to kill all the Jews of ancient Persia by plotting against them, and suggests that Sarid deserves a similar end to Haman, namely execution. In this speech, Yosef not only attacks the secular Israeli politicians in the person of Sarid, but also Palestinians in the person of Darwish. By collapsing two groups that he perceives as the "enemy," Yosef condemns both groups severely to the point of dehumanizing them. Unlike the previous example where Yosef's *psika* on "Ceding Territory in Order to Save Lives" supported a reconciliatory position, in this instance he used his religious influence to exclude and disparage political opponents. This type of religious vilification seriously undermines any liberal-democratic public debate that is supposed to be based on values of tolerance, mutual respect and respect for rule of law.

Yosef directed similar condemnations to the judges serving in the Supreme Court, especially during justice Aharon Barak's term as the president of the Court (1995–2006). During this period, the Supreme Court extended the scope of individual rights by embracing a liberal interpretation of the Basic Laws and took a more activist position in general.[101] Religious figures starkly criticized the Court and accused it of undermining the status-quo agreement (as discussed in Chapter 3) in favor of the secular through engaging in judicial activism. In this context, when Rabbi Ovadia Yosef called the Supreme Court judges "empty-headed and wanton evildoers, who are unclean and desecrate the Shabbath," the Attorney General opened a criminal investigation against Yosef for incitement.[102]

Shas also showed illiberal and anti-democratic tendencies in its approach toward the Reform and Conservative Jewish groups' demands for religious pluralism in Israel. In 2006, these groups sent a petition to the Supreme Court demanding the right to have access to public *mikvehs* (ritual baths) in order to perform ritual immersions for their convert candidates.[103] The Religious Affairs Minister Yitzhak Cohen from Shas not only opposed but also ridiculed the Conservative and Reform Movements when he said: "conversions of the Reform and Conservative organizations are virtual conversions, and therefore are deserving of a virtual immersion … the only immersion familiar to the Reform movement is baptism. … they should continue walking on water and leave the people of Israel alone."[104] Similarly in 2012, when the Attorney General announced that the government needed to follow the Supreme Court ruling on recognizing non-Orthodox rabbis and pay the wages of the those rabbis serving in regional councils, the party's reaction was harsh.[105] Shas MK Nissim Zeev stated that the decision marked "the beginning of the destruction of the Jewish people in the land of Israel."[106] The Shas MKs' dismissive and hostile attitudes toward Conservative and Reform Judaism show how Shas's ideology becomes exclusionary when it comes to the rights of religious minorities.

Third, the incorporation of Shas into successive coalition governments and the parallel increase in the party's electoral fortunes had an adverse effect on democratic stability by leading to the intensification of the secular–religious cleavage. The disproportionate funding Shas's civil society organizations receive through its entrenched patronage networks in several ministries troubled the secularist public in the 1990s. Moreover, Shas policies, such as the restriction of Conservative and Reform practices in public facilities, or curtailment of pork-selling rights, created the perception on the part of the secular public that their freedoms were at stake. As a result, secular segments of Israel began to voice more forcefully their criticism of ultra-Orthodox practices, and this paved the way for the rise of secular parties, particularly the Shinui.

A cursory look at the national political climate surrounding the 1999 and 2003 national elections shows how polarized the nation became over secular–religious issues in this period. The greatest testament to the escalation of the religious–secular conflict was the twin demonstrations organized by the ultra-Orthodox parties and secularist parties in Jerusalem on 14 February 1999 that brought the city to a halt. That day a quarter of a million ultra-Orthodox men came together to protest the decisions of the Supreme Court on the rights of the Reform and Conservative rabbis to serve on the religious councils and on the limitations put on draft exemptions for ultra-Orthodox men.[107] In this demonstration, which turned into a huge communal prayer event, Shas and other ultra-Orthodox parties fiercely criticized the Supreme Court judges for changing the status quo on the relationship between religion and state.

On the same day, the secular parties led by Meretz and Shinui also brought together 50,000 people in a nearby park to show their solidarity with the Supreme Court judges and protested the excessive political power the ultra-Orthodox exerted on the lives of Israeli citizens. In the midst of "freedom from religion" chants, Meretz Party leader Yossi Sarid explained the secularist fears: "You must understand this is a war, a war over the character of our beloved country."[108] In the 1999 election campaign, which immediately followed these demonstrations, secular parties' supporters voiced similar concerns. "*Rak Lo Shas*" (Anyone but Shas), became the most popular slogan among supporters of Meretz, Shinui and even One Israel (an electoral alliance led by Labor). These simmering tensions surfaced again in 2000, when the Supreme Court approved the jail sentence of Aryeh Deri. While Shas supporters organized continuing vigils next to the Ma'asiyahu prison to show their support for Deri and opposition to the Supreme Court, secular intellectuals made a public call for the creation of a Shas-free, secular "New Israel."[109]

A survey conducted in 1998 showed that 60 percent of the population thought the conflicts within Israeli society were much more dangerous than the conflict with the Palestinians. Of the domestic conflicts the religious–secular conflict was ranked first with 63 percent.[110] A post-election poll taken after the 1999 national elections, when Shas sent a record number of 17 representatives to the Knesset, showed that people expected all conflicts to improve except the religious–secular conflict.[111]

This heightened tension between the religious and secular segments paved the way for the rise of the secular Shinui as a party with a single domestic issue platform, namely secularization of the Israeli government. Shinui, which was part of the Democratic Movement of Change in the 1970s and of Meretz in the early to mid-1990s, started to run as a single party with a strict secularist program in 1996 under the leadership of Avraham Poratz and later Tommy Lapid. The party's political platform demanded the writing of a constitution, the curtailment of funding to ultra-Orthodox yeshivas and institutions, changing the law that exempts ultra-Orthodox men from military service, the running of public transportation during Shabbat, the institution of civil marriage, and the abolition of the Religious Affairs Ministry. Shinui's leader Tommy Lapid also declared that in no circumstance would his party sit in a coalition government with any ultra-Orthodox party—a promise he kept.

In a very short period, Shinui became the focal point of public discontent with the politics of Shas in particular and the ultra-Orthodox in general and won six and 15 seats in the 1999 and 2003 elections respectively. During the 2003 elections, the religious–secular cleavage was crystallized in the struggle between Shas and Shinui, where the latter presented itself as the representative of the secular and middle class interests. As one observer at the time wrote, Shas and Shinui had radically different visions for the future of Israeli society:

> The constituencies of the two parties have agendas that include issues that do not seem to be part of the national agenda: whether the country's character will be Jewish or democratic, Western or Mediterranean; whether the dominant way of life will be that symbolized by Tel Aviv or that of Netivot and the Har Nof neighborhood of Jerusalem … whether the voters of Shinui will continue to underwrite the way of life of Shas voters, and whether Shas's elected representatives will continue to dictate the way of life of Shinui voters. The two parties direct a great deal of mutual arrogance at each other.[112]

This sharp difference in worldviews and lifestyles with the harsh political rhetoric the party leaders employed toward each other created an important element of instability in the democratic system. The result of the 2003 national elections was a serious blow for Shas, not because of the election of a record number of Shinui MKs but because of Likud leader Ariel Sharon's decision to include Shinui in the coalition government at expense of the ultra-Orthodox parties, including Shas. While Shinui rapidly faded away due to internal dysfunctions and later merged with Kadima, today Yair Lapid—Tommy Lapid's son—is attempting to reclaim the anti-Shas, secularist mantle with his new party, Yesh Atid, founded in 2012.

The meteoric rise of Shinui as well as Shas's exclusion from the 2003 coalition government sent a serious message to Shas's leadership. Weighing the consequences of an aggressive stance toward secular political actors, Shas leaders decided to tone down their anti-secularist rhetoric in the aftermath of the 2003 elections. The chairman Eli Yishai demanded that all the party's MKs temper their criticism of secular actors, particularly state institutions, such as the Supreme Court. This new stance gave Shas a more moderate outlook. The party veteran Nissim Zeev's statement on the importance of the democratic regime is an example of this new moderation:

> Shas is representing a very big segment of the society and in general these people want the state to be a secular state. In the society there are traditional people and they want to respect the state as secular. We are talking to the traditional population. The secular people want to depict Shas as if Shas wants the State of Israel to be a Judaic state first and then a democratic state. But Shas wants to have first a democratic state, then a Judaic state.[113]

Nissim Zeev's statements prioritize democracy over Judaism, which is a sign of ideological moderation. In another interview, the local chairman of Shas in Sderot asserted how the party members' behavior toward secular individuals is conciliatory:

> It is impossible to forget that the representatives [of Shas] are composed of religious returnees. If you were to take a survey and take all of the Shas representatives in Israel, most served in the army, almost all of them … We relate to everything … we're not fanatics living in a cave. We're here, we want to learn Torah, we want to connect. Rav Ovadia instilled in the [Shas] representatives [the idea] that even if someone who doesn't keep the Torah or the mitzvoth sits next to you, a Jew, though a sinner, is still a Jew … That's our perspective. It's impossible to hate him, anyone from Israel … Make every effort so there won't be a conflict. Even if you're right, take a step back.[114]

This emphasis on a non-conflictual language and conciliation became visible among Shas representatives in the aftermath of the 2003 elections. A similar sentiment is expressed in the slogan "there are no religious, there are no seculars, we are all Jews" that appeared on a Shas election poster below a big picture of Ovadia Yosef. While there are various explanations posed in the literature for the moderation of religiopolitical actors, I argue that in this instance the moderation of Shas can be best explained with a rational choice model. The party leadership based its decision to tone down the party's rhetoric and embrace a more conciliatory approach on a cost–benefit analysis. Moderation was the most rational course of action, because improving the party's image in the eyes of the non-religious parties and constituents would prevent any future possibility of being left out of the coalition government and being cut from precious control of state resources.

Conclusion

Shas became a popular grassroots movement in the 1990s and 2000s by formulating an eclectic message that successfully appealed to Sephardi grievances. Shas activists created injustice frames, which blamed Labor Zionism for the separation of the Sephardim from their traditional heritage, their forced secularization, and ethnic marginalization. In order for Sephardim to overcome their perceived victimhood, Shas provided ideational empowerment by framing Rabbi Ovadia Yosef's *halachic* efforts as the restoration of Sephardi dignity and the creation of a reimagined religious past. Through its civil society networks, Shas provided extensive welfare support to disadvantaged groups, thereby showing how religious revival can be a cure to the everyday plight of lower class Sephardim. The modest background of prominent party activists made the movement's message of social justice credible in the eyes of ordinary citizens. In delivering its message, Shas utilized loosely connected networks. These included *hazara betshuva* preachers, rabbis in ethnic Sephardi synagogues, mystic Sephardi folk figures and ultra-Orthodox yeshiva students. These networks interpenetrated with Shas's own political and social organizations and deftly connected with traditional, ultra-Orthodox and even secular Sephardim. Shas activists saw their political activism as a *mitzvah*, which made them work with a sense of religious duty and engage in personal sacrifice. Shas's mobilization efforts also reveal that the movement's relationship to modernity is Janus-faced, similar to many other new religious movements. While Shas criticizes modernity as the source of the Sephardim's loss of tradition, social decay and gradual secularization, movement activists effectively use modern mediums of communication—including video cassettes, radio stations, television and websites—to transmit the movement's messages and mobilize constituencies. Politically, Shas carved a novel ideological space in Israel's political spectrum by embracing new interpretations and challenging long-standing categories.

Notes

1 http://shas.org.il/ [Hebrew].
2 Interview with Nisim Cohen, deputy Director of *El Hama'ayan*, Jerusalem, 12 December 2006; interview with Moshe Iluz, Director of *El Hama'ayan*, Jerusalem, 10 June 2012.
3 S. D. Baumel, *Sacred Speakers Language and Culture Among the Haredim in Israel*, New York: Berghahn Books, 2005, p. 150.
4 K. Caplan, 'Studying Haredi Mizrahim in Israel: Trends, Achievements, and Challenges', *Studies in Contemporary Jewry*, vol.22, 2008, 182.
5 J. Lupu, *Haim Tahzir Shas Atara LeYoshna? (Can Shas Restore Past Glory?)*, Jerusalem: Floersheimer Institute, 2004, p. 8 [Hebrew].
6 A. Picard, 'Soft Religiosity: The Identity of North African Youths in Israel', *The Journal for the Study of Sephardic and Mizrahi Jewry*, 2009, 132–68.
7 J. Lupu, *Haim Tahzir Shas*, p. 8.
8 Ibid., p. 8.
9 L. Weissbrod, 'Shas: An Ethnic Religious Party', *Israel Affairs*, vol.9, no.4, 2003, 92.
10 B. Lau, *Mimaran Ad Maran: Mishanto hahilkatit shel harav Ovadia Yosef*, Tel Aviv, 2004. Quoted in N. Leon, '"Zikui Harabim": Ovadia Yosef's Approach toward Religious Activism and His Place in the Haredi Movement within Mizrahi Jewry', *Studies in Contemporary Jewry*, vol.22, 2008, 152.
11 M. B. Shapiro, 'Mi Yosef ad Yosef Lo Kam ke-Yosef', *Meorot*, vol.6, no.1, 2006, 9.
12 O. Kamil, 'Rabbi Ovadia Yosef and his "Culture War" in Israel', *Middle East Review of International Affairs*, vol.4, no.4, 2000, 24.
13 A *psika* (singular form of *psakim*) is the decision of a religious legal scholar in matters on which the Jewish law has been inconclusive.
14 Interview with Shas activist Shmuel Amerusi, Elad, 12 June 2012.
15 S. C. Heilman and M. Friedman, 'Religious Fundamentalism and Religious Jews: The Case of the Haredim', in M. E. Marty and S. Abbelby (eds.), *Fundamentalisms Observed*, Chicago: Chicago University Press, 1991, p. 254; G. Denoeux, 'The Forgotten Swamp: Navigating Political Islam', *Middle East Policy*, vol.9, no.2, 2002, 63; M. Ayoob, *Many Faces of Political Islam: Religion and Politics in the Muslim World*, Ann Arbor: University of Michigan Press, 2008, pp. 2–4.
16 M. Ayoob, 'Deciphering Islam's Multiple Voice', in F. Volpi (ed.), *Political Islam: A Critical Reader*, New York: Routledge, 2011, pp. 44–54.
17 Interview with Shas chairman of Bat Yam branch Eli Ben Harer, Bat Yam, 25 June 2012.
18 Interview with Nisim Cohen, Deputy Director of *El Hama'ayan*, Jerusalem, 12 December 2006.
19 A. Willis, *Sephardic Torah Guardians: Ritual and the Politics of Piety*, unpublished Ph.D. dissertation, Princeton University, 1993, p. 176.
20 E. Don-Yehiya, 'Religion, Ethnicity and Electoral Reform: The Religious Parties and the 1996 Elections', *Israel Affairs*, vol.4, no.1, 1997, 86.
21 N. Leon, 'Zikui Harabim', p. 157.
22 Ibid., p. 158.
23 Interview with Shas chairman of Sderot branch Oren Malka, Sderot, 25 June 2012.
24 E. Bick, 'A Party in Decline: Shas in Israel's 2003 Elections', *Israel Affairs*, vol.7, no.4, 2004, 108.
25 D. Yosef, 'Parashat Emor: I will be Sanctified in the Midst of Benei Yisrael', *Aram Soba Newsletter*, Jerusalem, 1999.
26 M. B. Shapiro, 'Mi Yosef ad Yosef', p. 6.

27 Interview with Yigal Barzani, Jerusalem, 12 June 2012.
28 A. Willis, 'Shas-The Sephardic Torah Guardians: Religious "Movement" and Political Power', in A. Arian and M. Shamir (eds.), *The Elections in Israel-1992*, New York: SUNY Press, 1995, pp. 127–8.
29 E. Don-Yehiya, 'Religion, Ethnicity and Electoral Reform', pp. 86–7.
30 G. Hoffman, 'Shas Broke Law with Prayer for Soldier', *The Jerusalem Post*, 7 January 2009; S. Tepe and R. Baum, 'Shas's Transformation to "Likud with Kippa?": A Comparative Assessment of the Moderation of Religious Parties', in A. Arian (ed.), *The Elections in Israel-2006*, Piscataway: Transaction Publishers, 2008, p. 75.
31 G. Hoffman, 'Shas Broke Law with Prayer for Soldier', *The Jerusalem Post*, 7 January 2009.
32 Interview with NRP activist Yaacov Soler, Tel Aviv, 15 November 2006.
33 S. Deshen, 'The Emergence of the Israeli Sephardi Ultra-Orthodox Movement', *Jewish Social Studies*, vol.11, no.2, 2005, 82. Deshen argues that the difference between the stringency of Sephardi and Ashkenazi rabbinical authorities lies in the different socio-historical contexts in which modernity is conceived by Jews living in Europe and the Muslim world.
34 Z. Zohar, 'Oriental Jewry Confronts Modernity: The Case of Rabbi Ovadiah Yosef', *Modern Judaism*, vol.24, no.2, 2004, 143.
35 Interview with Moshe Iluz, Director of *El Hama'ayan*, Jerusalem, 10 June 2012.
36 K. Caplan, 'Israeli Haredi Society and Repentance (Hazarah Biteshuva) Phenomenon', *Jewish Studies Quarterly*, vol.8, 2001, 370.
37 Ibid., pp. 393–7.
38 L. Weissbrod, 'Shas: An Ethnic Religious Party', *Israel Affairs*, vol.9, no.4, 2003, 94; N. Leon, 'Zikui Harabim', p. 162; E. Bick, 'The Shas Phenomenon and Religious Parties in the 1999 Elections', *Israel Affairs*, vol.7, no.2–3, 2001, 61.
39 A. Picard, Review of *Soft Ultra-Orthodoxy: Religious Renewal in Mizrahi Jews* by Nissim Leon, Yad Yitzhak Ben Zvi, 2010, 30 June 2010. Online. Available at www.hartman.org.il/Research_And_Comment_View.asp?Article_Id=519&Cat_Id = 322&Cat_Type = Research_And_Comment.
40 Ibid.
41 'The Tora is our Platform: The Post's Aryeh Rubinstein talks to Shas leader Yitzhak Peretz', *The Jerusalem Post*, 3 August 1984.
42 N. J. Davis and R. V. Robinson, 'Overcoming Movement Obstacles by the Religiously Orthodox: The Muslim Brotherhood in Egypt, Shas in Israel, Comunione e Liberazione in Italy, and the Salvation Army in the United States', *American Journal of Sociology*, vol.114, no.5, 2009, 1302–49.
43 Interview with Shas chairman of Ofakim branch Shlomo Azran, Ofakim, 24 June 2012.
44 D. Izenberg, 'Fire and Brimstone in Bat Yam', *The Jerusalem Post*, 20 May 1997.
45 Some of the professionally prepared clips of Rabbi Amnon Yitzhak are available at his well-maintained website at www.shofar.net/site/index.asp. Some of the clips are available with English subtitles.
46 N. Leon, 'The Political Use of the Teshuva Casette Culture in Israel', *Contemporary Jewry*, vol.31, 2011, 98.
47 Ibid., p. 97.
48 E. Don-Yehiya, 'Religion, Social Cleavages, and Electoral Behavior: The Religious Parties in the Elections', in D. J. Elazar and S. Sandler (eds.), *Who's the Boss in Israel?: Israel at the Polls, 1988–9*, Detroit: Wayne State University Press, 1992, p. 115.
49 H. Keinon, 'Pamphlet: State Founders didn't want Sephardim', *The Jerusalem Post*, 19 January 1993.
50 Interview with Yigal Barzani, Jerusalem, 12 June 2012.

51 Interview with Eliezer Don-Yehiya, professor of sociology at the Bar-Ilan University, November 2006.
52 A. Willis, 'Shas-The Sephardic Torah Guardians', p. 123.
53 Interview with Moshe Iluz, Director of *El Hama'ayan*, Jerusalem, 10 June 2012.
54 'Lies and Videotape', *The Jerusalem Post*, 30 April 1999.
55 'Video Raises Ethnic Tensions', *The Toronto Star*, 30 April 1999.
56 D. Harman and L. Collins, 'Suissa, Lapid Trade Holocaust Insults', *The Jerusalem Post*, 28 April 1999.
57 Statements of David Tal in 'Netanyahu Ally Sentenced to Jail', *Associated Press Online*, 15 April 1999.
58 N. Leon, 'The Political Culture', p. 94.
59 P. Hirschberg, 'Alternate Reality', *The Jerusalem Report*, 12 April 1999.
60 In the mainstream public discourse, all immigrants from Soviet successor states are labeled "Russian" irrespective of whether they actually come from the Russian Federation. Here, I follow this usage.
61 Z. Geiltman, 'The "Russian Revolution" in Israel', in A. Dowty (ed.), *Critical Issues in Israeli Society*, Westport: Praeger, 2004, pp. 95–6.
62 Ibid., p. 95.
63 Y. Peled, 'Progressive Struggle under Religious Guise? The Shas Party in Israel', paper presented at the conference of the *Australasian Political Studies Association*, Canberra, October, 2000, 3.
64 R. Kampeas, 'Israelis Search for Election Issues', *Associated Press*, 2 May 1999. In the slogan Nash has a double-meaning. It refers to Nathan Sharansky, who was the leader of the Yisrael Ba'aliyah at the time. The word also means "our."
65 Ibid.
66 L. Collins and A. D. Cohen, 'PM brings Shas, Yisrael Ba'aliya', *The Jerusalem Post*, 7 May 1999.
67 D. Rosenthal, *Ordinary People in an Extraordinary Land: The Israelis*, New York: Free Press, 2003, p. 143.
68 *Mideast Mirror*, 23 November 1999.
69 D. Rosenthal, *Ordinary People*, p. 143.
70 'Rabbi Yosef: Lieberman Voters Support Satan', *Ynet News*, 9 February 2009.
71 'Document of Principles'. Online. Available at http://shas.org.il/Web/He/About/Platform/Default.aspx [Hebrew] (accessed on 12 August 2012).
72 Ibid.
73 Ibid.
74 Interview with Yitzhak Cohen on Israeli Army Radio *Federal News Service* 31 October 2006.
75 S. Tepe and R. Baum, 'Shas's Transformation', p. 75.
76 Ibid., p. 75.
77 Ibid., p. 76.
78 I. Marciano, 'Shas Election Jingles Reach Finals', *Ynet News*, 10 January 2006. Online. Available at www.ynetnews.com/articles/0,7340,L-3197823,00.html#n (accessed 15 June 2012).
79 L. Derfner, 'An A-to-Z Party', *The Jerusalem Post*, 1 August 1997.
80 Interview with Shas chairman of Bat Yam branch, Beni El Harer, Bat Yam, 25 June 2012.
81 Ibid.
82 Interview with Shas chairman of Ofakim branch, Shlomo Azran, Ofakim, 24 June 2012.
83 B. Lau, 'From Shop to Top "Maran Ovadia Yosef: Habiografia" by Nitzan Chen and Anshel Pfeffer', *Ha'aretz*, 1 October 2004.
84 D. Z. Harris, 'The Reluctant Prince', *The Jerusalem Post*, 20 August 1999.

85 Interview with an ex-Shas activist rabbi (the respondent wanted to stay anonymous), Sderot, 18 June 2012.

86 One of the earliest treatments of this argument can be found in A. Willis, 'Redefining Religious Zionism: Shas' Ethno-Politics', *Israel Studies Bulletin*, vol.8, no.2, 1992.

87 'The Tora is our Platform: The Post's Aryeh Rubinstein Talks to Shas Leader Yitzhak Peretz', *The Jerusalem Post*, 3 August 1984.

88 Interview with Shas chairman of Ofakim branch, Shlomo Azran, Ofakim, 24 June 2012.

89 Interview with Nissim Cohen, deputy director of *El Hama'ayan*, 12 December 2006.

90 N. Leon, 'Ethnic Synagogues of Mizrahi Jews in Israel: Ethnicity, Orthodoxy, and Nationalism', *Sociological Papers*, vol.13, 2008, 13.

91 K. Caplan, 'Studying Haredi Mizrahim in Israel: Trends, Achievements, and Challenges', *Studies in Contemporary Jewry*, vol.22, 2008, 171.

92 D. Lev, 'Rabbi Yosef: IDF Crucial for Torah Study', *Arutz Sheva*, 25 April 2012.

93 Interview with Shas MK Nissim Zeev, Jerusalem, 5 December 2006.

94 N. Jeffay, 'Shas Breaks Old Taboo, Join Zionists', *Forward Magazine*, 5 March 2010.

95 D. Schoenfeld, 'Formalism, Morality and Ovadia Yosef: A Response to Daniel Statman', *The Journal of the Society for Textual Reasoning*, vol.6, no.1, 2010. Online. Available at http://etext.virginia.edu/journals/tr/volume6/number1/TR06_01_schoenfeld.html.

96 Rabbi Ovadia Yosef, 'Nothing Must Stand in the Way of Saving Life', *The Jerusalem Post*, 6 October 1989.

97 Ibid.

98 H. Shapiro, 'Rabbinical Council Backs Chief Rabbis on not Surrendering the Land of Israel', *The Jerusalem Post*, 1 August 1989.

99 S. Honig, 'The Second Tape Savages Burgs, NRP, and Labor', *The Jerusalem Post*, 8 February 1993.

100 'I Hereby Instruct the Police to Investigate Rabbi Ovadia Yosef: Extracts from the Text of the Decision by the Attorney General, Elyakim Rubinstein, Instructing the Police to Conduct an Inquiry into Rabbi Ovadia Yosef', *Ha'aretz*, 28 March 2000.

101 Israel does not have a constitution. Instead, there are a number of Basic Laws which organize the functioning of state institutions or establish basic civil rights of citizens. These Basic Laws are treated as legislation that has primary status over other legislation. They are available at www.knesset.gov.il/description/eng/eng_mimshal_yesod1.htm.

102 N. Morris, 'Israel's Orthodox Demonstrate against Supreme Court Rulings', *Knight Ridder News Services*, 14 February 1999.

103 V. Bekker, 'Non-Orthodox Push for Access to Israeli Mikvehs', *The Forward*, 9 June 2006.

104 Ibid.

105 J. Sharon, 'In "Historic" Decision, State Agrees to Recognize, Pay Wages of Non-Orthodox Rabbis', *The Jerusalem Post*, 30 May 2012.

106 J. Sharon, 'Harsh Words Exchanged over State's Recognition of the Non-Orthodox Rabbis', *The Jerusalem Post*, 31 May 2012.

107 N. Norris, 'Israel's Orthodox Demonstrate against Supreme Court Rulings', *Knight Ridder News Services*, 14 February 1999.

108 D. Kraft, 'Religious Rallies Mark Turning Point in Israeli Culture War', *Associated Press*, 15 February 1999; D. Harman, 'Reflections in a Fun House Mirror', *The Jerusalem Post*, 15 February 1999.

109 N. Segal, 'Deri goes to Jail', *Canadian Jewish News*, 14 September 2000.

110 Survey conducted by Tami Steinmetz Center for Peace Research, Tel Aviv University, January 1998, in R. Hazan, 'Religion and Politics in Israel: The Rise and Fall of the Consociational Model', *Israel Affairs*, vol.55, no.1, 1999, 128.
111 Ibid., p. 130.
112 S. Ilan, 'A Fierce Fight on the Sidelines', *Ha'aretz*, 5 January 2003.
113 Interview with Shas MK Nissim Zeev, 5 December 2006.
114 Interview with the Sderot chairman of Shas Oren Malka, Sderot, 25 June 2012.

7 The Rise, Fall and Transformation of Political Islam in Turkey

From the 1990s to 2012

After the military regime, the NOM members formed the Welfare Party (WP) in 1983. Necmettin Erbakan was reelected as the leader of the party in 1987, when the law restricting the political rights of the pre-1980 era politicians was removed in a referendum. The WP won control of the municipalities of Ankara and Istanbul in the 1994 local elections, received the highest national vote share in the 1995 national elections by capturing 21.4 percent of the nation-wide vote, and became the senior coalition partner in the 1996–7 *Refahyol*[1] coalition government.

In addition to their accomplishments in the political arena, WP activists also succeeded in building a mass party with 4.5 million members[2] in 1998 and forming an elaborate, unprecedented party structure that reached most households in Turkey. Women's branches proved to be instrumental in the party's mobilization efforts, and the WP built close links with civil society organizations that connected the party leadership to the grass-roots in the mid-1990s. Similar to Shas's outreach work targeting Sephardi youngsters through *El Hama'ayan*, the WP used the *Milli Gençlik Vakfı* (National Youth Foundation) to provide shelter and education to disadvantaged youth and recruit them to the NOM. Moreover, the NOM operated a daily newspaper, *Milli Gazete*, a television station *TV5*, a research institute, the *Ekonomik ve Siyasi Araştırmalar Merkezi* (ESAM) (Economic and Political Research Center), and the *Avrupa Milli Görüş Teşkilatı* (European National Outlook Organization) that catered to Turkish immigrants in European countries. The WP also formed close links with religious-minded economic organizations, such as the trade union Hak-İş and the business association MUSIAD. After the shutting down of the WP in 1998 and its successor VP in 2001, the politicians who defected from the NOM formed the JDP and incorporated most of NOM's network web into the new political formation.

In common with Shas' ideology in Israel, National Outlook successfully blended religious, cultural, national and economic messages in order to address the grievances of the periphery in Turkey. This eclectic ideology targeted peripheral groups, which suffered economic, cultural and political exclusion. By framing political issues in ways that addressed the concerns of

Table 7.1 Vote share of National Outlook Parties in selected provinces in Eastern and Southeastern Anatolia (1973–99)

Year of elections	*1973*	*1977*	*1987*	*1991*	*1995*	*1999*
National average	11.8	8.6	7.2	16.9	21.4	15.4
Adıyaman	22.1	19.2	11.4	24.9	32.6	27.5
Bingöl	25.5	25.4	22.2	35	51.6	24.4
Erzincan	16.1	5.9	4	22	32.3	18.7
Elazığ	27.8	14	17.6	29.3	41.8	24.5
Erzurum	29.5	15.5	9.8	37	38.7	28.3
Bitlis	11.3	27.3	21.1	29.1	29	20.8
Nevşehir	18.4	9.9	10.7	26.4	28.4	18.4
Sivas	25.7	14	12.7	38.3	39.3	27.8
Şanlıurfa	17.6	19.5	11.9	18.4	26.2	21.4
Siirt	9.5	22	24.1	20.6	28	13.4

such groups, the WP constructed an alliance of those who felt they were marginalized in Turkish politics.

One of the sources of political support for the National Outlook parties in the 1990s was the underdeveloped provinces in Eastern and Southeastern Anatolia. By emphasizing regional inequalities in its party program and promising to take policy measures to remedy them, the NOM appealed to residents living in these regions. Like Shas's successes in development towns, the WP and the VP received votes above their national average in the national elections in these poor and underdeveloped parts of Turkey (see Table 7.1).

The party appealed in particular to Kurdish constituents in southeastern Anatolia and in the squatter settlements of the big cities. Instead of emphasizing a homogenizing Turkish nationalism that denied ethnic and cultural differences in the Turkish society, the parties of the National Outlook promoted the concept of Islamic brotherhood. By using this concept, National Outlook attracted the electoral support of many Kurds. In the post-1980 era the WP, VP and later the JDP were the only serious contenders for the Kurdish vote against the Kurdish nationalist parties in the predominantly Kurdish southeastern provinces, such as Diyarbakır, Siirt, Batman and Mardin. NOM activists presented Islamic brotherhood as an ideological construct that would help Kurdish constituents to overcome their sense of exclusion from the Kemalist nationalist narrative.

In the 1990s, the urban poor formed a significant part of the WP's popular base. The Islamists developed networks in the shantytowns of the metropolitan cities and appealed to those residents by rallying them around the concept of justice. For instance, in the 1992 partial elections the WP succeeded in capturing the municipalities of Güngören, Sultanbeyli and Bağcılar boroughs in Istanbul with a concentration of shantytowns, and Kağıthane, a traditional working class borough with a concentration of rural immigrant workers. The WP used its control of these municipalities to deliver essential social and material services to residents. During the 1994 municipal election campaign the WP capitalized on its experiences and successes in those municipalities. In both the 1991 and 1995 national elections, neighborhoods with a concentration of shantytowns preferred the WP.[3]

The NOM also represented the interests of the rising Islamic bourgeoisie. As discussed in Chapter 5, small and medium-sized manufacturing firms based in the Anatolian cities, such as Kayseri, Gaziantep, Denizli or Kahramanmaraş, benefited greatly from the export-oriented development strategy adopted by Özal in the post-1980 period. These new conservative businessmen rose to economic elite status, although culturally they were seen as part of the periphery.[4] A new set of Islamic bourgeois habits, such as alcohol-free coffeehouses, headscarf fashion shows, and segregated vacation resorts became cultural manifestations embraced by this new class to overcome their cultural and symbolic peripheralization. The veil also became much more visible in the public arena as more conservative women started to attend universities and entered the workforce after the 1980s.[5] The new Muslim middle class sees the veil and other cultural manifestations of Islamic piety as a form of social and cultural recognition.[6] The WP became the flag bearer of these cultural demands by embracing cultural Islamization at localities, encouraging cultural manifestations of Islamic piety among its members, and actively supporting relevant political issues such as opposing the headscarf ban in universities and state offices. The symbolic and political embrace of the Islamic bourgeoisie allowed the WP to empower the newly emerging Muslim middle class, who rose to an elite status in economic terms, yet were alienated in cultural terms, because their Islamic values were not compatible with the cultural norms of the center.[7] Since the NOM appealed to groups from various socioeconomic classes, some scholars have defined the movement as a cross-class alliance.[8]

The Religious Character of the NOM

The National Outlook parties have never explicitly expressed a religiopolitical ideology because the institutional context in which they operate, namely Turkey's state-imposed strict secularism, prohibits any self-declared religious political party. Hence, unlike Shas which openly defines itself as a Judaic movement, National Outlook parties have had to be more subtle in their use of Islam as a political reference point. The NOM expressed its Islamic character by using religious idioms in its political message. For instance, the word "*milli*"—which is at the core of the movement's platform *Milli Görüş* (National Outlook)—does not simply mean national, but is also used by the party cadres as an adjective that refers to a "religiously defined community."[9] Furthermore, the motto of the party's newspaper *Milli Gazete* reads: "*Hak gelince batıl zail olacak,*" meaning that falsehood will vanish with the advent of truth. The reference is to the NOM's rise to political power and the concomitant disappearance of other political parties that are construed as promoting superstitious materialism. The founder of the NOM, Necmettin Erbakan, was known as *Hoca* (teacher) among his followers. The term has a double meaning. It not only references Erbakan's status as a university professor of mechanical engineering, but also depicts him as a religious opinion leader, hence a religious teacher. Erbakan was also known to organize ceremonies after National Outlook's public meetings, where people take an oath of allegiance to the movement's cause. These ceremonies resembled the oath of obeisance (*biat*) followers take before religious leaders.[10] Erbakan also utilized the concept of *jihad* in his political speeches, and made his own interpretation of the concept. According to him, *jihad* meant "to work with all your abilities and until the end of your endurance for the formation of a godly/just order and to use all your wealth in this path."[11] In political rallies, supporters often chanted slogans calling Erbakan a *mujahiddin* (*mücahit*).

The religious vocabulary used by the National Outlook parties was in tune with the ideological tendencies of the movement's activists and supporters. The activists and elites in the WP distinguished themselves from others by expressing high levels of commitment to Islamic ideology. In a survey conducted in 1997–8, all 111 WP party cadres and activists questioned responded affirmatively to the claim that "Islam is the one ideal that can emancipate individuals from the chains of the current problems in the country."[12] A post-election survey conducted in 1999 showed that religious values were the most important predictor of the VP's vote.[13] The results of the survey indicated that voters who cast their ballot for the VP differed from other voters primarily in their emphasis on religious ideology.

One of the major components of the NOM's Islamism has been its critique of the Kemalist project of modernization. The NOM's civilizational critique starts with the late Ottoman period. According to the activists, the Ottoman Empire started to crumble when it decided to borrow practices from the West:

> We said that the prescriptions the West introduced into Turkey in the past two decades did not develop Turkey, caused Turkey to lose blood, and took Turkey backwards … The Tanzimat edict in 1839 was the importation of certain political projects into Turkey by pressure from the West. Thus, we started to import systems. First we said "let's import knowledge and technology," then we said that this knowledge and technology are part of a system and started to import systems. After 20 years, in 1856 with the Rescript of Reform we entered a bigger import period. After another 20 years in 1876 we started to import political systems … Certainly Turkey needed to take certain measures within its boundaries. Yet, since these were done with an import mentality and imposition of the West, but not with a mentality based on our own values, our own resources, our own opportunities, the Empire disintegrated. From 1839 to 1938, after 5–6 import packages, we could neither become rich nor do anything. On the contrary, we lost our political power, we lost our

> military power ... In conclusion, it is apparent that the Westernization process caused Turkey to regress, caused Turkey to disintegrate. This is a historical reality. These packages did not—as they [the Westerners] and their extensions in Turkey argue—make Turkey rich or develop Turkey. On the contrary they caused Turkey to regress and shrank the domain of freedom for our people who are attached to their own values.[14]

The above analysis, which claims Turkey's underdevelopment is caused by the Westernization practices the country adopted, lies at the core of the NOM's ideological worldview. In most of his speeches Erbakan called all the other political parties "imitators" in order to emphasize that they are unquestionably accepting of the Kemalist project of Westernization, while his party is proposing an alternative civilizational project that foregrounds the Islamic roots of Turkish society. Therefore, the NOM activists describe their parties as belonging to the category of "*hak*"—meaning truth, sacred and godly—while depicting all the other parties as belonging to the category of "*batıl*"—meaning false, spurious and irreligious.[15]

According to the NOM's ideologues, the Turkish education system depicts the West as the ultimate source of progress and human achievement and overlooks the contributions of Islamic societies to humanity in the scientific, legal and political realms. This admiration of Western culture and attempts to mimic it creates a lack of self-confidence on the part of the Turkish population.[16] These claims amount to an injustice frame that not only place the blame for the decline of Turkish society on the adaptation of Western practices, but also depict those practices as the source of corruption of the fair societal practices that reigned during the Ottoman era. As one of the old guards of the NOM asserts:

> We are not going to learn from the West how to govern a society. When we look to history, we see that we are the descendants of a governing cadre, which governed three continents for six centuries, and they have governed these places despite the diversity in ethnicities and religions. Hence, there is no point to look for salvation in the capitalism or socialism of the West. We need to foresee a governing system in which we elevate the right (*hak*) and justice and ensure the establishment of happiness among the entire nation and geography.[17]

Kazan attributes the peaceful coexistence of ethnicities and religious communities in the Ottoman Empire to the institution of the "*millet system,*" which accepted Greeks, Armenians and Jews as people of the book (*ehl-i kitap*), and therefore recognized them as official religious communities by granting each a certain degree of legal and administrative autonomy. This practice, according to National Outlook activists, is an indication that political practices were fairer during Ottoman times:

> Under the Ottomans, there was a democratic mechanism, because the Jews who came from Spain were living according to their laws, according to their beliefs, according to their values. So were the Christians, and the Muslims. Hence, everyone was living as they wished. It [the Ottoman state] only provided security, in a way it was an administrative mechanism. In a way it was enabling the different communities to live together, it was eliminating all the pressures among the communities. At that time there was a conception of democracy much more developed than today's. When we started to Westernize, we also started to lose this [conception of democracy], as I said we also lost our freedom. The racist system that they call the nation-state, which also affects the Turkish-Kurdish issue, came to us by the imposition of the West. Now for 100 years we have been trying to sort it out. This is not the product of our values and culture. We lived for 1000 years together, the Turks, Kurds, and even the Armenians and there was no problem. Whenever we brought from the West a racist system in the form of the nation-state, then the problem occurred.[18]

Taking the millet system of the Ottoman Empire as an example, Bahri Zengin designed a project for "multiple legal orders," which envisages the existence of plural legal systems for different ethno-religious communities in Turkey. According to this project, which was promoted by the WP on different political occasions, each citizen should have the right to choose the legal system of his choice and be tried according to the rules of this system.[19] Some in the movement also grounded the project in the Medina Charter, which refers to the legal arrangement Prophet Muhammad instituted between the Muslim, Jewish and pagan Arab tribes in Yathrib (later Medina) in order to establish public order in the city after his *hijra*.[20] NOM's attempt to create policy proposals by appropriating practices from an idealized Islamic past is analogous to Shas's attempts to reimagine the glorious Sephardi era from Andalucia. Just as Shas has sought to recreate the glorious Sephardi civilization from Andalucia to counter secular Zionism, the NOM proposes to create a civilization that would stand up to the Western civilization imposed on Turkish society by Republican elites.[21] NOM activists claim that their political program is a reflection of Turkish society's authentic values during the glory days of the Ottoman Empire. Thus, NOM activists construct prognostic frames which claim that a return to religious roots by refashioning practices from the Ottoman Empire and the time of Prophet Muhammad (*Asr-ı Saadet*) offers solutions to modern-day societal problems in Turkey.

One concept that the NOM activists use to indicate their attempt to create a religious society is "spiritual development" (*manevi kalkınma*). NOM activists contemplate that an emphasis on religious education would strengthen the spiritual character of Turkish society and citizens. As one activist asserts:

> First of all we think that the moral and spiritual fabric [of this nation] needs to be strengthened. This can be achieved through education. To

> state it more clearly it can be achieved through religious education, moral education … A union of fate, spiritual fabric of the society, deference to each other's traditions, these form the foundation of elements that keep a nation together. This is how a strong societal fabric can be built, this is how strong family is built. We name all of these as "spiritual development."[22]

In addition to using religious and moral education to create religious revival among Turkish citizenry (more in Chapter 8), the NOM activists also believe that the web of religious institutions under the purview of the Turkish state needs to be used more effectively to achieve these ends. The Directorate of Religious Affairs needs to coordinate this attempt at spiritual development, as a prominent NOM politician asserted:

> And certainly the Directorate of Religious Affairs needs to be made much more functional. In essence, the Turkish constitution is not a constitution that rejects religion. Just the contrary; article 24 envisages a compulsory religion class. This is an exceptional thing in a secular system … Hence in Turkey there is a legal foundation of religiosity, moreover, the Turkish Penal Code stipulates legal sanctions against the defamation of religion, defamation of religious people, and defamation of religious values … Even more important than these, the Political Parties Law states that a political party which puts the abolition of the Directorate of Religious Affairs in its party program should be closed down … Hence in Turkey both in the constitution and in the laws there is respect for religion and religious values. Yes there are deficiencies, but the main problem is in practice. For instance to remove the spiritual weakness, religion needs to be made much more functional, because—according to published statistics—in Turkey today 25 million people go to Friday prayers. Now, this is very important, such an organization does not exist in any other country. For the peace of the society, for the strengthening of the society, this opportunity needs to be used. Another issue, for instance today sixteen thousand mosques lack imams. These places need to be filled. Today, in Turkey there is a need for an additional thirty-five thousand "Religious Culture and Morality" teachers, these needs need to be met. In Turkey with a population of seventy million, there are twenty-five "Divinity Faculties." The curriculum of these Divinity Faculties needs to be reevaluated and the number of students accepted into them needs to be increased. … The Directorate of Religious Affairs need to be reinvigorated. The imam should not just be a person who leads the Friday payer and the five prayers, he also needs to be an opinion leader, he needs to be more active and functional.[23]

As these statements show, the aim of the NOM has never been to radically transform the institutional structure of the Turkish state as far as the religion–state relationship is concerned. The leaders and activists of the NOM know that the Turkish state already exerts an important authority over religious affairs. The Directorate of Religious Affairs appoints the imams in mosques and supervises the Friday sermons. Religious education is provided only through state institutions, such as the *Imam Hatip* schools under the authority of the Ministry of Education, and Quranic courses under the purview of the Directorate of Religious Affairs. As discussed in Chapter 3, the aim of this state control of religious affairs is the Kemalist view of keeping religious activity at bay and making sure that religiosity of society confirms the Kemalist tenets of the state. On the other hand, the aim of the NOM is to use these institutions already set in place by the Kemalist state to create a citizenry more in tune with its own political ideology. Hence, the aim of the movement is not to free religious activity from the state's control, but to use these state institutions to propagate a particular religious ideology.

Another dimension of the National Outlook's religious message can be seen in the movement's approach to the Kurdish question. In the 1990s, the parties of the NOM emerged as the only serious political alternative to Kurdish nationalist parties in the southeastern provinces with a Kurdish majority. The main reason behind the appeal of the WP was its inclusive approach toward Kurds, when all other mainstream parties in the 1990s embraced a homogenizing nationalist language that was exclusionary of Kurdish aspirations. The WP continually claimed—especially in the 1990s when radical Kurdish nationalism was on the rise and the activities of the Partiya Karkeren Kurdistan (PKK) were at the focus of national politics—that the concept of Islamic brotherhood should foreground the solution for the "Eastern Question."[24]

At its fourth party congress held on 10 December 1993, the WP represented the sources of the Kurdish question as "i) the materialist and racist character of Turkish nationalism; ii) economic underdevelopment of the region, and iii) the destruction of Islamic brotherhood by Republican policies of modernization without providing a substitute."[25] The press adviser of Erbakan at the time, Nazır Özsöz, stated that "the people of the Southeast have always been considered as a threat by the (Republican) Westernists simply because of their strong commitment to their faith (Islam) and their traditions and their resistance to the integration with the West."[26] With this and similar declarations, the WP attempted to construct a bond between the Kurds and the Islamists by emphasizing their exclusion and persecution at the hand of a common enemy, namely the Kemalist center. Furthermore, it suggested that the Islamic character of the Kurdish population constitutes an important reason for its exclusion by the Republican elites. Although it is true that Kurdish nationalism had religious overtones in the early Republican period, this close relation between Islam and Kurdish national awareness constitutes at best a half-truth.

According to the NOM, the solution to the Kurdish question needed to be found in the framework of a new national identity grounded in the concept of Islamic brotherhood. As a columnist of the *Milli Gazete* explains:

> Certainly, *Refah* (Welfare) will solve the Southeastern Question … by winning the population … not by a racist societal view, not by crushing them [the Kurdish citizens], not by putting pressure on them through the state's means, not by forcing them to leave their houses and villages, not by leaving them hungry and jobless. … by seeing them as Muslim brothers, by winning their hearts and minds.[27]

The National Outlook parties aim to create a more inclusive national identity that presents Sunni Islam as a social glue for different ethnicities. Some within the movement suggested that Islam subscribes to communal rights for different ethnic groups. As Yakup Hatipoğlu, a Kurdish WP parliamentarian elected from the Kurdish province Diyarbakır in the 1995 election, states:

> This problem needs to be solved in a logical, rational way. Military struggle can work up to a point. We need to find ways outside this. The solutions outside the military struggle can be done through mutual agreements. And this is granting certain rights. I see this as a human rights problem. If people's rights are given, this problem would be solved. What are human rights? Our religion has determined those. These are all necessary for a tribe, a race, and a nation. … The solution is in Islam. Whatever Islam says would happen, whatever Allah says would materialize. Rights and freedoms need to be granted.[28]

As seen in the above quotation, Hatipoğlu justifies the granting of certain communal rights to Kurds—albeit without specifying them—with Islamic scripture. This rather multiculturalist proposition, which is also embraced by a liberal minority in Turkey, is less homogenizing than NOM's proposal for creating a Turkish national identity intermeshed with Islamic brotherhood. However, despite these discursive appeals to solve the Kurdish question within an inclusive Islamic framework, the relationship between the National Outlook parties and their Kurdish constituents has not always been smooth. For instance, when the WP made an electoral alliance with the ultra-nationalist Nationalist Action Party before the 1991 national election, many Kurdish members either resigned from the WP or criticized the decision of the party leadership. Furthermore, the WP did not deliver its promises of an inclusive solution once it became the senior coalition partner and adopted the hardline official military approach to the Kurdish question.

The last aspect of the National Outlook's religiopolitical ideology is manifested in its foreign policy agenda. Unlike the Shas which mostly focused on domestic political issues, the National Outlook parties proposed a detailed foreign policy agenda that differs significantly from all other mainstream parties in Turkey. At the center of NOM's foreign policy lies an anti-imperialist analysis which asserts that the current international political system "puts might over right." Erbakan and the party leadership link the imperialist nature of the international political system to the Western civilization which promotes power, wealth, privilege and interest.[29] According to the leadership, this flawed system produces war, conflict, double standards, arrogance, exploitation and oppression for mankind.[30]

This Third Worldist critique of the international system aims to portray an international war against Muslim identity by imperial powers and evoke a sense of injustice among the Muslim constituents. To arouse this sense of victimization, the NOM parties successfully instrumentalized conflicts in the international arena, such as the first and second Gulf wars, the U.S. invasion of Afghanistan, the ethno-religious conflict between Armenia and Azerbaijan, the ethno-religious conflict in Bosnia, and the Palestinian plight under Israeli occupation. The most visible example of this was the huge humanitarian campaign spearheaded by the WP to help Bosnian Muslims in 1993. The WP constructed a victimized Muslim identity in the global arena around the Bosnian war in order to bolster the party's anti-Western, anti-EU stance, and call for international justice.

The NOM also proposes positive frames to remedy those injustices. According to Erbakan, an international system that "puts right over might" can only be created by an initiative from the Muslim world, as the West cannot be trusted for the salvation of humanity. Therefore, the NOM proposed the creation of a "United Nations of Muslim Countries" and "The Defense and Cooperation Organization of Muslim Countries."[31] According to Erbakan, these international organizations can "protect right and justice in the world as the Seljukis and the Ottomans did."[32] In this vision of foreign policy, the NOM attributes to Turkey a leadership role in the Muslim world as the inheritor of the Seljuki and Ottoman civilizations. This vision proposes the creation of a "Great Turkey" that stands on her feet and takes initiatives in the international arena as opposed to being "a satellite of the West which is run by racist and imperialist mentalities."[33] Thus, since its inception the NOM has been vehemently opposed to Turkey's joining the European Union and executing a Western-friendly foreign policy—except for a brief period during the VP.[34] The NOM's foreign policy vision goes hand in hand with its critique of the Kemalist modernization project. The NOM creates a binary between the injustice of the West and the virtue of the East and squarely situates Turkey's heritage within a "Muslim East."[35]

The NOM took practical steps to realize this vision for the first time during the *Refahyol* coalition government by forming a new international body named D-8, composed of the eight largest Muslim countries, namely Turkey, Pakistan, Bangladesh, Egypt, Nigeria, Iran, Indonesia and Malaysia. As stated by Necmettin Erbakan the aim of the D-8 was to break Western domination in the international system, become an alternative to the G-7, and institute "peace over war, dialogue over conflict, justice over double standards, equality over superiority, cooperation over exploitation, and human rights and democracy over force and imposition."[36] After the WP left office, the D-8 became, in the words of NOM activists, a shelved project and without any substantive achievements toward realizing its grandiose and utopic goals. The NOM's aims to create a "just international order" based on Islamic precepts reveals that the movement's religious project is not confined to national boundaries, but also aims to address the *umma*, the transnational Islamic community, although Turkey and its Ottoman past are seen to be at the center of the *umma*.[37]

Another central theme of Erbakan's political speeches and the National Outlook's critique of the international system is Zionism. Echoing anti-Semitic conspiracy theories, Erbakan links every international injustice and exploitation to Zionism and its alleged aim to create a Greater Israel. A segment from the FP's latest election declaration is a typical example of this stance:

> The great game of the racist imperialism is to institute its world dominance and turn all people into servants and slaves to itself by establishing a Greater Israel ... The great game of the racist imperialism is to establish the Greater Israel that would include the entire promised land between the Euphrates and the Nile, to control the government of all 28 countries from Morocco to Indonesia in order to institute its [Greater Israel's] security, to get rid of any independent state that is the inheritor of the Seljuks and Ottomans and could be a threat to Israel, hence to destroy our Turkey. This is the great game. This is their religion, there is no bargaining on this, there is no adaptation on this, there is no negotiation on this, [this is their] 5767 year old aim.[38]

This type of analysis has been part of the NOM's ideological view since its inception and figured prominently in its leaders' speeches and various party publications. This type of anachronistic foreign policy vision differentiates the NOM's political discourse from all other mainstream political parties in Turkey. This vision has some popular appeal as it provides simplified answers to complex realities and plays to a victimization mentality by attributing all the blame for the Muslim world's problems to non-Muslim political ideologies and actors.[39]

Framing the NOM's socioeconomic message

In the 1990s, the WP embraced a populist rhetoric and emphasized themes of poverty and socioeconomic inequality to appeal to socioeconomically disadvantaged strata. The WP's leaders used injustice frames by defining the economic system of Turkey as an "order of exploitation" (*sömürü düzeni*) and claiming that the WP represented the oppressed.[40] These themes struck a chord with rural migrants, who had a hard time climbing the economic ladder and coping with the difficulties of city life. A WP activist explains the socioeconomic consequences of rural–urban migration and the need to implement social security nets to manage the demographic changes:

> The inequities between social layers need to be eradicated ... [P]eople in Kars immigrate to İstanbul, to İzmir, to Ankara and settle in *gecekondu*

> neighborhoods. This is the picture in Altındağ, this is the picture in Mersin. When you go to Adana, this is the [same] picture, in İstanbul this is the [same] picture. Why is this so? Why do 15 million people live there [in İstanbul]? Because people are hungry there [in the villages]. Certainly, there will be demographic movement, it is unavoidable. Yet the people's needs should be met at the minimum level … You have to manage the transition, you cannot abandon people to wild capitalism.[41]

In its party programs and electoral campaigns, the WP emphasized the social and moral consequences of unfettered capitalism and economic inequalities. In the 1987 and 1991 elections the WP activists criticized the MP for its neo-liberal economic policies emphasizing the strong link between economic policies and the cultural-moral realm. A WP activist contrasts the WP's economic outlook with the MP's:

> [National Outlook] stands more for social justice and is more egalitarian [than the Motherland Party]. Particularly in terms of receiving a fair share from the budget, it protects the rights of low-wage, poor milieus … Yet the MP was not like this … for instance Özal's claims such as "I like the rich very much" distinguished us from the MP … [National Outlook] was a movement that opposed the economic policies [of the MP] and also exposed that this economic model would corrupt national values and the understanding of morality … The MP just supported free market economy, but did not put any filter to it … we, however, stand for a free market order that is for social justice and is morally equipped … These criteria set us apart from the MP. Inevitably this understanding in economy was reflected in social life and moral sphere.[42]

Accordingly, WP activists emphasized throughout the election campaigns of 1987 and 1991 that MP policies paved the way for wild capitalism, which in turn weakened citizens in the moral realm. In the WP's election rallies, Necmettin Erbakan explained these concerns in simple terms: "You see the Motherland Party. Isn't it this MP that opens casinos and induces more than half a million of our women into prostitution? The paint came off the tin,"[43] or "[during the MP governments] the disease that is called AIDS is coming here from Europe. Youngsters are starting to use drugs in their schools. From the six channels in the national television, dirt is flowing. In Turkey divorces are increasing 28 percent each year. In ten years there won't be any notion of 'family' in Turkey."[44]

As an antidote to economic inequalities and hyper-modernization, the WP adopted in its third party congress in 1990 a policy document named "Just Order" (*Adil Düzen*),[45] which defined both capitalism and socialism as exploitative systems that put "might over right," one promoting exploitation at the hands of capital, the other promoting exploitation at the hands of political power.[46] Instead, the WP assigned the state an active role in the creation of an egalitarian income distribution, provision of credit to the private sector, and the creation of basic infrastructure for heavy industries, while still considering the private sector as the main engine of growth.[47] The WP claimed that capitalist economic practices, such as interest rate-taking, credit systems and exchange rate systems were at the root of economic injustice.[48] However the WP was careful in differentiating between "rentier capitalism" that exploited the lower classes and a free market economy that was composed of small business enterprises interested in creating jobs and building the economy. The WP's program argued that in a "Just Economic Order," Islamic economic institutions and practices, which are predicated on assumptions that Turkish citizens would rise to a mature level of moral development, would replace the current exploitative economic relations based on materialist assumptions.[49]

The promise of a more egalitarian future appealed to the urban lower classes whose economic conditions had worsened as the share of urban wages and salaries in the GDP declined significantly from the late 1970s to the early 1990s.[50] The WP's critique of rentier capitalism and its promise of replacing it with a just economic order also appealed to the owners of SMEs who were members of MUSIAD. Although the number and organizational power of these SMEs rose significantly in the 1990s, these businesses did not receive nearly as much credit from the state as the big industrialists and the owners still perceived themselves as the "step-children of the state."[51] The Just Order's emphasis on religious morality also appealed to MUSIAD, whose members were committed to synthesizing Muslim values and business ethics.[52] As a result, MUSIAD threw its electoral, organizational and financial support behind the WP, while the WP supported MUSIAD members' candidacies to leadership positions in the Chambers of Commerce and Industry.[53]

The WP complemented its message of a "Just Order" with an emphasis on the importance of a clean society (*temiz toplum*). In the post-1980 era, the WP could run on an anti-corruption agenda, because it did not become part of any government until 1996, when all other mainstream parties were involved in corruption scandals while serving in highly unstable coalition governments.[54] The WP repeatedly claimed that it was the only party that fought bribery and corruption and believed in government accountability. The WP also had the opportunity to prove that these themes were more than election promises when it won the municipalities of four big boroughs in Istanbul, namely Kağıthane, Bahçelievler, Sultanbeyli and Bağcılar, in the 1992 interim local elections. In these four municipalities, the party meticulously worked to show that it could deliver services to the residents without getting involved in corruption or bribery charges. New mayors of these municipalities became famous for hanging banners on municipality buildings that read: "Bribes cannot enter through this door."[55] The anti-corruption efforts of these municipalities and interviews with the mayors on their achievements were continuously represented in the *Milli Gazete* before the elections.[56]

In the mid-1990s, the WP presented itself as the champion of the cause for "justice" (*adalet*), and was able to form an alliance from various marginalized societal segments around this conception of justice. A closer look at the WP's electoral campaigns in 1991 and 1995 shows that the NOM began to reach out to all segments who felt excluded from society. For instance, in the text of one of the 1991 electoral ads, individuals from various walks of life voiced their concerns about the injustice of the political system:

> farmers, civil servants, small-scale retailers, and workers who complain about rising inflation, low salaries, and high taxes; an industrialist who goes bankrupt and is unable to pay even the interest of the credit he took; the youngster who cannot find a job; the retired person who could not find peace; and the student with a headscarf who demands that her human rights would be respected.[57]

These messages in the electoral campaigns aimed to reach the "man on the street" who felt excluded from the system.[58] An activist, who joined the NOM during the VP era, defines the WP as an alliance of the excluded:

> Hence in the '91 and '95 election campaigns this left [rhetoric] was enormous … [They] wanted justice and opposed poverty, wrongfulness, injustice … Indeed the WP is a coalition [composed of] everyone who wants justice. [One says] I want justice, because Islam, our civilization is wronged … the other had to work hard in the past, he wants justice. The other is homeless, he wants justice. Hence, in the "Just Order," this is very clear, [it is] a coalition.[59]

This promise of bringing justice also extended to non-observant and non-traditional voter groups. During the mid-1990s, the WP is known to have engaged in extensive political propaganda and canvassing in taverns (*meyhanes*) and even in brothels in the slums of big cities.[60] Anecdotal evidence suggests that these slums supported the WP candidates in various elections.[61] My interviewees suggested that these non-traditional, non-observant voters supported the party because their program, "Just Order," captured their imagination and addressed their sense of exclusion from the society and longing for a better future. For instance, during his candidacy for the mayor of Istanbul in 1994 Recep Tayyip Erdoğan explained his opposition to the operation of brothels by empathizing with the sex workers and stating that they were enslaved and exploited by the brothel owners.[62] This strategy of the WP to reach out to the socially marginalized strata is analogous to Shas's engagement with drug addicts and ex-prisoners in the development towns and big city slums in Israel.

One of the significant reasons why the WP's message of justice resonated with various groups is the messengers. The modest background of many of the party's activists played a central role in convincing people that the promise of the WP to create a new just, egalitarian order was genuine. For instance, Recep Tayyip Erdoğan, the son of a rural immigrant who grew up in one of the lower class neighborhoods of Istanbul, had to work in the informal economy in order to support his own education through high school.[63] Despite his modest background, Erdoğan worked his way up the party ranks and became Istanbul's mayor at the young age of 40. As one activist explains, the WP's message became more credible in the eyes of the people, since activists like Erdoğan voiced it:

> In that period, during the 28 February [process], videotapes of Şevki Yılmaz and Tayyip Erdoğan were circulated. [Those in the media said] these are supporting sharia … But the people on the street did not listen to what the media said. [They said] these men are crying out, they are crying out for us. He is one of us, someone from Kasımpaşa … The more these tapes were shown on TV, the more the WP strengthened. Hence someone similar to us is crying out, [they did not care] if he was religious or not … The prostitute in the brothel, the drug user on the street [thought] [they are] crying out for "me."[64]

While the modest background of WP activists was imperative in reaching out to non-traditional groups, the WP was able to mobilize pious people by incorporating religious rhetoric in its call to justice. The WP's ability to mobilize citizens around the concept of economic and social justice can in part be explained by the activists' ability to explain the problems of poverty and inequality to the people on the street with religious idioms:

> These people lived in Turkey and were expecting service eventually. Despite the limited opportunities at the time the Welfare Party members were able to find solutions to their problems. Hence, they tried to help those people in the shantytowns, those people who came from the rural areas. … And our prophet commands that "the one who sleeps with a full stomach while his neighbor sleeps hungry is not one of us" … Thus, a concept developed within the party organization. There were many people who got a religious education in the *Imam Hatip* schools or in the Quranic courses. They received this religious education, but could not apply it in real life. The Welfare Party became an instrument for them to apply this in their social lives … In our faith, our prophet says "the one who sleeps with a full stomach while his neighbor sleeps hungry is not one of us." This person [with a religious education] knew this, but could not implement it. Upon entering the WP, he started to implement it. Henceforth, the interest in the WP grew.[65]

As the above quotation shows, WP activists used the Prophet Muhammad's hadith, "the one who sleeps with a full stomach while his neighbor sleeps hungry is not one of us," to communicate their egalitarian message to people residing in poor communities. The usage of religious idioms in framing the party's social message shows how the movement used local beliefs and practices for mobilization. The religious framing of social issues also provided emotional incentives for pious activists to participate in the movement's mobilization efforts. Many WP activists made personal and financial sacrifices for the party as they perceived their active engagement in the WP as fulfilling the Islamic commandment of "enjoining the good and forbidding the evil."[66] One WP activist explained the dedication of party activists with this anecdote:

> When I served in the Trabzon party organization [of the WP], I had a friend who answered people who were curious about the sources of our revenue. [He used to say]: "One third of my earnings goes to the state as taxes, one third goes to the [Welfare] Party, and the remaining third is for me." Thus, other political parties had rich members, but were themsleves poor. On the other hand, the WP members were from lower and lower-middle classes, but the WP was a rich party.[67]

Erbakan and the party's leadership continuously emphasized that working for the WP constituted a good deed that would be rewarded by God (*sevap*).[68] The *Milli Gazete* and party cadres stressed the significance of working for the movement and helping the poor by referring to the hadith: "the most auspicious among human beings is the one who is beneficial to others."[69] Many of the grassroots activists embraced this sense of religious mission and stated that they worked for the WP for "God's sake" (*Allah rızası için*), not for any individual gain or prestige.[70]

Party Networks as Means of Mobilization

The WP turned its egalitarian message to concrete social action thanks to the extensive party organization it built in the 1990s. Unlike the NSP whose popular appeal was rather limited, the WP succeeded in becoming a mass party by developing a highly disciplined, sophisticated party network that was known as the "prayer bead model" (*tespih modeli*). At the top of the party hierarchy was the Central Decision and Executive Board which has always been controlled by an old guard of politicians—e.g. Şevket Kazan, Fehim Adak, Oğuzhan Asiltürk, Temel Karamollaoğlu, Cevat Ayhan and Recai Kutan—known for their complete loyalty to Erbakan since the 1970s. The top brass appointed activists who would be in charge of each administrative district. In each province (*il*), the party maintained an executive council with 50 regular and 50 associate members that acted as the center of decision-making.[71] Moreover, one regular and one associate WP representative was appointed to each province (*il*), each borough (*ilçe*), and finally each neighborhood (*mahalle*) or village (*köy*). Before the 1995 national elections, the WP had representatives in 80,000 neighborhoods and villages.[72] In addition, in each neighborhood, five members, including one president, were appointed for each voting booth. These five voting booth observers (*sandık müşahiti*) were active not only during election campaigns, but also in between elections. They met every week to discuss how to reach out to citizens in their designated district and met every month with WP members in their district.[73] In 1995, the number of these booth observers in neighborhoods and villages surpassed 200,000.[74] As a result of this extensive work at the grassroots, the WP increased its membership from 800,000 in 1991 to over four million in 1995, surpassing any other party in Turkey.[75]

The booth observers provided information on all voters and potential members residing in their district which was entered into a large database at party headquarters. This database helped activists to locate and register potential supporters and turn them out to vote during elections.[76] Moreover, the highly disciplined and penetrating nature of these networks enabled the party to hang hundreds of thousands of election posters overnight or to distribute ads to tens of thousands of homes.[77] The WP also employed close to 10,000 teachers and preachers (*öğretmen ve hatipler*) to whom it provided professional training in oratory so that they would communicate the party's message at election rallies and other smaller gatherings.[78]

The WP's extensive political network was especially successful in initiating face-to-face contacts with citizens. WP representatives made frequent visits to homes and coffeehouses in the *gecekondu* neighborhoods in the big metropolitan cities. Before his election as the mayor of Istanbul in 1994, Recep Tayyip Erdoğan attended hundreds of house conversations (*ev sohbetleri*) as the head of WP's Istanbul organization.[79] Furthermore, the WP members attended social occasions, such as funerals or weddings in the neighborhoods, to construct a human connection with the residents and show that the party cares for them. As a WP activist stated:

> People say that the RPP is a social democratic party, but the social democrats do not have any involvement with the social life. They did not consider if these people in the shanties were hungry, thirsty, or if they needed anything. But those in the Welfare Party did not act like this. They went from door to door, they handed out roses during Women's Day. They brought presents on Mother's Day ... With their limited means, the borough organizations, the district organizations engaged in these endeavors. They prepared talks in the coffeehouses, they held conversations in apartments ... With these developments, every day new people joined the WP.[80]

In addition to forming personal relations with the citizenry, the WP's party organization together with welfare municipalities pinpointed poor households in the urban neighborhoods and provided material help by providing hot meals to the needy, distributing coal to low-income households before winter, and supplying cloth and food packages before Ramadan.[81] The WP municipalities alone provided extensive welfare services, including free health care services, discount supermarkets, free food through food houses, circumcision services, scholarships for education, in kind help for orphans, marriage and dowry support for the poor youth.[82] Similar to Shas's activities catering to the poor in the impoverished development towns in Israel, the NOM's focus on social welfare provisions in the deprived *gecekondu* neighborhoods drew many urban poor to the WP.

In addition to providing economic benefits, the WP also formed dense informal networks in these neighborhoods to earn the confidence of the citizens. For instance, the National Youth Foundation (*Milli Gençlik Vakfı*)—which had an organic relation with the WP and acted as its youth branch—built popular, hierarchical organizations in high schools in *gecekondu* neighborhoods and drew pupils to the Foundation by offering them scholarships, tutoring in English and math, lunches, and health services.[83] The Foundation also provided shelter to underprivileged youngsters by organizing social gatherings, training in combat sports and finding employment.[84] Similar to *El Hama'a-yan*'s aim to raise a religiously informed Sephardi youth, the National Youth Foundation sought to "promote a new civilizational understanding of Islam and nurture the spirituality of the Muslim youth."[85] The foundation had 1,800 branches and 350,000 members before it was targeted during the 28 February Process (more below) and eventually closed down by courts.[86]

The efforts of women party members also played a key role in successful political mobilization. Women were very active in the party organization and dedicatedly worked in women's branches named "Ladies Commissions." Despite their exclusion from party leadership positions, women activists participated in the WP in order to "carve out new areas of autonomy within the traditional expectations of their community."[87] The Ladies Commissions were designed parallel to the party's central organizational structure by establishing committees at the province, borough and neighborhood levels. All these branches were tied vertically to the organizational center of the commission in Ankara.[88] By the end of 1996, WP's women activists were organized in all of the 79 provinces in Turkey.[89] In Istanbul alone the WP Ladies Commission had 377,888 members in 1997, constituting over one-third of the party's Istanbul membership.[90]

In metropolitan cities, WP women organized groups at apartment levels, which proved to be key in gaining access to households.[91] Women activists could access homes, most of which become gender segregated spaces during day time, where male activists could not visit. They conducted visits for condolences, for newborns, for engagements, and for tea chats in order to communicate the movement's message.[92] As one of the prominent NOM activists suggested, the effect of women in mobilization was unmistakable:

> The women's committees became an instrument of reaching out to a big audience, especially to households. Very silently, without making much noise, by knocking on doors, [by giving] a daisy, or 50 grams of coffee,

> [the women working for the WP said] this is our position, we don't want your vote, we want your heart. Many people were contacted in this way.[93]

Women also organized women-only Islamic conversations and lessons at homes and "referred upward [the party hierarchy] any problems that they have noticed in the families they visited."[94] According to the chair of the WP's Istanbul women's branch Sibel Eraslan, the WP's women numbered 18,000 and organized 200,000 face-to-face meetings in the month prior to the 1994 municipal election.[95]

The WP and Democratic Governance

The relationship between the WP and democratic governance has been multifaceted and shows parallels to the Shas experience. In several ways the NOM has deepened democracy in Turkey. As with Shas's integration of Sephardi concerns, the WP became the voice of the economic, political and cultural concerns of the periphery at the center of Turkish politics.[96] As discussed above, many groups who experienced socioeconomic and/or cultural exclusion felt empowered thanks to the representation of their concerns in the parliament and municipalities by WP and VP representatives in the 1990s. By constructing a new Islamic identity around the concept of justice, the WP managed to address both the socioeconomic marginalization of the urban poor and the demands of the newly emerging Islamic bourgeoisie for cultural recognition. To the dismay of secularist actors, cultural symbols of the periphery started to gain visibility in the political sphere thanks to the Welfare and Virtue politicians. The hegemony of Kemalism as a homogenizing moral code in the public sphere has been undermined, if not broken, as a result of the WP and VP's political prominence.

In contrast to this positive role, some of the rhetoric the party leaders used against their opponents undermined democratic political culture in Turkey. The exclusivist rhetoric Erbakan and party leaders employed against their opponents is akin to Rabbi Ovadia's jabs against Shas's opponents that undermined norms of democratic debate in Israel. One of the infamous statements of Erbakan was his reference to other party supporters as unbelievers:

> If you don't want to serve *Refah* [Welfare] Party, none of your prayers will be accepted … We, the entire community of believers, shall obey the orders of *Refah* and join this army. Those who don't join [are not Muslims, but they] belong to the potato religion … *Refah* is the army. You will work for the growth of this army. If you don't, then you belong to the potato religion. It is your religious duty to obey this call for jihad.[97]

This and similar statements reveal the undemocratic and exclusivist tendencies of the NOM leadership and its lack of respect for democratic rivals. It shows how Erbakan used his position of religiopolitical authority to dismiss the

NOM's rivals. Erbakan continued to use dismissive rhetoric when he became prime minister and his WP was the senior coalition partner. As a response to the infamous Susurluk car crash—which revealed traces of the deep state (*derin devlet*)[98] by uncovering close connections between the mafia and state officials—the public demanded that the government investigate the matter and started to protest, for example by turning their lights on and off every evening at 9 p.m. Erbakan, as the prime minister, called these protests trivial (*fasa fiso*) and said that the protesters are "like children doing the gulu gulu dance."[99] The Justice Minister, Şevket Kazan, added insult to injury by likening these protests to the alleged game of "*mum söndü*" (snuff out the candle).[100] These remarks showed the WP leadership's lack of democratic political culture and their trivialization of democratic grassroots demands when those conflicted with their agenda.

Another aspect of the WP's politics that was anathema to democratic governance was the totalistic approach some party activists embraced with regard to the Turkish state and society. As the general discussion in this chapter suggests, the WP was not a monolithic entity. One of the groups within the movement, which was led by Bahri Zengin, saw the NOM as a civilianization project (*sivilleşme projesi*). According to this view the NOM would create a grassroots movement and create a bottom-up change in Turkish society. This group usually criticizes the Turkish state for being too powerful and argues that the strong state tradition stymies any attempt at creating a social movement for change. According to Zengin, the Islamist movement can be most successful if the role of the society is maximized in the government and the role of the state is curbed.[101] The project of the "people's assemblies," which connected citizens to the elected officials, was a project that exemplified Zengin's vision and was implemented by several WP municipalities in Istanbul.[102]

Yet another, more influential group within the movement, finds fault in the official ideology of the state, rather than state institutions' extensive power over the society. One critical activist criticizes this top-down approach eloquently:

> The modernism of the WP comes from this: they aim to capture the government and transform the society from top-down. They want [to create] the "Great Turkey." In this manner they are similar to the Kemalists, hence they want a strong, developed, industrialized Turkey. There is only one difference: Muslim morality, spiritual development. They aim to come to government with their spiritually developed cadres and to rehabilitate Turkey with these cadres. This is the ideological basis. Hence this is the basis of the conflict. There is an authoritarian state … and there is an ideology named Kemalism within this state … They [the WP activists] do not challenge the authoritarian state. They oppose the totalitarian ideology in this authoritarian state, namely Kemalism. Hence they will take out Kemalism and put in an ideology that is inspired by Islam.[103]

Parallel to Bekaroğlu's claims many NOM activists perceive the state as a "sacred" institution. Like Kemalist elites, they think that a strong state is crucial for running the affairs of the society.[104] For instance, many of my interviewees claimed that the Directorate of Religious Affairs, which administers most religious affairs in Turkish society, should be kept as it is or even be strengthened. Similarly, many argued that the state should be the sole provider of religious education, and this authority should not be shared with different religious communities (*cemaatler*). This argument, which is also frequently used by many Kemalists, assumes that there is one correct interpretation of Islam, and that the state should disseminate this correct interpretation through its institutions. Hence, the NOM, with the exception of a small group led by Zengin, did not question the "strong state" ethos of the Turkish Republic, but only wanted to command the institutions of the "strong state" to implement its own worldview from top-down.

Religious-Secular Polarization, the "28 February Process" and the Breakdown of Democracy in Turkey

One of the consequences of the WP's increasing electoral and political success was the polarization of Turkish politics along a secular–religious axis in the 1990s. When the WP emerged as the largest party in the 1995 national election, receiving 21.4 percent of the national vote and 158 seats in the 550-seat parliament, alarm bells started to ring in secularist circles. Many in the mainstream media and center political parties immediately made the claim that in democracies the will of 21 percent of the population could not preside over the will of 79 percent.[105] This statement implied not only that the WP lacked any mandate to rule despite its first-place finish in the electoral race, but also that all the votes cast for other parties constituted a total rejection of the WP.

The polarization of Turkish politics was also reflected in the political campaigns in the wake of the elections, when all the mainstream parties and the WP positioned themselves along the religious–secular spectrum. Before the elections the Democratic Left Party (DLP), the Social Democratic Populist Party (SDPP), the True Path Party (TPP) and the MP declared that they would not participate in any coalition government with the WP.[106] In their election campaigns, each political party also portrayed its platform as the only safeguard against the Islamists.

Erbakan, on the other hand, made a sharp distinction between his party and the others by portraying the WP as the only rightful party and the other parties as imitators of the West. Moreover, he made it clear in campaign speeches that he did not see the WP in the same league with other parties by refusing to participate in TV debates.[107] When asked which party would follow WP in its vote share after the elections, he stated that the other parties were "invisible"[108] and referred to other party supporters as believers in a "potato religion," a mocking expression implying a superstitious belief system.[109]

Despite these polarizing pre-election statements, heavy opposition from the mainstream media and after a brief center-right coalition government, the WP formed a coalition government with the center-right TPP in June 1996, and Erbakan became the first Islamist prime minister of Turkey. During its short-lived government, the WP faced an ardent secularist coalition composed of mainstream media outlets, the military establishment and members of the judiciary who maintained an organized public campaign against the WP in order to undermine the party's legitimacy and to communicate the message that the lifestyle of the secular segments of Turkish public was under serious threat. The excerpts below from an op-ed by Oktay Ekşi, the lead columnist in Turkey's then most-widely circulated daily, reflects the secularists' sense of urgency:

> The military academy, air force academy, and naval academy started the new academic year yesterday. Yet, yesterday they made a start different than other years. The information passed to us by some of our friends was that in all three academies the content of the first class was "secularism" … Moreover Atatürk's statement "You should understand very well that the Republic of Turkey won't be a country of sheikhs, dervishes and disciples" was hung on the wall of the room in which the ceremony of the air force academy was held. This is not all. Yesterday, some universities had opening ceremonies. In most of them either the first class was on "secularism" or a speech given in the ceremony emphasized secularism … It is also reported that the chief justice of the Constitutional Court Yekta Güngör Özden mentioned the danger of sharia in the speech he gave in one of the ceremonies in Ankara and said: "before it is not too late, we need to wake up and take steps." As Yekta Güngör Özden says now without losing time we need to take action in order to save the secular republic.[110]

In this period, the media closely scrutinized the WP's actions and statements in the government and heavily criticized political statements and events that challenged the secular symbols of the Republic. On the foreign policy front, Erbakan visited Libya's now-ousted president Muammar Qaddafi in his tent and quietly listened to his anti-Republican tirade and criticism of Turkey's NATO membership.[111] The WP also hosted representatives from Islamist political formations Hamas and the Muslim Brotherhood at its fifth party congress.[112] On the domestic front, the WP politicians declared their support for lifting the ban on the headscarf in universities and state offices, publicly deliberated the building of a mosque at the center of the Taksim square in Istanbul—which is construed as creeping Islamization by secular actors—and proposed a law for allowing the donation of the hides of sheep sacrificed for the Festival of Sacrifices to institutions other than the Turkish Aeronautical Association.[113] Erbakan also threw an *iftar* (fast-breaking) dinner for religious order leaders in the prime ministry. These events challenged the secular imagery of the Republic and convinced the military and judiciary that the secular nature of the regime was under grave threat.

On 4 February 1997, tanks rolled on the streets of Sincan, a borough of Ankara, as the army's warning against the "Jerusalem Night" which was organized by the WP's Sincan mayor Bekir Yıldız and attended by the Iranian ambassador Reza Mohammed Baghari who gave a speech praising Islamic rule.[114] While this did not lead to an overt coup, the institutional and social opposition leveled against the WP government culminated in the meeting of the National Security Council (NSC) on 28 February 1997, when the military members of the NSC defined "backwardness" (*irtiça*) as the biggest internal threat Turkey faced and listed a number of political measures the government needed to implement. Since the NSC asked Erbakan to fully implement these decisions or face the consequences, they clearly constituted a memorandum and marked the beginning of what is known as a "soft coup."[115] When the government dragged its feet in complying with the measures in the following months, the political scene became more tense, and the military started to pressure MPs from the TPP to resign in the summer of 1997 in an attempt to dissolve the coalition government. Erbakan's resignation in June 1997 spelled the end of the WP's short-lived government.

The NSC's decisions initiated what is known as the "28 February Process,"[116] when the military tried to reorient the Turkish political scene by curtailing the public manifestations of Islam and eradicating the social networks formed by the WP and other Islamic actors throughout the 1990s. The initial 20 point decision taken by the NSC at the 28 February meeting included among other things:

1) the enforcement of the dress code initiated during the Turkish revolution;
2) the closing of the religious orders;
3) the transfer of all the dormitories, schools and foundations with a connection to religious orders to the ministry of education; and
4) closing of the middle-school sections of the *Imam Hatip* schools by passing the eight-year compulsory education law.

The next coalition government headed by the MP's Mesut Yılmaz implemented these measures, which included the closure and illegalization of many religious foundations, including the National Youth Foundation, and the closure of the middle sections of *Imam Hatip* high schools (for further details see Chapter 8). The enforcement of the headscarf ban in universities was tightened with the Higher Education Council's directives. Veiled students who insisted on attending universities while wearing headscarves were sometimes interrogated in the infamous "persuasion rooms" next to the university gates, where state administrators tried to persuade them to uncover their heads.[117]

Moreover, a controversial body named the West Working Group (WWG) (*Batı Çalışma Grubu*) was formed within the Turkish Armed Forces (TAF) "with the task of collecting information regarding the political orientations of politicians, intellectuals, academics, and bureaucrats."[118] The WWG also tried to alter the dynamics in the civil society by closely monitoring the political leanings and activities of foundations, newspapers, dormitories, newspapers, radio and TV stations that were deemed to pose a "threat of backwardness."[119] Over a hundred companies run by Muslim businessmen also became the targets of the military's campaign.[120]

On the political front, the WP was charged with becoming the center of anti-secular activities and was closed down by the Constitutional Court on 22 February 1998. Erbakan and several other WP heavyweights received a political ban for five years. A year later, Istanbul's popular mayor Recep Tayyip Erdoğan was imprisoned for inciting religious hatred when he recited a poem from Ziya Gökalp during a public speech in Siirt.

During the 28 February Process the media sphere was also heavily polarized. A critical discourse analysis conducted in February and March 1997 on 44 texts that had appeared in the secular *Cumhuriyet* and Islamist *Akit* newspapers shows how both systematically communicated an ideological stance, in which they represented negatively the outer group and positively the inner group.[121] In the secularist *Cumhuriyet* "pro-Shariat," "backwards," "darkness" or "obstructionist" were the most used words to describe the Islamists, while *Akit* portrayed the secular camp as "oppressive," "brutal," "having an interventionist (military) mentality" or "having an aim to eradicate believers from the political scene."[122] Similar frames appeared in the Islamic-leaning *Zaman* and *Yeni Şafak*, while secularist newspapers, *Milliyet*, *Hürriyet* and *Yeni Yüzyıl* painted a picture of a rising Islamic threat.

The NOM Splits: From the WP to the JDP

When the Constitutional Court outlawed the WP and imposed a five-year ban from politics for several of party's leaders, including Erbakan, the party organizations and the MPs reorganized themselves into the Virtue Party (VP). The VP, now headed by Erbakan's close associate Recai Kutan, adopted a new political discourse that incorporated global concepts, such as human rights, democracy, rule of law and international law. During its short political tenure, the VP emphasized the importance of human rights, expansion of political liberties, and the constitution of "real democracy" in Turkey.[123] Unlike its predecessor, the VP also explicitly embraced Turkey's efforts for EU membership in its party platform.[124] The primary impetus for the VP's discursive change came from the party leadership's belief that Turkey's EU membership would limit the role of the military in politics and extend the scope of its constituents' freedoms against the hostile reaction they faced from the military, judiciary and the secularist media during the 28 February Process.[125] Erbakan even appealed the Constitutional Court's decision that outlawed the WP to the European Court of Human Rights (ECHR).[126]

Despite this discursive move, the VP's political life ended very abruptly, when the public prosecutor Vural Savaş opened a case against the VP for being the center of anti-secular activities. Savaş opened the case primarily for one incident, namely the entrance of Merve Kavakçı, a newly elected female VP deputy, into the GNA with her headscarf during the swearing-in ceremony. On 2 May 1999, Kavakçı endured "get out" chants of secularist parliamentarians from the DLP, and the then-prime minister Bülent Ecevit reprimanded her from the stage of the parliament. Later that month, her parliamentary immunity, membership of parliament and Turkish citizenship were revoked.[127] Kavakçı's case and later the closure of the VP in 2001 by the Constitutional Court were a testament that the "28 February Process" was still alive.

The VP's closure marked a major split within the NOM, which had important consequences for political Islam in Turkey. This split goes back to a power struggle between the old guard and a new generation of reformers within the VP. The young generation led by politicians such as Recep Tayyip Erdoğan, Bülent Arınç and Abdullah Gül, and supported by organizations like the Foundation of Unity (*Birlik Vakfı*), argued for the adoption of a more integrationist approach that would require the NOM to shed some of its core ideological premises, such as the fundamental critique of Kemalism and creation of a new civilization.[128] When the first congress of the VP was held on 14 May 2000, the young generation coalesced around the candidacy of Abdullah Gül who ran against the old guard's nominee Recai Kutan. While Kutan was reelected as the leader of the VP, the reformers gained a major success, because Gül received more than 40 percent of the delegates' votes despite Erbakan's clear support of Kutan. This leadership conflict within the VP culminated in a split, when the VP was closed down in 2001.

The new generation of reformers formed the Justice and Development Party (JDP), while the old guard organized around the Felicity Party (FP) continuing the ideological premises of the NOM and staying loyal to Erbakan. The split led to the marginalization of the FP, which gained only 2.5 percent of the vote in the 2002 elections. As Asef Bayat argues: "While sharing state power may enable social movements to turn some of their ideas into public policy, failure to do so, even though due to opponents' sabotage, would undermine their support base, thus rendering them powerless."[129] The failure of the WP to stay in the government and the subsequent closure of the WP and VP led many voters to lose trust in the NOM's ability to deliver any meaningful political change. As a result NOM's popular support shifted to the newly formed JDP.

The JDP and the Transformation of Political Islam in Turkey

Unlike the FP, the JDP became the largest political party in Turkey winning all three national elections it entered by receiving respectively 34.4, 46.7 and 49.8 percent of the vote and forming a single-party government after each of the elections. The JDP broadened the popular base it received from the NOM by gradually capturing the center-right vote in Turkey. While discussing various aspects of JDP's ideology and political behavior would go beyond the scope of this chapter, it is nevertheless important to identify some of JDP's departures from and continuities with the NOM in order to understand the transformation of religious politics in Turkey.

When the JDP was formed on 14 August 2001, the party leaders declared that they were cutting their ideological ties with the NOM and wrote a new political program that significantly departed from Erbakan's "National Outlook" (*Milli Görüş*).[130] Unlike the WP, the JDP eschewed the use of conflictual language or charged symbolism in its political discourse such as had antagonized the secularist institutional and political actors.[131] In order to diffuse political tensions with the Republican establishment, the JDP emphasized its commitment to Republican institutions, the secular state, individual rights and gradualist change. During its first term (2002–7) in government, the JDP refrained from addressing some of the significant cultural issues for its constituency, such as the removal of the headscarf ban, in order to diffuse secular–religious tensions and assure the secularist establishment of JDP's systemic credentials. While some scholars criticized this strategy as a "politics of avoidance" that prevented any meaningful public deliberation on how Islam can be incorporated into the public sphere, others referred to it as the "politics of patience."[132]

The JDP's approach toward the role of religion in politics also departed significantly from the NOM. In his various speeches, JDP's leader Erdoğan stated that using religion in politics constituted one of his party's "red lines," implying that this would be outside the boundaries of his party's political discourse.[133] The party leaders also mentioned on various occasions that their political party does not have a religious identity nor does it endorse any religious ideology:

> While attaching importance to religion as a social value, we [the JDP] do not think it right to conduct politics through religion, to attempt to transform government ideologically by using religion, or to resort to organizational activities based on religious symbols. To make religion an instrument of politics and to adopt exclusive approaches to politics in the name of religion harms not only political pluralism but also religion itself. Religion is a sacred and collective value. This is how we should interpret it, how we should understand it. It should not be made the subject of political partisanship causing divisiveness.[134]

The JDP politicians even refuse to use labels such as moderate political Islam or a Muslim democrat to define their party's political identity. Instead, they define the JDP as a conservative democrat party. This term was developed in a document authored by Erdoğan's advisor Yalçın Akdoğan—who later entered the GNA from the JDP.[135] Based on this newly adopted political position, the party elites claim that their aim is to reproduce the universal standards of political conservatism within the social and cultural context of

Turkey.[136] The party documents foreground a number of democratic and liberal values, such as limited government, universal human rights, the rule of law, primacy of civil society, and the significance of pluralism.[137] Akdoğan argues that a commitment both to these liberal values and to local conservative values is possible as typified by the Conservative Party in the United Kingdom and the Republican Party in the United States.[138] The JDP's aim of forging a synthesis is voiced by Erdoğan:

> A significant part of the Turkish society desires to adopt a concept of modernity that does not reject tradition, a belief in universalism that accepts localism, an understanding of rationalism that does not disregard the spiritual meaning of life, and a choice of change that is not fundamentalist. The concept of conservative democracy is, in fact an answer to the desires of the Turkish people.[139]

The JDP claims that "conservative democracy" represents this synthesis between modernity and tradition, universalism and localism. According to the party leaders, this concept constitutes a useful means to bridge the gap between the state and society, the center and the periphery.[140] While creating a synthesis between modernity and tradition, universalism and localism, is an admirable goal, the JDP elites are ambivalent on the values that would inform this synthesis and how this synthesis can be achieved.[141]

The JDP's foreign policy vision also represents a fundamental break with the foreign policy of the NOM. The JDP rejects the anti-Western stance of the NOM and its totalistic analysis of the international system based on a critique of Western civilization.[142] Instead, it emphasizes the importance of civilizational dialogue explicitly criticizing Samuel Huntington's "clash of civilization" approach.[143] Perhaps more importantly, the JDP embraced and actively pursued Turkey's EU membership. This pro-EU stance was strategically important for the JDP's domestic platform, as the party presented the pursuance of EU membership as working for the Kemalist aim of "reaching the level of contemporary civilization."[144] Moreover, the bid for EU accession necessitated reforms in the areas of democratization and human rights that were instrumental for the JDP to weaken the power of the military in Turkish politics and to open a political space for itself that is less susceptible to attacks by non-elected institutions. Therefore, when the JDP came to power in 2002, it prioritized the start of accession talks with the EU and passed six "harmonization packages" in parliament between 2002 and 2004 in order to bring Turkish law in accord with the EU's political criteria.

These harmonization packages presented by the government and approved by the GNA led to the enhancement of safeguards for the rights of prisoners, enhancement of freedom of association, changes in party laws that would make the closure of political parties more difficult, provisions allowing the use of languages other than Turkish in political propaganda, removal of the military members from the Higher Education Council, diminishing the powers of the NSC, taking away the authority of military courts over civilians, removal of any reference to the death penalty including military offences, and extension of the power of the ECHR.[145] The GNA also adopted a new Civil Code that reinforced gender equality, particularly on women's rights in marriage.[146] As a result of these harmonization packages and legal changes, the EU officially opened accession talks with Turkey in October 2005 during the first JDP government. However, the adoption of the reform packages slowed down considerably from 2005 due to resistance toward Turkey's membership among European public opinion and increasing Euro-skepticism in Turkey.

In addition to its pursuit of EU membership, the JDP also aims to increase Turkey's soft power and make it a significant regional player in the Middle East and North Africa. The JDP's foreign policy architect Ahmet Davutoğlu—who has been serving as Turkey's foreign minister since May 2009—argues that due to its unique geographical position, Turkey holds a special central country status and has unique historical and cultural bonds with Europe, Asia and Africa.[147] Therefore, Turkey is "a Middle Eastern, Balkan, Caucasian, Central Asian, Caspian, Mediterranean, Gulf, and Black Sea country" and should "[take] on a more active, constructive role to provide order, stability and security in its environs."[148]

Based on this vision, the JDP departed from Turkey's traditional foreign policy approach that kept a certain distance from the politics of the Middle East, and pursued a more proactive agenda in its relations with countries in the region in order to bolster its soft power. Under the JDP governments, Turkey sent troops to the UNIFIL II force stationed in Lebanon in 2006 after the war between Israel and Lebanon, mediated indirect peace talks between Syria and Israel in 2008,[149] and became the co-president of the U.S. initiated Greater Middle East Initiative—and actively supported the Broader Middle East Initiative as it was renamed in 2004—that aimed to promote economic liberalization and democratization in the region as an antidote to terrorism.[150] This policy of democracy promotion continued during the recent Arab uprisings, when the JDP government actively supported popular revolutionary forces. The JDP leaders suggested that their own political experience can be a role model for the development of democracy in Muslim-majority countries in the Middle East.[151] Turkey's active engagement in the Middle East—including Erdoğan's vocal criticism of Israel during the Gaza operations of 2008–9 and 2012—bolstered Erdoğan's popularity at home and in the Arab world. This increased engagement with the Middle East and the presumed leadership role undoubtedly instills pride among a significant part of the party's constituents and to a certain extent fulfills NOM's aspiration of creating a "Great Turkey." However, attempts to export political philosophy or experiments to countries which have different sociohistorical circumstances may backfire as illustrated in the Prime Minister's recent visit to Cairo. In an interview with a private TV station, when Erdoğan said to the Egyptian people: "Do not be wary of secularism. I hope there will be a secular state in Egypt,"[152] and added that a person can be both Muslim and govern a secular state, the Muslim Brotherhood declared that Turkey should not interfere in the transition process in Egypt, and that they did not need to be instructed about democracy by foreign powers.[153]

How to Understand the JDP's New Political Identity? Sources of Ideological Moderation

As the above discussion shows, both ideologically and practically the JDP has diverged from the ideological tenets of the NOM significantly. Therefore, it is not surprising that the FP, as the new face of the NOM, is one of the fiercest critics of the JDP in the domestic and foreign policy arenas. Most FP activists I interviewed accused the JDP of becoming just another mainstream party and being co-opted by secularist actors at home and hegemonic powers in the international arena.[154] The JDP's ideological transformation brings two important questions to the fore: What is the JDP's relation to political Islam? What are the causes of JDP's moderation?

Scholars who study the JDP have employed a number of different labels, such as Islamist, post-Islamist, pro-Islamic, moderately Islamist, mildly Islamist, Muslim democrat, to describe the party's newly formed political identity. I think that the category of "post-Islamism" developed by Asef Bayat best captures the ideological transformation of the JDP. According to Bayat, post-Islamism represents a moment:

> [Post-Islamism] refers to a political and social condition where, following a phase of experimentation, the appeal, energy, and sources of legitimacy of Islamism get exhausted even among its once-ardent supporters. Islamists become aware of their system's anomalies and inadequacies as they attempt to normalize and institutionalize their rule. The continuous trial and error makes the system susceptible to questions and criticism. Islamism becomes compelled, both by its own internal contradictions and by societal pressure, to reinvent itself, but does at the cost of a qualitative shift.[155]

The emergence of the JDP corresponds to a political moment in Turkish political history that is akin to what Bayat describes above. The JDP is the product of historical circumstances where WP's Islamism failed to become a credible governing ideology, instigated a harsh response from the Kemalist establishment, and faced robust internal criticism from its own dedicated members and supporters. But for Bayat post-Islamism is not only a moment, but also a project:

> Post-Islamism is a conscious attempt to conceptualize and strategize the rationale and modalities of transcending Islamism in social, political, and intellectual domains. Yet, post-Islamism is neither anti-Islamic, un-Islamic, nor is it secular. Rather it represents an endeavor to fuse religiosity and

> rights, faith and freedom, Islam and liberty. It is an attempt to turn the underlying principles of Islamism on its head by emphasizing rights instead of duties, plurality in place of a singular authoritative voice, historicity rather than fixed scriptures, and the future instead of past. It wants to marry Islam with individual choice and freedom, with democracy and modernity (something post-Islamists stress), to achieve what some have termed an "alternative modernity."[156]

Parallel to Bayat's discussion, the JDP represents a strategic and conceptual transcendence of Islamism. Similar to other post-Islamist political formations, such as various reformist groups in Iran and *al Wasat* (the Center) party in Egypt, the JDP tries to forge a synthesis between religiosity and rights, faith and freedom as described above. However, unlike these post-Islamist formations in Iran and Egypt, the JDP elites are ambivalent on the values that would inform this synthesis and do not make overt references to Islam.[157] What then is the role of Islam in JDP's identity? While the JDP avoids using any explicit attribution to Islam in political debates, the party's cadres engage in pious acts in the public sphere, such as participation in religious activities with veiled family members. Jenny White refers to this type of politics via increasing manifestations of Islamic piety in the public and political spheres as the "Muslimhood Model."[158] As a former JDP minister states: "AKP [JDP] is a political movement and the movement's actors have a very warm, close relationship, primarily as individuals, to … religious experience … At the moment, I believe that all ministers are fasting."[159] Yavuz argues that JDP members are engaged in a struggle over the definition of symbols and meanings that inform social institutions and values through this politics of piety.[160]

What then explains this transformation from NOM's Islamism to the JDP's post-Islamism? Two main explanations that can shed light on the likely causes of political Islam's ideological transformation in Turkey are the rational actor model and the structural explanation. The cadres that formed the JDP broke away from the NOM's ideology after the 28 February Process, when they realized that embracing a conflictual path with secularist actors would harm their short- and long-term interests. They observed that the 28 February Process not only led to the closure of the WP and VP as the representatives of political Islam, but also turned into an attempt to uproot Islamic social and economic networks. Therefore, the new leadership decided to accept the ideological constraints Turkey's strict secularist legal and historical legacy imposed on politics. Accordingly, the JDP adopted a new ideology that did not make reference to Islam in the political discourse, showed commitment to EU membership and embraced the broadening of individual rights. Hence, the JDP represents "the withdrawal of Islam from the political sphere in return for safeguarding its social network which forms the basis for the party's conservatism."[161] According to the JDP "individual freedom means the removal of state intervention and constraints from the community."[162]

However, while individual rights are seen as a significant instrument that would liberate community groups from state interference, the social position of vulnerable individuals within these community groups is not addressed by the JDP.[163] By focusing on the protection of societal actors from the state, the JDP aims to create a civil sphere, in which Islamic life choices, social, and economic networks can thrive without state interference. The construction of a political discourse foregrounding individual rights, the rule of law and democracy helped the JDP to forge a political alliance with liberal intellectuals and to increase its legitimacy in the eyes of global powers, such as the EU and the United States.[164]

The second major explanation for the JDP's ideological moderation is the role of structural factors. As discussed above, the WP was a cross-class coalition that brought together the urban poor and the rising Islamic bourgeoisie by constructing an eclectic political message and a fuzzy economic program. As the Islamic bourgeoisie thrived economically, it began to find NOM's Islamism harmful for its desire to live in a stable political system and NOM's economic program as anathema to its desires for integration in the neo-liberal economic system. Thus, MUSIAD, as the representative of this new economic class, actively supported the reformers within the VP. For instance, at MUSIAD's congress held in 2000, reformists of the VP dominated the congress, and the association's founder Erol Yarar gave a speech highly critical of NOM's old guard.[165] After the closure of the VP by the Constitutional Court, the reformers started to work for the formation of a new party, and the members of parliament from the VP had to decide whether they wanted to join the reformers' new party or stay with the FP. 28 out of 31 businessmen parliamentarians chose to side with the reformers and their new party.[166] When the reformers formed the JDP, about ten MUSIAD businessmen became founding members of the party, and during the 2002 elections 21 MUSIAD members were elected to the GNA from the JDP.[167] MUSIAD also helped the JDP organizationally "as numerous members of the association joined the AKP [JDP] to complete the organization of the local offices of the party in Anatolian cities."[168]

As a result of this organic relationship, the JDP embraced a neo-liberal economic agenda and worked for Turkey's full integration into the global economy through extensive privatization. During the JDP governments, MUSIAD businessmen also had unprecedented access to public contracts.[169] Yıldız Atasoy explains the class basis of the JDP's ideological break from the NOM:

> The divergence of the AKP [JDP] from the Islamic national view [outlook] ideology of Erbakan represents a change in class relations of Islamist capital groups in Turkey. Newly rich Islamist capitalists want to integrate into the processes of capital accumulation as a culturally distinct group within a global capitalist economy. They believe that the basic economic interests of Islamic enterprises will thrive within the global economy. In contrast to the rhetoric of national view ideology, Turkish Islamists now

raise the possibility that Turkey may very well become an industrial and economic powerhouse in the region, and play a dominant role in connecting the Islamic world to the West as partners in a global economy. The AKP's push for Turkey's full membership in the EU reinforces this as a political possibility—that Islamist capitalists be incorporated into a broadening of the political alliances of corporate regulation.[170]

The Clash between the JDP and the Secular State

Despite its ideological moderation, several political developments brought the JDP onto a collision course with the military and other secularist institutional actors in 2007–8. Since the JDP's formation, the secular sectors of Turkish society voiced skepticism as to JDP's ideological transformation and accused the party of concealing its true intentions of creating an Islamic state. On 24 April 2007, Abdullah Gül's nomination to the presidency, an institution the secularists saw as their last bulwark against "creeping Islamism," rang alarm bells among secularist circles, because the JDP held the GNA majority needed to elect the president. On 29 April a mass protest organized by Atatürkist civil society organizations and secularist political parties in Çağlayan square was attended by over a million people who protested Gül's candidacy, and the fact that his wife donned the Islamic veil—a particular concern for the secularists.[171] The JDP nevertheless went ahead with the election process in the parliament, in which a presidential candidate needed to receive two-thirds of the votes in the first two rounds, while a simple majority was sufficient to get elected in the third and fourth rounds. When Gül failed to receive two-thirds of the votes in the first round, the RPP—which did not enter the GNA session for the election—applied to the Constitutional Court for the annulment of the first round by claiming that two-thirds quorum was required not only for the election of the candidate but even for the opening of the GNA session.[172] On the same day of the first round, the military issued a warning on its website harshly criticizing Gül's bid for the presidency. On 1 May 2007, the Constitutional Court invalidated the first round by claiming that the vote needed to take place in front of two-thirds of the GNA, making the election of a new president virtually impossible. The Constitutional Court's decision—which according to most constitutional scholars was in direct variance with the literal and teleological interpretations of the constitution[173]—was yet another attempt to block Gül's presidency. As a response, the JDP went to early parliamentary elections in June. The election results, where the JDP increased its vote share to 46.7 percent of the national vote, showed that the secularist pressures on the JDP backfired. Gül was elected president on 28 August 2007, with the votes of the newly elected parliament.

After winning the elections in a landslide, the reassured JDP started to focus on cultural issues that were important for its constituency, such as the abolition of the headscarf ban in universities. The headscarf debate in

Turkey involves different interpretations of secularism. As discussed in Chapter 3, Turkish secularism, which is designed along the lines of the French principle of *laïcité*, primarily aims to create a secular public sphere by eradicating signs of religious particularism from the public space. The JDP opposes this interpretation of the concept, known as assertive secularism, and says that Turkey needs to adopt defensive secularism as it is implemented in the United States.[174] Unlike assertive secularism, defensive secularism is tolerant of the manifestations of religious piety in the public and political sphere, hence it is more liberal. As Bülent Arınç, the current deputy prime minister from the JDP, claims: "We would like Turkey to apply secularism as it is in the world, because secularism in America, Anglo-Saxon secularism … do[es] not interfere with [people's] clothing."[175]

In line with its commitment to defensive secularism, the JDP made changes to paragraph 4 of article 10 and to paragraph 6 of article 42 of the Turkish Constitution with the parliamentary support of the Nationalist Action Party (NAP) on 9 February 2008. The aim of these changes—which expanded the limits of equality before the law and extended anti-discrimination measures in the right to education—was to allow veiled students to attend universities. The RPP took the amendments straight to the Constitutional Court, and the Court annulled the constitutional amendments claiming they would harm the principle of secularism.

On 14 March 2008, the public prosecutor Abdurrahman Yalçınkaya opened a case against the JDP and demanded the outlawing of the party. The Court decided not to outlaw the JDP,[176] but found it guilty of becoming the center of anti-secularist activities. As a result of this ruling, the JDP received a serious warning from the Court for undermining Turkey's secularism, primarily for its stance on the headscarf issue, and half of its public funding was cut.

The events surrounding Gül's candidacy, the constitutional amendments for the headscarf, and the JDP closure case reveal that the judiciary—and to a lesser extent the military—tried to block the JDP's ascendance and shrink the domain of civilian political power. Due these developments, the political scene was again polarized around the religious–secular cleavage. This is a testament that the intensification of the religious–secular cleavage not only depends on the ideology (moderate/radical) of the religiopolitical actors, but also (maybe more so) on the size of their political power and the threat perception on the part of the secular political actors.

Limits of the JDP's Democratic Discourse and Challenges of Democratic Consolidation in Turkey

Toward the end of its second term in government, the JDP's reform efforts slowed down, and the party's stance toward opposition actors gradually became more intolerant. This illiberalization is not related to the JDP's relation to religion, but rather stems from a lack of democratic consolidation in Turkey. The JDP's super majority in the parliament, the weakness of effective and constructive opposition parties, and the polarization of Turkish politics along secular–religious lines made the leadership more and more intolerant of any criticism.[177]

Immediately after the closure case in 2008, a number of high profile arrests of retired and active-duty military officers, civil society organizers, journalists and media figures were made in the context of what is known as the "Ergenekon trial." Ergenekon is the name given to a clandestine ultra-nationalist organization—that is seen as part of the deep state—allegedly engaged in plots to destabilize the democratic regime and overthrow civilian government. While the JDP's constituency and liberal social actors argued that the Ergenekon trial is an attempt to dismantle the deep state and military tutelage over the democratic regime, the pro-secular critics claimed that it is used as a tool of intimidation and suppression of opposition against the JDP. While initially the trial created an opportunity to civilianize and democratize Turkey by showing that "finally the 'untouchables' of the 'deep state' no longer have impunity but can be brought before the court,"[178] lately skepticism has increased regarding the trial's credibility, intentions and scope. Many civil society organizers and journalists are detained based on evidence that appears to be suspect, and some of the evidence seems fabricated.[179] The long pre-trial detention periods after arrest effectively become jail times for the arrested individuals. While, as the government claims, the trial is run by the judiciary and not by the government, both the JDP and the main opposition party RPP do not hesitate to politicize the trial. In the social sphere, the trial became an asset in a zero-sum discursive war between mutually distrustful pro-secular and religious conservative actors.[180] Some JDP officials, ministers and the party's conservative supporters in media circles do not refrain from labeling any criticism directed toward the JDP as supporting military tutelage, or being a member of clandestine Ergenekon organization, in an attempt to stifle legitimate criticism toward the party.[181]

In the past three years the JDP's hegemonic tendencies increased, and Erdoğan's governing style as the unchallenged leader of his party became more intolerant, particularly in his approach to the media and freedom of expression. For instance, Erdoğan asked his supporters to boycott the Doğan media group, one of the biggest media conglomerates, after its newspapers published reports on the JDP's alleged ties to a religious charity organization that faced trial for fraud in Germany. Immediately after Erdoğan's call for boycott, the Doğan group was charged with a tax-evasion case and fined $2.5 billion, which was later dropped to $600 million.[182] The Doğan group had to sell some of its assets, including the daily *Milliyet*, in 2011 in order to meet the fine.[183]

Similarly, Erdoğan filed numerous high-profile defamation lawsuits against journalists critical of him, which became a significant source of intimidation for others.[184] Some ardent JDP critics were fired and lost their newspaper columns due to the government's active pressure on media outlets to discipline their personnel.[185] Erdoğan did not refrain from publicly condemning a popular soap opera on the ground that it distorted Ottoman history or even chastising the British magazine *The Economist* in his election rallies for a news report it published before the 2012 elections. Erdoğan's statements after his controversial visit to the Middle East Technical University reveals his narrow-minded approach toward the media's role in a democracy: "We have a problem with the media. It is their mission to announce good things to my people. This is what I want. But tomorrow you'll see headlines saying the prime minister slammed the media."[186] The utterance of these statements by a prime minister is anathema to the media's role to act as a check against the power of the government in any healthy democracy.

Erdoğan's intolerant tendencies are reminiscent of Adnan Menderes's rigid governing style that developed toward the end of his second term, and peaked in his third term, as prime minister. Similar to Menderes, Erdoğan embraces a majoritarian definition of democracy and equates his party's decisions—and he is the ultimate decision-maker due to lack of internal party democracy in the JDP—with the "will of the people" dismissing opposition concerns.

Due to the stalling of reform efforts for the EU, the JDP's recent back-pedaling on the Kurdish question and increasing intolerance toward legitimate opposition, the alliance between the liberals and the JDP has started to crumble of late. Even some of the party's ardent liberal supporters, who praised the JDP's efforts to break the military tutelage over Turkish democracy, accused Erdoğan of acting like the Vladimir Putin of Turkey.[187] As Nuray Mert states, the dismantling of military tutelage over civilian rule—which is steadily taking place under the JDP—is a necessary, but not a sufficient, condition for democratic consolidation in Turkey.[188] The weakness of the "pro-secular and 'effective and constructive' opposition parties, particularly in the style of [a] European social democratic party" also plays a role in the JDP's recent liberal-democratic deficit.[189] Currently, Turkish politics is stuck between secularist opposition actors who try to securitize politics by embracing a "rigid understanding of secularism and national sovereignty"[190] and an all-powerful JDP government which is increasingly unaccepting of a multi-vocal political and social sphere.

Conclusion

In the 1990s, the WP rallied a diverse array of groups who felt political, social or economic exclusion by constructing injustice frames around domestic and international events. NOM activists formulated empowerment and prognostic frames by successfully blending religious, cultural and social messages and promising a just future. Populations residing in the underdeveloped provinces in eastern and southeastern Anatolia, Kurds, the urban poor, and the rising Islamic bourgeoisie constituted a popular alliance that supported the WP. The elaborate network of party organizations that penetrated into many households, the door-to-door canvassing of the WP's women branches, outreach work among underprivileged youth through the National Youth Foundation, welfare provisions delivered to the urban poor through local party offices and municipalities, and the anti-corruption campaigns of the WP municipalities gave credence to the party's promise of creating a "just order." The activists' modest backgrounds also bolstered the credibility of this message.

While the WP's rise to power incorporated the demands of the periphery into the political system and challenged the premises of strict state-imposed secularism, the exclusivist rhetoric party leadership adopted toward its political opponents, the trivialization of opposition demands, and the party's embrace of the "strong state ethos" contributed to the poverty of the democratic political culture in Turkey. The WP's political success triggered a backlash from secularist actors leading to the polarization of the political spectrum along secular–religious lines, and ultimately leading to a democratic breakdown, known as the "soft coup" in 1998.

The birth of the JDP as an offshoot of the VP signified the emergence of post-Islamism in Turkey. The JDP's ideological change can best be explained by the rational assessment of party elites of their political constraints and structural factors, particularly the role of the Muslim bourgeoisie in pushing for a more integrative, neo-liberal ideology. However, despite the moderation of religiopolitical actors and perhaps in particular because of the JDP's electoral successes, the relations between secularist actors and the JDP remain one of uneasy coexistence at best. The opposition actors' rigid conceptualization of secularism and nationalism together with the JDP's increasing intolerance toward democratic opposition—thanks to the party's unchecked super-majority in the parliament—are anathema to democratic consolidation in Turkey.

Notes

1 Refahyol is a Turkish compound word used to describe the coalition between the WP and the True Path Party (TPP). It is composed of the words *Refah* (Welfare) and *Yol* (Path), taken from both parties' names.
2 Interview with Numan Kurtulmuş, 5 March 2007.
3 Ş. I. Özler, 'The Political Choices of Urban Squatters in National Elections', *Turkish Studies*, vol.1, no.2, 2000, 39–58.
4 N. Göle, 'Secularism and Islamism in Turkey: The Making of Elites and Counter-Elites', *Middle East Journal*, vol.51, no.1, 1997, 46–58.
5 J. S. Walsh, 'Gender Equality and Islamic Headscarves', Social Science Research Council blog, Immanent Frame, 2008. Online. Available athttp://blogs.ssrc.org/tif/2008/02/10/gender-equality-and-islamic-headscarves/; A. Kadıoğlu, 'The Headscarf and Citizenship in Turkey', Social Science Research Council blog, Immanent Frame, 2008. Online. Available at http://blogs.ssrc.org/tif/2008/04/23/the-headscarf-and-citizenship-in-turkey/.
6 N. Göle, 'The Civilizational, Spatial and Sexual Powers of the Secular', in J. Vanantwerpen and G. Calhoun (eds.), *Varieties of Secularism in a Secular Age*, Cambridge, MA: Harvard University Press, 2010, p. 258.
7 N. Göle, 'Authoritarian Secularism and Islamist Politics: The Case of Turkey', in A. R. Norton (ed.), *Civil Society in the Middle East*, vol.2, Leiden: E. J. Brill Publishing, 1996.

8 Z. Öniş, 'The Political Economy of Islamic Resurgence in Turkey: The Rise of Welfare Party in Perspective', *Third World Quarterly*, vol.18, no.4, 1997, 743–66.
9 H. Yavuz, *Islamic Political Identity in Turkey*, New York: Oxford University Press, 2003, p. 208
10 F. Çalmuk, 'Necmettin Erbakan', in Y. Aktay (ed.), *İslamcılık*, Istanbul: İletişim Yayınları, 2004, p. 566.
11 R. Çakır, 'Milli Görüş Hareketi', in Y. Aktay (ed.), *İslamcılık*, Istanbul: İletişim Yayınları, 2004, p. 568.
12 B. Yeşilada, 'Realignment and Party Adaptation: The Case of the Refah and Fazilet Parties', in S. Sayarı and Y. Esmer (eds.), *Politics, Parties, and Elections in Turkey*, Boulder: Lynne Rienner, 2002, p. 171.
13 Y. Esmer, 'At the Ballot Box: Determinants of Voting Behavior', in S. Sayarı and Y. Esmer (eds.), *Politics, Parties, and Elections in Turkey*, Boulder: Lynne Rienner, 2002, p. 111.
14 Interview with Bahri Zengin, 7 March 2007.
15 H. Yavuz, *Islamic Political Identity*, p. 223.
16 *Bahri Zengin'le On the Record Sistemin Anatomisi Üzerine Söyleşiler*, 2001, p. 37.
17 Interview with Şevket Kazan, 2 March 2007.
18 Interview with Bahri Zengin, 7 March 2007.
19 B. Zengin, *Özgürleşerek Birlikte Yaşamak*, Ankara: Birleşik Yayıncılık, 1995, pp. 87–93, cited in A. Yayla, 'Turkey's Leaders-Erbakan's Goals', *Middle East Quarterly*, vol.4, no.3, 1997, 21.
20 A. Bulaç, 'Medina Vesikası Hakkında Genel Bilgiler', *Birikim*, vol.38–9, 1992, 102–11.
21 A. Yayla, 'Turkey's Leaders', pp. 19–20.
22 Interview with Cevat Ayhan, 22 February 2007. Ayhan has been elected as an MP from the NSP, WP and VP. He is still an active member of the FP.
23 Interview with Şeref Malkoç, 22 February 2007.
24 For example, 'İşte Kurtuluş Reçetesi', *Milli Gazete*, 6 December 1995; 'RP Seçim Beyannamesi Özet 1', *Milli Gazete*, 8 December 1995.
25 B. Duran, 'Approaching the Kurdish Question via Adil Duzen: An Islamist Formula of the Welfare Party For Ethnic Coexistence', *Journal of Muslim Minority Affairs*, vol.18, no.1, 1998, 113.
26 *Milli Gazete*, 26 July 1994. B. Duran, 'Approaching the Kurdish Question', p. 114.
27 Huseyin Tanrıkulu, 'Anlamak', *Milli Gazete*, 15 December 1995.
28 'Refah'ın yumuşak karnı: Kürt sorunu', *Nokta*, 11–17 August 1996, pp.20–3.
29 N. Erbakan, *İslam-Batı Diyaloğu ve Geleceği*, Istanbul: Milsan Basın A.Ş., 2006, p. 11.
30 Ibid., pp. 20–3.
31 N. Erbakan, *Gayemiz Bütün Beşeriyetin Saadetidir*, Ankara: ESAM, 2005, pp. 19–21.
32 Ibid., p. 21.
33 Ibid., p. 27.
34 Ali Y. Sarıbay, *Türkiye'de Modernleşme Din ve Parti Politikası: Millî Selâmet Partisi Örnek Olayı*, Istanbul: Alan Yayınları, 1985, pp. 127–8; İ. Dağı, *Kimlik Söylem ve Siyaset Doğu-Batı Ayrımında Refah Partisi Geleneği*, İstanbul: İmge Yayınları, 1998, p. 24.
35 İ. Dağı, *Kimlik Söylem ve Siyaset*, pp. 24, 28.
36 ESAM, 'Opening Speech of Necmettin Erbakan at the Meeting of the Union of Muslim Communities on 28 May, 2006', in *Konuşmalar*, Ankara: ESAM, 2006.
37 İ. Dağı, *Kimlik Söylem ve Siyaset*, pp. 30–1.
38 *Saadet Partisi 2007 Seçim Beyannamesi*, p. 21. Online. Available at www.sp.org.tr/download.asp?subid=25.
39 İ. Dağı, *Kimlik Söylem ve Siyaset*, pp. 35–6.
40 'RP Seçim Beyannamesi Özet 1', *Milli Gazete*, 8 December 1995.
41 Interview with Cevat Ayhan, 22 February 2007.

42 Interview with Şeref Malkoç, 22 February 2007.
43 S. A. Ezer, 'Koydukları barajlarda boğulacaklar', *Tercüman*, 9 November 1987.
44 'Erbakan: aileyi mahvettiler', *Tercüman*, 18 October 1991.
45 *Adil Düzen* is a social and economic program that is based on a project prepared by university professors living a communal Islamic life in Akevler, Izmir. This project, which was prepared by Professor Arif Ersoy, Assistant Professor Süleyman Akdemir and Süleyman Karagülle, was adopted by Erbakan in 1985 and first used as the political program of the WP in the 1991 national elections.
46 Refah Partisi, *Adil Düzen:21 Soru 21 Cevap*, Ankara: Refah Partisi, 1994.
47 Z. Öniş, 'The Political Economy of Islamic Resurgence: The Rise of the Welfare Party in Perspective', *Third World Quarterly*, vol.18, no.4, 1997, 753.
48 Refah Partisi, *Adil Düzen*.
49 Hasan Aksay, 'Adil Düzen', *Milli Gazete*, 20 March 1994.
50 H. Gülalp, 'Globalization and Political Islam: The Social Bases of Turkey's Welfare Party', *International Journal of Middle Eastern Studies*, vol.33, 2001, 441.
51 Ibid., p. 439.
52 A. Yıldırım, *Muslim Democratic Parties: Economic Liberalization and Islamist Moderation in the Middle East*, unpublished Ph.D. dissertation, Ohio State University, 2010, p. 128.
53 Celil Çakır, 'İnancın Zaferi', *Milli Gazete*, 4 December 1995.
54 H. Gülalp, 'Globalization and Political Islam', p. 438.
55 'Rüşvet kapılarını kapattık', *Milli Gazete*, 11 March 1994.
56 *Milli Gazete*, 11 March 1994; 17 March 1994; 19 March 1994; 20 March 1994.
57 A. Alemdaroğlu, 'Refah Partisi'ni Yeniden Düşünmek: 1991 Reklam Kampanyasının Analizi' paper delivered at the Sixth National Social Science Congress of the *Turkish Social Science Association*, November 1999.
58 Ibid.
59 Interview with Mehmet Bekaroğlu, 6 March 2007.
60 'RP'de amaç her kesime hitap etmek', *Tercüman*, 13 October 1991.
61 For instance see 'Beyoğlu'nda genelev sokağından RP çıktı', *Nokta*, 9–15 January 1994, pp. 16–18.
62 Interview with Recep Tayyip Erdoğan, *Milli Gazete*, 8 March 1994.
63 M. Pamuk, *Yasaklı Umut Recep Tayyip Erdoğan*, Birey Yayıncılık, 2001, pp. 20–1.
64 Interview with Mehmet Bekaroğlu, 6 March 2007.
65 Interview with Ali Turan, 1 March 2007.
66 R. Çakır and F. Çalmuk, *Recep Tayyip Erdoğan: Bir Dönüşüm Öyküsü*, Istanbul: Metis Yayınları, 2001, p. 48.
67 Interview with Şeref Malkoç, 22 February 2007.
68 Şakir Bayramoğlu, 'Milli Görüşçü olmak bir sevdadır', *Milli Gazete*, 10 December 1995.
69 Ş. Kazan, *Refah Gerçeği*, vol.1, Ankara: Keşif Yayınları, 2006, p. 212; C. Tuğal, *Passive Revolution: Absorbing the Islamic Challenge to Capitalism*, Stanford: Stanford University Press, 2009, pp. 61–2.
70 Y. Arat, *Political Islam in Turkey and Women's Organizations*, Istanbul: Tesev Yayınları, 1999, pp. 36–7; Y. Arạt, *Rethinking Islam and Liberal Democracy Islamist Women in Turkish Politics*, Albany: State University of New York Press, 2005, pp. 62–4.
71 B. Yeşilada, 'Realignment and Party Adaptation', p. 173; Y. Akdoğan, *Siyasal İslam: Refah Partisi'nin Anatomisi*, Istanbul: Şehir Yayınları, 2000, p. 270.
72 Y. Akdoğan, *Siyasal İslam*, p. 270.
73 R. Çakır and F. Çalmuk, *Recep Tayyip Erdoğan*, p. 49.
74 B. Yeşilada, 'The Refah Party Phenomenon in Turkey', in B. Yeşilada (ed.), *Comparative Political Parties and Party Elites*, Ann Arbor: University of Michigan Press, 1999, p. 134.
75 Ibid., p. 134.

76 R. Çakır, *Ne Şeriat Ne Demokrasi: Refah Partisini Anlamak*, Istanbul: Metis Yayınları, 1994, p. 52.
77 R. Çakır and Fehmi Çalmuk, *Recep Tayyip Erdoğan*, p. 49.
78 Y. Akdoğan, *Siyasal İslam*, p. 270.
79 R. Çakır and Fehmi Çalmuk, *Recep Tayyip Erdoğan*, p. 49.
80 Interview with Ali Turan, 1 March 2007.
81 Interview with Muzaffer Doğan, Mayor of Bahçelievler from the WP, *Milli Gazete*, 17 March 1994; *Hizmetlerle Dolu 5 Altın Yıl: Sosyal, Kültürel ve Sportif Faaliyetler* (Booklet published by Gaziosmanpaşa Municipality, 1999), p. 32; R. Çakır, *Ne Şeriat Ne Demokrasi*, p. 185.
82 *Hizmetlerle Dolu 5 Altın Yıl*, pp. 26–31; … *ve 27 Mart 1994* (Booklet published by Gaziosmanpaşa Municipality, 1999), p. 15; Ş. Kazan, *Refah Gerçeği*, vol.1, p. 211; B. Eligür, *The Mobilization of Political Islam in Turkey*, New York: Cambridge University Press, 2010, pp. 172–3.
83 C. Tuğal, *Passive Revolution*, p. 60.
84 Ibid., p. 60; interview with Ali Turan, 1 March 2007.
85 H. Yavuz, *Islamic Political Identity*, 2003, p. 228.
86 T. Karapınar, 'Hoca'nın son kalesi sonunda kapatıldı', *Milliyet*, 4 June 2004.
87 J. White, *Islamist Mobilization in Turkey: A Study in Vernacular Politics*, Seattle: University of Washington Press, 2002, p. 234.
88 Y. Arat, *Rethinking Islam*, p. 43.
89 Ibid., p. 45.
90 Y. Arat, *Political Islam*, p. 23.
91 Y. Arat, *Rethinking Islam*, p. 45.
92 Y. Arat, *Political Islam*, pp. 25–6.
93 Interview with Numan Kurtulmuş, 5 March 2007.
94 J. White, *Islamist Mobilization*, p. 199.
95 Y. Arat, 'Feminism, Islamists, and Political Change in Turkey', *Political Psychology*, vol.19, no.1, 1999, 124.
96 N. Göle, 'Authoritarian Secularism'.
97 H. Gülalp, 'The Poverty of Democracy in Turkey: The Refah Party Episode', *New Perspectives on Turkey*, vol.21, 1999, 40.
98 Deep state is the name given to individuals and groups with connections to the state, who committed the dirty work of the state and fought against the perceived enemies of the state in extra-judicial ways.
99 H. Gülalp, 'The Poverty of Democracy', p. 49.
100 These remarks of Kazan were especially offensive to the Alevis in Turkey, although they were not directed at Alevis. The usage of "*Mum söndü*" implies that there are inappropriate sexual relations between females and males during Alevi ritual practice. This is a public myth that is invented by those who are hostile toward the religious practices of the Alevis, especially the lack of gender segregation in their places of worship.
101 For the civilianization manifesto of this group see B. Zengin, *Sivil Anayasa Yeni Bir Toplum Sözleşmesi Önerisi*, Ankara: Mart Matbaacılık, 2001.
102 'Refah Gelecek yüzler gülecek', *Milli Gazete*, 10 December 1995; … *ve 27 Mart 1994* (Booklet published by Gaziosmanpaşa Municipality, 1999), p. 16.
103 Interview with Mehmet Bekaroğlu, 7 March 2007.
104 For an argument on the similarity of statisms between the Kemalist and Islamist actors see Y. Navaro-Yashin, *Faces of the State: Secularism and Public Life in Turkey*, Princeton: Princeton University Press, 2002.
105 For example, T. Halman, 'İslami Çum-huriyet', *Milliyet*, 3 July 1996.
106 'Saygısızlar', *Milli Gazete*, 17 December 1995; A. Kardam and S. Tüzün, *Türkiye'de Siyasi Kutuplaşmalar ve Seçmen Davranışları*, Ankara: Veri Araştırma, 1998, p. 69.

107 'Erbakan: Refah yanardağ gibi', *Milli Gazete*, 13 December 1995.
108 Fehmi Koru, 'RP lideriyle Güneydoğuda', *Zaman*, 20 December 1995.
109 Ş. Alpay, 'RP iktidara yürüyor', *Milliyet*, 6 June 1996.
110 Oktay Ekşi, *Hürriyet*, 1 October 1996, quoted in Ş. Kazan, *Refah Gerçeği*, vol.3, Ankara: Keşif Yayınları, 2006, p. 94.
111 S. Çevikcan, 'Tam Bir Fiyasko', *Milliyet*, 7 October 1996; T. Akyol, 'Libya Faciası', *Milliyet*, 8 October 1996.
112 'Refah kongresinde 'İhvan' ağırlığı', *Milliyet*, 10 October 1996; 'Hamas Skandalı', *Milliyet*, 15 October 1996.
113 'Türkiye Geriye Gidemez', *Milliyet*, 1 February 1996; Ş. Kazan, *Refah Gerçeği*, vol.3, p. 95. The law stipulated that the skins of sacrifices made during the Festival of Sacrifices had to be donated to the Aeronautical Association. This law basically aimed to curb the potential financial gains of religious civil society organizations that might benefit from such donations.
114 'Bagheri'nin şok sözleri', *Milliyet*, 3 February 1997.
115 Some social scientists also refer to what occurred in the aftermath of the NSC meeting as "postmodern coup." It indicates that the intervention occurred behind the scenes and even without the recognition of some parts of Turkish population.
116 Ü. Cizre and M. Çınar, 'Turkey 2002: Kemalism, Islamism, and Politics in the Light of the February 28 Process', *South Atlantic Quarterly*, vol.102, 2003, 310.
117 G. D. Özer, *Psikolojik Bir İşkence Metodu Olarak İkna Odaları*, Istanbul: Beyan Yayınları, 2005.
118 Ü. Cizre and M. Çınar, 'Turkey 2002', p. 330.
119 'İşte Tartışılan Belgeler', *Milliyet*, 11 July 1997; A. Bayramoğlu, 'Belgelerle Ergenekon'un Ruhu Olarak 28 Şubat', *Yeni Şafak*, 16 April 2008.
120 H. Yavuz, *Islamic Political Identity*, p. 246.
121 S. Yağcıoğlu (ed.), *1990 Sonrası Laik-Antilaik Çatışmasında Farklı Söylemler: Disiplinler Arası Bir Yaklaşım*, İzmir: Dokuz Eylül Yayınları, 2002.
122 Ibid., pp. 171–4.
123 M. Quinn, 'From the Ashes of Virtue, a Promise of Light: The Transformation of Political Islam in Turkey', *Third World Quarterly*, vol.25, no.2, 2004, 346.
124 Fazilet Partisi, *Günışığında Türkiye, 18 Nisan 1999 Seçim Beyannamesi*, p. 45. Quoted in B. Eligür, *The Mobilization of Political Islam in Turkey*, p. 237.
125 A. T. Kuru, 'Globalization and Diversification of Islamic Movements: Three Turkish Cases', *Political Science Quarterly*, vol.120, no.2, 2005, 270.
126 Ibid., p. 270.
127 M. Kavakçı, 'Headscarf Heresy', *Foreign Policy*, vol.142, 2004, 66.
128 F. Atacan, 'Explaining Religious Politics at the Crossroad: AKP-SP', *Turkish Studies*, vol.6, no.2, 2005, 195–6.
129 A. Bayat, *Making Islam Democratic: Social Movements and the Post-Islamist Turn*, Stanford: Stanford University Press, 2007, p. 196.
130 A. Karakuş, 'Milli Görüş'ü terk ettiler: AKP geçmişini unutuyor', *Milliyet*, 17 May 2003.
131 M. Çınar, 'Turkey's Present *Ancien Regime* and Justice and Development Party', in M. Casier and J. Jongerden (eds.), *Nationalisms and Politics in Turkey: Political Islam, Kemalism and the Kurdish Issue*, London: Routledge, 2011, p. 22.
132 S. Tepe, 'A Pro-Islamic Party? Promises and Limits of Turkey's Justice and Development Party', in H. Yavuz (ed.), *The Emergence of a New Turkey Democracy and the AK Parti*, Salt Lake City: University of Utah Press, 2006, pp. 123–8; B. Duran, 'The Justice and Development Party's "New Politics": Steering toward Conservative Democracy, a Revised Islamic Agenda or Management of New Crises', in Ü. Cizre (ed.), *Secular and Islamic Politics in Turkey: The Making of the Justice and Development Party*, London: Routledge, 2008, p. 95.

133 'Geçmişte dini istismar yanlışına biz de düştük', *Milliyet*, 2 March 2004; S. Oğuz, 'Başbakanın sözleri açık yürekli itiraf!', *Milliyet*, 3 March 2004; M. Yılmaz, 'Başbakan'ın İslamcılık Özeleştirisi', *Milliyet*, 4 March 2004.
134 R. T. Erdoğan, 'Conservative Democracy and the Globalization of Freedom', speech delivered to American Enterprise Institute on 29 January 2004. Online. Available at www.aei.org/events/filter.all,eventID.735/transcript.asp.
135 Y. Akdoğan, *Muhafazakar Demokrasi*, Ankara: AKP Yayınları, 2003.
136 R.T. Erdoğan, 'Giriş', in Y. Akdoğan, *Muhafazakar Demokrasi*, Ankara: AKP Yayınları, 2003, p. 3.
137 Y. Akdoğan, *Muhafazakar Demokrasi*, pp. 4–7; W. Hale and E. Özbudun, *Islamism, Democracy and Liberalism in Turkey: The Case of AKP*, London: Routledge, 2011, p. 24.
138 Y. Akdoğan, 'The Meaning of Conservative Democratic Identity', in H. Yavuz (ed.), *The Emergence of a New Turkey: Democracy and the AK Parti*, Salt Lake City: University of Utah Press, 2006, p. 57.
139 R. T. Erdoğan, 'Conservative Democracy'.
140 W. Hale and E. Özbudun, *Islamism, Democracy*, p. 25; R. T. Erdoğan's opening speech to the Symposium on Conservatism and Democracy, held on 10–11 January 2004 in Istanbul. Online. Available at www.akparti.org.tr/site/haber/3173/muhafazakarlik-ve-demokrasi-sempozyumu-basbakan-erdogan-ak-parti-siyaseti-r.
141 S. Tepe, 'A Pro-Islamic Party', p. 122.
142 The FP returned to the culturalist, anti-Western, anti-EU foreign policy vision, after the brief period when the VP adopted a pro-EU stance.
143 For an example, see Erdoğan's opening speech to the Symposium on Conservatism and Democracy, held on 10–11 January 2004 in Istanbul. Available at www.akparti.org.tr/site/haber/3173/muhafazakarlik-ve-demokrasi-sempozyumu-basbakan-erdogan-ak-parti-siyaseti-r. Turkey also became the co-sponsor of the U.N. initiative "Alliance of Civilizations" with Spain, and Erdoğan served as the co-chair of this initiative in 2005–7 with the Spanish Prime Minister Zapatero.
144 B. Duran, 'The Justice and Development Party's "New Politics"', p. 83.
145 İ. Dağı, 'The Justice and Development Party: Identity, Politics, and Human Rights Discourse in the Search for Security and Legitimacy', in H. Yavuz (ed.), *The Emergence of a New Turkey: Democracy and the AK Parti*, Salt Lake City: University of Utah Press, 2006, pp. 98–101; J. Lagendijk, 'Turkey's Accession to the European Union and the Role of the Justice and Development Party', in A. Kuru and A. Stepan (eds.), *Democracy, Islam & Secularism in Turkey*, New York: Columbia University Press, 2011, pp. 167–8.
146 W. Hale and E. Özbudun, *Islamism, Democracy*, p. 62.
147 A. Davutoğlu, 'Turkish Foreign Policy Vision: An Assessment of 2007', *Insight Turkey*, vol.10, no.1, 2008, 78–9.
148 Ibid., p. 79.
149 M. B. Altunışık, 'The Possibilities and Limits of Turkey's Soft Power in the Middle East', *Insight Turkey*, vol.10, no.2, 2008, 50–2.
150 İ. Duman, 'What is Turkey's Position in the Greater Middle East Initiative', *World Bulletin*, 25 March 2011. Online. Available at www.worldbulletin.net/?aType=haber& ArticleID = 71637.
151 AK Parti, *AK Parti 2023 Siyasi Vizyonu: Siyaset, Toplum, Dünya*, 30 September 2012. Online. Available at www.akparti.org.tr/upload/documents/akparti2023siyasivizyonuturkce.pdf [accessed 28 December 2012].
152 'Egypt's Muslim Brotherhood Criticizes Erdogan's Call for a Secular State', *Al Arabiya News*, 14 September 2011.
153 Ibid.; J. Cole, 'Muslim Brotherhood Rebukes Erdogan for Advocacy of Secularism', *Informed Comment*, 15 September 2011. Online. Available at www.juancole.com/2011/09/muslim-brotherhood-rebukes-erdogan-for-advocacy-of-secularism.html.

154 The interviews were conducted before the closure case was initiated against the JDP in the Constitutional Court.
155 A. Bayat, 'What is Post-Islamism', *ISIM Review*, vol.16, 2005, 5.
156 Ibid., p. 5.
157 S. Tepe, 'A Pro-Islamic Party', p. 122.
158 J. White, 'The End of Islamism? Turkey's Muslimhood Model', in R. W. Hefner (ed.), *Remaking Muslim Politics: Pluralism, Contestation, Democratization*, Princeton: Princeton University Press, 2005, pp. 87–111.
159 Quoted in ibid., p. 87.
160 H. Yavuz, *Secularism and Muslim Democracy in Turkey*, New York: Cambridge University Press, 2009, pp. 5, 12.
161 İ. Dağı, 'The Justice and Development Party', p. 90.
162 H. Yavuz, *Secularism and Muslim Democracy*, p. 94.
163 Ibid., p. 95.
164 Ibid., p. 96.
165 M. Bekaroğlu, *"Adil Düzen"den "Dünya Gerçekleri"ne: Siyasetin Sonu*, Elips Kitap, 2007, pp. 223–4.
166 Ş. Gümüşçü and D. Sert, 'The Power of the Devout Bourgeoisie: The Case of the Justice and Development Party in Turkey', *Middle Eastern Studies*, vol.45, no.6, 2009, 964.
167 M. Şen, 'Transformation of Turkish Islamism and the Rise of the Justice and Development Party', in B. Yeşilada and B. Rubin (eds.), *Islamization of Turkey under the AKP Rule*, London: Routledge, 2011, p. 69; G. Bakırezer and Y. Demirer, 'AK Parti'nin Sosyal Siyaseti', in İ. Uzgel and B. Duru (eds.), *AKP Kitabı: Bir Dönüşümün Bilançosu*, Ankara: Phoenix Yayınevi, 2009, p. 164.
168 Ş. Gümüşçü and D. Sert, 'The Power of the Devout Bourgeoisie', p. 964.
169 J. Jang, *Taming Political Islamists by Islamist Capital: The Passions and Interests in Turkish Islamic Society*, unpublished Ph.D dissertation, University of Texas at Austin, 2005, cited in M. Şen, 'Transformation of Turkish Islamism', p. 71.
170 Y. Atasoy, *Turkey, Islamists and Democracy: Transition and Globalization in a Muslim State*, London: I. B. Tauris, 2005, p. 182.
171 'Çağlayan meydanı doldu taştı', *Sabah*, 29 April 2007.
172 This interpretation was first publicly proposed by Sabih Kanadoğlu, an ardent Kemalist former Public Prosecutor, in order to block Gül's election to the presidency. Later, the RPP adopted this proposal as a political strategy.
173 E. Özbudun, 'The Turkish Constitutional Court and Political Crisis', in A. Kuru and A. Stepan (eds.), *Democracy, Islam & Secularism in Turkey*, New York: Columbia University Press, 2011, p. 159.
174 The terms assertive and defensive secularism are coined by Ahmet Kuru. For example see A. Kuru, *Secularism and State Policies toward Religion: The United States, France, and Turkey*, New York: Cambridge University Press, 2009.
175 'Gerçek Laikliği Gerçekleştirdik', *TRT Haber*, 24 April 2011. Online. Available at www.trt.net.tr/haber/HaberDetay.aspx?HaberKodu=b38c8aca-8412-4808-9413-46d5c603d0b8 (accessed 31 May 2011).
176 There were six votes cast for the closure of the JDP and five against. Since the decision required a three-fifths majority, the JDP survived closure with one vote.
177 M. Somer, 'Moderate Islam and Secularist Opposition in Turkey: Implications for the World, Muslims and Secular Democracy', *Third World Quarterly*, vol.28, no.7, 2007, 1271–89; M. Somer, 'Democratization, Clashing Narratives, and "Twin Tolerations" between Islamic-Conservative and Pro-Secular Actors', in M. Casier and J. Jongerden (eds.), *Nationalisms and Politics in Turkey: Political Islam, Kemalism and the Kurdish Issue*, London: Routledge, 2011, pp. 28–47.
178 J. Lagendijk, 'Turkey's Accession', p. 180.

179 G. Jenkins, 'The Fading Masquerade: Ergenekon and the Politics of Justice in Turkey', *Turkey Analyst*, vol.4, no.7, 4 April 2011. Online. Available at www.silkroadstudies.org/new/inside/turkey/2011/110404B.html.
180 M. Somer, 'Democratization, Clashing Narratives', pp. 33–43.
181 Nuray Mert, 'Muhafazakar Cumhuriyet', *Milliyet*, 5 January 2012.
182 D. Filkins, 'The Deep State', *The New Yorker*, 12 March 2012.
183 N. Ognianova, *Turkey's Press Freedom Crisis: The Dark Days of Jailing Journalists and Criminalizing Dissent*, New York: United Book Press, 2012, p. 12.
184 Ibid., p. 6; O. K. Cengiz, 'Prime Minister's Lawsuits will Backfire', *Today's Zaman*, 1 January 2013.
185 E. Temelkuran, 'Turkish Journalists are Very Frightened—but We Must Fight this Intimidation', *Guardian*, 27 January 2012; C. Özdemir, 'Nuray Mert'in gazetede basılmayan yazısı anlatıyor', *Radikal*, 21 February 2012; N. Ognianova, *Turkey's Press Freedom Crisis*, pp. 11–12.
186 'Shame on Professors: The Turkish PM', *Hürriyet Daily News*, 22 December 2012.
187 A. Altan, 'Rahat Batıyor', *Taraf*, 14 March 2012.
188 N. Mert, 'Muammalı bir hesaplaşma devri', *Milliyet*, 12 January 2012.
189 M. Somer, 'Democratization, Clashing Narratives', p. 41.
190 Z. Öniş, 'Conservative Globalism at the Crossroads: The Justice and Development Party and the Thorny Path to Democratic Consolidation in Turkey', *Mediterranean Politics*, vol.14, no.1, 2009, 24–5.

8 Politics of Religious Schooling

Schools are spaces where various ideologies compete to shape a society's collective memory and future. Therefore, debates on schooling are never only about education, but ultimately about ideology. Educational institutions constitute arenas where competition for hegemony takes place between different social, political and religious actors.[1] Ongoing political debates regarding the status and funding of religious education in Israel and Turkey illustrate that religious schooling has emerged as a highly contested, emotional and polarizing issue between the religious and secular actors in both countries.

Building on these debates, in this chapter I demonstrate how *Ma'ayan* schools in Israel and *Imam Hatip* schools in Turkey have become vehicles for political mobilization for religious parties over the past three decades. A focus on state-funded religious schools provides leverage to illustrate the interaction between political opportunity structures, meaning-making and networks, as schools constitute institutions where micro-practices of identity formation and macro political forces interact. After a brief introduction to the history of religious education, the comparative discussion of religious schooling in the chapter will mirror the theoretical framework that underlines the book.

Foundations of Educational Pluralism in Israel

The existence of separate educational streams for secular Zionists, modern Orthodox and ultra-Orthodox Jews goes back to the *Yishuv* period in Palestine, even before the formation of the British Mandate. The establishment of the British Mandate in 1920 reinforced the operation of separate educational facilities. In 1926, the Mandate administration began partly funding Jewish education by giving money to a National Board (*Va'ad Leumi*),[2] which transferred funds to the educational institutions of the General Zionists, Labor Zionists and Religious Zionists. These three streams, which were organically tied to the political party of each group, were administered through the cooperation of National Board officials, British administrators and trend leaders.[3] The British did not intervene in education pedagogically, but organizationally.[4] The ultra-Orthodox Agudah schools, on the other hand, did not accept any funds from the National Board in order to retain full autonomy over their education system. In 1947, the Agudah sought funding and recognition for its schools from the National Board for the first time, when the ultra-Orthodox community lost most of its financial funds from abroad because of the Holocaust. This demand was rejected, because the ultra-Orthodox party was not ready to give enough concessions to a central secular authority. However one year later, at the height of the Independence War, the Israeli government declared the Agudah network a recognized stream placing hardly any limitations on its autonomy.[5]

During the first five years of the establishment of the Israeli state, the ideological autonomy of the four separate educational streams and their organic connection to political parties continued. In this period, fierce competition ensued between the different streams for the recruitment and socialization of Sephardi immigrants' children. Most of these Middle Eastern Jews were unaware of the ideological differences between the political camps and were open to manipulation by these parties. The political camps did not miss the opportunity to "use means of pressure and enticements to attract immigrant children to their schools and that diverged from the rules of fair, open competition as set forth during the *Yishuv* period."[6] The concentration of the newly arriving immigrants in camps and *ma'abarot* (temporary settlements) made the Oriental Jews easier targets for these coercive strategies, especially for the governing Mapai. Mapai was accused by the religious parties of misleading the new immigrants through use of heavy anti-religious propaganda in the *ma'abarot*. The conflict came to a peak when Mapai instituted a religious sub-trend within the socialist educational stream,[7] and started to provide education to the children of religious immigrants. This issue became so critical that it led to a coalition crisis and finally to the resignation of the incumbent government in 1951. In order to solve this problem, in 1953, the new government passed the State Education Law, which stripped the different educational streams of their political affiliations and placed them under the jurisdiction of the state:

> State education is defined as education provided by the state on the basis of the curriculum approved by the Minister of Education, without attachment to a party, communal body, or other non-government organization, and is under the supervision of the Minister of Education … The State education system consists of two trends: "State education," and "State-religious education."[8]

According to this new legal arrangement, the General Zionist and socialist educational streams were merged into a *secular state education* system, while the Religious-Zionist educational stream was transformed into a *state religious education* system. While both of these newly created educational streams became public systems and were officially part of the Education Ministry, the ultra-Orthodox Agudah stream did not become official and remained a private system.

Ma'ayan Hahinuch Hatorani (The Wellspring of Torah Education): An Education Network for Ultra-Orthodox Sephardim in Israel

As discussed in detail in Chapter 3, Sephardim who attended one of the three main streams faced discrimination or marginalization in one way or another. As a response, Shas established ultra-Orthodox Sephardi educational institutions in 1986. These schools were initially built in an ad hoc manner and operated under the umbrella of Shas's civil society organization, *El Hama'ayan*. The schools became a full-fledged, autonomous education network and received the name *Ma'ayan Hahinuch Hatorani* in 1988.

Ma'ayan schools quickly succeeded in attracting a significant number of religious, traditional and non-religious Sephardi students and became the jewel of the Shas movement. Thanks to Shas's political leverage in coalition governments, the network started to receive ad hoc state funding in 1988, and in 1992 funding for the network was institutionalized. This was possible primarily due to a provision in the 1953 Law of Education that gave the Education Minister the authority to recognize unofficial educational institutions—that is schools outside of the secular state and state religious educational streams—if these institutions adopted 75 percent of a basic curriculum (*liba*),[9] and the training of their staff conformed to that in the official schools. The minister of education could decide to grant a certain amount of funding to these "*unofficial recognized*" institutions based on how much of the basic curriculum the schools adopted. The overwhelming majority of Shas schools belong to the "*unofficial recognized*" category eligible for full state funding, unlike the "*non-recognized*" or "*exempt*" institutions, which provide education that is not recognized by the State of Israel.

The decision for allocation of funding to "*unofficial recognized*" schools was made on an administrative level and lacked any clear criteria.[10] The administrative nature of this funding decision makes it vulnerable to political pressure, and Shas has exploited this to secure more funding for its schools. Accordingly, the funds Shas received from the Education Ministry increased from 9.8 million NIS in 1989 to 331 million NIS in 1998.[11] In 1997, *Ma'ayan* schools received more funding per pupil than any educational network in Israel.[12] In 1993–2000, the number of students in *Ma'ayan* elementary schools increased from 4,400 to 16,642, the number of classes increased from 253 to 846, and the number of teachers increased from 300 to 2,000.[13] In 2006, the network operated 111 elementary schools and 233 kindergartens with 20,765 and 9,753 pupils respectively.[14] In addition, *Ma'ayan Hahinuch Hatorani* operates a limited number of junior high schools, and there are ultra-Orthodox Sephardi senior high schools that are ideologically connected with *Ma'ayan*, but not under its direct supervision.[15]

This proliferation and overfunding of *Ma'ayan* schools was closely linked to Shas's inclusion in coalition governments and the party's increasing electoral share. Shas leaders signaled very clearly that they were willing to adopt a flexible stance on national issues, such as the peace process, in order to

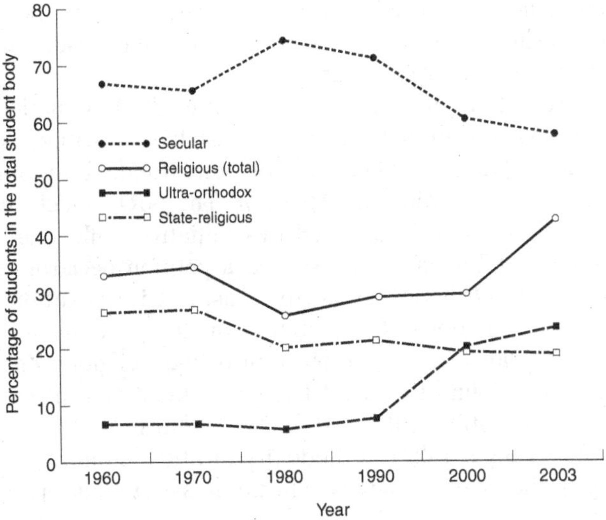

Figure 8.1 Percentage of students in different primary educational streams in Israel (1960–2003).
Source: *Statistical Abstract of Israel*, 2003, Central Bureau of Statistics

become a suitable coalition partner for both the Labor and the Likud. As a result, Shas was offered a place in most governing coalitions, and received important ministerial positions, including positions in the Education Ministry (see Chapter 4). In the Education Ministry, Shas single-mindedly pursued a particularistic agenda of channeling state resources to its educational network.

The practice of allocating state funding to autonomous ultra-Orthodox education did not start with the *Ma'ayan* schools, however. Since 1953 the Agudah channeled state resources to its own Independent Education network. Yet the institutionalization of *Ma'ayan Hahinuch Hatorani* drew more attention and criticism from other political actors, especially those in the Religious Zionist and secular camps, because, the network targeted not only ultra-Orthodox children, but also traditional and non-religious children. As a result, the spread of *Ma'ayan* schools considerably increased the share of pupils in ultra-Orthodox schools among the overall student body in Israel's elementary schools (see Figure 8.1).

Some of the political criticisms voiced against the *Ma'ayan* schools reveal the perceived threat felt by Religious Zionist parties. For instance, relations between the NRP and Shas turned sour during the budget debate in 1991 on special allocations for the *Ma'ayan* network, when both parties were part of Yitzhak Shamir's coalition government.[16] The NRP fiercely opposed special allocations to the *Ma'ayan* network, although it did not object to allocations to Agudah's school network.[17] The main concern of the NRP was *Ma'ayan*'s target audience, which was more expansive than Agudah's and intersected with the state-religious network's target population.[18] This political conflict over special allocations to *Ma'ayan* schools continued for several weeks, until the NRP had to give in to Shas's demands.[19]

In the next coalition government, formed after the 1992 national elections, an ultra-Orthodox education authority was established within the Education Ministry to institutionalize allocation of state funding to different ultra-Orthodox networks, including the *Ma'ayan*. The NRP, which remained outside of the coalition, fiercely opposed this initiative. Influential NRP MKs, Shaul Yahalom and Yitzhak Levy, started a petition declaring that the formation of the ultra-Orthodox authority constituted a violation of the 1953 Education Law.[20] Yahalom's fierce attacks on the government decisions on school funding is indicative of the reaction of the Religious Zionist community toward losing ground to Shas: "The government and the education minister were, and are still, willing to seriously harm Religious Zionism by establishing the *Haredi* [ultra-Orthodox] education authority, which would have damaged the State-Religious education system and religious-Zionist culture."[21]

Religious Zionists were not the only group concerned about the steep growth of the *Ma'ayan*. Secularist parties, such as Shinui and Meretz, often criticized the concessions the state authorities gave to the *Ma'ayan*. In 1999, a major crisis broke out within Ehud Barak's governing coalition, when the *Ma'ayan* network declared bankruptcy and demanded that the government pay off its debt. Yosi Sarrid, the education minister from Meretz, resisted this demand for a long time despite the threat of resignation by 17 Shas MKs from the coalition government if their demand was not met. Due to this conflict over the financial allocations to the *Ma'ayan* schools, the 2000 budget remained in limbo for six weeks.[22] The parties then reached a compromise deal, requiring the treasury to cover most of *Ma'ayan*'s debt. In return, Shas agreed that the *Ma'ayan* schools would adopt a financial restructuring plan, devote more time to secular and technical subjects, and abide with specific teacher–student ratios.[23]

This compromise deal did not end the contentious relations between Meretz and Shas over school funding. When the *Ma'ayan* management evaded its obligations specified in the deal, relations between the two political parties deteriorated, culminating in a showdown right before the Camp David II peace talks. All ten of the MKs from Meretz, including the Education Minister Sarid, were forced to resign from the coalition on 24 June 2000, so that the 17 member Shas would stay in the government. As a result of this resignation, Shas secured $6 million additional government funding for its schools and the Shasnik deputy Education Minister Meshulam Nahari was given sole oversight over *Ma'ayan Hahinuch Hatorani*'s internal dealings.[24] This episode is a revealing example of how Shas single-mindedly pursues the allocation of state resources for its education network by its pragmatic stance on national security issues. Barak could dispense with Meretz, because he could depend on Meretz's support for any peace settlement even from outside the government, while Shas used its support for any possible peace agreement as a bargaining chip for more funding for its schools.

Ma'ayan Schools and Social Provisions

While Shas's access to the material resources of the state played an important role in the sustenance and proliferation of the *Ma'ayan* schools, another major reason for the success of the network was its ability to attract low-income parents to its schools irrespective of their religiosity. The schools, mainly located in low-opportunity urban neighborhoods and development towns, provide economic incentives, such as smaller classes, free hot lunches and subsidized transportation for pupils. Furthermore, the school day is longer compared to the secular-state and state-religious schools. The pupils study until 4 p.m. in the *Ma'ayan* schools, while in the secular-state schools the school day usually finishes at 1 p.m. The extra hours the *Ma'ayan* schools provide also prompted action by the Ministry of Education, which adopted a pilot initiative of extending school hours in public education in some of the peripheral cities. For example, the state-religious schools in Beit Shemesh added two hours to each school day by extending the school closing hour from 1:30 p.m. to 3:30 p.m., in order to be more competitive with the *Ma'ayan* schools in the city.[25] More and more working-secular parents, living in low-opportunity neighborhoods, are sending their children to the kindergartens operated by *Ma'ayan Hahinuch Hatorani* for the lack of a better option.

A report published by the Ne'eman committee in 1999 found that the average number of pupils in the *Ma'ayan* institutions is smaller than the average number of pupils in the secular-state and state-religious schools (125 compared to 387). Moreover, the *Ma'ayan* schools had a smaller average class size (20 compared to 29) and a smaller number of pupils per teacher (13 compared to 19).[26] Another report published in 2004 by the Central Bureau of Statistics revealed that the ultra-Orthodox schools, including those that belong to the *Ma'ayan* network, receive significantly more funding than the state and state-religious schools per pupil.[27]

One of the main reasons for this discrepancy in funding is Shas's ability to evade state supervision over its educational network through its leverage in the Education Ministry. The lack of state supervision gives the *Ma'ayan* administration the flexibility to allocate state funding to different needs. For instance, the teachers in the state and state-religious schools receive their salaries directly from the state, while in the *Ma'ayan* schools the teachers are paid by the principals.[28] This arrangement gives the *Ma'ayan Hahinuch Hatorani* the opportunity to pay smaller salaries to its teachers and divert the remaining funds to other services, such as providing longer hours and free meals. The teachers in the *Ma'ayan* network are likely to accept the smaller salaries, because they are usually under-qualified, have a high level of ideological commitment to the Shas movement, and are therefore willing to work for less. For example, during the 1999 near bankruptcy of the *Ma'ayan* network, the teachers continued to work without pay for months.

Cultural Empowerment through *Ma'ayan* Schools: Creation and Circulation of Frames

While social provisions provided by *Ma'ayan Hahinuch Hatorani* attracted socioeconomically disadvantaged Sephardim to the network's schools and turned Shas into a new power broker between the poor Sephardim and the state, framing processes in and around the schools helped the party to foster a new Sephardi identity among pupils and parents.

As discussed in Chapter 4, one of the major motifs that Shas emphasizes to address the historic ethnic grievances of Sephardim is "injustice." This sense of injustice is also injected into debates on *Ma'ayan* schools to deepen the feeling of ethnic persecution. During governmental debates over school funding, Shas activists often claim that their schools lack funds because of the secular establishment's bias against their schools—although this is generally not accurate. A weekly Torah newsletter published by Shas's network makes this point rather well:

> One unanswerable question arises from the *parashah* [Torah portion] of the Egyptian exile, the bondage, the plagues, and Pharaoh's stubbornness and indecisiveness: why, on what basis? … [Pharoah] slaughtered three hundred children each day in order to bathe in a tub full of their blood. … Pharaoh had no need to justify his actions. His decision to do something was enough.
>
> Such governmental procedures remind us so much of different times and different rulers. We have the good fortune of living in a country of equality, where there exists a law of mandatory, free education. The ultra-Orthodox sector makes up around 13% of the Israeli population, but its portion of the budget—around 3%! Why? Because this is how it is! Is there any wonder that the general education budget is balanced, while the Torah educational network is accumulating a heavy deficit? Yet, when a request is submitted to cover the expenses, we are considered greedy … Eight hundred psychologists are set aside for general education. Good—these schools suffer from violence, drugs and crime. But for the "*Ma'ayan Hahinuch*" schools only part-time workers were provided … This is outright discrimination, but somehow it is always the religious who are greedy and draining resources.[29]

As the interpretation of the weekly Torah portion above shows, Shas rabbis skillfully present the issue of school funding as a matter of persecution at the hands of the government by drawing a parallel between the Egyptian tyrant, Pharoah's actions and the Israeli government's budget decisions.

However, the main strength of the frames created in and around Ma'ayan schools is not the sense of victimization they evoke, but the sense of pride they instill both in students and in parents. Unlike Ashkenazi ultra-Orthodox networks, *Ma'ayan* schools include specific Sephardi traditions in the curriculum, and therefore teach their pupils to be proud of their Sephardi heritage in contrast with the Sephardi pupils' loss of self-respect in other educational streams. A Shas MK emphasizes the contrast between *Ma'ayan* schools and the others: "Our public wants to learn specifically more about traditional Judaism. They want to understand specific traditions."[30] In this way, *Ma'ayan* schools play a central role in bringing Ovadia Yosef's legal-political project to the masses by teaching specific Sephardi values, such as family cohesion, respect for the father and the rabbi, and respect for Jewish law in accordance with Sephardi traditions.

Ma'ayan activists go from door to door to recruit students for their school network by maintaining that the main value they teach to the pupils is "respect for parents." Sometimes, *Ma'ayan* officials sign agreements with non-religious parents to ensure appropriate behavior at home, such as not smoking on Sabbath or cursing.[31] Although these agreements are scarcely enforced, they are shown as indicators of the schools' high propriety standards. Based on these practices, Shas activists depict *Ma'ayan* schools as safe havens from the corrupting influences of secular society. As one activist claims:

> Secular schools are already in bankruptcy, all the violence going on there and all the rapes. *Ma'ayan*'s religious education with all its values is a different world, a different league ... A boy who comes out of our education system comes out as a complex of things, where he is ready to begin his Jewish life.[32]

These schools are portrayed as institutions that protect pupils from secularization and teach them how to be good Jews in order to cope with problems in the larger society. To their credit, *Ma'ayan Hahinuch Hatorani* deliberately opens institutions in poverty stricken parts of Israel, where crime and drug use are rampant. These institutions—together with the clubs of *El Hama'ayan*—cater to disadvantaged Mizrahi children who could be otherwise drawn to the streets.

Lastly, *Ma'ayan* activists use frames which depict religious education taught in their schools as a catalyst for positive societal change. Activists are proud that their education system emphasizes respect for figures of religious authority:

> When the lecturer goes into the classroom, all the students are quiet and stand up for the teacher out of respect. They have to stand up when he goes out. It is a small thing, but it has a big impact. It is very symbolic. Does this happen in a secular school? ... [Here] the student learns how to respect the rabbis and this also influences the home, it continues outside.[33]

According to this frame, *Ma'ayan* pupils do not simply adopt appropriate behavioral traits in their schools but also become agents of societal change. The Shas activists that I interviewed told various stories about how children who attend elementary schools, kindergartens or even child care centers, play a role in bringing their parents close to religion. As one Shas activist explains:

> About 40 years ago when Sephardim came to Israel, their religious commitments weakened … Through *Ma'ayan Hahinuch Hatorani*, Shas returned many people back to the [Sephardi] heritage … There are thousands of students [attending to *Ma'ayan* schools] in development towns. In Ber Sheva, in Ofakim, in Netivot, in Sderot, city by city these educational institutions increased in number, and people strengthened [in their religious commitment], and returned to religion, and slowly and slowly that amounted to a revolution.[34]

Myth and truth are mixed in these embellished stories of Shas activists to promote Shas's sociopolitical agenda. However, it is important to understand how this type of prognostic frames (narratives that offer a solution) completes injustice frames (narratives that identify victims) and therefore depicts *Ma'ayan* education as a means of return to Judaism. According to this grand-narrative, Sephardi parents who lost their traditional roots due to forced secularization are returning to their heritage thanks to their children who are receiving a proper religious education in the *Ma'ayan* schools. This change at home is then depicted as the first step in the Judaization of Israeli society.

Social networks formed around the Ma'ayan schools play a critical role in extending these frames to further constituents and become a source of political support. Schiffman (2005) found that the vote share of Shas is significantly higher in the districts with a *Ma'ayan* school than the party's national vote share.[35] However, the vote share of Shas cannot solely be explained by the political support of parents, because it far exceeds the number of parents whose children study in *Ma'ayan* schools. According to Schiffman, the greater political support for Shas can be explained by the presence of secondary webs that are formed around these schools:

> Non-ultra-orthodox Jews who support the existence of *Ma'ayan Hahinuch Hatorani* without partaking of its services constitute a larger group than the few thousand non-ultra-orthodox parents who enroll their children in schools in the network. Those with secondary ties to the network include friends and neighbors of families with enrolled children, as well as school bus drivers, custodians, secretaries, and shopkeepers near schools who do business with parents of enrolled children.[36]

Through these secondary beneficiaries, the provisions provided by the *Ma'ayan* schools extend to others living in school neighborhoods. A Shas activist had a similar observation:

> Maintaining schools requires teachers, janitors, clients, and all the activities surrounding it. Kindergarten teachers, assistants, maintenance and repair people. It employs a large number of people that enter the circle. And the circle expands constantly.[37]

These expanding circles are similar to what the SMT calls mobilizing structures or social networks. These social networks not only offer material benefits but also communicate the mobilizing frames constructed around *Ma'ayan* education to larger groups. For instance, *Ma'ayan* kindergartens are used in the evenings as community meeting points, where people "gather and exchange information about community life."[38] Other civil society organizations affiliated with Shas also extend these messages to Sephardim who participate in their extra-curricular activities. Through these networks, many Sephardim hear Shas's ethno-religious message, which resonates with their sociocultural grievances.

Ma'ayan Education and Social Mobility

While these frames are used by Shas activists to appeal to constituents, there are significant misgivings about the strength and quality of education provided in *Ma'ayan* schools. That many of the Shas MKs prefer to send their children to more prestigious Ashkenazi ultra-Orthodox schools rather than to their own educational network raises doubts about the quality of education provided in *Ma'ayan* schools.[39] As an ex-bureaucrat in state religious education candidly claimed graduates from *Ma'ayan*'s elementary schools who continue to state-religious high schools have much lower basic skills in mathematics, reading, comprehension or writing compared to their peers who graduate from state-religious schools.[40]

In addition to doubts about the quality of education in *Ma'ayan* schools, the schools are also seen as fostering a culture of dependency among the Shas constituents, especially among secular and traditional Sephardim, who would not otherwise receive an ultra-Orthodox education. While most *Ma'ayan* schools have to teach a minimum number of secular subjects, such as mathematics, English or social studies as part of the basic curriculum, Education Ministry officials admit that the supervision of *Ma'ayan* schools over their administration of the basic curriculum is far from reliable.[41] Because of the primacy of the religious curriculum and the paucity of secular subjects in the curriculum, the students do not become active participants in the workforce. The schools do not train the students for white-collar jobs other than teaching or administrative positions in the *Ma'ayan Hahinuch Hatorani* network.[42] Therefore most graduates do not continue to college, which constitutes a significant impediment to upward mobility.

However, recently some initiatives have been taken to integrate graduates into the mainstream workforce thanks to the efforts of Adina Bar-Shalom—the eldest daughter of Ovadia Yosef—who opened a women's college in 2001.

The education of girls in the Shas movement is different from that of boys, because Torah study is not encouraged for girls.[43] Girls' high schools include more secular subjects, and women become the breadwinners in ultra-Orthodox Sephardi families, where the men are committed to life-long Torah study and earn nothing other than a small stipend. According to the Central Bureau of Statistics, 55 percent of ultra-Orthodox women worked outside the home in 2008.[44] However, while a very small portion of women who graduate from religious high schools obtain teaching or administrative positions in the *Ma'ayan* network, most have to settle for low-paid or part-time jobs.[45]

Aware of this socioeconomic reality and the aspirations of some Shas women, Bar-Shalom opened a Haredi College for Women in 2001 in Jerusalem. The college later also opened its doors to ultra-Orthodox men, and currently offers 11 degree programs for women and four degree programs for men.[46] Last year, the college had 820 female and 400 male students.[47] The nature of the degree programs offered by the college is closely monitored by Shas's Council of Torah Sages, and strict gender separation is enforced within the school.[48] The Shas activists I interviewed were very proud of running a university that provides degrees in communications, psychology and computer studies and is recognized by the Education Ministry. Adina Bar-Shalom, who still serves as the university's president, explains the socioeconomic significance of this effort in plain terms:

> The requirement in the workplace today is an academic education. You can't earn a decent salary without it. So I decided that my task was to provide such a high-level academic education, but to create it within a strict haredi environment so that our young women and men could feel at ease while acquiring such an education.[49]

While the size of this ultra-Orthodox university is relatively modest, it surely provides a significant path for economic self-sufficiency for some ultra-Orthodox Sephardim. Whether this limited attempt to integrate the Shas constituency into the mainstream workforce would widen and have transformative effects on the Sephardi ultra-Orthodox community remains to be seen. The college could also potentially lead to social and political empowerment of ultra-Orthodox Sephardi women by providing access to university education.

The Origins of the *Imam Hatip* Schools in Turkey

In contrast to Israel, there was no pluralism in the education system of Turkey during the state formation period. The Law on Unification of Education, passed on 3 March 1924, abolished the Ottoman pluralism in education and established total state control over the new unified education system. Just after the passage of this law, all the *madrasas* (religious schools) were shut down. The implementation of the Law on Unification of Education meant that all the students of the new Republic would be educated according to the new secularist, modernist worldview. The Republican elites were keen to use education as a political tool through which they could mold the younger generations into the future citizens of modern Turkey.

Nevertheless, Article 4 of the Law on the Unification of Education stipulated that vocational schools for the training of religious functionaries needed to be opened under the Ministry of Education. Subsequently, in 1924, the state opened 29 new vocational schools under the title "*Imam Hatip* schools" (preacher and prayer leader schools) in order to train religious functionaries. The number of *Imam Hatip* schools, which provided a four-year education similar to other middle schools, decreased in the 1920s due to a lack of demand, and the last two schools were closed down in 1930.

In 1947, one year after the introduction of the multiparty system, the RPP introduced some reforms in the area of religious education and reopened these schools in the form of "*Imam Hatip* programs." These new programs provided ten months of education and a certificate to middle-school graduates who wanted to become religious functionaries.[50] After the transition to multiparty politics, under the DP governments (1950–60) the *Imam Hatip* programs were transformed into full-fledged vocational high schools, which provided students with seven years of education. Between 1951 and 1972, the student body of these state-based religious high schools increased. Despite this increase, the number of *Imam Hatip* students as a percentage of the entire student body was low and never exceeded 4 percent.

Politicization of Religious Education

The NSP's coalition partnerships in the latter half of the 1970s, first with Ecevit's RPP and then twice with Demirel's JP, was an important turning-point for state religious education in Turkey. In this period, both the number and status of *Imam Hatip* schools changed significantly. During the ten months of the RPP-NSP government, 29 new schools were opened bringing the total number of *Imam Hatip* schools to 101. Because of the NSP's key role in the Nationalist Front governments in the second half of the 1970s, the opening of new *Imam Hatip* schools speeded up, and in 1980, *Imam Hatip* school students constituted over 9 percent of all middle and high school students.

In addition to the quantitative changes in the number of students, the NSP succeeded in changing the public's perception of these state religious schools. The NSP never hid its interest in the *Imam Hatip* schools and saw them as a tool, through which it could realize its self-declared goal of spiritual development (*manevi kalkınma*) for Turkey. In the coalition agreement of 1975, NSP attributed to *Imam Hatip* graduates new roles. According to this agreement:

> the morality lessons in the elementary and high schools will be foremost taught according to their philosophy by the graduates of the divinity faculty, Institute of Islamic Higher Education or *Imam Hatip* schools; the

> place of religious functionaries in [the Turkish] society will be recognized by utilizing them in social and economic development.

Many Islamist activists I interviewed claimed that religious education was a significant source of Turkey's moral transformation:

> First of all, we think that the moral and spiritual fabric [of this nation] needs to be strengthened. This can be achieved through education. To state it more clearly, it can be achieved through religious education, moral education. A shared destiny, spiritual fabric, morals, respect for one another's rights … these are at the basis of the elements that keep a nation together. This is how a sound social fabric and family structure are formed; this is how people with strong moral and spiritual values, a strong society, a strong family, comes into being … For that reason, we call all of these [elements] spiritual development.[51]

In its political propaganda, NSP activists portrayed graduates from the *Imam Hatip* schools as "a new and moral generation,"[52] which would transform Turkey. By depicting the *Imam Hatip* schools as the source of spiritual awakening, Erbakan's NSP politicized the issue of religious education in Turkey in the late 1970s. Many pious families started to perceive the *Imam Hatip* schools as an educational alternative to the secular schools, rather than as vocational institutions. During the latter half of the 1970s, which was a period of extreme political volatility in Turkey, the campuses of these schools became places where the youth organizations of different political parties struggled for hegemony. The main competitors were *Ülkücüler*, the youth organization of the ultranationalist Nationalist Action Party (NAP) and the *Akıncılar*, the youth organization of the NSP. It was the latter which most frequently held control over the campuses of the *Imam Hatip* schools.[53]

In the 1980s, during the MP governments, the number of religious schools did not considerably increase—partly because of the remaining military influence in politics—although the quality and capacity of these schools improved significantly. Rather than opening new schools, education ministers opened new buildings as annex campuses to already existing high schools. When the MP assumed power in 1983, 207,006 students attended *Imam Hatip* high schools, while in the 1990–91 academic year, their number had increased to 309,553.[54] Moreover, the MP established "Anatolian *Imam-Hatip*" high schools, which provided a more elite education including instruction in a foreign language. Some, such as the Kartal Anatolian *Imam Hatip* school, became the school of choice for the children of the Islamic bourgeoisie.[55]

In the 1990s, political discussion around these schools became more heated with the increasing political fortunes of the WP. The secularist parties and social actors constantly accused the *Imam Hatip* schools of being the Islamists' political "backyard" or even the Trojan horse within the Turkish state. After the military ousted Erbakan's coalition government in 1997 with a soft

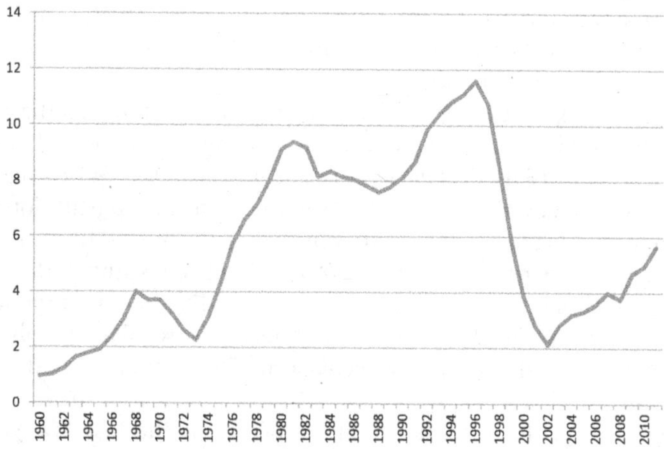

Figure 8.2 Number of students in *Imam Hatip* schools as percentage of all students in secondary education (1960–2011). Calculated by the author.
Sources: National Education Statistics, 2000–2001 through 2011–2012, Education Ministry; National Statistics Indicators 1923–2005, Turkish Statistical Institute; A. Ünsür, *Imam-Hatip Liseleri Kuruluşundan Günümüze*, Istanbul: Ensar Neşriyat, 2005

coup, it demanded that the new government, now led by Mesut Yılmaz, implement the 28 February Decisions, which included the closing of the middle-school sections of the *Imam Hatip* schools and a change in the status of vocational schools in the university entrance examination (see Chapter 7 for more information). This latter provision, which specifically targeted the *Imam Hatip* schools, practically prevented all *Imam Hatip* graduates from entering any department other than the Divinity Faculty in higher education. After 1998, the middle-school sections of the *Imam Hatip* schools were closed down and the number of students who attended the remaining high-school sections plummeted due to the difficulties imposed on graduates in the university entrance examinations (see Figure 8.2).

Imam Hatip students and graduates became disgruntled with these restrictions. The JDP governments have been more sympathetic to the concerns of the *Imam Hatip* community. Considering that many JDP politicians are themselves *Imam Hatip* graduates, this should not come as a surprise. According to the party program of the JDP, "the graduates of all high schools and equivalent institutions would be accorded equality in the university entrance examinations."[56] This stipulation meant getting rid of the restrictions placed on *Imam Hatip* schools by the 28 February Decisions and granting their graduates equal opportunities with secular schools in university entrance examination.

The JDP acted on its commitment and passed a bill that would ease *Imam Hatip* graduates' entry into the university department of their choice on 13 May 2004. However, the bill was vetoed by Turkey's former president, Ahmet

Necdet Sezer, on the basis that it violated the principle of secularism.[57] Afterwards, Prime Minister Erdoğan, who himself is an *Imam Hatip* graduate, said that they were shelving the law.[58]

Up until recently, the JDP has not taken any measures on the status of *Imam Hatip* schools, so as to avoid drawing any anti-secularism charges from the judiciary upon itself. This caution is not unwarranted. When the Republican Prosecutor Yalçınkaya filed the closure case in the Constitutional Court in 2008, remarks made by the prime minister, ministers, JDP parliamentarians and mayors regarding the *Imam Hatip* schools constituted an important part of the indictment. According to the Public Prosecutor's argument, the promotion of *Imam Hatip* schools as alternatives to secular schools violated Turkey's constitutional principle of secularism. The document used the words "*Imam Hatip*" 70 times.

However, due to its increased political power in the last few years and considerable weakening of the secularist actors, particularly the higher judiciary and the army, the JDP passed a new law on educational reform on 30 March 2012. The new law, which is popularly known as the 4+4+4 formula, increases compulsory education to 12 years, where pupils have to study four years in an elementary school, followed by another four years of middle school, and four years of high school education. According to this new educational reform, the middle sections of the *Imam Hatip* schools will be reopened, and the pupils will be able to receive religious education at an earlier age. These new educational provisions which came into effect in the 2012–13 academic year have been drawing much criticism from educational experts and parents because of the lack of infrastructural and pedagogical preparation to accommodate such a major restructuring in such a short period. Although not explicitly stated, the major aim of the JDP in this education overhaul was to reopen the middle sections of the *Imam Hatip* schools. This political bickering illustrates that religious education and the status of *Imam Hatip* schools is still a salient and contentious political issue.

After the NSP first politicized state-religious education by increasing state funding for religious schools and changing the public's perception of *Imam Hatip* schools, the debate on state religious education has become ever more contentious. However, in order to understand how *Imam Hatip* schools became so popular among pious Muslims and a successful vehicle of political mobilization one needs to illustrate how these schools addressed the economic needs of the periphery through social provisions and cultural aspirations through identity construction.

Imam Hatip Schools and Social Provision

As discussed in Chapter 3, the sociocultural hierarchies between the periphery and the center became more pronounced in the urban encounters of rural immigrants with "modernized" city-dwellers. The changing residential backgrounds of *Imam Hatip* students also reflect the movement of the periphery from the villages to the cities. Akşit (1986) found that 55.8 percent of *Imam Hatip* students were from rural backgrounds in 1977, while Akşit and Coşkun (2004) found in their study that this was the case for only 14 percent of the students 1997.[59]

In this context, *Imam Hatip* schools attracted students from disadvantaged neighborhoods in big cities by providing scholarships and free boarding opportunities. Since the *Imam Hatip* schools are state educational institutions, they receive income from the state budget. However, they also receive material resources from societal sources. From the 1970s onwards, grassroots organizations around these schools proliferated.[60] Civil society organizations provided material and logistical support to students and graduates alike. For instance, the Association for the Dissemination of Knowledge (*İlim Yayma Cemiyeti*), which has 85 branches in 45 cities across Turkey, has provided material help to *Imam Hatip* students and successful graduates who continue to university.[61] The organization also runs 60 boarding houses, which provide accommodation for the students in secondary and higher education. Similarly, the Alumni Association of *Imam Hatip* High Schools (*ÖNDER*) and the Ensar Foundation provide scholarships primarily for *Imam Hatip* students based on need and academic merit.

Furthermore, social organizations collected donations from citizens in order to construct new buildings for the *Imam Hatip* schools. Accordingly, 65 percent of the school buildings of *Imam Hatip* schools were built solely by private donations, while only a little over 9 percent were built by the state with no help from citizens.[62] For instance, Ünsür's (2005) study shows that Üsküdar *Imam Hatip* High School, a prestigious religious school in one of the densely populated districts of Istanbul, received three times more money from the Istanbul Üsküdar *Imam Hatip* Beneficent Society (*Istanbul Üsküdar Imam Hatip Lisesi Koruma Derneği*) than from the state budget. These funds were used to contribute to the infrastructural needs of the school and to help students from underprivileged families.[63]

In the academic year 1996–97, 28.1 percent of all boarding facilities in primary and secondary education belonged to the General Religious Education Administration, even though *Imam Hatip* students constituted only 12 percent of the entire student population in the same year.[64] Even after the closure of the middle sections of *Imam Hatip* schools, these schools received more boarding facilities per pupil. In the 2011–12 academic year, over 10 percent of all the boarding facilities were designated to *Imam Hatip* schools and the percentage of *Imam Hatip* students who stayed in boarding facilities free of charge amounted to 12 percent of all free student boarders, even though *Imam Hatip* graduates numbered a little over 5 percent of the student body that academic year.[65] This shows that the boarding facilities available for *Imam Hatip* students far exceeded those available for other students. This difference is partly due to the fact that many of the boarding houses are donated to the state by civic associations or private foundations to be used specifically as boarding facilities for *Imam Hatip* schools.[66]

These material incentives made *Imam Hatip* schools attractive for students from a lower socioeconomic background and provided a venue for upward mobility. A JDP politician maintained:

> [In the past in Turkey], a big segment of the population could not send their children to the schools. They could not do that due to a lack of material opportunities ... *Imam Hatip* schools constituted the most important social project in the history of the Republic ... Hence, [these schools] became the only place where the poor and deprived masses could get an education.[67]

This shows how the provision of socioeconomic opportunities through religious schools is used by religious entrepreneurs to respond to the everyday needs of Turkish citizens from the lower classes. While some parents chose to send their children to *Imam Hatip* schools due to economic accessibility and a good quality of education, others preferred it due to the expectation that their children would potentially receive a job in the Directorate of Religious Affairs once they graduated.[68]

Framing Processes and Cultural Empowerment through *Imam Hatip* Schools

Material incentives were not the only reason for the increasing popularity of the *Imam Hatip* schools. As with *Ma'ayan* schools, cultural motives also played a significant role. Many conservative families preferred to send their children to *Imam Hatip* schools because these schools constructed—through empowerment frames—a positive collective identity for pious Muslims, which the republican elites tried to erase for many years. This positive collective identity partly stemmed from the socialization process within the schools and was expressed in different ways. Some of the *Imam Hatip* graduates whom I interviewed pointed to a special consciousness that existed within the schools. Zeynep, a graduate from Kütahya Anadolu Imam Hatip High School, said that there was a different type of atmosphere in her school compared to the secular schools.[69] This atmosphere, which she called "emotions" (*hissiyat*), inculcated spiritual principles in the students, such as valuing others because they are Allah's creations. Another graduate, Metin, claimed that there was a spiritual atmosphere in his school because "we could talk with others about religious matters, we could pray in the mescid [mosque] within the school."[70] This spiritual atmosphere created a consciousness of being an *Imam Hatip* member (*İmam Hatiplilik şuuru*). According to Metin, this consciousness is "not something that is taught in the classes, rather it is a situation that emerges during your years of education in the school."

This atmosphere on the school campuses affects the religiosity and ideological orientations of the students. Akşit (1986) reported that during the 1977–8 academic year, *Imam Hatip* students were a lot more religious compared to secular school students. Akşit and Coşkun (2004) reported that their survey conducted in the 1997–8 academic year showed a significant cultural and ideological variance between the students in the *Imam Hatip* schools and the students in secular high schools. For instance, while more than 55 percent of the *Imam Hatip* students read Islamic/conservative newspapers, in secular high schools only 5 percent did. Similarly, Onay (2005) found in his survey, conducted among university students in the 1999–2000 academic year, a significant difference between the *Imam Hatip* school graduates and secular high-school graduates in their level of attitudinal and behavioral religiosity.

Imam Hatip schools are also credited for becoming the only venue for the education of pious girls, since they offer a dignified educational context for them. Many conservative families choose to send their daughters to these schools due to their propriety standards.[71] The spatial segregation between the sexes in curricular and extra-curricular activities played an important role in the maintenance of these propriety standards.[72] While girls were accepted to the *Imam Hatip* schools for the first time in the 1977–8 academic year, the number of girls in religious education rose exponentially in the following years. In the academic years after 1990, girls have always constituted at least 40 percent of all *Imam Hatip* students.[73]

Secularist circles in Turkey often voice dismay about the education of girls in the *Imam Hatip* schools, since it is impossible for them to become either *Imams* or *Hatips.* Most female graduates from *Imam Hatip* schools, like most of the boys, move to secular professions or attend universities to study secular subjects. In this way, the female graduates from the *Imam Hatip* schools played an important role in the upward mobility of the periphery. Moreover, this has led to the increasing visibility of Islamic symbols, such as the headscarf, in professional jobs and institutions of higher learning.

Another frame, which is almost identical to those constructed around the *Ma'ayan* schools in Israel, depicts the *Imam Hatip* schools as safe havens from the ill effects of the secular world, such as violence, criminal activities or drug use. These frames are not only constructed within the school, but also reproduced by religious newspapers and Islamist politicians. As a NOM activist maintains:

> One of the reasons why people prefer *Imam Hatip* schools is because of criminal activities, such as drug abuse, physical injuries, that were occurring in secular schools … In *Imam Hatip* schools, students who are engaged in these types of activities don't pass one percent [of the school's student body].[74]

These accounts portray *Imam Hatip* schools as institutions that remedy the ill-effects of modernization, while students continuing to secular schools are depicted as more prone to illicit activities and improper behavior due to a lack of religious teaching. Metin, an *Imam Hatip* graduate, sums up this claim eloquently:

> Currently, you can observe that students engage in strange movements, such as Satanism, or commit homicides. I think this happens due to a lack of religious knowledge. Let me give you an example. For instance, you tell people not to steal. Yet, if you cannot make the person internalize this, if this person cannot assimilate this spiritually and conscientiously, then [this instruction] is to no avail. Hence, I want to say that education is not solely mental. Today, you see that people who received a very good education go and rob banks, embezzle state resources, steal. Why? And [they do these] despite the fact that you gave them a good education … The reason is because you approach education one-dimensionally.[75]

This narrative is sometimes supplemented by a more activist claim that emphasizes the proactive social role *Imam Hatip* students should take in their larger social setting. Accordingly, *Imam Hatip* students and graduates are expected to be role models for the larger Turkish society. As one graduate puts it: "Once you say that you are an *Imam Hatip* member (*imam hatipli*), you need to be aware of your behaviour, because you subscribe to a mission. Hence, you develop an auto-control mechanism."[76] This model of exemplary behavior is expected to have larger social consequences, such as cleansing the society from corruption, terror and so forth. NOM politicians contend that these schools raise students who would rule Turkey without getting engaged in corruption.[77] Similarly, a JDP parliamentarian currently stated that an increase in the number of *Imam Hatip* graduates would mean that "diplomats who do not sell the future of the country and who are respectful of the country's heritage and culture would lead this country."[78]

Others go further and claim that the *Imam Hatip* generation should be seen as the engine of societal Islamization in Turkey. Hayreddin Karaman, a graduate of the *Imam Hatip* schools and an authoritative figure in *Imam Hatip* circles, summarizes this argument very cogently:

> How does Islamization occur? What is the means to achieve Islamization? … According to my opinion, Islamization occurs through education and instruction. It occurs through generating faith and action among those we educate … As a result our people will become Muslims again … Those who are deficient Muslims will become complete Muslims. The more you turn people into complete Muslims, the more the country becomes Muslim with her morality, with her image, with her actuality, with her institutions, and with her order … But who will undertake this effort? … We claim that under current conditions the most suitable community for this job is the *Imam Hatip* community, this generation.[79]

Last, as with the *Ma'ayan* schools in Israel, the *Imam Hatip* schools were placed at the center of injustice frames, which portray these religious schools as victims at the hands of the secular establishment. After the 28 February Decisions, this frame became much more prevalent, with the closing of the middle sections of *Imam Hatip* schools defined as "oppression" (*zulüm*).[80] However, victimization as a major narrative by conservative media and politicians long preceded the 28 February Decisions. According to this frame, the reason for the proliferation of *Imam Hatip* schools was society's embrace of Islamic values. In spite of the demand from society for more *Imam Hatip* schools and religious education, secular intellectuals and state elites, who are alienated from their Turkish-Islamic roots and aspire to become Westerners, try to malign these schools by depicting them as sources of religious extremism.[81] Furthermore, throughout the 1980s and 1990s, religious newspapers, like *Tercüman*, *Zaman* and the *Milli Gazete*, have periodically published reports about *Imam Hatip* school buildings, which were donated to the state by private initiatives and awaited the approval of the education minister to open.[82] The subtext of these news reports emphasizes state–society tensions. According to this message, the *Imam Hatip* schools represented the demands of the society for more religious education. Nonetheless, these demands were not sufficiently met by the authoritarian Turkish state, which was controlled by a powerful secular minority elite. Hence, the *Imam Hatip* schools were at the center of this injustice frame that portrayed the victimization of a religious society at the hands of a powerful secular state. Even when the JDP became the government, JDP politicians continuously used this state–society binary. Prime Minister Erdoğan has maintained that the graduates faced "discrimination and humiliation for long years."[83]

Social Networks and the Dissemination of Frames

Social networks formed around the *Imam Hatip* schools were essential to disseminate these frames to the larger society and translate meaning making into social and political power. Unlike the Shas's relation to *Ma'ayan* schools in Israel, there is no organic relationship between the *Imam Hatip* schools and the NOM or the JDP. However, the graduates of the *Imam Hatip* schools form a loose community by coming together around several associations and foundations. The Ensar Foundation, Alumni Association of Imam Hatip High Schools (*ÖNDER*), Community for the Dissemination of Knowledge, the Foundation for the Dissemination of Knowledge (*İlim Yayma Vakfı*), and Turkey Imam Hatip Members Foundation (*Türkiye İmam Hatipliler Vakfı*) are the main organizations that bring the *Imam Hatip* community together.

These organizations provide several opportunities for social and political mobilization. Through their publications and events they actively circulate the frames formed around the *Imam Hatip* schools to the larger society. Prime Minister Erdoğan is the most prominent *Imam Hatip* graduate in Turkey. Erdoğan as well as other JDP politicians attend events of Alumni Societies and foster the sense of pride around being an *Imam Hatip* member. In his speech to the sixth general assembly of the Alumni Association of *Imam Hatip* Schools in 2010, Erdoğan used the theme of empowerment quite explicitly:

> Throughout my life I have proudly kept in my heart that I am a graduate of an *Imam Hatip* school. God permitting, I will keep this honor and pride of being a member of the *Imam Hatip* community until my last breath.[84]

Similar statements are circulated on *ÖNDER*'s website. Abdurrahman Dilipak, an Islamist journalist, writes: "To be an Imam Hatip member does not only give you 'the will to live as a Muslim,' but also gives you the mission to explain and spread this [will]."[85] *ÖNDER* has close to two million members that consist of both students and graduates.[86] The organization publishes a quarterly magazine called *Tohum* (Seed), which discusses the concerns of *Imam Hatip* schools, as well as the successes of its students. Ensar Foundation has a prolific publishing house that prints books on religious subjects and voices the concerns of the *Imam Hatip* community.

Through their participation in these social networks *Imam Hatip* graduates are also able to talk about and act on political issues which are their common concerns, such as the headscarf ban in universities. Naturally, these social networks engage in debates regarding policies concerning religious education. For example, on 11 May 1997, the Ensar Foundation, *ÖNDER*, and the Community for the Dissemination of Knowledge organized a rally against the 28 February Decisions in Sultanahmet Square. In this rally, 300,000 people, including many prominent figures from the NOM, gathered to protest the change in the education law.[87]

Finally, these social networks provide spaces, where the members of religious political parties and *Imam Hatip* graduates can physically meet and interact. Many members of the NOM and the governing JDP are *Imam Hatip* graduates. These politicians preserve their ties with other alumni, who have become prominent members in other social or business circles. Mukadder Başeğmez, a member of the Turkish National Assembly from the WP in 1991–9, explains how social networks of *Imam Hatip* graduates turned to political and economic networks:

> I am a graduate from the *Imam Hatip* [schools]. The most effective aspect of the *Imam Hatip* [schools] is this—we received a better education than other schools in all subjects such as physics, chemistry, foreign language, biology, law, health. But at the same time, we were also learning religious sciences. For this reason, we were raised as individuals who had a strong social side, but at the same time we knew the religion. Afterwards, these [*Imam Hatip* schools] have proliferated. Their proliferation was not forced. People were giving the money themselves, they were building [the schools] themselves. Hence, this was a popular demand. *But those who could not create such organizations felt uneasy. These cadres [from the schools] became at the same time political cadres, at the same time commercial cadres.*[88]

As Başeğmez mentions, the secular camp, which lacked similarly effective networks to mobilize its supporters, felt uneasy about the social, economic and political potential of the *Imam Hatip* graduates, and therefore perceived these schools as the breeding ground of political Islam. In 1996, 60 percent of the WP's 158 deputies in the Grand National Assembly were *Imam Hatip* graduates, and one-third of the JDP's 340 deputies in 2007.[89] In 2002–6, the JDP also appointed more than 1,100 *Imam Hatip* graduates to posts in several ministries.[90] Many of these JDP parliamentarians and bureaucrats attend events prepared by the *Imam Hatip* community and preserve ties with students as well as other graduates who become prominent members in social or business circles.

Conclusion

Incorporation of the NSP and Shas into governmental structures in the 1970s and 1980s increased religious actors' access to state resources and led to the creation of alternative educational spheres, namely *Ma'ayan* schools in Israel, or the transformation of already existing institutions to alternative educational tracks, namely *Imam Hatip* schools in Turkey.

Using this new political opportunity, religious entrepreneurs formulated strategic frames within and around these alternative educational institutions. These frames depicted religious schools as victims of a secular state, as safe havens from the corruptive effects of the modern world, as the source of societal transformation and of cultural pride. These frames played an important role in creating an affirmative religious Sephardi/conservative Muslim identity and empowering those who felt culturally excluded. These frames, which were in line with the ideologies of the religiopolitical actors, also challenged official secularist state ideologies, formed counter-hegemonic discourses, and provided an ideological repertoire for the nurturing of counter-elites.

Social networks formed around religious schools, such as alumni associations, foundations, civil society organizations or extra-curricular clubs, also aided political mobilization by disseminating those frames to larger audiences, by providing social provisions to the economically marginalized—thereby showing that a religious project can solve everyday problems—and by forming sources of political recruitment and solidarity.

The discussion above also provides some insights for the SMT regarding frame formation. The comparative discussion of *Imam Hatip* and *Ma'ayan* schools demonstrates that state (funded) institutions can be appropriated by oppositional forces to create and transmit frames that emphasize injustices inflicted by the state itself. This is a counterintuitive finding. While some SMT scholars have studied how state elites constructed counter-frames in order to weaken the appeal of opposition movement frames,[91] the formation of frames within state institutions that are critical of the state has not been studied. This finding reveals that the state is not a monolithic entity, and different institutional spaces within state structures can at times communicate ideas that are in dissonance with each other.

Notes

1 M. M. Ringer, 'Education in the Middle East: Introduction', *Comparative Studies of South Asia, Africa and the Middle East*, vol.21, no.1–2, 2001, 3–4.
2 The National Board was the governing body of the Jewish population in Palestine during the British Mandate. It became the government of Israel after 1948.
3 H. L. Schachter, 'Educational Institutions and Political Coalitions: The Case of Israel', *Comparative Education*, vol.16, no.3, 1972, 464–6.
4 S. Shamai, '"Cultural Shift": The Case of Jewish Religious Education in Israel', *British Journal of Sociology of Education*, vol.21, no.3, 2000, 405.
5 Z. Zameret, *Across a Narrow Bridge: Shaping the Educational System during the Aliyah*, Sde Boqer: Ben Gurion University of the Negev Press, 1997, cited in ibid., p. 406.
6 E. Don-Yehiya, *Religion and Political Accommodation in Israel*, Jerusalem: Floersheimer Institute for Policy Studies, 1999, p. 58.
7 A. F. Kleinberger, *Society, Schools, and Progress in Israel*, Oxford: Pergamon Press, 1969, p. 118.
8 'State Education Law'. Online. Available at: http://cms.education.gov.il/EducationCMS/Units/Owl/English/Legislation/Principal/STATE+EDUCATION+LAW.htm.
9 The basic curriculum consists of four course clusters: Heritage (*tanach*) and social studies; languages (Hebrew and English); mathematics, nature, science and technology; and physical education. The Education Ministry asks the schools to teach a given number of hours from this basic curriculum. In first grade, the *Ma'ayan* schools have to teach 11 hours of core curriculum courses, while in second and third grades, they have to teach 13, and fourth and fifth grade 15 hours. Source: Education Ministry.
10 A. Maoz, 'Religious Education in Israel', *University of Detroit Mercy Law Review*, vol.83, no.5, 2006, 710.
11 R. Tesler, *Beshem hashem: Shas ve hamahapecha hadatit*, Jerusalem: Keter Publishing, 2003, p. 415.
12 *Budget Directives for 1997*, Education Ministry, cited in V. Schiffer, *The Haredi Education in Israel: Allocation, Regulation, and Control*, Jerusalem: The Floersheimer Institute for Policy Studies, 1997, p. 14.
13 R. Tesler, *Beshem hashem*, p. 410.
14 The figures are provided by the Department of Unofficial Recognized Education under the Education Ministry. The *Ma'ayan* network officials on the other hand claim to have around 50,000 students in their schools. There is always a discrepancy between the numbers published by the Education Ministry and the numbers provided by the *Ma'ayan* network, since the number of students determine the state funding allocated to schools.
15 S. D. Baumel, *Sacred Speakers: Language and Culture Among the Haredim in Israel*, New York: Berghahn Books, 2005, pp. 154–5.
16 A. Odenheimer, 'Panel Still Trying to Find Solution to Special Allocations', *The Jerusalem Post*, 28 November 1991; A. Odenheimer, 'Shamir to Push NRP on Allocations', *The Jerusalem Post*, 1 December 1991.
17 Interview with Yitzhak Levy cited in D. Izenberg, 'Where Angels Fear to Tread', *The Jerusalem Post*, 6 December 1991.
18 Ibid.
19 D. Izenberg, 'Budget Passes First Reading in 48–47 Vote', *The Jerusalem Post*, 12 December 1991.
20 D. Izenberg, 'High Court Blocks Haredi School Authority. Government Says NRP Challenge Could Easily be Overcome', *The Jerusalem Post*, 31 August 1992.
21 Ibid.

22 D. Z. Harris, 'Majority to Support Budget as Shas's Demands are Met', *The Jerusalem Post*, 29 December 1999.
23 D. Z. Harris, 'The Future of Shas's Schools', *The Jerusalem Post*, 29 December 1999.
24 N. Morris, 'Israel Coalition Preserved as Barak, Shas Make Deal', *San Diego-Union Tribune*, 23 June 2000.
25 D. Lehmann and B. Siebzehner, *Remaking Israeli Judaism: The Challenge of Shas*, London: Oxford University Press, 2006, pp. 172–3.
26 *The Jerusalem Post*, 24 September 1999.
27 *Ha'aretz*, 6 August 2004. In E. Schiffman, 'The Shas School System in Israel', *Nationalism and Ethnic Politics*, vol.11, 2005, 105.
28 Interview with a high-level official in the Recognized Unofficial Education Department on December 10, 2006. The interviewee requested anonymity.
29 'Parashat Bo: Stop Discrimination', *Aram Soba Newsletter*, Jerusalem, 2001.
30 Interview with Nissim Zeev, Jerusalem, December 5, 2006. Nissim Zeev also serves as the head of *Nevat Yisrael*, which is a religious seminary for Sephardi girls. While *Nevat Yisrael* is not under the umbrella of *Ma'ayan Hahinuch Hatorani*, there are ideological ties between the two.
31 D. Lehmann and B. Siebzehner, *Remaking Israeli Judaism*, p. 177.
32 Interview with Nissim Cohen, Deputy Director of *El Hama'ayan*, Jerusalem, December 12, 2006.
33 Ibid.
34 Interview with Ofakim chairman of Shas Shlomo Azran, Ofakim, June 24, 2012.
35 E. Schiffman, 'The Shas School System', pp. 105–6.
36 Ibid., p. 107.
37 Interview with Bat Yam chairman of Shas Beni El Harer, Bat Yam, June 25, 2012.
38 H. D. Kalev, 'Bargaining with Spiritual Hierarchy: Women in the Shas Movement in Israel', in P. S. Anderson (ed.), *New Topics in Feminist Philosophy of Religion: Contestations and Transcendence Incarnate*, London: Springer, 2010, pp. 91–2.
39 'Eyfo hayeladim shel Shas: Be yeshivot shel haashkenazim', *Yediot Aharonot*, 23 November 2006.
40 Interview with Mati Dagan, the former head of State Religious Education, 7 December 2006.
41 Interview with a high-level official in the Recognized Unofficial Education Department on 10 December 2006. The interviewee requested anonymity.
42 S. D. Baumel, *Sacred Speakers*, p. 147.
43 H. D. Kalev, 'Bargaining with Spiritual Hierarchy', p. 95.
44 M. Lidman, 'A Study of the Nonemployment Crisis', *The Jerusalem Post*, 9 July 2010.
45 K. Ben-Shimon, 'Deferentially Progressive', *Jerusalem Report*, 3 July 2011.
46 M. Lidman, 'A Study of the Nonemployment Crisis', *The Jerusalem Post*, 9 July 2010.
47 K. Ben-Shimon, 'Deferentially Progressive', *Jerusalem Report*, 3 July 2011.
48 P. Cidor, 'Head of the Class', *The Jerusalem Post*, 1 October 2010.
49 Ibid.
50 H. Ayhan, *Türkiye'de Din Eğitimi*, Istanbul: Dem Yayınları, 2004, p. 186.
51 Interview with Cevat Ayhan, 22 February 2007.
52 H. Yavuz, *Islamic Political Identity in Turkey*, New York: Oxford University Press, 2003, pp. 126–7.
53 M. A. Gökaçtı, *Türkiye'de Din Eğitimi ve İmam Hatipler*, Istanbul: İletişim Yayınları, 2005, p. 224.
54 M. Öcal, *Imam Hatip Liseleri ve İlk Öğretim Okulları*, Istanbul: Ensar Neşriyat, 1994, pp. 68–9.

55 M. Gündem, 'Muhafazakar burjuvazinin tercihi … ', *Milliyet*, 4 May 2004.
56 Cited in W. Hale, 'Christian Democracy and the JDP: Parallels and Contrasts', in H. Yavuz (ed.), *The Emergence of a New Turkey: Democracy and the AK Parti*, Salt Lake City: University of Utah Press, 2006, p. 78.
57 'YÖK'e İmam Hatip Vetosu', *Milliyet*, 29 May 2004.
58 W. Hale, 'Christian Democracy', p. 79.
59 B. Akşit, 'Imam-Hatip and Other Secondary Schools in the Context of Political and Cultural Modernization of Turkey', *Journal of Human Sciences*, vol.5, no.1, 1986, 25–41; B. Akşit and M. A. Coşkun, 'Türkiye'nin Modernleşmesi Bağlamında Imam Hatip Okulları', in Y. Aktay (ed.), *İslamcılık*, Istanbul: İletişim Yayınları, 2004, pp. 394–410.
60 H. Yavuz, *Islamic Political Identity*, p. 124.
61 'İlim Yayma Cemiyeti'. Online. Available at www.iyc.org.tr/ (accessed 25 November 2010).
62 A. Ünsür, *Kuruluşundan Günümüze İmam Hatip Liseleri*, Istanbul: Ensar Neşriyat, 2005, pp. 202–3.
63 Ibid., pp. 209–11.
64 R. Çakır, İ. Bozan and B. Talu, *İmam Hatip Liseleri Efsaneler ve Gerçekler*, Istanbul: TESEV Yayınları, 2004, p. 73.
65 *National Education Statistics 2011–2012*, Education Ministry.
66 If a building is donated for a specific purpose to the Education Ministry, it cannot be used for another purpose.
67 Interview with Numan Kurtulmuş, 4 March 2007. Kurtulmuş was in NOM at the time of the interview. Later he found and led a new splinter party. Currently he is a member of the JDP.
68 R. Çakır, İ. Bozan and B. Talu, *İmam Hatip Liseleri Efsaneler*.
69 All the names used in the text for the *Imam Hatip* graduates are pseudonyms.
70 Interview, 31 March 2007.
71 S. Pak, *At the Crossroads of Secularism and Islamism*, unpublished Ph.D. dissertation, University of Wisconsin, Madison, 2002.
72 Ibid., pp. 184–5.
73 R. Çakır, İ. Bozan and B. Talu, *İmam Hatip Liseleri Efsaneler*, p. 13.
74 Interview with Osman Yumakoğlu, Istanbul, 23 March 2007.
75 Interview, 31 March 2007.
76 Cited in R. Çakır, İ. Bozan and B. Talu, *İmam Hatip Liseleri Efsaneler*, p. 126.
77 M. A. Gökaçtı, *Türkiye'de Din Eğitimi*, p. 219.
78 'Okulları imam hatip yapma şansı yakaladık', *Milliyet*, 24 August 2012.
79 H. Karaman, *İmam Hatiplilik Şuuru*, Istanbul: Ensar Neşriyat, 2005, pp. 11–12.
80 H. Karaman, *Laik Düzende Dini Yaşamak 4*, Istanbul: İz Yayıncılık, 2006.
81 C. Çiçek, 'Milletin Gözüyle İmam Hatip Okulları ve Beklentileri', in *Kuruluşunun 43. Yılında İmam Hatip Liseleri*, Istanbul: Ensar Neşriyat, 1994, pp. 73–83.
82 For an example see: 'Binaları Tamamlanan İmam Hatipler Neden Açılmıyor?', *Milli Gazete*, 4 October 1993.
83 'PM: Imam-Hatip Graduates Snubbed for Many Years', *Today's Zaman*, 6 December 2010.
84 'Erdoğan İmam Hatipliler Kurultayında Konuştu', *Hürriyet*, 5 December 2010.
85 A. Dilipak, 'İmam Hatipler Geliyor', 10 August 2012. Online. Available at www.onder.org.tr/index.php?option=com_content& view = article& id = 304:abdurrahman-dilipak-yazd& catid = 1:usthaber (accessed 16 August 2012).
86 Interview with Yusuf Kara, 20 March 2007.
87 'İmam Hatipe Yakışır Şekilde', *Zaman*, 12 May 1997.
88 Interview with Mukadder Başeğmez, 26 February 2007.
89 I. Özgur, *Islamic Schools in Modern Turkey: Faith, Politics, and Education*, New York: Cambridge University Press, 2012, pp. 131–2.

90 Ibid., p. 147.

91 J. A. Noakes, 'Official Frames in Social Movement Theory: The FBI, HUAC, and the Communist Threat in Hollywood', in H. Johnston and J. A. Noakes (eds.), *Frames of Protest: Social Movements and the Framing Perspective*, Lanham: Rowman & Littlefield, 2005, pp. 89–112.

9 Conclusion

I started this book by posing three interrelated questions:

1 Why does the electoral strength of religiopolitical actors increase in democratic settings?
2 What factors contribute to the continuing success of religious parties in democratic politics?
3 What is the effect of the increasing power of religiopolitical actors on democratic governance and stability?

The comparative analysis of Shas and the National Outlook Parties' successful political trajectories provides significant clues to answer these questions and improves our understanding as to how religiopolitical movements mobilize popular support in democratic regimes in the Middle East.

Adopting an SMT approach, this book has argued that the interaction between ripe political opportunity structures (POS), framing processes and mobilizational networks best explains successful political mobilization by religiopolitical actors in Israel and Turkey. Sharpened sociocultural grievances due to social changes, increased access of religious actors to state resources and economic liberalization created ripe POS for religious movements. Using these POS, religious entrepreneurs constructed frames that addressed already-heightened grievances of the peripheral groups. Lastly, formal and informal networks were instrumental in successful mobilization by penetrating the society, providing welfare provisions to marginalized constituents and circulating the movements' frames.

As discussed in Chapter 3, a sociocultural cleavage was created both in Israel and Turkey during the state formation period. This sociocultural cleavage—between the Ashkenazim and Sephardim in Israel and the center and the periphery in Turkey—became politicized by processes of socioeconomic change. In Israel, the increasing literacy rates of the Sephardim and the concomitant attempts to integrate Sephardi students in each of the three existing educational streams created a backlash from Ashkenazi parents and increased the cultural frustrations of Sephardim. Similarly, in Turkey the sociocultural divide was politicized when accelerating rural–urban immigration led to increasing social contact between the periphery and center. Rural immigrants, most of whom started to live in *gecekondu* neighborhoods and work in the informal economic sector, were stigmatized by the urban middle classes for posing a cultural threat to their own existence. When the negative representations of rural immigrants became part of mainstream middle-class urban discourse, the grievances of the second- and third-generation rural immigrants, who already found it hard to climb the economic ladder due to stagnant opportunities, became more acute. In these contexts, Shas was formed in Israel in 1983, and the NOM was formed in Turkey in 1970 with a claim to appeal to the social, economic and cultural frustrations of the lower class Sephardim and the periphery.

The incorporation of Shas and NOM into state institutions provided another set of political opportunities for these fledgling religiopolitical movements. In Israel, Shas was incorporated into almost every coalition government, because the movements' leaders pursued a very particularistic agenda focused on the needs of their constituents, while also acting pragmatically on national issues, such as the peace process. Shas's occupation of the ministries of the Interior and Religious Affairs provided access to the cultural and material resources of the state. Through its grip on the Interior Ministry, Shas could claim that it acted to "protect the Jewish character" of the Israeli state. To that end, Shas's interior ministers challenged the citizenship status of Russian immigrants who lacked necessary documentation to prove their Judaism or fought for the deportation of undocumented non-Jewish African immigrants. More significantly, Shas's grip on the two ministries was critical for creating extensive patronage networks within the state. The party channeled funds, legally and extra-legally, to its own educational network and affiliated non-profit civil society organizations providing religious services. Moreover, through its control over the Religious Affairs Ministry, Shas established control over the religious economic sector and provided employment opportunities, such as kosher food inspectors, ritual bath managers, religious court judges and yeshiva school administrators, to its ultra-Orthodox constituents.

In Turkey, state incorporation of religious actors occurred in three successive periods and provided a significant political opportunity for the WP in the 1990s. First, Erbakan's NSP became part of three coalition governments during the 1970s. During its coalition partnerships in the Ecevit government and in the two Nationalist Front governments, the NSP used its ministries and governmental agencies to create patronage networks, which survived into the post-1980 political era.

The military government (1980–3) forged a symbiotic relationship with a conservative think-tank, the Hearth of Intellectuals, and aimed to marry Turkish nationalism with selective elements appropriated from Islam. This new religious nationalism, known as the Turkish-Islamic Synthesis, aimed to depoliticize a Turkish society that had been blighted by ideological polarization in the pre-coup period. During the period of military rule, Hearth members were appointed to the higher echelons of the state bureaucracy and shaped the cultural and educational policies of the Turkish state.

The next governments formed by Özal's MP (1983–91) also incorporated religious actors into the state by allocating important ministerial positions to a conservative faction, most of whom were former NSP members. During this period, state institutions such as the education ministry, national television, family consultation centers, and the Atatürk Culture, Language and History Higher Institution emerged as institutional sites where a conservative ideology was constructed and communicated to the larger public. As a consequence of these efforts, religious political actors found a receptive cultural environment to increase their public appeal, especially at a time when leftist political actors still faced restrictions.

On the other hand, the instrumental use of religion by the state triggered a different dynamic. Religious actors outside the state, such as religious newspapers, the WP and Islamist intellectuals criticized the instrumentalization of Islam by the MP and the military. WP ideologues and Islamist intellectuals argued that both the military government's Turkish Islamic synthesis and the MP's lip service to conservative constituents aimed to prevent the rising Islamic tide and contaminated authenticity of Islamic expression. These criticisms discredited the MP in the eyes of conservative constituents, who started to shift their support to the WP. At the same time, the gradual resignation of conservative politicians and party organizations from the MP and their entry to the WP in early 1990s boosted the latter's organizational and political strength.

Implementation of economic liberalization measures created yet another set of opportunity structures for both religiopolitical actors. Neo-liberal restructuring, which started during the 1977 Likud coalition government and crystallized in the Economic Stabilization Plan of 1985, retrenched Israel's welfare state by slashing social provisions, such as food subsidies, child allowances and unemployment benefits. Shas filled the subsequent social vacuum by providing social welfare to lower class and ultra-Orthodox Mizrahim, two groups further marginalized as a result of these policies. The party's occupation of the Labor and Social Welfare Ministry and the Health Ministry as well as its civil society organizations, including its school network *Ma'ayan Hahinuch HaTorani*, were critical to its ability to provide welfare to these groups.

Similarly, Turkey embraced a neo-liberal restructuring after 1980 which disproportionately hurt the urban poor. The WP municipalities in collaboration with party networks provided extensive social provisions to the needy, particularly in *gecekondu* neighborhoods, filling the vacuum created by economic restructuring. Moreover, Turkey's economic liberalization under Özal benefited SMEs in the provincial cities leading to the formation of a pious Muslim middle class, which became one of the main drivers of the WP in the next decade.

While delineating political opportunity structures is important in understanding how a favorable sociopolitical context provides openings for religiopolitical movements, it is the religious entrepreneurs who translate these opportunities to collective action. For successful mobilization, the movement activists had to articulate and disseminate frames that resonated with the grievances of potential supporters.

Shas and the NOM activists appealed to the sense of injustice the Sephardim and pious Muslims faced during the state formation period under secular hegemonic ideologies, namely Labor Zionism and Kemalism. Shas activists blamed Labor Zionism for the separation of the Sephardim from their traditional heritage, their forced secularization, economic underachievement, and social marginalization. For the NOM activists, the Republican modernization project was culpable for most of the modern ills of Turkish society and politics. According to NOM activists, blind imitation of the West had severed Turks from their core values, distanced the state from the society, discriminated against pious citizens and led to the adoption of an uncompromising nationalism that excluded Kurds. By dubbing all the secular parties "imitators of the West" and by defining Turkey's regime as an "order of exploitation," the WP became a vocal critic of the headscarf ban and restrictions imposed on religious education in the 1990s and designated itself as the representative of the oppressed.

These injustice frames not only targeted pious segments in both societies but also those who felt socioeconomic marginalization. Therefore the movements actively reached out to the socioeconomically disadvantaged primarily concentrated in development towns and *gecekondu* neighborhoods, and even to non-traditional groups such as drug addicts, ex-prisoners or sex workers. In Turkey, the NOM also reached out to Kurds, while to a much lesser extent Shas appealed in its earlier years to Israeli Arabs. Hence both movements were successful in forging an alliance composed of groups who felt excluded by their respective governments around the concept of justice.

In order for movement frames to capture the imagination of societal groups, the targeted groups should not only feel wronged, but also need to be inspired to correct these injustices. To achieve this, both Shas and the NOM proposed political projects grounded in a reimagined religious past. For many lower class Sephardim, Shas's motto, "returning the crown to its past glory" (*Lehahzir Atara Leyoshna*) meant the restoration of the dignity of Sephardim in social and political life. Similarly, the NOM's promise to create an alternative civilization inspired by the glory days of the Ottoman Empire and to institute a "Just Order" resonated with the periphery's sense of cultural marginalization and socioeconomic discontent.

Both Shas and the NOM saw religious education as an important part of their religiopolitical project. To that end, movement entrepreneurs formulated empowerment and prognostic frames within and around state-funded religious schools. Religious entrepreneurs framed the *Ma'ayan* schools in Israel and the *Imam Hatip* schools in Turkey as safeguards against the corrupting influences of secular modernity, the source of a morally equipped generation with a transformative mission, and the engine of societal Judaization/

Islamization. These frames became a source of pride for students, alumni and movement activists and forged a sense of community among them. Two major factors increased the credibility of the movements' messages of justice and empowerment. The modest backgrounds of religious activists helped the masses to associate easily with them while the extensive welfare services provided to the underprivileged became a testament that a religious project can respond to the everyday needs of the marginalized. Prominent Shas leaders, such as Rabbi Ovadia Yosef, Ariyeh Deri and Eli Yishai, grew up in poor families and worked their way up to become influential political figures. Therefore, many Shasniks claimed that the Sephardi public perceived the Shas leaders as of their own and could see eye to eye with them. Moreover, Shas engaged in extensive welfare service provisions in the development towns and in the slums of the big cities. Through its network of civil society organizations, Shas provided affordable day care to working-class parents, offered cheap education in its kindergartens and primary schools, delivered free meals and school supplies to needy families, opened discount markets, and offered extra-curricular activities to the underprivileged youth.

Similarly WP leaders who came to political prominence from unprivileged backgrounds—most noticeably Recep Tayyip Erdoğan who worked in the informal economy in order to support his own high school education—played an important role in providing credibility to the NOM's message of a "Just Order." Ordinary people could associate with these figures who did not refrain from interacting frequently with the "man on the street." Moreover, the WP attended to the needs of the poor, especially in *gecekondu* neighborhoods, by engaging in extensive welfare work through its municipalities and party networks. Among other things, the WP delivered food supplies to poor residents before Ramadan, distributed coal packages and hot meals, offered free health care services, and even provided marriage and dowry support to the underprivileged youth. Thus, both Shas and the WP convinced many people through numerous small-scale welfare initiatives that their message of justice was genuine and that religious revival could provide the answer to everyday social and economic problems.

Finally, the political success of Shas and the WP depended on their elaborate party networks that forged close links between constituents and insiders. While the WP had a hierarchical, disciplined party organization along the lines of modern mass political parties, Shas's organizational structure was quite diffused.[1] In its mobilization efforts, Shas tapped into ultra-Orthodox Sephardi rabbis and yeshiva students in the immediate orbit of Rabbi Ovadia Yosef who loyally propagated Ovadia Yosef's message at election times, used ethnic synagogues and mystic folk figures, such as Baba Baruch or late Rabbi Kedouri to gain the support of traditional Sephardim, and maintained a close affiliation with *hazara betshuva* movements and returnee preachers to connect with and convert potential secular constituents. These networks interpenetrated with Shas's own political and social organizations thereby forming a loose, but effective instrument for mobilization.

The WP, on the other hand, maintained a highly disciplined, hierarchically structured party organization which came to be known as the "prayer bead model." According to this model, the party was horizontally organized from the largest administrative levels to the smallest districts. The party maintained an executive council in each province and appointed representatives to each province, borough, village or neighborhood. Moreover, in each neighborhood five observers were appointed to each voting booth, and tasked with meeting all year around and reaching out to registered citizens in their designated district. Women and youth were also organized in a parallel fashion and were linked to the main party organization. As a result of this elaborate party organization, the WP became the only mass political party in Turkey. Despite this difference between the party structures, both Shas and WP activists construed their political activism for their respective movements as "working for God's sake." This shared sense of religious mission and personal sacrifice differentiated these religiopolitical activists from their counterparts working in mainstream secular parties and became an organizational asset to the respective movements.

The comparative causal narratives that draw on the interaction between political opportunity structures, framing processes and mobilizational networks reveal the inadequacy of explanations emphasizing the primacy of one variable—political, social or economic—in understanding the complex processes of religious mobilization in democratic settings. To understand how grievances, which exist in every society, translate to political mobilization, it is necessary to weave together sociopolitical context, idea-making and resource mobilization. The parallel trajectories of a Judaic and Islamic political movement also show that religious activism is not tied to the essence of a religious tradition/scripture as some culturalist theories contend, but is very much shaped by context, agency and interpretation.

The comparative approach implemented in this book is an attempt to rethink the political study of Turkey and Israel which have tended to be viewed as exceptional cases with Israeli or Turkish politics conceptualized as sui generis. To expand our knowledge of Middle Eastern politics, there is a need to go beyond single case studies and situate Israeli and Turkish political systems in a comparative framework with their Middle Eastern counterparts.

The comparative narratives delineated in the book also provide insights into how religiopolitical actors interact with democratic institutions. Studies that look to the relationship between religious politics and democratization in the Middle East mainly draw their inferences from the trajectories of Islamist movements functioning in non-democratic settings. These inferences are limiting as they have to focus their attention on the limited spaces of contestation that exist in authoritarian regimes. Focusing on religious politics in the two democracies of the Middle East provides more credible insights into the complex relationship between religious actors and the democratic process.

On the one hand, the experiences of Shas, the NOM, and later the JDP, show that religiopolitical actors can deepen democratic practice. Both religiopolitical movements used religion as a meta-narrative to question the ideological tenets of homogenizing, secular state ideologies, namely Labor Zionism and Kemalism. In the political and sociocultural spheres, these actors carved ideological spaces where they asserted pride around a positive Sephardi and pious Muslim identity and critiqued their state's ideals of assimilation. By doing so, they carried the voice of the culturally marginalized to the center of the politics. This politics of identity paved the way for increased recognition of peripheral identities in the public arena and restored some sense of self-respect to groups who had been deprived of dignity in the public sphere. In this regard, these religiopolitical actors show some resemblance to protest movements that strive for recognition of difference and political inclusion of peripheral identities.

In the Turkish context, where the public sphere is much less accomodationist of religious expression than is the case in Israel, the WP, VP, and later the JDP, aimed, and to certain extent succeeded, in expanding the assertive secularist parameters of the public debate regarding the relationship between religion and politics. They introduced a language of rights and freedoms when discussing issues that mattered to pious constituencies. For instance, as the annulled constitutional amendments passed by the JDP-controlled GNA in 2008 showcase, the wearing of the headscarf in universities was conceptualized in the context of equality before the law and freedom of education. Similarly demands to lift the restrictions on access to religious education in the Quranic courses and *Imam Hatip* schools appealed to notions of freedom of religion and accommodation of different lifestyles, norms prevalent in liberal democracies. While these arguments pluralized the public debate by engendering robust discussions such as the limits of state encroachment into religious affairs, the extent of freedom of religious expression in the democratic public sphere, and the collective right to religious education, their effect on transforming the assertive secularist premises of the legal sphere has been limited.

On the other hand, Shas and NOM leaders eroded boundaries of civil discourse when they employed an exclusionary language toward their opponents with reference to religious idioms. These attacks, which can primarily be traced in the speeches of Rabbi Ovadia Yosef and Erbakan, undermined liberal-democratic political culture. More importantly, the Israeli and Turkish cases demonstrate how the electoral strengthening of religious parties in democracies with long-standing secular traditions can undermine democratic stability. The rise of the WP to power in 1996 and Shas's unprecedented electoral success in the 1999 elections increased the anxiety level of secular sociopolitical actors in both societies. The heightened threat perception led to the formation of secularist political blocs and led to the polarization of politics along secular–religious lines.

While polarization ensued in both contexts, a significant difference exists between the Israeli and Turkish cases as to how politico-legal arrangements dealt with this political polarization in general and with the role of religion in the public arena in particular. Since its formation, the Turkish state had tried to prevent the participation of religious actors in the political arena by restricting even implicit public appeals to religion by political actors and limiting the role of religious social actors. In the last two decades, the strict interpretation of this constitutional principle *laïcité* (*laiklik*) by the Turkish Constitutional Court and the political influence of the Turkish military as an assertively secularist actor exacerbated the already heightened secular–religious polarization of the 1990s. This restrictive approach toward religion's public manifestations led to the breakdown of Turkish democracy during the "28 February Process" and the consequent shutting down of the WP and the VP. Even after the JDP's adoption of a post-Islamist ideology, which signifies the moderation of religiopolitical actors, the secularist opposition to Erdoğan's party led to major politico-legal crises as manifested during the presidential elections of 2007 and the closure case opened against the JDP in the Constitutional Court in 2007–8. Partly as a reaction to the rigid definition of secularism by the state and political actors, and partly due to its unchecked legislative power thanks to Turkey's rather majoritarian political system, the JDP leaders have embraced an increasingly illiberal political language toward the opposition in the recent years. These developments pose a significant challenge for the consolidation of democracy in Turkey.

By contrast, the Israeli state has adopted a more accommodationist approach toward political manifestations of religion since the state's formation. Permitting explicit religious expression in the political field, recognizing autonomous religious education as a premise of pluralism, and securing consensualism through proportional electoral laws gave the Israeli system a flexibility that Turkey lacked. Therefore the secular–religious polarization—although raising powerful emotions on both sides—was successfully contained within legitimate legal-political parameters and did not lead to any democratic breakdown. These two cases suggest that the combination of political accommodation of religious difference in the political sphere and consensual political mechanisms is more conducive for democratic containment of secular–religious polarization than exclusion of religious difference and majoritarian political arrangements.

Lastly, the comparative analysis of religious politics in Israel and Turkey provides some insights as to why religiopolitical actors undergo ideological or strategic moderation. The main moderation of religiopolitical actors occurred in Turkey, when the reformers broke away from the VP and in 2001 formed the JDP with a post-Islamist outlook.

The moderation of the JDP does not lend support to the inclusion–moderation thesis. On the contrary, the moderation of religiopolitical actors in Turkey followed a period of exclusion, which was exemplified by the removal of the WP from power by a "soft coup" and the respective bans of the WP and VP by the Constitutional Court. I contend that a rational actor model better explains the moderation of the JDP. Based on their assessment of the political and institutional constraints posed on religious parties in Turkey and the detrimental effects of the 28 February Process on religious civil society networks, the JDP leaders decided that it would be in their long-term interest to continue to participate in Turkish politics with a more moderate ideology. By embracing a more reconciliatory discourse towards the secular state, refraining from using Islam as a political referent, showing commitment to Turkey's EU membership, and embracing the broadening of individual rights, the party leadership aimed to come to terms with the secular power structures, to ensure its political survival, and to safeguard religious civil society networks which were significantly harmed by the 28 February Process.

In Israel, the Shas leadership also underwent a moderation of sorts when the party leadership started to adopt less conflictual language toward pro-secular actors after the 2003 elections. Shas's decision to tone down its uncompromising rhetoric was also based on a cost–benefit analysis and a rational assessment of the political situation. The party leadership realized that its vocal, non-conciliatory approach toward secular actors led to the alienation and strengthening of the pro-secular camp, which cost Shas a place in Ariel Sharon's 2003 coalition government and thereby access to vital state resources. When the leadership assessed this political reality, it decided to tone down its vocal criticism of secular actors in order to benefit from the perks of government participation.

While the rational actor model can explain similarities between the moderation processes in Turkey and Israel, the different levels of moderation between Shas and the JDP require some other explanation. The discussions in Chapters 7 and 8 of this volume show that there is a significant qualitative difference between the two cases. While the JDP engaged in a serious critique of Islamism, attempted to create a synthesis between liberal and conservative values and embraced a post-Islamist character, Shas's moderation was only strategic and did not entail any ideological transformation. The difference can be explained by structural factors, in other words by looking to the social bases of the two parties.

The most influential social actor that supported the reformers in their attempt to break away from the VP and to form the JDP was MUSIAD, which represented the owners of SMEs who became prosperous in the 1980s and 1990s. This new Muslim middle class, which was part of the NOM's cross-class coalition in the 1990s, actively supported the ideological transformation of the JDP. This Islamic bourgeoisie, which was fully integrated into the world economy through its engagement in exports, desired a stable democratic system, integration to international neo-liberal system and a pro-EU foreign policy, and therefore perceived NOM's Islamism as restrictive and anathema to its class interests.

In contrast, lower class and ultra-Orthodox Sephardim, the backbone of Shas's constituency, are not economically integrated into the mainstream Israeli socioeconomic structures, let alone to the global economy. For instance most of the graduates from *Ma'ayan* schools are not prepared to enter the Israeli workforce or universities, in sharp contrast to *Imam Hatip* graduates who take up professions in various sectors and gain upward social mobility. *Ma'ayan* graduates usually work in the religious sector jobs created and maintained by the Israeli state. Hence most of Shas's constituencies are still on the economic periphery—despite some limited attempts at integration, such as the formation of an ultra-Orthodox university by Adina Bar Shalom. Shas's policies of state patronage and cultural segregation intensify the social and economic barriers between its constituencies and mainstream Israeli society, thereby preventing any social impetus for meaningful ideological moderation.

Note

1 I would like to thank Nissim Leon for pointing out the contrast to me.

Bibliography

Abadi, J., 'Ethnicity and Religion in Israeli Politics: Emergence of the Shas Party', in S. C. Saha (ed.), *Religious Fundamentalism in the Contemporary World Critical Social and Political Issues*, pp. 235–263, New York: Lexington Books, 2004.

Ahmad, F., 'The Political Economy of Kemalism', in E. Özbudun and A. Kazancıgil (eds.), *Atatürk: Founder of Modern Turkey*, pp. 145–63, Hamden: Archon Book, 1981.

——'Islamic Reassertion in Turkey', *Third World Quarterly*, vol.10. no.2, 1988, 750–69.

——'Politics and Islam in Modern Turkey', *Middle Eastern Studies*, vol.27, no.1, 1991, 3–21.

——*Demokrasi Sürecinde Türkiye (1945–1980)*, Istanbul: Hil Yayın, 1992.

Akdoğan, Y., *Siyasal İslam: Refah Partisi'nin Anatomisi*, Istanbul: Şehir Yayınları, 2000.

——*Muhafazakar Demokrasi*, Ankara: AKP Yayınları, 2003.

——'The Meaning of Conservative Democratic Identity', in H. Yavuz (ed.), *The Emergence of a New Turkey Democracy and the AK Parti*, pp. 49–65, Salt Lake City: University of Utah Press, 2006.

AK Parti, *AK Parti 2023 Siyasi Vizyonu: Siyaset, Toplum, Dünya*, 30 September 2012. Online. Available at www.akparti.org.tr/upload/documents/akparti2023siyasivizyonuturkce.pdf.

Akşit, B. 'Imam-Hatip and Other Secondary Schools in the Context of Political and Cultural Modernization of Turkey', *Journal of Human Sciences*, vol.5, no.1, 1986, 25–41.

Akşit, B. and Coşkun, M. A., 'Türkiye'nin Modernleşmesi Bağlamında Imam Hatip Okulları', in Y. Aktay (ed.), *İslamcılık*, pp. 394–410, Istanbul: İletişim Yayınları, 2004.

Alemdaroğlu, A., 'Refah Partisi'ni Yeniden Düşünmek: 1991 Reklam Kampanyasının Analizi', paper presented at the Sixth National Social Science Congress of the *Turkish Social Science Association*, November, 1999.

Allouche, J., *The Oriental Communities in Israel, 1948–2003: The Social and Cultural Creation of an Ethnic Group*, Geneva: Institut universitaire de hautes études internationals, 2003.

Alper, E. and Göral, O. S., 'Aydınlar Ocağı', in A. Çiğdem (ed.), *Muhafazakârlık*, pp. 583–89, Istanbul: İletişim Yayınları, 2003.

Altunışık, M. B., 'The Possibilities and Limits of Turkey's Soft Power in the Middle East', *Insight Turkey*, vol.10, no.2, 2008, 41–54.

Anderson, L., 'The State in the Middle East and North Africa', *Comparative Politics*, vol.20, no.1, 1987, 1–18.

Arat, Y., 'Social Change and the 1983 Governing Elite in Turkey', in M. Kıray (ed.), *Structural Change in Turkish Society*, pp. 163–78, Bloomington: Indiana University Press, 1991.

——'Feminism, Islamists, and Political Change in Turkey', *Political Psychology*, vol.19, no.1, 1999, 117–31.

——*Political Islam in Turkey and Women's Organizations*, Istanbul: Tesev Yayınları, 1999.

——*Rethinking Islam and Liberal Democracy Islamist Women in Turkish Politics*, Albany: State University of New York Press, 2005.

Atacan, F., 'Explaining Religious Politics at the Crossroad: AKP-SP', *Turkish Studies*, vol.6, no.2, 2005, 187–99.

Atasoy, Y., *Turkey, Islamists and Democracy: Transition and Globalization in a Muslim State*, London: I. B. Tauris, 2005.

Ayhan, H., *Türkiye'de Din Eğitimi*, Istanbul: Dem Yayınları, 2004.

Ayoob, M., *Many Faces of Political Islam: Religion and Politics in the Muslim World*, Ann Arbor: University of Michigan Press, 2008.

——'Deciphering Islam's Multiple Voices: Intellectual Luxury or Strategic Necessity?', in F. Volpi (ed.), *Political Islam: A Critical Reader*, pp. 44–54, New York: Routledge, 2011.

Bakırezer, G. and Demirer, Y., 'AK Parti'nin Sosyal Siyaseti', in İ. Uzgel and B. Duru (eds.), *AKP Kitabı: Bir Dönüşümün Bilançosu*, pp. 153–78, Ankara: Phoenix Yayınevi, 2009.

Barlas, D., *Etatism and Diplomacy in Turkey: Economic and Foreign Policy Strategies in an Uncertain World, 1929–1939*, New York: Brill, 1998.

Baumel, S. D., *Sacred Speakers: Language and Culture Among the Haredim in Israel*, New York: Berghahn Books, 2005.

Bayat, A., 'Islamism and Social Movement Theory', *Third World Quarterly*, vol.26, no.6, 2005, 891–908.

——'What is Post-Islamism', *ISIM Review*, vol.16, 2005, 5.

——*Making Islam Democratic: Social Movements and the Post-Islamist Turn*, Stanford: Stanford University Press, 2007.

Bekaroğlu, M., *"Adil Düzen"den "Dünya Gerçekleri"ne: Siyasetin Sonu*, Elips Kitap, 2007.

Benbassa, E. and Rodrigue, A., *Sephardi Jewry: A History of the Judeo-Spanish Community, 14th–20th Century*, Berkeley: University of California Press, 2000.

Benford, R. D. and Snow, D., 'Framing Processes and Social Movements: An Overview and Assessment', *Annual Review of Sociology*, vol.26, 2000, 611–39.

Berger, P., *The Sacred Canopy: Elements of a Sociological Theory of Religion*, Garden City: Doubleday, 1967.

——'Desecularization of the World: A Global Overview', in P. Berger (ed.), *The Desecularization of the World: Resurgent Religion and World Politics*, pp. 1–18, Grand Rapids: Eerdmans Publishing, 1999.

Berman, E., 'Sect, Subsidy and Sacrifice: An Economist's View of Ultra-Orthodox Jews', *NBER Working Papers*, no.6712, National Bureau of Economic Research Inc., 1998, 1–47.

Bick, E., 'The Shas Phenomenon and Religious Parties in the 1999 Elections', *Israel Affairs*, vol.7, no.2–3, 2001, 55–100.

——'A Party in Decline: Shas in Israel's 2003 Elections', *Israel Affairs*, vol.7, no.4, 2004, 98–129.

Birand, M. A. and Yalçın, S., *The Özal: Bir Davanın Öyküsü*, Istanbul: Doğan Kitapçılık, 2001.

Blass, N. and Amir, B., 'Integration in Education: The Development of a Policy', in Y. Amir and S. Sharan (eds.), *School Desegregation: Cross-Cultural Perspectives*, pp. 63–98, Hillsdale: Lawrence Erlbaum Associates Publishers, 1984.

Bora, T. and Can, K., '12 Eylül'ün resmi ideolojisi, faşist entelejensiya ve "Türk-İslam Sentezi', *Birikim*, vol.18, 1990, 27–39.

Boratav, K. 'Kemalist Economic Policies and Etatism', in E. Özbudun and A. Kazancıgil (eds.), *Atatürk: Founder of Modern Turkey*, pp. 165–90, Hamden: Archon Book, 1981.

——'İktisat Tarihi', in S. Akşin, B. Tanör and K. Boratav (eds.), *Yakınçağ Türkiye Tarihi 1908–1980*, pp. 189–245, Istanbul: Milliyet Yayınları, 2003.

Brown, C. L., *Religion and State: The Muslim Approach to Politics*, New York: Columbia University Press, 2000.

Buğra, A., 'Political Sources of Uncertainty in Business Life', in M. Heper (ed.), *Strong State and Economic Interest Groups: The Post-1980 Turkish Experience*, pp. 151–62, New York: Walter de Gruyter, 1991.

——'The Immoral Economy of Housing in Turkey', *International Journal of Urban and Regional Research*, vol.22, no.2, 1998, 283–302.

Bulaç, A., *Din ve Modernizm: Tarihin Kırılma Anında Tufan*, Istanbul: Endülüs Yayınları, 1990.

——'Medina Vesikası Hakkında Genel Bilgiler', *Birikim*, vol.38–39, 1992, 102–11.

Çakır, R., *Ayet ve Slogan Türkiye'de İslami Oluşumlar*, Istanbul: Metis Yayınları, 1990.

——*Ne Şeriat Ne Demokrasi: Refah Partisini Anlamak*, Istanbul: Metis Yayınları, 1994.

——'Milli Görüş Hareketi', in Y. Aktay (ed.), *İslamcılık*, pp. 544–75, Istanbul: İletişim Yayınları, 2004.

Çakır, R. and Çalmuk, F., *Recep Tayyip Erdoğan: Bir Dönüşüm Öyküsü*, Istanbul: Metis Yayınları, 2001.

Çakır, R., Bozan, İ. and Talu, B., *İmam Hatip Liseleri Efsaneler ve Gerçekler*, Istanbul: TESEV Yayınları, 2004.

Çalmuk, F. 'Necmettin Erbakan', in Y. Aktay (ed.), *İslamcılık*, pp. 550–67, Istanbul: İletişim Yayınları, 2004.

Caplan, K., 'Israeli Haredi Society and Repentance (Hazarah Biteshuva) Phenomenon', *Jewish Studies Quarterly*, vol.8, 2001, 369–98.

——'Studying Haredi Mizrachim in Israel: Trends, Achievements, and Challenges', *Studies in Contemporary Jewry*, vol.22, 2008, 169–92.

Chetrit, S. S., *Intra-Jewish Conflict in Israel: White Jews, Black Jews*, London: Routledge, 2010.

Cemal, H., *Özal Hikayesi*, Ankara: Bilgi Yayınevi, 1989.

Çiçek, C., 'Milletin Gözüyle İmam Hatip Okulları ve Beklentileri', in *Kuruluşunun 43. Yılında İmam Hatip Liseleri*, Istanbul: Ensar Neşriyat, 1994.

Çınar, M., 'Turkey's Present *Ancien Regime* and Justice and Development Party', in M. Casier and J. Jongerden (eds.), *Nationalisms and Politics in Turkey: Political Islam, Kemalism and the Kurdish Issue*, pp. 13–27, London: Routledge, 2011.

Cizre, Ü. and Çınar, M., 'Turkey 2002: Kemalism, Islamism, and Politics in the Light of the February 28 Process', *South Atlantic Quarterly*, vol.102, 2003, 309–32.

Clark, J., 'Social Movement Theory and Patron-Clientelism: Islamic Social Institutions and the Middle Class in Egypt, Jordan, and Yemen', *Comparative Political Studies*, vol.37, no.8, 2004, 941–68.

Çolak, Y., 'Language Policy and Official Ideology in Early Republican Turkey', *Middle Eastern Studies*, vol.40, no.6, 2004, 67–91.

Collier, D. 'The Comparative Method', in A. Finter (ed.), *Political Science: The State of the Discipline II*, pp. 105–19 Washington, D.C.: American Political Science Association, 1993.

Copeaux, E., *Tarih Ders Kitaplarında (1931–1993) Türk Tarih Tezinden Türk-İslam Sentezine*, A. Berktay (trans.), Istanbul: Tarih Vakfı Yurt Yayınları, 2000.

Dağı, İ., *Kimlik Söylem ve Siyaset Doğu-Batı Ayrımında Refah Partisi Geleneği*, İstanbul: İmge Yayınları, 1998.

——'The Justice and Development Party: Identity, Politics, and Human Rights Discourse in the Search for Security and Legitimacy', in H. Yavuz (ed.), *The Emergence of a New Turkey: Democracy and the AK Parti*, pp. 88–106, Salt Lake City: University of Utah Press, 2006.

Davis, N. J. and Robinson, R. V., 'Overcoming Movement Obstacles by the Religiously Orthodox: The Muslim Brotherhood in Egypt, Shas in Israel, Comunione e Liberazione in Italy, and the Salvation Army in the United States', *American Journal of Sociology*, vol.114, no.5, 2009, 1302–49.

Davutoğlu, A., 'Turkish Foreign Policy Vision: An Assessment of 2007', *Insight Turkey*, vol.10, no.1, 2008, 77–96.

Delacoura, K., *Islamist Terrorism and Democracy in the Middle East*, New York: Cambridge University Press, 2011.

Demir, A. İ., *Cumhuriyet Dönemi Aydınlarının İslam'a Bakışı*, Istanbul: Ensar Neşriyat, 2004.

Demir, Ö., Acar, M. and Toprak, M., 'Anatolian Tigers or Islamic Capital: Prospects and Challenges', *Middle Eastern Studies*, vol.40, no.6, 2004, 166–88.

Denoeux, G. 'The Forgotten Swamp: Navigating Political Islam', *Middle East Policy*, vol.9, no.2, 2002, 56–81.

Deshen, S., 'The Emergence of the Israeli Sephardi Ultra-Orthodox Movement', *Jewish Social Studies*, vol.11, no.2, 2005, 77–101.

Dilipak, A., *Bu Din Benim Dinim Değil*, Istanbul: İşaret Yayınları, 1991.

Don-Yehiya, E., 'Religion, Social Cleavages, and Electoral Behavior: The Religious Parties in the Elections', in D. J. Elazar and S. Sandler (eds.), *Who's the Boss in Israel?: Israel at the Polls, 1988–9*, pp. 83–129, Detroit: Wayne State University Press, 1992.

——'Religion, Ethnicity and Electoral Reform: The Religious Parties and the 1996 Elections', *Israel Affairs*, vol.4, no.1, 1997, 73–102.

——*Religion and Political Accommodation in Israel*, Jerusalem: The Floersheimer Institute for Policy Studies, 1999.

Dowty, A., *The Jewish State a Century Later*, Berkeley: University of California Press, 2001.

Duran, B., 'Approaching the Kurdish Question via Adil Duzen: An Islamist Formula of the Welfare Party For Ethnic Coexistence', *Journal of Muslim Minority Affairs*, vol.18, no.1, 1998, 111–28.

——'The Justice and Development Party's "New Politics": Steering toward Conservative Democracy, a Revised Islamic Agenda or Management of New Crises', in Ü. Cizre (ed.), *Secular and Islamic Politics in Turkey: The Making of the Justice and Development Party*, pp. 80–106, London: Routledge, 2008.

Ediş, T., 'Islamic Creationism in Turkey', *Creation/Evolution*, vol.34, no.1, 1994, 1–12.

Efron, N. J., *Real Jews: Secular Versus Ultra-Orthodox and the Struggle for Jewish Identity in Israel*, New York: Basic Books, 2003.

Elazar, D. J., *The Other Jews: The Sephardim Today*, New York: Basic Books, 1989.

Eligür, B., *The Mobilization of Political Islam in Turkey*, New York: Cambridge University Press, 2010.

Erbakan, N., *Gayemiz Bütün Beşeriyetin Saadetidir*, Ankara: ESAM, 2005.

——*İslam-Batı Diyaloğu ve Geleceği*, Istanbul: Milsan Basın A.Ş., 2006.

Erdoğan, R. T., 'Conservative Democracy and the Globalization of Freedom', speech delivered to American Enterprise Institute on 29 January 2004. Online. Available at www.aei.org/events/filter.all,eventID.735/transcript.asp.

Erman, T., 'The Politics of Squatter (*Gecekondu*) Studies in Turkey: The Changing Representations of Rural Migrants in the Academic Discourse', *Urban Studies*, vol.38, no.7, 2001, 983–1002.

Erman, T. and Eken, A., 'The "Other of the Other" and "Unregulated Territories" in the Urban Periphery: Gecekondu Violence in the 2000s with a Focus on the Esenler Case, Istanbul', *Cities*, vol.21, no.1, 2004, 57–68.

ESAM, *Konuşmalar*, Ankara: ESAM, 2006.

Esmer, Y. 'At the Ballot Box: Determinants of Voting Behavior', in S. Sayarı and Y. Esmer (eds.), *Politics, Parties, and Elections in Turkey*, pp. 91–114, Boulder: Lynne Rienner, 2002.

Esposito, J. and Voll, J., *Islam and Democracy*, New York: Oxford University Press, 1996.

Evren, K., *Türkiye Cumhuriyeti Cumhurbaşkanı Kenan Evren'in Söylev ve Demeçleri/ 12 Eylül 1982–9 Kasım 1983*, Ankara: TBMM Basımevi, 1985.

Findley, C. V., *Turkey, Islam, Nationalism, and Modernity: A History, 1789–2007*, New Haven: Yale University Press, 2010.

Fox, J., 'World Separation of Religion and State Into the 21st Century', *Comparative Political Studies*, vol.39, no.5, 2006, 537–69.

Friedman, M., 'The NRP in Transition—Behind the Party's Electoral Decline', in D. Caspi, A. Diskin and E. Guttman (eds.), *The Roots of Begin's Success*, pp. 270–95, London: Croom Helm, 1983.

——'The Ultra-Orthodox and Israeli Society', in J. Peters and K. Kyle (eds.), *Whither Israel: The Domestic Challenges*, pp. 177–201, London: I. B. Tauris & Company, 1993.

Gamson, W., Fireman, B. and Rytina, S., *Encounters with Unjust Authority*, Homewood: Dorsey Press, 1982.

Gaziosmanpaşa Belediyesi (Gaziosmanpaşa Municipality), *Hizmetlerle Dolu 5 Altın Yıl: Sosyal, Kültürel ve Sportif Faaliyetler*, Istanbul, 1999.

—— *… ve 27 Mart 1994*, Istanbul, 1999.

Geiltman, Z., 'The "Russian Revolution" in Israel', in A. Dowty (ed.), *Critical Issues in Israeli Society*, pp. 95–108, Westport: Praeger, 2004.

Genelkurmay Başkanlığı (General Staff), *Atatürkçülük*, Istanbul: Milli Eğitim Basımevi, vol.1, 1988.

——*Atatürkçülük*, Istanbul, Milli Eğitim Basımevi, vol.3, 1988.

Giladi, G. N., *Discord in Zion: Conflict Between Ashkenazi & Sephardi Jews in Israel*, London: Scorpion Publishing, 1990.

Gökaçtı, M. A., *Türkiye'de Din Eğitimi ve İmam Hatipler*, Istanbul: İletişim Yayınları, 2005.

Gökalp, Z., *Türkleşmek, İslamlaşmak, Muasırlaşmak*, F. Kaynak (ed.), Istanbul: Eflatun, 2004.

Goldscheider, C., *Israel's Changing Society Population, Ethnicity, and Development*, Boulder: Westview Press, 2002.

Göle, N., 'Authoritarian Secularism and Islamist Politics: The Case of Turkey', in A. R. Norton (ed.), *Civil Society in the Middle East*, vol.2, pp. 17–44, Leiden: E. J. Brill Publishing, 1996.

——*The Forbidden Modern: Civilization and Veiling*, Ann Arbor: University of Michigan Press, 1997.

——'Secularism and Islamism in Turkey: The Making of Elites and Counter-Elites', *Middle East Journal*, vol.51, no.1, 1997, 46–58.

——'The Civilizational, Spatial and Sexual Powers of the Secular', in J. Vanantwerpen and G. Calhoun (eds.), *Varieties of Secularism in a Secular Age*, pp. 243–64, Cambridge, MA: Harvard University Press, 2010.

Gonen, A., 'The Changing Ethnic Geography of Israeli Cities', in A. Weingrod (ed.), *Studies in Israeli Ethnicity: After the Ingathering*, pp. 25–37, New York: Gordon & Breach, 1985.

Gorenberg, G., *The Accidental Empire: Israel and the Birth of Settlements, 1967–1977*, New York: Times Books, 2006.

Greilsammer, I., 'Campaign Strategies of the Israeli Religious Parties, 1981–84', in A. Arian and M. Shamir (eds.), *The Elections in Israel 1984*, pp. 79–96, Jerusalem: Ramat Publishing, 1986.

Gülalp, H., 'The Poverty of Democracy in Turkey: The Refah Party Episode', *New Perspectives on Turkey*, vol.21, 1999, 35–59.

——'Globalization and Political Islam: The Social Bases of Turkey's Welfare Party', *International Journal of Middle Eastern Studies*, vol.33, 2001, 433–48.

Gümüşçü, Ş. and Sert, D., 'The Power of the Devout Bourgeoisie: The Case of the Justice and Development Party in Turkey', *Middle Eastern Studies*, vol.45, no.6, 2009, 953–68.

Gürsel, S., 'Cumhuriyet Döneminde Türkiye Ekonomisi', in M. Tunçay (ed.), *75 yılda düşünceler tartışmalar*, Istanbul: Türk Tarih Vakfı Yayınları, 1999.

Haberfeld, Y. and Cohen, Y., 'Gender, Ethnic, and National Earnings Gaps in Israel: The Role of Rising Inequality', *Social Science Research*, vol.36, 2007, 654–72.

Hale, W., 'Christian Democracy and the JDP: Parallels and Contrasts', in H. Yavuz (ed.), *The Emergence of a New Turkey: Democracy and the AK Parti*, pp. 66–87, Salt Lake City: University of Utah Press, 2006.

Hale, W. and Özbudun, E., *Islamism, Democracy and Liberalism in Turkey: The Case of AKP*, London: Routledge, 2011.

Hanioğlu, Ş., *A Brief History of the Late Ottoman Empire*, Princeton: Princeton University Press, 2008.

——*Atatürk: An Intellectual Biography*, Princeton: Princeton University Press, 2011.

Hazan, R., 'Religion and Politics in Israel: The Rise and Fall of the Consociational Model', *Israel Affairs*, vol.55, no.1, 1999, 109–37.

Hedges, C., *American Fascists: Christian Right and the War on America*, New York: Free Press, 2007.

Heilman, S. C., 'The Orthodox, the Ultra-Orthodox, and the Elections for the Twelfth Knesset', in A. Arian and M. Shamir (eds.), *The Elections in Israel-1988*, pp. 135–53, Boulder: Westview Press, 1990.

Heilman, S. C. and Friedman, M., 'Religious Fundamentalism and Religious Jews: The Case of the Haredim', in M. E. Marty and S. Abbelby (eds.), *Fundamentalisms Observed*, pp. 197–264, Chicago: Chicago University Press, 1991.

Herzog, H., 'Political Factionalism: The Case of Ethnic Lists in Israel', *The Western Political Quarterly*, vol.39, no.2, 1986, 285–303.

Huntington, S., *The Clash of Civilizations and the Remaking of World Order*, New York: Simon & Schuster, 1996.

Jang, J., *Taming Political Islamists by Islamist Capital: The Passions and Interests in Turkish Islamic Society*, unpublished Ph.D. dissertation, University of Texas at Austin, 2005.

Jenkins, G., 'The Fading Masquerade: Ergenekon and the Politics of Justice in Turkey', *Turkey Analyst*, vol.4, no.7, 4 April 2011. Online. Available at www.silkroadstudies.org/new/inside/turkey/2011/110404B.html.

Kalev, H. D., 'Bargaining with Spiritual Hierarchy: Women in the Shas Movement in Israel', in P. S. Anderson (ed.), *New Topics in Feminist Philosophy of Religion: Contestations and Transcendence Incarnate*, pp. 85–102, London: Springer, 2010.

Kalyvas, R., *The Rise of Christian Democracy in Europe*, Ithaca: Cornell University Press, 1996.

——'Commitment Problems in Emerging Democracies: The Case of Religious Parties', *Comparative Politics*, vol.32, 2000, 379–98.

Kamil, O., 'Rabbi Ovadia Yosef and his "Culture War" in Israel', *Middle East Review of International Affairs*, vol.4, no.4, 2000, 22–9.

Kandiyoti, D. A., 'Emancipated but Unliberated? Reflections on the Turkish Case', *Feminist Studies*, vol.13, no.2, 1987, 317–38.

Kaplan, S., 'Din-u Devlet All Over Again? The Politics of Military Secularism and Religious Militarism in Turkey', *International Journal of Middle East Studies*, vol.34, 2002, 113–27.

——'"Religious Nationalism": A Textbook Case from Turkey', *Comparative Studies of South Asia, Africa and the Middle East*, vol.25, no.3, 2005, 665–76.

Karaman, H., *İmam Hatiplilik Şuuru*, Istanbul: Ensar Neşriyat, 2005.

——*Laik Düzende Dini Yaşamak 4*, Istanbul: İz Yayıncılık, 2006.

Kardam, A. and Tüzün, S., *Türkiye'de Siyasi Kutuplaşmalar ve Seçmen Davranışları*, Ankara: Veri Araştırma, 1998.

Karpat, K. H., *The Gecekondu: Rural Migration and Urbanization*, New York: Cambridge University Press, 1976.

——*Politicization of Islam: Reconstructing Identity, State, Faith, and Community in the Late Ottoman Empire*, New York: Oxford University Press, 2001.

Kavakçı, M., 'Headscarf Heresy', *Foreign Policy*, vol.142, 2004, 66.

Kazan, Ş. *Refah Gerçeği*, Ankara: Keşif Yayınları, vol.1, 2006.

——*Refah Gerçeği*, Ankara: Keşif Yayınları, vol.3, 2006.

Keddie, N. R., 'New Religious Politics: Where, When, and Why do Fundamentalisms Appear?', *Comparative Studies in Society and History*, vol.40, no.4, 1998, 696–723.

Keyder, Ç., *Türkiye'de Devlet ve Sınıflar*, Istanbul: İletişim, 2000.

Keyman, F., 'On the Relation between Global Modernity and Nationalism: The Crisis of Hegemony and (Islamic) Identity in Turkey', *New Perspectives on Turkey*, vol.13, 1995, 93–120.

Kleinberger, A. F., *Society, Schools, and Progress in Israel*, Oxford: Pergamon Press, 1969.

Kuru, A. T., 'Globalization and Diversification of Islamic Movements: Three Turkish Cases', *Political Science Quarterly*, vol.120, no.2, 2005, 253–74.

——*Secularism and State Policies toward Religion: The United States, France, and Turkey*, New York: Cambridge University Press, 2009.

Lagendijk, J., 'Turkey's Accession to the European Union and the Role of the Justice and Development Party', in A. Kuru and A. Stepan (eds.), *Democracy, Islam & Secularism in Turkey*, pp. 166–88, New York: Columbia University Press, 2011.

Lee, R. D., *Religion and Politics in the Middle East Identity, Ideology, Institutions, and Attitudes*, Boulder: Westview Press, 2010.

Lehmann, D. and Siebzehner, B., *Remaking Israeli Judaism: The Challenge of Shas*, London: Oxford University Press, 2006.

——'Self-exclusion as a Strategy of Inclusion: The Case of Shas', *Citizenship Studies*, vol.12, no.3, 2008, 233–47.

Leon, N., 'Ethnic Synagogues of Mizrahi Jews in Israel: Ethnicity, Orthodoxy, and Nationalism', *Sociological Papers*, vol.13, 2008, 1–17.

——'"Zikui Harabim": Ovadia Yosef's Approach toward Religious Activism and His Place in the Haredi Movement within Mizrahi Jewry', *Studies in Contemporary Jewry*, vol.22, 2008, 150–68.

——'The Political Use of the Teshuva Casette Culture in Israel', *Contemporary Jewry*, vol.31, 2011, 91–106.

Lerner, D., *The Passing of the Traditional Society Modernizing the Middle East*, Glencoe: The Free Press, 1958.

Lewis, B., *The Political Language of Islam*, Chicago: Chicago University Press, 1988.

——*The Emergence of Modern Turkey*, New York: Oxford University Press, 2002.

——*What Went Wrong: The Clash between Islam and Modernity in the Middle East*, New York: Oxford University Press, 2002.

Lupu, J., *Haim Tahzir Shas Atara LeYoshna? (Can Shas Restore Past Glory?)*, Jerusalem: Floersheimer Institute, 2004.

Maalouf, A., *In the Name of Identity: Violence and the Need to Belong*, New York: Penguin Books, 2003.

McAdam, D., *Political Process and the Development of Black Insurgency, 1930–1970*, Chicago: University of Chicago Press, 1982.

McAdam, D., McCarthy, J., and Zald, M. N., 'Introduction: Opportunities, Mobilizing Structures, and Framing Processes-toward a Synthetic Comparative Perspective on Social Movements', in D. McAdam, J. McCarthy and M. Zald (eds.), *Comparative Perspectives on Social Movements: Political Opportunities, Mobilizing Structures, and Cultural Framings*, pp. 1–22, New York: Cambridge University Press, 1996.

Magnarella, P. J., *Human Materialism: A Model of Sociocultural Systems and a Strategy for Analysis*, Gainesville: University Press of Florida, 1993.

Mahmood, S., *Politics of Piety: The Islamic Revival and the Feminist Subject*, Princeton: Princeton University Press, 2005.

Maoz, A., 'Religious Education in Israel', *University of Detroit Mercy Law Review*, vol.83, no.5, 2006, 679–728.

Mardin, Ş., 'Center-Periphery Relations: A Key to Turkish Politics', *Daedalus*, 1973, 169–90.

——'Religion and Secularism in Turkey', in E. Özbudun and A. Kazancıgil (eds.), *Atatürk: Founder of Modern Turkey*, pp. 191–219, Hamden: Archon Book, 1981.

——'Religion and Secularism in Turkey', in A. Hourani, P. S. Khoury and M. C. Wilson (eds.), *The Modern Middle East*, pp. 347–74, Berkeley: University of California Press, 1993.

——'Türkiye Siyasasini Açıklayabilecek Bir Anahtar: Merkez-Çevre İlişkileri', in M. Türköne and T. Önder (eds.), *Şerif Mardin Bütün Eserleri 6: Türkiye'de Toplum ve Siyaset*, pp. 9–76, Istanbul: İletişim Yayınları, 2004.

Martin, D., *A General Theory of Secularization*, New York: Harper & Row, 1979.

Marty, M. E. and Appelby, R. S. (eds.), *Fundamentalisms Observed*, Chicago: University of Chicago Press, 1994.

Massad, J., 'Zionism's Internal Others: Israel and the Oriental Jews', *Journal of Palestine Studies*, vol.25, no.4, 1996, 53–68.

Meyer, D. S., 'Protest and Political Opportunities', *Annual Review of Sociology*, vol.30, 2004, 125–45.

Migdal, J., *State in Society: Studying How States and Societies Transform and Constitute One Another*, New York: Cambridge University Press, 2001.

Moore, B. Jr., *Social Origins of Democracy and Dictatorship: Lord and Peasant in the Making of the Modern World*, Boston: Beacon Press, 1966.

Mousalli, A., *The Islamic Quest for Democracy, Pluralism, and Human Rights*, Gainesville: The University of Florida Press, 2003.

Munson, M., 'Gush Emunim and the Israeli Settlers of the Occupied Territories: A Social Movement Approach', *Strategic Insights*, 2008.

Munson, Z., 'Islamic Mobilization: Social Movement Theory and the Egyptian Muslim Brotherhood', *The Sociological Quarterly*, vol.42, no.4, 2001, 487–510.

Navaro-Yashin, Y., *Faces of the State: Secularism and Public Life in Turkey*, Princeton: Princeton University Press, 2002.

Noakes, J. A., 'Official Frames in Social Movement Theory: The FBI, HUAC, and the Communist Threat in Hollywood', in H. Johnston and J. A. Noakes (eds.), *Frames of Protest: Social Movements and the Framing Perspective*, pp. 89–112, Lanham: Rowman & Littlefield Publishers, 2005.

Öcal, M., *Imam Hatip Liseleri ve İlk Öğretim Okulları*, Istanbul: Ensar Neşriyat, 1994.

Ognianova, N., *Turkey's Press Freedom Crisis: The Dark Days of Jailing Journalists and Criminalizing Dissent*, New York: United Book Press, 2012.

Onay, A., 'Imam Hatip Liselerindeki Din Eğitimi ve Dindarlık Yansımaları', in M. Zengin (ed.), *Imam Hatip Liselerinde Eğitim ve Öğretim*, pp. 97–112, Istanbul: Dem Yayınları, 2005.

Öncü, A., 'Global Consumerism, Sexuality as Public Spectacle, and the Cultural Remapping of Istanbul in the 1990s', in D. Kandiyoti and A. Saktanber (eds.), *Fragments of Culture: The Everyday of Modern Turkey*, pp. 171–90, New Brunswick: Rutger University Press, 2002.

Öniş, Z., 'The Political Economy of Export-Oriented Industrialization in Turkey', in Ç. Balım (ed.), *Turkey: Political, Economic, and Social Challenges in the 1990s*, pp. 107–29, Leiden: Brill, 1995.

——'The Political Economy of Islamic Resurgence: The Rise of the Welfare Party in Perspective', *Third World Quarterly*, vol.18, no.4, 1997, 743–66.

——'Conservative Globalism at the Crossroads: The Justice and Development Party and the Thorny Path to Democratic Consolidation in Turkey', *Mediterranean Politics*, vol.14, no.1, 2009, 21–40.

——'The Triumph of Conservative Globalism: The Political Economy of the AKP Era', *Turkish Studies*, vol.13, no.2, 2012, 135–52.

Oran, B., *Kenan Evren'in Yazılmamış Anıları*, Ankara: Bilgi Yayınevi, 1989.

Oz, A., *In the Land of Israel*, New York: Harcourt Brace Jovanovich Publishers, Inc., 1983.

Özbudun, E., 'The Institutional Decline of Parties in Turkey', in L. Diamond and R. Gunther (eds.), *Political Parties and Democracy*, pp. 238–65, Baltimore: Johns Hopkins University Press, 2001.

——'The Turkish Constitutional Court and Political Crisis', in A. Kuru and A. Stepan (eds.), *Democracy, Islam & Secularism in Turkey*, pp. 149–65, New York: Columbia University Press, 2011.

Özbudun, E. and Keyman, F., 'Cultural Globalization in Turkey: Actors, Discourses, Strategies', in P. Berger and S. Huntington (eds.), *Cultural Globalization in the Contemporary World*, pp. 296–319, New York: Oxford University Press, 2002.

Özer, G. D., *Psikolojik Bir İşkence Metodu Olarak İkna Odaları*, Istanbul: Beyan Yayınları, 2005.

Özgür, I., *Islamic Schools in Modern Turkey: Faith, Politics, and Education*, New York: Cambridge University Press, 2012.

Özler, Ş. I., 'The Political Choices of Urban Squatters in National Elections', *Turkish Studies*, vol.1, no.2, 2000, 39–58.

Özyeğin, G., 'The Doorkeeper, the Maid and the Tenant: Troubling Encounters in the Turkish Urban Landscape', in D. Kandiyoti and A. Saktanber (eds.), *Fragments of Culture: The Everyday of Modern Turkey*, pp. 43–72, New Brunswick: Rutgers University Press, 2002.

Pak, S., *At the Crossroads of Secularism and Islamism*, unpublished Ph.D. dissertation, University of Wisconsin, Madison, 2002.

Pamuk, M., *Yasaklı Umut Recep Tayyip Erdoğan*, Birey Yayıncılık, 2001.

Parla, T., *Ziya Gökalp, Kemalizm ve Türkiye'de Korporatizm*, Istanbul: İletişim, 1989.

——*Türkiye'nin Siyasal Rejimi 1980–1989*, Istanbul: İletişim Yayınları, 1995.

Peled, Y., 'Towards a Redefinition of Jewish Nationalism in Israel? The Enigma of *Shas*', *Ethnic and Racial Studies*, vol.21, no.1, 1998, 703–27.

——'Progressive Struggle under Religious Guise? The Shas Party in Israel', paper presented at the conference of the *Australasian Political Studies Association*, Canberra, October, 2000.

Picard, A., 'Soft Religiosity: The Identity of North African Youths in Israel', *The Journal for the Study of Sephardic and Mizrahi Jewry*, vol.2, no.2, 2009, 132–68.

——Review of *Soft Ultra-Orthodoxy: Religious Renewal in Mizrahi Jews* by Nissim Leon. Yad Yitzhak Ben Zvi, 2010. Online. Available at www.hartman.org.il/Research_And_Comment_View.asp?Article_Id=519&Cat_Id = 322&Cat_Type = Research_And_Comment.

Pipes, D., 'There Are No Moderates: Dealing With Fundamentalist Islam', *National Interest*, no.41, 1995, 48–57.

Putnam, R., *Making Democracy Work: Civic Traditions in Modern Italy*, Princeton: Princeton University Press, 1994.

Quinn, M., 'From the Ashes of Virtue, a Promise of Light: The Transformation of Political Islam in Turkey', *Third World Quarterly*, vol.25, no.2, 2004, 339–58.

Rabasa, A. M. (ed.), *The Muslim World after 9/11*, Arlington: Rand Corporation, 2004.

Rafael, E. B. and Sharot, S., *Ethnicity, Religion, and Class in Israeli Society*, Cambridge: Cambridge University Press, 1991.

Ragin, C. J., *The Comparative Method: Moving beyond Qualitative and Quantitative Strategies*, Berkeley: University of California Press, 1987.

Ravitzky, A., *Messianism, Zionism, and Jewish Religious Radicalism*, Chicago: University of Chicago Press, 1999.

Refah Partisi, *Adil Düzen:21 Soru 21 Cevap*, Ankara: Refah Partisi, 1994.

Riaz, A., '"God Willing": The Politics and Ideology of Islamism in Bangladesh', *Comparative Studies of South Asia, Africa, and the Middle East*, vol.23, no.1&2, 2003, 301–20.

——'Three Arguments about the Religion-politics Nexus', in A. Riaz (ed.), *Religion and Politics in South Asia*, pp. 1–24, London: Routledge, 2010.

Richards, A. and Waterbury, J., *A Political Economy of the Middle East*, Boulder: Westview Press, 1996.

Ringer, M. M., 'Education in the Middle East: Introduction', *Comparative Studies of South Asia, Africa and the Middle East*, vol.21, no.1–2, 2001, 3–4.

Rodrigue, A., *Images of Sephardi and Eastern Jewries in Transition: The Teachers of the Alliance Israélite Universelle, 1860–1939*, Seattle: University of Washington Press, 1993.

Rosenthal, D., *Ordinary People in an Extraordinary Land: The Israelis*, New York: Free Press, 2003.

Roth, G., *The Social Democrats in Imperial Germany: A Study in Working-Class Isolation and National Integration*, Somerville: Bedminster Press, 1963.

Rubin, A., 'The Status of Religion in Emergent Political Regimes: Lessons from Turkey and Israel', *Nations and Nationalism*, 2012, 1–20.

Rucht, D., 'The Impact of National Contexts on Movement Structures: A Cross-Movement and Cross-National Comparison', in D. McAdam, J. McCarthy and M. Zald (eds.), *Comparative Perspectives on Social Movements: Political Opportunities, Mobilizing Structures, and Cultural Framings*, pp. 185–204, New York: Cambridge University Press, 1996.

Sarıbay, A. Y., *Türkiye'de Modernleşme Din ve Parti Politikasi: Millî Selâmet Partisi Örnek Olayı*, Istanbul: Alan Yayınları, 1985.

Schachter, H. L., 'Educational Institutions and Political Coalitions: The Case of Israel', *Comparative Education*, vol.16, no.3, 1972, 462–73.

Schiffer, V., *The Haredi Education in Israel: Allocation, Regulation, and Control*, Jerusalem: The Floersheimer Institute for Policy Studies, 1997.

Schiffman, E., 'The Shas School System in Israel', *Nationalism and Ethnic Politics*, vol.11, 2005, 89–124.

Schoenfeld, D., 'Formalism, Morality and Ovadia Yosef: A Response to Daniel Statman', *The Journal of the Society for Textual Reasoning*, vol.6, no.1, 2010. Online. Available at http://etext.virginia.edu/journals/tr/volume6/number1/TR06_01_schoenfeld.html.

Schwedler, J., *Faith in Moderation: Islamist Parties in Yemen and Jordan*, New York: Cambridge University Press, 2006.

Şen, M., 'Transformation of Turkish Islamism and the Rise of the Justice and Development Party', in B. Yeşilada and B. Rubin (eds.), *Islamization of Turkey under the AKP Rule*, pp. 57–82, London: Routledge, 2011.

Shahak, I. and Mezvinsky, N., *Jewish Fundamentalism in Israel*, London: Pluto Press, 2004.

Shalev, M., 'Have Globalization and Liberalization "Normalized" Israel's Political Economy?', *Israel Affairs*, vol.5, no.2–3, 1998, 121–55.

Shamai, S., '"Cultural Shift": The Case of Jewish Religious Education in Israel', *British Journal of Sociology of Education*, vol.21, no.3, 2000, 401–17.

Shapiro, M. B., 'Mi Yosef ad Yosef Lo Kam ke-Yosef', *Meorot*, vol.6. no.1, 2006, 1–17.

Shavit, Y., 'Segregation, Tracking, and the Educational Attainment of Minorities: Arabs and Mizrahi Jews in Israel', *American Sociological Review*, vol.55, no.1, 1990, 115–26.

Shils, E. A., 'Centre and Periphery', in *The Logic of Personal Knowledge: Essays Presented to Michael Polanyi on his Seventieth Birthday*, pp. 117–130, London: Routledge, 1961.

——*Center and Periphery: Essays in Macrosociology*, Chicago: University of Chicago Press, 1975.

Shohat, E., 'Perspectives on Mizrachiut. The Shaping of Mizrahi Studies: A Relational Approach', *Israel Studies Forum*, vol.17, no.2, 2002, 86–93.

Singerman, D., 'The Networked World of Islamist Social Movements', in Q. Wicktorowicz (ed.), *Islamic Activism: A Social Movement Theory*, pp. 143–63, Bloomington: Indiana University Press, 2004.

Smooha, S., *Israel, Pluralism and Conflict*, Berkeley: University of California Press, 1978.

Snow, D. A. and Benford, R. D., 'Ideology, Frame Resonance, and Participant Mobilization', *International Social Movement Research*, vol.1, 1988, 197–217.

Snow, D., Rochford, E. B., Worden, S. K. and Benford, R. D., 'Frame Alignment Processes, Micromobilization, and Movement Participation', *American Sociological Review*, vol.51, no.4, 1986, 464–81.

Somer, M. 'Moderate Islam and Secularist Opposition in Turkey: Implications for the World, Muslims and Secular Democracy', *Third World Quarterly*, vol.28, no.7, 2007, 1271–89.

——'Democratization, Clashing Narratives, and "Twin Tolerations" between Islamic-Conservative and Pro-Secular Actors', in M. Casier and J. Jongerden (eds.), *Nationalisms and Politics in Turkey: Political Islam, Kemalism and the Kurdish Issue*, pp. 28–47, London: Routledge, 2011.

Stepan, A., 'Religion, Democracy, and the "Twin Tolerations"', *Journal of Democracy*, vol.11, no.4, 2000, 37–57.

Sternhel, Z., *The Founding Myths of Israel: Nationalism, Socialism, and the Making of the Jewish State*, Princeton: Princeton University Press, 1998.

Taşkın, Y., 'Muhafazakâr Bir Proje Olarak Türk-İslam Sentezi', in A. Çiğdem (ed.), *Muhafazakârlık*, pp. 381–401, Istanbul: İletişim Yayınları, 2003.

Tepe, S., 'A Pro-Islamic Party? Promises and Limits of Turkey's Justice and Development Party', in H. Yavuz (ed.), *The Emergence of a New Turkey: Democracy and the AK Parti*, pp. 107–35, Salt Lake City: University of Utah Press, 2006.

——*Beyond Sacred and Secular: Politics of Religion in Israel and Turkey*, Stanford: Stanford University Press, 2008.

Tepe, S. and Baum, R., 'Shas's Transformation to "Likud with Kippa?": A Comparative Assessment of the Moderation of Religious Parties', in A. Arian (ed.), *The Elections in Israel-2006*, pp.69–101, Piscataway: Transaction Publishers, 2008.

Tesler, R., *Beshem hashem: Shas ve hamahapecha hadatit*, Jerusalem: Keter Publishing, 2003.

Tessler, M., 'The Political Right in Israel: Its Origins, Growth, and Prospects', *Journal of Palestine Studies*, vol.15, no.2, 1986, 12–55.

Tibi, B., 'Why They Can't be Democratic', *Journal of Democracy*, vol.19, no.3, 2008, 43–8.

Timuroğlu, V., *12 Eylül'ün Eğitim ve Kültür Politikasi Türk-İslam Sentezi*, Istanbul: Başak Yayınları, 1991.

Toprak, B., 'The State, Politics and Religion in Turkey', in M. Heper and A. Evin (eds.), *State, Democracy and Military: Turkey in the 1980s*, pp. 119–35, New York: W. de Gruyter, 1988.

Toprak, B. and Birtek, F., 'The Conflictual Agendas of Neo-Liberal Reconstruction and the Rise of Islamic Politics in Turkey: The Hazards of Rewriting Modernity', *Praxis International*, vol.13, 1993, 192–212.

Tuğal, C., 'Transforming Everyday Life: Islamism and Social Movement Theory', *Theory and Society*, vol.38, 2009, 423–58.

——*Passive Revolution: Absorbing the Islamic Challenge to Capitalism*, Stanford: Stanford University Press, 2009.

Tzfadia, E., 'Public Policy and Identity Formation: The Experience of Mizrahim in Israel's Development Towns', *The Journal for the Study of Sephardic and Mizrahi Jewry*, 2007, 57–82.

Tzfadia, E. and Yiftachel, O., 'Between Urban and National: Political Mobilization among Mizrahim in Israel's "Development Towns"', *Cities*, vol.21, no.1, 2004, 41–55.

Ünsür, A., *Kuruluşundan Günümüze İmam Hatip Liseleri*, Istanbul: Ensar Neşriyat, 2005.

Weissbrod, L., 'Shas: An Ethnic Religious Party', *Israel Affairs*, vol.9, no.4, 2003, 79–104.

White, J., *Islamist Mobilization in Turkey: A Study in Vernacular Politics*, Seattle: University of Washington Press, 2002.

——'State Feminism, Modernization, and the Turkish Republican Woman', *NWSA Journal*, vol.15, no.3, 2003, 145–59.

——'The End of Islamism? Turkey's Muslimhood Model', in R. W. Hefner (ed.), *Remaking Muslim Politics: Pluralism, Contestation, Democratization*, pp. 87–111, Princeton: Princeton University Press, 2005.

Wickham, C. R., *Mobilizing Islam: Religion, Activism and Political Change in Egypt*, New York: Columbia University Press, 2002.

——'Interests, Ideas, and Islamist Outreach in Egypt', in Q. Wicktorowicz (ed.), *Islamic Activism: A Social Movement Theory*, pp. 231–49, Bloomington: Indiana University Press, 2004.

——'The Path to Moderation: Strategy and Learning in the Formation of Egypt's Wasat Party', *Comparative Politics*, vol.36, no.2, 2004, 205–28.

Wiktorowicz, Q., 'Introduction: Islamic Activism and Social Movement Theory', in Q. Wicktorowicz (ed.), *Islamic Activism: A Social Movement Theory*, pp. 1–36, Bloomington: Indiana University Press, 2004.

Willis, A., *Sephardic Torah Guardians: Ritual and the Politics of Piety*, unpublished Ph.D. dissertation, Princeton University, 1993.

——'Shas-The Sephardic Torah Guardians: Religious "Movement" and Political Power', in A. Arian and M. Shamir (eds.), *The Elections in Israel-1992*, pp. 121–41, New York: SUNY Press, 1995.

Wilson, B., *Religion in Secular Society*, London: Watts, 1966.

——*Contemporary Transformations of Religion*, Oxford: Oxford University Press, 1976.

Yadgar, Y., 'Jewish Secularism and Ethno-National Identity in Israel: The Traditionist Critique', *Journal of Contemporary Religion* vol.26, no.3, 2011, 467–81.

Yağcıoğlu, S. (ed.), *1990 Sonrası Laik-Antilaik Çatışmasında Farklı Söylemler: Disiplinler Arası Bir Yaklaşım*, İzmir: Dokuz Eylül Yayınları, 2002.

Yalçın, S., *Hangi Erbakan?*, Istanbul: Başak Yayınları, 1994.

Yalçıntan, M. C. and Erbaş, A. E., 'Impacts of "Gecekondu" on the Electoral Geography of Istanbul', *International Labor & Working-Class History*, vol.64, 2003, 91–111.

Yaşar, M. E., 'Dergh'tan Parti'ye, Vakıf'tan Şirkete Bir Kimliğin Oluşumu ve Dönüşumü: İskenderpaşa Cemaati', in Y. Aktay (ed.), *İslamcılık*, pp. 323–39, Istanbul: Iletişim, 2004.

Yavuz, H., *Islamic Political Identity in Turkey*, New York: Oxford University Press, 2003.

——*Secularism and Muslim Democracy in Turkey*, New York: Cambridge University Press, 2009.

Yayla, A., 'Turkey's Leaders-Erbakan's Goals', *Middle East Quarterly*, vol.4, no.3, 1997, 19–25.

Yeşilada, B., 'The Refah Party Phenomenon in Turkey', in B. Yeşilada (ed.), *Comparative Political Parties and Party Elites*, pp. 123–50, Ann Arbor: University of Michigan Press, 1999.

——'Realignment and Party Adaptation: The Case of the Refah and Fazilet Parties', in S. Sayarı and Y. Esmer (eds.), *Politics, Parties, and Elections in Turkey*, pp. 157–78, Boulder: Lynne Rienner, 2002.

Yıldırım, A., *Muslim Democratic Parties: Economic Liberalization and Islamist Moderation in the Middle East*, unpublished Ph.D. dissertation, Ohio State University, 2010.

Young, I. M., *Justice and the Politics of Difference*, Princeton: Princeton University Press, 1990.

——*Inclusion and Democracy*, Oxford: Oxford University Press, 2000.

Zald, Mayer N., 'Culture, Ideology, and Strategic Framing', in D. McAdam, J. McCarthy and M. Zald (eds.), *Comparative Perspectives on Social Movements: Political Opportunities, Mobilizing Structures, and Cultural Framings*, pp. 261–74, New York: Cambridge University Press, 1996.

Zameret, Z., 'Fifty Years of Education in the State of Israel', Israel Ministry of Foreign Affairs, 1998. Online. Available at www.mfa.gov.il/MFA/History/Modern%20History/Israel%20at%2050/Fifty%20Years%20of%20Education%20in%20the%20State%20of%20Israel (accessed 3 December 2008).

Zartman, W., 'Democracy and Islam, the Cultural Dialectic', *Annals of the Academy of Political and Social Science*, vol.524, 1992, 181–91.

Zengin, B., *Özgürleşerek Birlikte Yaşamak*, Ankara: Birleşik Yayıncılık, 1995.

——*Sivil Anayasa Yeni Bir Toplum Sözleşmesi Önerisi*, Ankara: Mart Matbaacılık, 2001.

Zohar, Z., 'Oriental Jewry Confronts Modernity: The Case of Rabbi Ovadiah Yosef', *Modern Judaism*, vol.24, no.2, 2004, 120–49.

——'Sephardim and Oriental Jews in Israel: Rethinking the Sociopolitical Paradigm', in Z. Zohar (ed.), *Sephardic and Mizrahi Jewry: From Golden Age of Spain to Modern Times*, pp. 300–27, New York: New York University Press, 2005.

Zürcher, E., *Turkey: A Modern History*, London: I. B. Tauris, 2004.

Index

Note: page numbers in **bold** refer to tables; page numbers in *italics* refer to figures.